団体向け
テストプログラム

# TOEFL ITP® TEST 実戦問題集【改訂版】

順天堂大学国際教養学部教授
**ポール・ワーデン**
株式会社リンクアンドモチベーション
**ロバート・ヒルキ**
リベラルアーツ私塾 武蔵野自由英学塾
**松谷偉弘**

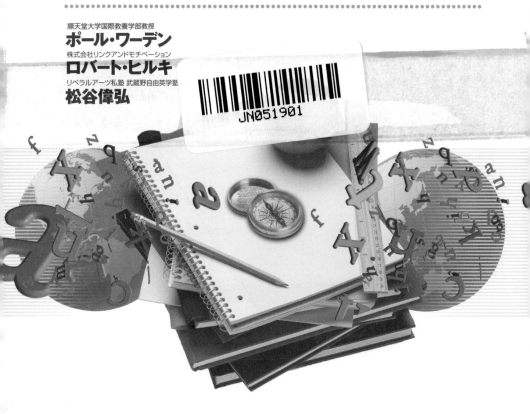

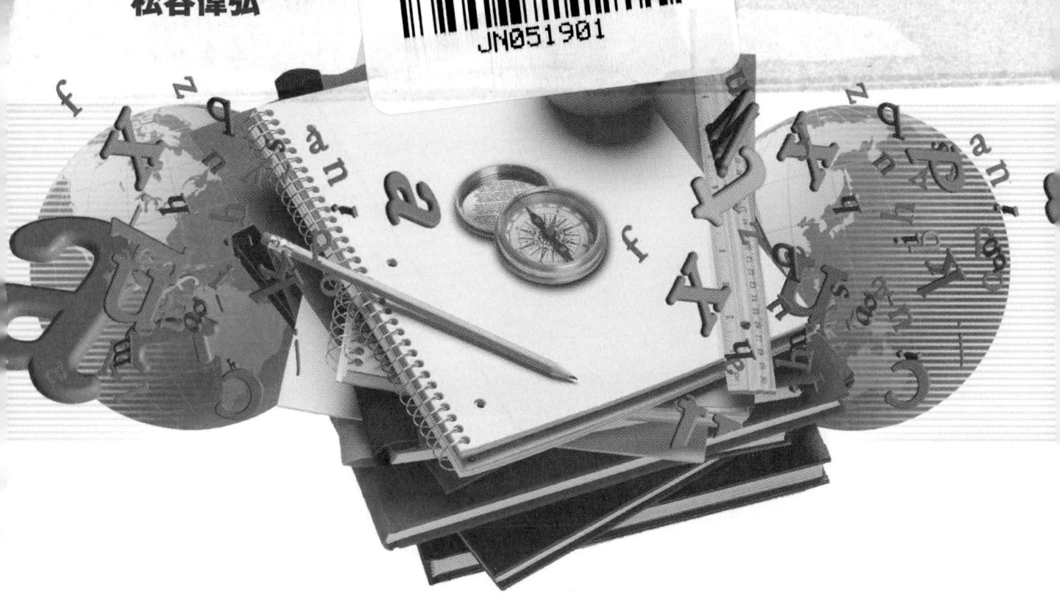

語研

本書は，弊社刊『TOEFL ITP® TEST 実戦問題集』を TOEFL ITP® TEST の出題形式，出題傾向に即して改訂し，加筆修正したものです。

# はじめに

TOEFL ITP® は主に大学のクラス分けや単位認定，大学院入試，留学者選抜試験などのために利用されている団体向けテストプログラムです。国内で採用している教育機関や企業は500 以上にのぼります。

TOEFL ITP® でスコアアップを図るには，適切な教材で受験準備をすることが絶対条件です。私たちは，これまでに 50 冊以上の TOEFL 対策書を日本やアジア各国で出版してきました。教材が実際の TOEFL を正確に反映するよう，私たちは自ら TOEFL を受験することはもちろん，TOEFL 問題作成者と定期的にミーティングの機会を持ち，また過去の問題を詳細に分析して，その結果を教育誌に発表してきました。本書は，私たちのそうした分析の最新成果です。TOEFL ITP® をはじめて受験する方，なかなかスコアが上がらずに苦労している方，短期間でのスコアアップをめざす方のために，3 回分の模試（計 420 問）を用意し，すべての問題に詳細な解説と解き方を示してあります。

TOEFL ITP® でスコアアップを実現するためには，まず Listening Comprehension, Structure and Written Expression, Reading Comprehension の 3 セクションのすべてについて効果的な受験ストラテジー（攻略法）を身につける必要があります。そのうえで，実際のテストの出題傾向を忠実に反映した良質の問題を数多く，しかも繰り返し解きながら，身につけたストラテジーを実際そのままの受験環境の中で 100 パーセント発揮できる「受験力」を高めなければなりません。

⇨ 良質な模試 3 回分（計 420 問）

⇨ 本物に限りなく近い出題傾向とコンテンツ

⇨ ハイクオリティの音声データ

本書のこれらの要素が皆さんのスコアアップ，ひいては大学生活，留学生活を成功させる一助となることを願っています。

2024 年 4 月

著者

# 目 次

【装丁】山田 英春
【CD 吹き込み】Edith Kayumi
Josh Keller
Jack Merluzzi
Carolyn Miller

## 音声について (音声無料ダウンロード)

◆ 本書の音声は無料でダウンロードすることができます。下記の URL または QR コードからアクセスしてご利用ください。

https://www.goken-net.co.jp/catalog/card.html?isbn=978-4-87615-431-9

◆ 実戦問題 3 回分の Listening Comprehension に対応する音声が収録されています。

### ⚠ 注意事項 ⚠

● ダウンロードで提供する音声は，複数のファイル・フォルダを ZIP 形式で 1 ファイルにまとめています。ダウンロード後に復元してご利用ください。ダウンロード後に，ZIP 形式に対応した復元アプリを必要とする場合があります。

● 音声ファイルは MP 3 形式です。モバイル端末，パソコンともに，MP 3 ファイルを再生可能なアプリ，ソフトを利用して聞くことができます。

● インターネット環境によってダウンロードできない場合や，ご使用の機器によって再生できない場合があります。

● 本書の音声ファイルは，一般家庭での私的使用の範囲内で使用する目的で頒布するものです。それ以外の目的で本書の音声ファイルの複製・改変・放送・送信などを行いたい場合には，著作権法の定めにより，著作権者等に申し出て事前に許諾を受ける必要があります。

# TOEFL ITP® テスト<br>について

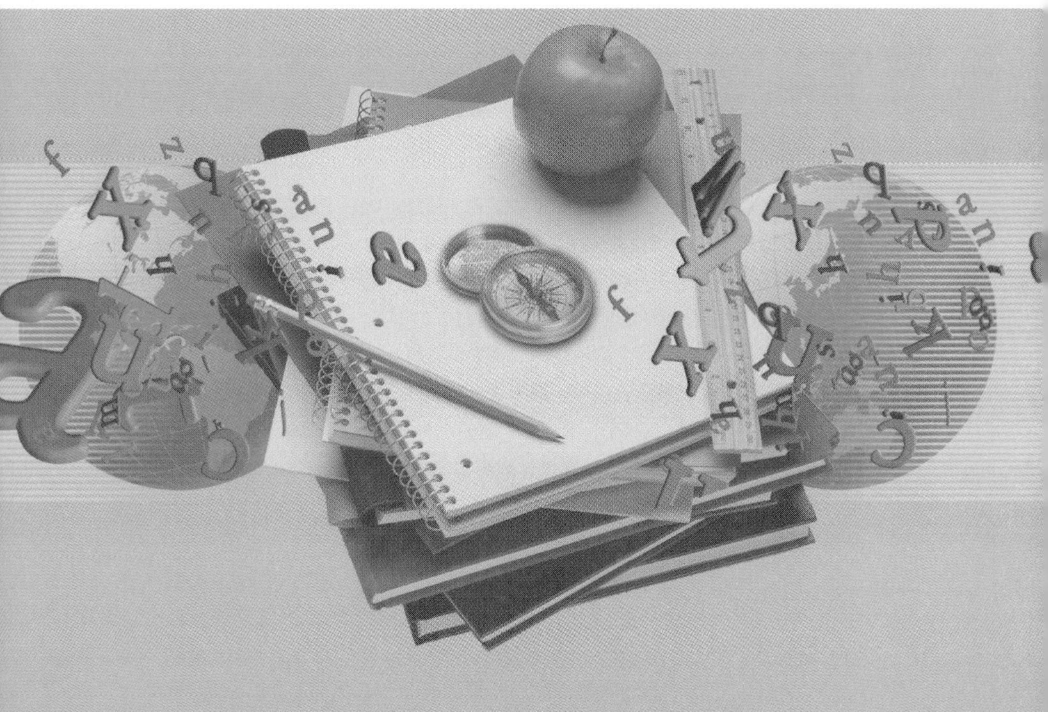

## 1. TOEFL ITP® テストとは

TOEFL（Test of English as a Foreign Language）は米国，カナダの大学，大学院への留学を希望する，英語を母国語としない人々に課される英語能力評価テストです。アメリカの標準化テスト開発機関 ETS（Educational Testing Service）が問題を作成し，日本での運営は ETS Japan 合同会社が行っています。

TOEFL は本来，留学希望者の英語能力を評価する目的で作成されているため，その内容もキャンパスでの会話，大学でのディスカッション，アメリカ史や地学などの大学での講義内容を素材として，アカデミズム指向の強い試験となっています。

TOEFLはこれまで，PBT（Paper-Based Test），CBT（Computer-Based Test），iBT（internet-Based Test）とさまざまな形式を取り入れてきましたが，2006 年以降は，留学希望者に対しては TOEFL iBT® のみの受験が義務付けられています。

TOEFL ITP®（Test of English as a Foreign Language Institutional Testing Program）は団体受験に限って実施されているテストで，マークシート方式のペーパー版と，インターネット接続できるコンピュータを使用したデジタル版があります。2020 年から導入されたデジタル版は，問題数およびスコアスケールがペーパー版と同一です。TOEFL ITP® は，主に大学，短期大学，語学学校でのクラス分けや大学院入試のために活用されています。受験結果は公式の TOEFL スコアとしては認定されないため，留学志望先には提出できません（TOEFL iBT® のスコアを提出する必要があります）。しかし，過去のペーパーテスト版 TOEFL（PBT）の問題を再利用し，採点方法なども TOEFL iBT® に準じているため，TOEFL iBT® のスコアと高い相関関係があるとされています。そのため，現在 500 以上の教育機関（高校・大学・大学院など）や団体，企業で実施されています。生徒や社員の英語力の測定，交換留学の選抜試験，社員の研修，クラス分けのために利用されています。また，TOEFL iBT® に比べ，受験料も安くて受験しやすいため，TOEFL iBT® の受験準備にも多く利用されています。TOEFL ITP® は団体受験限定ですので，受験申し込みは所属している団体や教育機関にご確認ください。

## 2. TOEFL ITP® の構成

TOEFL ITP® は Listening Comprehension, Structure and Written Expression, Reading Comprehension の3つのセクションで構成されています。TOEFL ITP® には Level 1 と Level 2 があり，Level 2 は初中級者向けにやさしめに作られたテストです。本書では，過去の PBT 問題をそのまま利用した Level 1 を対象としています。

| ◆Section 1 | *Listening Comprehension*（所要時間：約35分　設問数：50問） |
|---|---|
| Part A | 短い会話を聞き，その内容についての設問に答える。<br>（約15分　30問） |
| Part B | 長めの会話を聞き，その内容についての設問に答える。<br>（約7分　8問または9問，会話は2題） |
| Part C | 講義，学術的なトークなどを聞き，その内容についての設問に答える。<br>（約12分　12問または11問，トークは3題） |
| ◆Section 2 | *Structure and Written Expression*（所要時間：25分　設問数：40問） |
| Structure | 空所補充問題（15問） |
| Written Expression | 誤文訂正問題（25問） |
| ◆Section 3 | *Reading Comprehension*（所要時間：55分　設問数：50問） |
| パッセージ（250～350語程度）を読み，その内容あるいは語彙についての設問に答える。<br>（50問，パッセージは5題または6題） | |

試験時間は約2時間，問題は全部で140問あります。試験監督官の指示に従い，最初に Listening Comprehension を解き，その後に Structure and Written Expression と Reading Comprehension に移ります。試験監督官の指示に従って，指定されたセクションだけを解かなければなりません。他のセクションを無断で解いていると判断された場合には，スコアが無効になる可能性があります。

なお，減点法は採用されていませんので，必ず全問を解くように心がけてください。どうしても正答がわからない場合は，必ず選択肢のひとつにマークしてから次の問題に進みます。その際は常に特定の選択肢にマークしても，そのつどマークする選択肢を変えても，それが偶然に正答になる確率は変わりません。

## 3. TOEFL ITP® と TOEFL iBT® の違い

| | TOEFL ITP® | | TOEFL iBT® | |
|---|---|---|---|---|
| | 設問数 | 時間 | 設問数 | 時間 |
| Listening (Comprehension) | 50 問 | 約 35 分 | 28 問<br>講義：3 題（各 6 問）<br>会話：2 題（各 5 問） | 36 分 |
| Structure and Written Expression | 40 問 | 25 分 | | |
| Reading (Comprehension) | 50 問 | 55 分 | 20 問<br>2 パッセージ（各 10 問） | 35 分 |
| Speaking | | | 4 問<br>Independent task 1 問<br>Integrated tasks 3 問 | 16 分 |
| Writing | | | 2 問<br>Integrated task 1 問<br>Academic Discussion task 1 問 | 29 分 |
| 合計 | 140 問 | 約 115 分 | 54 問 | 約 2 時間 |

TOEFL ITP® は Listening Comprehension, Structure and Written Expression, Reading Comprehension の 3 部構成です。TOEFL iBT® には Structure and Written Expression はありませんが，Writing と Speaking があります。

## 4. スコアについて

スコアレポートは1～2週間で発送されます。スコアはListening ComprehensionとStructure and Written Expressionが31～68点，Reading Comprehensionが31～67点で計算されます。合計点の算出方法は，

**(Listening + Structure + Reading)×10÷3**

という計算式で，最低310点，最高677点になります。

一般的に，大学での交換留学に必要な最低基準は500点，アメリカやカナダの大学への正規留学には最低500-550点，大学院への留学では最低550-600点が必要となります。

## 5. TOEFL ITP® テスト デジタル版に関する注意点

TOEFL ITP® テストデジタル版は、TOEFL ITP® と同様に団体受験に限って実施されているテストで，大学や大学院，専門学校等で活用されています。受験結果が公式のスコアとしては認められない点も TOEFL ITP® と同様です。

デジタル版の受験は要件を満たしたパソコンのみ使用が認められています。タブレットやスマホでの受験はできません。

問題数，スコアスケール，スコアの見方はペーパー版と同じです。ただし，Structure and Written Expression と Reading Comprehension のセクションでは受験者が時間内に解答を終えれば，次のセクションに進んだり，試験を終了したりできるため，所定の解答時間より早く終わることがあります。

Listening Comprehension のセクションについては，本書は主としてペーパー版試験の解法を示しています。デジタル版については，各会話やトークが始まるときに設問と選択肢が一緒に表示される形式へ切り替えられてきています。その場合，設問を先読みする時間はほとんどありませんが，それでも設問の最初の疑問詞，主語，動詞などに素早く目を通し，設問の答えに関連する情報を聞き取るように努めるとよいでしょう。

また，デジタル版では申し込み時に追加オプションを選択することで，Speaking セクションが受験できます。問題数は全 4 問で，音読問題が 1 問，提示されるトピックスについて話す問題が 2 問，会話を聞いて内容について話す問題が 1 問出題されます。所要時間は約 15 分です。スコアは 31 ～ 68 点で計算されます。

Speaking セクションのサンプル問題は ETS の Web サイトから確認できます。

# Practice Test 1
# 第1回実戦問題

# Section 1—Listening Comprehension

Section 1 is designed to measure your ability to understand spoken English. This section has three parts: short conversations, long conversations, and talks. Each short conversation is followed by one question, and each long conversation and talk is followed by four questions. There are 50 questions in this section.

## Part A

Listen to the short conversations that follow. After each short conversation, choose the best answer to the question about that conversation.



Go on to the next page

002

**1.** What does the woman mean?

(A) She would like to bet on the game.

(B) She will go to the game tomorrow.

(C) She also bought some lottery tickets.

(D) She is surprised at what the man said.

003

**2.** What does the woman say about Professor Collins?

(A) She appeared on a news program.

(B) She just joined the science faculty.

(C) She had a problem with her computer.

(D) She is quitting her position at the university.

004

**3.** What are the speakers discussing?

(A) What they will do tomorrow

(B) The schedule of TV programs

(C) The weather forecast

(D) A bad accident on the news

005

**4.** What does the woman ask the man to do?

(A) Complete some documents

(B) Come back later

(C) Re-apply next year

(D) Estimate how much money he needs

**Go on to the next page**

006

**5.** What does the woman mean?

(A) The party will end relatively early.

(B) The man can probably attend the party later.

(C) Many people have been invited to the party.

(D) Saturday evening is the best time for a party.

007

**6.** What can be inferred about the man?

(A) He is finished reading the book.

(B) He needs to exchange the text.

(C) He is studying a foreign language.

(D) He will graduate later in the year.

008

**7.** What seems to be true about Professor Robertson?

(A) His lectures are hard to follow.

(B) His grading policy is strict.

(C) His course is becoming popular.

(D) His class is rather dull.

009

**8.** What does the woman mean?

(A) She feels about the same as usual today.

(B) She forgot to take out the trash this morning.

(C) She is extremely frustrated with her car.

(D) She does not like her sociology class.

【第1回】実戦問題 【第2回】実戦問題 【第3回】実戦問題 【第1回】実戦問題解説 【第2回】実戦問題解説 【第3回】実戦問題解説

Go on to the next page

010

**9.** Why is the man upset?

(A) He does not like the seat he has been assigned.

(B) He will not be able to attend the lecture.

(C) The woman forgot to reserve the seats.

(D) The woman could not obtain the concert tickets.

011

**10.** What can be inferred from the conversation?

(A) The woman will not tour with the orchestra.

(B) The internship is not available this year.

(C) A new office will be opened in New York.

(D) The woman does not play a musical instrument.

012

**11.** What does the man imply about Karen?

(A) She has a good sense of humor.

(B) She has not contacted him for a while.

(C) She usually does not get such good grades.

(D) She enjoys studying mathematics.

013

**12.** What does the man mean?

(A) He cannot meet the woman until tomorrow.

(B) He finds his psychology course challenging.

(C) He is thinking of dropping the class.

(D) He does not have time to study for the test.

**Go on to the next page**

014

**13.** What will the man probably do during spring break?

(A) Take a trip with his friends

(B) Visit his family in California

(C) Work on an important paper

(D) Go surfing with the woman

015

**14.** What do the speakers mean?

(A) They both like drinking coffee.

(B) The cafeteria is out of cake.

(C) Most students do not go to the cafe.

(D) They agree the cake is excellent.

016

**15.** What can be inferred about the man?

(A) He is preparing to become a teacher.

(B) His children are enrolled in a day-care center.

(C) His teacher gave him a high evaluation.

(D) He just received his teaching credential.

017

**16.** What had the woman assumed?

(A) Art would give her a ride to the dance.

(B) The man does not like dancing.

(C) The report was not about art.

(D) The man had an assignment to complete.

Go on to the next page ➡

018

**17.** What was the problem with the meeting?

(A) It was attended by few people.

(B) Its purpose was unclear.

(C) It went on longer than expected.

(D) It was called on short notice.

019

**18.** What does the man mean?

(A) He probably will not have time to help the woman.

(B) He would like the woman to join him for dinner.

(C) He will give the woman a hand this evening.

(D) He cannot solve the woman's problem.

020

**19.** What does the woman imply about the man?

(A) He often tries to avoid exercise.

(B) He stayed up too late last night.

(C) He should go jogging by himself.

(D) He ought to get a health check-up.

021

**20.** What can be inferred from the conversation?

(A) There is a new dry cleaner near the park.

(B) The paint store has gone out of business.

(C) The man will not have time to attend the concert.

(D) The woman may not be able to wear the dress she wanted to.

**Go on to the next page**

022

**21.** What does the man imply?

(A) He has been eating out a lot recently.
(B) He does not like the cafeteria's food.
(C) He is too busy to go off campus tonight.
(D) He does not want to go downtown.

023

**22.** What can be inferred about the woman?

(A) She was planning on using a credit card.
(B) She just went to the bank this morning.
(C) She is not taking classes this term.
(D) She has already purchased what she needed.

024

**23.** What will the man likely do next?

(A) Take a seat next to the woman
(B) Read a periodical
(C) Check out a book
(D) Look for another place to sit down

025

**24.** What does the man mean?

(A) Some dorm members cannot sing in tune.
(B) The dorm really needs a new piano.
(C) The piano will not be delivered for another week.
(D) Dorm students should not play the piano so much.

Go on to the next page

026

**25.** What does the man imply?

(A) He will likely fail the course he is taking.

(B) He should have studied more than he did.

(C) He could not complete all of the exam questions.

(D) He found his calculator was broken.

027

**26.** What can be inferred about the woman?

(A) She is somewhat irresponsible.

(B) She already gave her class presentation.

(C) She completed the preparation last night.

(D) She will ask the professor to change the schedule.

028

**27.** What does the woman mean?

(A) She regrets not shopping at Steve's.

(B) She could not afford to buy her textbooks.

(C) She prefers to use new textbooks.

(D) She thinks Steve's is also expensive.

029

**28.** What does the man mean?

(A) He would love to see the woman's rehearsal.

(B) He does not know his schedule for the day.

(C) He hopes he can meet the woman later.

(D) He does not have time to give the woman a ride.

Go on to the next page ➡

030

**29.** Why were the students late for class?

(A) The bus drivers went on strike.

(B) There were no open parking spaces.

(C) There was a bus accident.

(D) They had to work overtime.

031

**30.** What does the man mean?

(A) He needs to continue searching for work.

(B) He hopes he can find a better job.

(C) He did not receive any job offers.

(D) He has to choose which company to work for.

**This is the end of part A.**

**Go on to the next page ➡**

NO TEST MATERIAL ON THIS PAGE

Go on to the next page ➡

## Part B

Listen to the conversations that follow. After each conversation, choose the best answer to each of the four questions about that conversation.



Go on to the next page

033 034

## Questions 31-34

**31.** What does the man want the woman to do?

(A) Meet him later to study in the library

(B) Help him look for a new place to live

(C) Recommend a reliable moving company

(D) Suggest someone to move in with him

**32.** Why is Linda moving?

(A) She does not get along with her roommates.

(B) She can save money by living with her parents.

(C) She wants to live in an apartment closer to campus.

(D) She is not happy with the place she lives now.

**33.** What can be inferred about the dormitory?

(A) It is noisy.

(B) It is expensive.

(C) It is convenient.

(D) It is crowded.

**34.** What will the man probably do next?

(A) Give Jennifer a call

(B) Ask Linda not to leave

(C) Speak with his parents

(D) Look at the dorm contract

Go on to the next page

035 036

## Questions 35-38

**35.** Why is the man talking to the woman?

(A) To discuss a presentation topic

(B) To ask about a missed assignment

(C) To request an introduction

(D) To receive help on an essay

**36.** What subject is the man studying?

(A) American literature

(B) United States history

(C) Modern economics

(D) Contemporary sociology

**37.** What initial problem did the man have in researching his topic?

(A) He could not find many sources.

(B) He did not know what to focus on.

(C) He chose a theme that was too broad.

(D) He could not use the library databases.

**38.** What final suggestion does the woman make to the man?

(A) He should start writing as soon as possible.

(B) He should ask the library staff for help.

(C) He should come back and see her again later.

(D) He should focus on the organization of his essay.

**This is the end of part B.**

**Go on to the next page ➡**

NO TEST MATERIAL ON THIS PAGE

Go on to the next page

## Part C

Listen to the talks and lectures that follow. After each talk or lecture, choose the best answer to the four questions about it.



Go on to the next page

038 039

## Questions 39-42

**39.** What is the main purpose of the talk?

(A) To give an overview of contemporary chemistry

(B) To describe changes to the field of chemistry

(C) To identify problems facing modern chemistry

(D) To explain how to conduct research in chemistry

**40.** What point does the professor make about the field of chemistry compared to other sciences?

(A) It is the oldest.

(B) It is theoretically the most challenging.

(C) It has the greatest effect on human life.

(D) It requires the most sophisticated research.

**41.** What aspect of chemical investigation does the professor say is most crucial?

(A) Chemical change

(B) Elemental analysis

(C) Physical make-up

(D) Atomic composition

**42.** According to the professor, how is most research conducted in chemistry?

(A) By individuals

(B) By teams

(C) By academic researchers

(D) By corporate laboratories

Go on to the next page ➡

## Questions 43-46

**43.** According to the professor, when did the first peoples arrive in America?

(A) About 3,000 years ago

(B) About 13,000 years ago

(C) About 30,000 years ago

(D) About 33,000 years ago

**44.** How does the professor regard the theory that early peoples may have crossed from Europe to America?

(A) With enthusiasm

(B) With skepticism

(C) With curiosity

(D) With surprise

**45.** What does the professor's description of Siberia suggest about the various peoples there?

(A) They may have communicated with each other.

(B) They benefited from discoveries elsewhere in Asia.

(C) They shared common ancestors.

(D) They were unusually isolated and cut off.

**46.** What does the professor conclude about Native American groups?

(A) They were extremely diverse in character.

(B) They were culturally very inventive.

(C) Their languages were closely related.

(D) Their physical appearance was surprisingly similar.

Go on to the next page ➡

042 043

## Questions 47-50

**47.** What was particularly important about the early amphibians?

(A) They were the first creatures to lay eggs.

(B) They were able to breathe both under water and on land.

(C) They were the first creatures with hard backbones.

(D) They were the organisms from which land creatures evolved.

**48.** According to the professor, how many species of amphibians have been identified?

(A) 1,500

(B) 3,000

(C) 5,000

(D) 7,500

**49.** Approximately how many new species of amphibians are discovered every year?

(A) 50

(B) 150

(C) 500

(D) 850

**50.** According to the professor, why are large numbers of amphibians dying off?

(A) Changes in weather patterns

(B) Environmental pollution

(C) Loss of habitat

(D) Emergence of new diseases

**This is the end of Section 1.**

**Stop work on Section 1 now.**

---

**Go on to the next page ➡**

# Section 2—Structure and Written Expression

**Time: 25 minutes**

Section 2 is designed to measure your knowledge of the grammar and usage of written English. This section has two parts: Structure and Written Expression.

## Structure

For each of the sentences that follow, choose the answer that best completes the sentence.



Go on to the next page ➡

**1.** —— possible temperature is called absolute zero.

(A) Low

(B) The low

(C) The lower

(D) The lowest

**2.** —— the Neolithic Period, humans learned to make pottery, which enabled them to more easily and efficiently store food and water.

(A) At

(B) When

(C) During

(D) Between

**3.** Parkinson's disease, —— in people over the age of fifty, is a degenerative disease of the brain affecting muscular control.

(A) mainly that is seen

(B) seen mainly

(C) it is seen mainly

(D) which seen mainly

**4.** —— small businesses operating in North America are sole proprietorships, meaning they are owned by one person.

(A) Most of the

(B) Most of

(C) The most

(D) Almost

**Go on to the next page ➡**

**5.** Tarragon, a bushy herb with narrow leaves, contains an aromatic oil which makes it an excellent spice for flavoring salads, pickles, and ——.

(A) flavoring tartar sauce

(B) used for tartar sauce

(C) tartar sauce

(D) the tartar sauce

**6.** Robert Penn Warren, ——, was originally a member of the Fugitive Group of young Southern writers.

(A) who eventually became America's first poet laureate

(B) he eventually became America's first poet laureate

(C) America's first poet laureate he eventually became

(D) became eventually America's first poet laureate

**7.** The auditory canal, a tube leading to the outer ear opening, is found only in animals having eardrums inside —— skulls.

(A) itself

(B) themselves

(C) its

(D) their

**8.** —— as overweight, an adult male or female should have a body weight 10 to 20 percent greater than other adults of the same size and sex.

(A) Defined

(B) Defining

(C) To define

(D) To be defined



Go on to the next page ➡

**9.** Volcanic soils, ——, are often some of the richest and most fertile.

(A) by eruptions deposited

(B) they are deposited by eruptions

(C) deposited by eruptions

(D) the eruptions deposit them

**10.** Research suggests that bears that attack humans are rarely hunting for food —— rather defending their cubs or their territory.

(A) but

(B) yet

(C) however

(D) consequently

**11.** Founded in 1565 by the Spanish explorer and admiral Pedro Menéndez de Avilés, St. Augustine, Florida is —— continually inhabited city in the United States.

(A) the old

(B) the oldest

(C) older

(D) old

**12.** The telegraph, ——, was used to establish the first direct link between the West and East coasts of the United States in 1861.

(A) the first electric communication device produced by humans

(B) humans produced this first electric communication device

(C) it is the first electric communication device produced by humans

(D) which is the first produced electric device by humans

**Go on to the next page ➡**

**13.** —— the many important functions of the liver are the producing of proteins and the cleaning of the blood.

(A) That

(B) Between

(C) For

(D) Among

**14.** Residents of the District of Columbia —— and members of a city council, as well as one non-voting delegate to the Congress of the United States.

(A) election of a mayor

(B) they elect the mayor

(C) elect a mayor

(D) the mayor is elected

**15.** It is the arrangement of the electrons, ——, which determines the formation of a compound.

(A) they are different for each element

(B) different for each element

(C) each element is different

(D) that is different for each element

## Written Expression

For each of the sentences that follow, choose the underlined portion of the sentence (A, B, C, or D) that contains a grammar, usage, or word choice error.

Go on to the next page ➡

**16.** The triode, invented (A) by the American engineer Lee De Forest, it (B) was used in amplifiers until (C) it was superseded by the (D) transistor during the 1950's.

**17.** It is estimation (A) that there are (B) about 1 billion bicycles in use (C) throughout the world, compared (D) to about 1.5 billion automobiles.

**18.** Asset (A) stripping is the sale (B) or exploitation of the assets of a business, often those (C) that has been intentionally (D) acquired for that purpose.

**19.** The Esch-Cummins Act of 1920, also known as (A) the Railroad Transportation Act, returning (B) the railroads to (C) private operation (D).

**20.** The planet Uranus has at least (A) ten rings, which is (B) composed mainly (C) of jagged (D) rocks and icy boulders.



Go on to the next page ➡

**21.** The fathom, a unit of measurement once used both at sea including on
A B
land, approximates the distance between an adult man's outstretched
C D
hands.

**22.** Heavy industry, such as that involving the manufacture of steel,
A
petroleum, and rubber, require high capitalization and the production of
B C D
large quantities of materials.

**23.** Although the paintings of Morris Louis do not feature recognizable
A B
people, landscapes, or objects, their form and energy have a power effect
C D
on the viewer.

**24.** Much different micro-organisms can be classified as germs since they
A B C D
cause disease.

**25.** An audit may be conducted by either a member of the organization as an
A B
internal audit and an outsider as an independent audit.
C D

Go on to the next page ➡

**26.** The city of Long Beach is home to the largest commercial port in
A B C
California there.
D

**27.** The most significantly provider of retirement income in the United States
A B C
is the Social Security Administration, which oversees a non-voluntary

pension plan.
D

**28.** William Buckley, a writer conservative and editor, founded *The National*
A B
*Review* in 1955 as a forum for his right-wing political views.
C D

**29.** In the mid-19th century, the industrial revolution marked the beginning of
A B C
mass production, technological innovation, and transportation of the public.
D

**30.** An amphibian must spend part of its life cycle in the water, there its eggs
A B C
are laid and fertilized.
D

**31.** Regarded as the great American playwright, Tennessee Williams
A
wrote about the consequences of intense passion and pain as well as the
B C
gradual deterioration of Southern gentility.
D

**32.** Hibernation is a state which occur in some mammals, such as bats and
A B
gophers, during which the animals' heart rate and respiration slow down.
C D

**33.** Collectivist societies place emphasis on the optimal performance of the
A B
group instead the outstanding achievements of the individual.
C D

**34.** One of the distinguishing characteristic of the Hudson River School
A
of Painting was its focus on vast landscapes, especially mountains and
B C D
rivers.

**35.** The phrase "The Roaring Twenties" was employed to characterize the
A B
society, artistic, and cultural dynamism of the 1920's.
C D

**Go on to the next page ➡**

**36.** The most significant accomplishment of Eli Whitney, famous for his
A
invention of the cotton gin, it was actually his achievement of producing
B C
equipment with interchangeable parts.
D

**37.** Charles Monroe Schultz was an American artist which *Peanuts* cartoons
A B
brought him worldwide fame.
C D

**38.** The market price of palladium, like those of gold or silver, is determined
A B
by a combination of factors including current supply, future production,
C
and projected demand.
D

**39.** With requiring that dogs be vaccinated while they are young, public
A B
health officials have been able to bring rabies and other canine diseases
C D
under control.

**40.** For half a century the logging of timber plays an important role in
A B C
Michigan's economy, though its influence is now negligible.
D

**This is the end of Section 2.**

**Stop work on Section 2 now.**

**Go on to the next page ➡**

NO TEST MATERIAL ON THIS PAGE

Go on to the next page

# Section 3—Reading Comprehension

**Time: 55 minutes**

Read the passages that follow. After each passage, respond to the questions by choosing the best answer to each question.



**Go on to the next page** ➡

## Questions 1-10

Line

Joseph Pulitzer is now mainly known for the writing prizes which bear his name, but he exemplified "the American Dream": the notion that anyone could, through diligence and perseverance, become a success regardless of national origin or background. As a teenager, Pulitzer immigrated from Hungary and fought for the Union during the Civil War.

After the war, Pulitzer, who could speak German and French, moved to Missouri, drawn by the growing German community there. At first, like many others, he struggled to make ends meet, performing a range of menial tasks and working as a waiter, a taxi driver, and even a caretaker of mules. Finally, in 1868 he landed an office job with a railroad company. The young Pulitzer impressed the company's lawyers so much that they encouraged him to become an attorney himself. In a quick rise that would foreshadow his future success, he completed his studies within a year and was admitted to the bar to practice law. But due to his youth, odd appearance, worn clothes, and imperfect English, Pulitzer attracted few clients. He did, however, manage to come to the attention of Carl Schurz, chief reporter and co-owner of the influential German-language newspaper in the community, who admired Pulitzer's intensity and his affinity for hard work.

When Schurz was elected to the United States Senate, he was forced to devote more of his time and effort to politics. Consequently, the newspaper needed to hire a new reporter to take over some of his duties. Pulitzer was the choice, and he proved to be indefatigable, often working late in the night. He was such a prolific writer and showed such a mastery of his job that within the year he was promoted to help run the newspaper. Assigned to cover the Missouri state legislature, he made himself well known as a critic of the Democrats who controlled the legislature. In 1871, Pulitzer was chosen partly as a joke by the Republican party to run as a candidate in the upcoming election for the state legislature. The Republicans felt they had no chance of winning the election, but they relished the thought of the relentless Pulitzer campaigning against the Democrats. Pulitzer surprised everyone by winning an improbable victory in the general election. At age 21, he was four years too young to officially assume his seat in the state senate; nonetheless, no one objected to his participating, and Pulitzer went on to exert his influence for many years, politically as well as journalistically.

**1.** The word "menial" in line 8 is closest in meaning to

(A) extraordinary
(B) challenging
(C) profitable
(D) humble

**2.** According to the passage, Pulitzer moved to Missouri because of

(A) a particularly good job offer
(B) the chance to purchase land
(C) the presence of European immigrants
(D) the recommendation of a famous journalist

**3.** Why was Pulitzer unsuccessful as a lawyer?

(A) He failed to pass the bar exam.
(B) He did not look like a lawyer.
(C) No law firms would hire him.
(D) He was unfamiliar with Missouri law.

**4.** The word "foreshadow" in line 12 is closest in meaning to

(A) prevent
(B) predict
(C) aid
(D) justify

**5.** It can be inferred from the passage that Pulitzer's success in winning election to the state senate was

(A) regretful
(B) misguided
(C) ironic
(D) futile

Go on to the next page ➡

**6.** The word "indefatigable" in line 21 is closest in meaning to

(A) tireless

(B) reliable

(C) exemplary

(D) adept

**7.** It can be inferred from the passage that the minimum age to serve in the Missouri state legislature was

(A) 21

(B) 25

(C) 30

(D) 35

**8.** Which of the following generalizations is supported by the passage?

(A) Politics and journalism do not mix.

(B) America attracted many immigrants during the 18th century.

(C) German immigrants greatly influenced American history.

(D) Anyone could succeed if he or she works hard enough.

**9.** The author organizes the discussion according to what principle?

(A) Chronology

(B) Comparison

(C) Classification

(D) Contrast

**10.** A paragraph following the passage would most likely discuss

(A) a change in the Missouri legislature's age requirements

(B) Pulitzer's accomplishments in his subsequent career

(C) Pulitzer's campaign in the upcoming senate election

(D) Missouri's increasing influence on national politics

**Go on to the next page ➡**

## Questions 11-20

Electrical lighting played a major role in transforming the world in the 20th century because it allowed humans to basically transcend the limitations of the natural lighting of the Sun and to continue their activities at night. The history of the electric light bulb, since its "first invention" by Thomas Edison in 1879, has been one of slow and steady progress as gradually technology has given humans more light for less cost, becoming cheaper but brighter, decade after decade.

The first light was the incandescent lamp, which radiates light from a thread or filament heated by passing an electric current through it until it glows. Although Sir Joseph Wilson Swan in England fabricated an incandescent lamp one year prior to Edison, Edison constructed a complete lighting system and thus was given credit for the bulb's invention. Among the subsequent improvements to Edison's bulb were replacing the original carbon filaments with tungsten filaments for longer life, coiling them for improved efficiency, and frosting the interior of the glass bulb to soften its light.

In the late 19th century, French physicist Georges Claude discovered that a vapor tube filled with neon gas under low pressure produces intense orange-red light. He also found that additional colors could be produced by adding small amounts of other substances to a tube containing neon gas, gaseous sodium, or mercury. Even at that time Claude recognized the value of his invention for commercial signs. Neon signs became popular for this reason in the 1920's, and they are still used in the same way today.

During the 1930's, fluorescent lamps first came into use. These long tubes contain mercury vapor that fluoresces, or glows, when subjected to the radiation of the mercury discharge. Fluorescent lamps, which are far more efficient and longer-lived than incandescent lamps, were the first vapor-tube lamps to be used indoors.



Go on to the next page

**11.** What is the main purpose of the passage?

(A) To identify the inventor of the first light bulb
(B) To analyze the influence of the light bulb on human society
(C) To outline the technological evolution of the light bulb
(D) To compare the shortcomings of various kinds of light bulbs

**12.** Which of the following statements can be inferred from the first paragraph?

(A) The development of electrical lights significantly influenced modern society.
(B) The technology of electrical lighting was advanced by sudden breakthroughs.
(C) Electrical lighting has changed the biological rhythms of humans.
(D) Electric lights were reluctantly accepted by many people.

**13.** In the second paragraph, what do we learn about the invention of electric lighting?

(A) Thomas Edison invented the first light bulb.
(B) The first light systems used tungsten filaments.
(C) A British inventor created the first electric lamp.
(D) The first electrical lights had soft tones.

**14.** The word "subsequent" in line 11 is closest in meaning to

(A) later
(B) unexpected
(C) innovative
(D) expensive

**15.** What is most likely the main use of the neon light?

(A) Street lighting
(B) Indoor lighting
(C) Advertising
(D) Heating

Go on to the next page ➡

**16.** What type of gas is contained in fluorescent lights?

(A) Neon
(B) Sodium
(C) Mercury
(D) Fluoride

**17.** According to the passage, what was the first vapor-tube lamp to be used inside buildings?

(A) The incandescent bulb
(B) The neon lamp
(C) The fluorescent light
(D) The carbon filament lamp

**18.** The phrase "subjected to" in line 23 is closest in meaning to

(A) exposed to
(B) condensed by
(C) dissolved by
(D) fused to

**19.** Where in the passage does the author refer to the relationship between the development of lighting and its price?

(A) Paragraph 1
(B) Paragraph 2
(C) Paragraph 3
(D) Paragraph 4

**20.** The tone of the passage could best be described as

(A) cynical
(B) neutral
(C) anxious
(D) skeptical

Go on to the next page ➡

## Questions 21-30

The music called "the blues" is difficult to define. Some people think of the blues as a type of music that embodies a particular feeling (the blues); others regard it primarily as a musical genre characterized by a special blues scale which contains twelve bars and three chords in a particular order. The blues also involves particular characteristics of voice and movement and could be described as poetry set to dance music. Whatever the exact definition, its influence on jazz, gospel music, theater music, rock, and almost every subsequent form of popular music in the 20th century was incalculable.

The blues cannot be traced to a specific composer or particular date, but as an identifiable form of music it originated in the Mississippi Delta region of Louisiana towards the end of the 19th century. The earliest appearance of printed music recognizable as the blues was the publication of W.C. Handy's "the Memphis Blues" in 1912, and Handy himself said he had first heard the blues along the lower Mississippi River in 1890. Early blues singers composed their own songs, accompanying themselves on a piano or a guitar. They played solo, inventing verses and borrowing also from other singers, and they were probably the first American artists to express the feelings of social and personal alienation from modern life, and to rise above them through their art. By singing about frustration, mistreatment, or misfortune, and often by overcoming it with irony, blues singers helped themselves and their listeners to deal with the problems of life, whether frustrated and angered by cheating lovers, ignorant bosses, crooked shopkeepers, police brutality, inadequate pay, unemployment, or racism. Blues singers fought human adversity by asserting human creativity, by turning life into art through ironic rebuttal, by linking themselves through their traditional art to others in the community, and by holding out a future hope for freedom and better times down the road. Blues lyrics represent an oral poetry of considerable merit, perhaps one of the finest genres of home-grown poetry in the English language.

Go on to the next page ➡

**21.** What is the main purpose of the first paragraph?

(A) To summarize the history of the blues

(B) To describe the origin of the blues

(C) To offer a general definition of the blues

(D) To contrast different styles of blues

**22.** In paragraph 1, the author implies that

(A) blues in its purest form is an instrumental music

(B) blues affected many types of modern music

(C) blues has yet to be fully appreciated as music

(D) blues is an exclusively African American music

**23.** The word "exact" in line 6 is closest in meaning to

(A) general

(B) required

(C) contemporary

(D) precise

**24.** According to the author, where did the blues begin?

(A) Memphis

(B) St. Louis

(C) Large eastern cities

(D) The southern Mississippi River

**25.** According to the passage, what was distinct to early American blues singers?

(A) They reflected a modern sense of social isolation.

(B) They produced songs of vigorous political protest.

(C) They performed in collaborations with other artists.

(D) They received adequate compensation for their work.

Go on to the next page ➡

**26.** What can be inferred about early blues singers from paragraph 2?

(A) They usually copyrighted their music.
(B) They played individually.
(C) They used many different instruments.
(D) They performed before large audiences.

**27.** Which of the following is NOT mentioned as a topic of blues songs?

(A) Lack of money
(B) The difficulty in finding a job
(C) The frustrations of love
(D) Respect for authority

**28.** The word "recognizable" in line 12 is closest in meaning to

(A) identifiable
(B) achievable
(C) released
(D) disputed

**29.** The author mentions English language poetry because

(A) the blues was widely recognized by literary critics
(B) blues songs were often written down and published as poems
(C) blues lyrics can be regarded as a form of sung poetry
(D) the blues was based in part upon rural English verse

**30.** The word "them" in line 18 refers to

(A) early blues singers
(B) verses
(C) other singers
(D) the feelings

**Go on to the next page ➡**

## Questions 31-40

The leaf is one of the three types of organs that collectively make up a typical plant found on land. The other two are the roots, which serve to anchor the plant and absorb water, and the stem, which supports the leaves and bears water and other materials, such as minerals and other nutrients, to and from them. The leaf is the plant's photosynthetic organ, the place where light is used to manufacture the food necessary for the plant to live. In its strictest sense, the term "leaf" is applied only to the photosynthetic organs of vascular plants, which have specialized systems to conduct food, water, and other materials. In a loose sense, however, the term is sometimes informally used to refer to the leaf-like structures of mosses and some liverworts. These structures do indeed carry on photosynthesis, but since they do not possess a vascular system, they are more properly classified as something other than leaves.

To perform their photosynthetic function, true leaves are typically thin and flat in order to maximize the amount of surface area available to absorb light and to facilitate the exchange of gases with the atmosphere. They are usually green because the color of the major photosynthetic element, chlorophyll, is green. A typical leaf consists of a flattened surface and an internal stalk. The arrangement of leaves on a stem is not random: the most important principle of leaf arrangement is that the leaves are oriented so that each leaf is exposed to the light with a minimum of interference from neighboring leaves.



Go on to the next page ➡

**31.** The main purpose of the passage is to

(A) describe the function of leaves
(B) offer a definition of a plant
(C) identify different kinds of leaves
(D) demonstrate the importance of plants

**32.** The word "them" in line 5 refers to

(A) roots
(B) leaves
(C) other materials
(D) minerals

**33.** The word "conduct" in line 8 is closest in meaning to

(A) absorb
(B) replace
(C) transport
(D) isolate

**34.** According to the passage, one function of the root is to provide

(A) stability to the plant
(B) access to sunlight
(C) synthesis of nutrients
(D) protection from fungi

**35.** According to the first paragraph, all of the following are organs of plants on land EXCEPT

(A) leaves
(B) roots
(C) stems
(D) seeds

Go on to the next page ➡

**36.** Referring to moss as "having leaves" would most likely be regarded by the author as

(A) a misunderstanding of function
(B) an overly strict interpretation
(C) a suitable usage among specialists
(D) technically inappropriate

**37.** It can be inferred from the passage that the physical appearance of a leaf primarily depends on

(A) the function it is designed to perform
(B) the color of the chlorophyll it contains
(C) the amount of usable sunlight it can receive
(D) the number of leaves attached to one stem

**38.** It can be inferred that a leaf is most similar in operation to which of the following?

(A) A factory
(B) A highway
(C) A warehouse
(D) A conduit

**39.** The word "oriented" in line 19 is closest in meaning to

(A) incorporated
(B) aligned
(C) dressed
(D) adhered

**40.** According to the passage, how are leaves on a particular stem generally arranged?

(A) In a pattern unique to that particular species of plant
(B) At equal intervals around the circumference of the stem
(C) In a manner that avoids blocking the light to adjacent leaves
(D) With the larger leaves attached highest on the stem

Go on to the next page ➡

## Questions 41-50

The history of Canadian literature is interesting chiefly as the record of a young nation's attempts to establish its own cultural identity, to find its own language, and to come to terms with its own environment. There have been no giant literary figures among Canadian writers. To be sure, a few writers have come to the attention of the world community for their work, but in all cases their reputations have faded with time. The quantity and quality of Canadian writing have made steady progress, even spectacular progress, but no serious literary critic would claim that the literature of Canada rivals that of England, France, Russia, or the United States.

This fact is partially attributable to the youth of Canada, which celebrated its first centennial in 1967 and is only around 150 years old today. But there are other reasons. The country and its culture have had to grow up in the shadow of not one but two founding nations—England and France—and of its great neighbor to the south, the United States. It has been difficult for Canadian authors to avoid imitating the styles of these more established literary traditions and to find a distinctive "Canadianism" which is not a mere compromise among them. This was certainly understandable in the early literature of Canada, since the writers of the 18th and early 19th century were themselves citizens of the colonial powers. In fact, it was not until the latter half of the 19th century that anything even approaching a national literature began to appear. Furthermore, unlike the United States and France, Canada has had no revolution; hence, there has been no great national crisis to shock it into self-awareness.

Until very recently, almost all Canadian poetry has been predominantly landscape poetry, strongly influenced by the overpowering presence of the country's magnificent and varied vistas. Until the 1920's, almost all novels were overly simplified historical romances designed to give Canadians a sense of their past and some hope for the future. Beginning in the mid-1920's, however, Canadian writers at last began to turn towards more realistic themes and the symbolic, even satirical, exploration of contemporary life. Since the end of World War II, this trend became particularly pronounced and, without question, is a positive sign for the future of Canadian literature.

Go on to the next page

**41.** What is the main purpose of paragraph 1?

(A) To imply that Canada is incapable of producing high-quality literature
(B) To maintain that Canada has no distinctive national identity
(C) To show that some Canadian writers have gained international attention
(D) To suggest that Canadian literature has yet to achieve a high standing

**42.** What does the author claim has happened to those Canadian writers who have gained international recognition?

(A) Their fame did not last long.
(B) Their work was below acceptable standards.
(C) They ignored their own cultural environment.
(D) They rival their counterparts in other countries.

**43.** Which of the following is NOT cited by the author as a reason why it has been difficult for Canada to develop a unique literary tradition?

(A) The influence of other nations
(B) The lack of a defining national crisis
(C) The country's relatively short history
(D) The country's lack of large cities

**44.** The word "spectacular" in line 7 is closest in meaning to

(A) visible
(B) compatible
(C) steadfast
(D) striking

**45.** According to the passage, when did Canadian literature first display elements of a national literature?

(A) In the late 18th century
(B) In the early 19th century
(C) In the late 19th century
(D) In the early 20th century

Go on to the next page ➡

**46.** The word "it" in line 20 refers to

(A) the United States
(B) Canada
(C) revolution
(D) national crisis

**47.** The word "pronounced" in line 29 is closest in meaning to

(A) mentioned
(B) maintained
(C) multiplied
(D) marked

**48.** The author's attitude toward the early Canadian novels can best be described as

(A) neutral
(B) critical
(C) appreciative
(D) indifferent

**49.** Where in the passage does the author refer to the major influence on traditional Canadian poetry?

(A) Lines 6-8
(B) Lines 9-10
(C) Lines 17-19
(D) Lines 22-24

**50.** With which of the following statements would the author most likely agree?

(A) Meaningful literature employs a degree of symbolism.
(B) Contemporary life cannot be realistically portrayed.
(C) Much of Canada's early literature has been unfairly neglected.
(D) The literary trends of the 1920's have unfortunately died out.

**This is the end of the test.**

# Practice Test 2
# 第2回実戦問題

# Section 1—Listening Comprehension

Section 1 is designed to measure your ability to understand spoken English. This section has three parts: short conversations, long conversations, and talks. Each short conversation is followed by one question, and each long conversation and talk is followed by four questions. There are 50 questions in this section.

## Part A

Listen to the short conversations that follow. After each short conversation, choose the best answer to the question about that conversation.



Go on to the next page

045

**1.** What does the woman mean?

(A) She would like to hear the music play a little longer.
(B) She thinks the design of the department is nice.
(C) She likes the clothes the actors wear in the drama.
(D) She feels the performance is unusually good.

046

**2.** What are the speakers discussing?

(A) What the weather will be like tomorrow
(B) What they ate for breakfast this morning
(C) What TV programs will be on this afternoon
(D) What they are planning to do today

047

**3.** What does the man imply?

(A) His tests should not be too difficult tomorrow.
(B) He has a lot of studying to do tonight.
(C) He does not think the concert will be very good.
(D) His classes require only a few tests this term.

048

**4.** What does the man mean?

(A) He is not going to give the class lecture a second time.
(B) He does not yet know all the students in the class.
(C) He does not understand why so many students are missing class.
(D) He will not give the woman another warning.

Go on to the next page

049

**5.** What can be inferred from the conversation?

(A) The man did not work hard last year.
(B) The class requires a lot of effort.
(C) The woman missed the last class.
(D) The professor is an easy grader.

050

**6.** What does the woman imply about Mike?

(A) He should study more than he does.
(B) He often goes to the library.
(C) He works for the local newspaper.
(D) He has a lot of classes.

051

**7.** What will the woman probably do tonight?

(A) Cook dinner for her roommates
(B) Study for an important examination
(C) Eat dinner at the school cafeteria
(D) Conduct a chemistry experiment

052

**8.** What does the man mean?

(A) The woman should not worry so much.
(B) He will not be in the lab for a while.
(C) He will be sure to lock the facility.
(D) The woman should take care of the laboratory.



Go on to the next page

053

**9.** What do the speakers imply about Paul?

(A) He is taking too many classes this term.

(B) He enjoys watching basketball.

(C) He has to improve his grades.

(D) He needs some variety in his life.

054

**10.** What can be inferred about the woman?

(A) She spent her vacation in Florida.

(B) She moved back into the dorm.

(C) She worked over the summer.

(D) She ran out of spending money.

055

**11.** What does the woman mean?

(A) Nobody knew what the homework was today.

(B) Somebody must have borrowed her textbook.

(C) Professor Morris stayed home today.

(D) The class assignment is too demanding.

056

**12.** What is the problem?

(A) The seminar room is already being used.

(B) The man forgot to contact the woman.

(C) The woman did not receive the man's message.

(D) The lecture was mistakenly canceled.

**Go on to the next page** ➡

057

**13.** What does the woman want to know?

(A) The meaning of a specialized term
(B) The reason for a recent tax increase
(C) The current tax rate on luxury cars
(D) The assignment for an economics class

058

**14.** What does the woman mean?

(A) The man should choose a different graduate program.
(B) The man should consider going to the job fair.
(C) The man should finish his applications as soon as possible.
(D) There may not be any good jobs available now.

059

**15.** What does the man plan to do?

(A) Put off writing his papers
(B) Read two newspapers
(C) Meet with the group next week
(D) Sign up for a better literature class

060

**16.** What does the man imply?

(A) It does not matter that the woman missed class.
(B) He would like to talk to the woman at once.
(C) The class did not start on time again today.
(D) The woman is frequently late.

Go on to the next page ➡

061

**17.** What does the woman suggest the man do?

(A) Come back later in the afternoon

(B) Attend her lecture series

(C) Visit her office later

(D) Review the proposal with his research partner

062

**18.** What will the speakers probably do later?

(A) Watch a television program

(B) Take a boat through the channel

(C) Copy some documents

(D) Have dinner around 7 o'clock.

063

**19.** Why is the man so happy?

(A) He won a lottery prize.

(B) His vacation has started.

(C) He did well on his finals.

(D) His professor canceled an exam.

064

**20.** What does the man suggest the woman do?

(A) Enroll in his course next term

(B) Study harder to follow the course topics

(C) Be more enthusiastic about her studies

(D) Take some more economics classes

**Go on to the next page**

065

**21.** What does the woman mean?

(A) The man can borrow her notes.

(B) She does not have any extra paper.

(C) The man should not use so much paper.

(D) She will give the man a notebook.

066

**22.** What does the man imply about the woman?

(A) She should not change her major so often.

(B) She would have been successful in business.

(C) She should consider becoming an anthropology major.

(D) She will find her new major too difficult.

067

**23.** What can be inferred about the man's research paper?

(A) It is already finished.

(B) Its topic may be too broad.

(C) It needs to be more deeply researched.

(D) Its length is inadequate.

068

**24.** What does the man tell the woman about Professor Stein?

(A) She has announced her plans to retire early.

(B) She has been appointed to the university administration.

(C) She is applying to be a full-time researcher.

(D) She will become the vice president of a private company.



**Go on to the next page**

069

**25.** How is the man feeling?

(A) Delighted

(B) Disappointed

(C) Nervous

(D) Frustrated

070

**26.** What does the woman imply about the man's presentation partner?

(A) She is not very good at public speaking.

(B) She is very busy with her part-time work.

(C) She does not prepare well enough in advance.

(D) She is very hard to communicate with.

071

**27.** What does the woman mean?

(A) She has finished making the calculations.

(B) She never received the calculations.

(C) She already returned the man's calculator.

(D) She forgot completely about the calculator.

072

**28.** What does the man suggest the woman do?

(A) Talk to the political science faculty

(B) Contact the mayor's office for an interview

(C) Get some advice from the senior students

(D) Apply for the position next year

Go on to the next page

073

**29.** What does the woman plan to do?

(A) Pick up some office supplies

(B) Go shopping with the man

(C) Stay home and write

(D) Copy some computer files

074

**30.** What does the woman mean?

(A) She was very disappointed with her test results.

(B) She is glad she finally completed the biology class.

(C) She was sad that Mark was not able to meet her.

(D) She has been under a lot of pressure this term.



**This is the end of part A.**

**Go on to the next page ➡**

**NO TEST MATERIAL ON THIS PAGE**

Go on to the next page ➡

## Part B

Listen to the conversations that follow. After each conversation, choose the best answer to each of the four questions about that conversation.



Go on to the next page

076 077

## Questions 31-34

**31.** Where is the man going?

(A) To football practice

(B) To a dance performance

(C) To the student center

(D) To a job recruitment fair

**32.** What kind of club does the man belong to?

(A) Classical ballet

(B) Social dance

(C) American football

(D) Aerobic exercise

**33.** What kind of problem is the man's club experiencing?

(A) A shortage of new members

(B) A loss of financial support

(C) An imbalance between sexes

(D) A lack of practice space

**34.** What does the woman say she will do?

(A) Talk to members of the football team

(B) Take a new exercise course

(C) Telephone the man tomorrow

(D) Reserve a studio for the dance club's practice

Go on to the next page ➡

## Questions 35-38

**35.** Why did the woman decide not to apply for a scholarship?

(A) She missed the application deadline.

(B) She could not gather enough information.

(C) She found out her grades were too low to qualify.

(D) She did not think it was worth the effort.

**36.** How did the woman obtain the money she needed?

(A) She asked her parents.

(B) She borrowed it.

(C) She won a scholarship.

(D) She worked overtime.

**37.** What does the man recommend that the woman do?

(A) Ask her advisor about scholarships within the university

(B) Discuss her need for funds with the financial aid office

(C) See if her department might grant her a research assistantship

(D) Check with the student services department about part-time jobs

**38.** What does the woman plan to do next?

(A) Apply for a job

(B) Go to the bank

(C) Study at the library

(D) Meet with her advisor

**This is the end of part B.**

**Go on to the next page ➡**

NO TEST MATERIAL ON THIS PAGE

## Part C

Listen to the talks and lectures that follow. After each talk or lecture, choose the best answer to the four questions about it.



Go on to the next page

081 082

## Questions 39-42

**39.** What does the talk mainly discuss?

(A) Designing a research methodology

(B) Choosing a research topic

(C) Types of research subjects

(D) New fields of biological research

**40.** According to the professor, what particular characteristic of fruit flies was used to establish principles of heredity?

(A) Size

(B) Sex

(C) Life span

(D) Eye color

**41.** According to the professor, what advantage do mice offer medical researchers?

(A) They develop quickly.

(B) They require little care.

(C) Their genes mutate more rapidly than humans.

(D) Their nervous systems do not feel pain.

**42.** What kind of research does the professor suggest is unique to primates?

(A) Evolutionary

(B) Reproductive

(C) Genetic

(D) Emotional

Go on to the next page

083
084

## Questions 43-46

**43.** What was Frederick Taylor's main area of expertise?

(A) Product planning
(B) Factory operations
(C) Finance
(D) Marketing

**44.** Under Taylor's plan, which of the following jobs might become unnecessary?

(A) Assembly-line supervisor
(B) Company president
(C) Cost accountant
(D) Production worker

**45.** What does the professor say about Taylor's book, *The Principles of Scientific Management*?

(A) It was an immediate sensation.
(B) It was widely criticized by business managers.
(C) It was published long after it was written.
(D) It was really authored by someone else.

**46.** According to the professor, what was one of the shortcomings of Taylor's book, *The Principles of Scientific Management*?

(A) Insufficient data collection
(B) Outdated managerial techniques
(C) Overuse of personal observations
(D) Unsystematic analysis



Go on to the next page

## Questions 47-50

**47.** What is the main topic of the talk?

(A) The origin of jazz
(B) Bop music and musicians
(C) Types of bop solos
(D) Miles Davis's musical career

**48.** According to the professor, what was an unusual characteristic of bop?

(A) It was usually played by large orchestras.
(B) It was often performed at an unusually fast speed.
(C) It emphasized group harmony over individual performance.
(D) It became the most popular music of the 1930's.

**49.** What instrument did Charlie Bird Parker play?

(A) The piano
(B) The trombone
(C) The saxophone
(D) The trumpet

**50.** What will the professor do next?

(A) Personally perform a Miles Davis song
(B) Talk about Charlie Parker's career
(C) Discuss the post-bop era
(D) Play various examples of bop

**This is the end of Section 1.**

**Stop work on Section 1 now.**

**Go on to the next page**

# Section 2—Structure and Written Expression

**Time: 25 minutes**

Section 2 is designed to measure your knowledge of the grammar and usage of written English. This section has two parts: Structure and Written Expression.

## Structure

For each of the sentences that follow, choose the answer that best completes the sentence.



Go on to the next page ➡

**1.** —— Jackson Pollock was widely regarded as an accomplished painter, he abandoned the use of brushes and began pouring the paint straight onto the canvas.

(A) Despite

(B) That

(C) Nonetheless

(D) Although

**2.** A musical suite is a set of instrumental pieces —— from a stage work such as a ballet or an opera.

(A) they are often assembled

(B) which assemble often

(C) often assembled

(D) are assembled often

**3.** —— many indigenous cultures used germ-killing medicines made from plants.

(A) Even before the invention of antibiotics

(B) The invention even before of antibiotics

(C) Antibiotics even before the invention of

(D) Before even antibiotics of the invention

**4.** Destruction of habitat is —— to many endangered species.

(A) the greatest one threat

(B) one of the greatest threats

(C) a threat of the greatest

(D) greatest of one of the threats

**Go on to the next page ➡**

**5.** In economics, the decline in the domestic purchasing power of a nation's currency —— as inflation.

(A) is referred to

(B) referring to

(C) refers

(D) is referred

**6.** As most of its —— for farming, northern Minnesota's economy is largely dependent upon tourism and timber.

(A) soil is too infertile or thin

(B) too infertile or thin soil is

(C) soil too infertile or thin is

(D) too infertile or is soil thin

**7.** According to botanists, a plant species —— depending upon air temperature, sunlight exposure, and soil fertility.

(A) they flourish

(B) flourishes

(C) flourishing

(D) flourish

**8.** The value of a company's stock is determined by both its current financial strength —— its expected future performance.

(A) or

(B) but

(C) nor

(D) and



Go on to the next page ➡

**9.** —— composition of a substance can vary from being made up of a single pure element to a combination of many different elements in a compound.

(A) Chemically

(B) The chemical

(C) Chemistry

(D) A chemistry

**10.** The question of whether alien species can play a positive role in an ecological system is still the subject of —— controversy among biologists.

(A) few

(B) much

(C) any

(D) many

**11.** During a recession, both the increase in unemployment rate and —— exert stress on an economy.

(A) the tax collection rate decrease

(B) rate of decreasing the tax collection

(C) the tax collection decreasing rate

(D) the decrease in tax collection rate

**12.** Of all of the Indo-European languages still spoken in Europe, Welsh is ——.

(A) old

(B) older

(C) the oldest

(D) an oldest

**Go on to the next page ➡**

**13.** The Federal Reserve Board —— seven members who are appointed by the president of the United States and who serve fourteen-year terms.

(A) is composed of

(B) which composes

(C) is composing

(D) composed of which

**14.** ——, the New Democratic Party was formed in Canada in a merger between two other political parties.

(A) When in 1961

(B) In 1961 it was

(C) It was 1961

(D) In 1961

**15.** —— the discovery of the electron, hundreds of kinds of particles have been found.

(A) Until

(B) When

(C) Since

(D) Then



Go on to the next page ➡

## Written Expression

For each of the sentences that follow, choose the underlined portion of the sentence (A, B, C, or D) that contains a grammar, usage, or word choice error.

Go on to the next page ➡

**16.** Manganese used chiefly in the making of steel alloys, but it also has
A B C
several important agricultural uses.
D

**17.** The small miniature size of solid-state circuits makes them ideally
A B C
suited for use in the cockpits of space vehicles and aircraft.
D

**18.** It is difficult for an author to detect minor errors in their own work, so a
A B
copy editor is usually asked to perform that task.
C D

**19.** Though he attended school only through the ninth grade, Richard Wright
A B
became a novelist, short-story writer, and he was also an essayist.
C D

**20.** Early American Colonial is a style of making furnitures which primarily
A B C
utilizes maple wood.
D

**21.** Perhaps the most skilled Native American horseback riders were the
A B C
Apache tribe of Southwest.
D

**22.** From 1978 to 1981 the Einstein telescope made important discoveries by
A B
using a complex set of reflecting surfaces to form an image of the sky
C
and transmit them back to Earth.
D

**23.** It was the painters of the Ashcan School abandoned romanticism for
A B
realism and rural beauty for urban reality.
C D

**24.** Solubility is a measure of the amount of solid or gas that will dissolve in
A B
a given amount of solvent, usual a liquid.
C D

**25.** Nomination by a political party is typically the first step in a process
A B C
on which a candidate gains political office.
D

**26.** Sugarcane, classified as a grass, it annually yields over nine tons of sugar
A B C
per acre.
D

Go on to the next page ➡

**27.** Albert Ryder developed one of the most original painting styles of his
A
time, using yellowish colors that gave his works an eerie, haunting
B C
qualities.
D

**28.** Great care must be taken when producing silicon chips, both to prevent
A B
contamination by dust or to avoid manufacturing defects.
C D

**29.** Richard Feynman won the Nobel prize in physics for himself work in
A B
developing principles to reliably predict the outcomes of sub-atomic
C D
events.

**30.** In biology, there are some unusual property associated with micro-
A B
organisms, such as rapid mutation and asexual reproduction.
C D

**31.** Typically, the weaker the immune system of an organism is, the great its
A B C
susceptibility to infection.
D

**32.** Some composers are spontaneous and imaginative in the way they create
A B
their music, while others are more orderly and methodically.
C D

**33.** Throughout American history, immigrants have typically been able to
A
support them only by taking the lowest paying jobs.
B C D

**34.** Jazz, which began to emerge at the end of the 19th century, is
A B
considered a first major musical form to originate in the United States.
C D

**35.** Because of its poor topsoil and sparse rainfall, the plains of eastern
A B
Montana are utilized more for grazing than farming.
C D

**36.** According to zoologists, the horseshoe crab is possible the oldest living
A B C
animal species on Earth.
D

**37.** It was not until 1920 during the Nineteenth Amendment was ratified that
A
American women were finally granted the right to vote.
B C D

Go on to the next page ➡

**38.** One of the most vocal supporter (A) of the principle (B) of civil disobedience, the philosopher Henry David Thoreau spent a (C) night in jail in 1846 for refusing (D) to pay taxes.

**39.** For (A) his study of the regulation (B) of cholesterol and fatty acid in the body, Conrad Bloch awarded (C) a Nobel Prize in medicine in (D) 1964.

**40.** William Jennings Bryan, an (A) American populist politician, is (B) best known for lose (C) presidential elections in (D) 1896, 1900, and 1908.

**This is the end of Section 2.**

**Stop work on Section 2 now.**

**Go on to the next page ➡**

**NO TEST MATERIAL ON THIS PAGE**

Go on to the next page ➡

## Section 3—Reading Comprehension

**Time: 55 minutes**

Read the passages that follow. After each passage, respond to the questions by choosing the best answer to each question.



**Go on to the next page ➡**

## Questions 1-10

Minerals are nutrients that exist in the body and in food in organic and inorganic combinations. All tissues and internal fluids of living things contain varying quantities of them. They are constituents of bones, teeth, soft tissue, muscle, blood, and nerve cells. They are important factors in maintaining physiological processes, strengthening skeletal structures, and preserving the vigor of the heart and brain as well as all muscle and nerve systems.

Within the body, minerals play a variety of significant roles. They act as a catalyst for many biological reactions, including muscle response, the transmission of messages through the nervous system, digestion, and the utilization of nutrients in foods. Furthermore, they are important in the production of hormones and thus influence physical growth. On a daily basis, they are necessary for the absorption of vitamins. Zinc, iron, copper, magnesium, and potassium are five minerals that are particularly involved in digestion and metabolism. Minerals also keep blood and tissue fluids from becoming either too acidic or too alkaline, and they permit other nutrients to pass into the bloodstream. In addition, they help draw chemical substances in and out of the cells, and they aid in the distribution of antibodies when a foreign or toxic element enters the body.

All the minerals known to be needed by the human body must be supplied in the diet: the body does not produce them. This is one of the underlying suppositions of sound diet and healthy nutrition. Among the most important minerals sometimes missing from diets are calcium, iron, and iodine. Shortages of these essential minerals over a long period of time can have serious health consequences. For example, calcium deficiency can cause bones to be brittle and to heal slowly when broken. Adequate calcium especially needs to be absorbed by middle-aged women and by both men and women as they progress into old age. Although the various minerals can be recognized individually, minerals cannot be considered separate with respect to their utilization since they influence each other. Simply stated, every mineral affects the function of other minerals.

Go on to the next page ➡

**1.** What does the passage mainly discuss?

(A) The chemical make-up of minerals
(B) The diseases caused by lack of minerals
(C) The minerals lacking in the common diet
(D) The use of minerals in the body

**2.** In the first paragraph, the author implies that minerals are found

(A) throughout the body
(B) mainly in the bone and skeletal system
(C) largely in fluid form
(D) in a limited number of combinations

**3.** The word "They" in line 3 refers to

(A) minerals
(B) organic and inorganic combinations
(C) all tissues
(D) living things

**4.** The word "catalyst" in line 8 is closest in meaning to

(A) barrier
(B) stimulant
(C) reversal
(D) foundation

**5.** In paragraph 2, the author mentions that minerals influence all of the following functions EXCEPT

(A) the sending of nerve impulses
(B) the digesting of food
(C) the producing of hormones
(D) the creation of new cells

Go on to the next page ➡

**6.** What does paragraph 2 imply about the relation between minerals and diseases?

(A) An excessive amount of a specific mineral can cause diseases.
(B) Diseases can enter the body with minerals.
(C) Minerals play a role in fighting diseases.
(D) Physicians prescribe particular minerals to treat diseases.

**7.** According to the passage, what is the main reason that minerals are so closely related to diet?

(A) They are essential to digesting food.
(B) They are only obtained through food.
(C) They can be lost during food digestion.
(D) They may not be present in most foods.

**8.** Which mineral appears to play the most important role in maintaining healthy bones?

(A) Iron
(B) Zinc
(C) Calcium
(D) Potassium

**9.** The word "Adequate" in line 25 is closest in meaning to

(A) abundant
(B) sufficient
(C) diminished
(D) vigorous

**10.** What does the author conclude about minerals?

(A) They have a complex relation to one another.
(B) They are the single most important factor in health.
(C) They are produced naturally by the body.
(D) They have the greatest importance during illness.

**Go on to the next page ➡**

## Questions 11-20

More than 70 percent of the world's businesses are owned and operated by a single person, mainly due to the ease of formation this type of business affords. Nevertheless, while the "sole proprietorship" remains by far the most common type of business organization today, there is no doubt that the dominant form of business in the world is the corporation. Although not all corporations are huge multi-national organizations, it can generally be said that the ability of corporations to influence the economy, politics, and culture of a nation greatly surpasses that of any other form of business.

The association of human beings in pursuit of a common objective is as old as history. However, the concept of a corporation as an entity separate and distinct from the individuals who constitute it occurred at the beginning of the colonial era, roughly the early 17th century. Legally, the corporation is an artificial "person," capable of conducting business transactions in the same way as the owner of a sole proprietorship would. Unlike the business owned by a single individual, though, the life of a corporation is potentially perpetual. It does not end when the owner dies or when its members change.

The principal reason why the corporation has become the most important form of business in the world is that it is the most practical type of organization for raising capital. Obtaining the manufacturing plants, the equipment, and the marketing outlets necessary to compete with other large concerns requires capital that may run into hundreds of millions of dollars, far more than any individual or even groups of individuals could supply. The system of shareholding, which allows for multiple owners, in conjunction with the development of a capital market for the impersonal purchase and sale of stock, has significantly assisted corporations to obtain the funds they need to operate on a wide scale.

Another advantage the corporation has over other forms of business enterprise is that it provides independent management; that is, business executives who, separate from the owners or shareholders, are paid to oversee and operate the company. This typically results in more professional and expert management and has evolved to be an increasingly important feature in corporate profitability.

Go on to the next page ➡

**11.** What is the main idea of the passage?

(A) The corporation is the most influential type of business organization.

(B) The corporation is the most common type of business organization.

(C) Corporations must be very carefully managed.

(D) Corporations have accumulated too much power.

**12.** Which of the following is true of corporations?

(A) They are as old as history.

(B) They are distinct from their owners.

(C) They can easily be separated into smaller entities.

(D) They exist primarily in the Western world.

**13.** The word "objective" in line 9 is closest in meaning to

(A) aim

(B) value

(C) norm

(D) belief

**14.** In line 13, the author's use of the phrase "artifical 'person'" implies that

(A) more than one person owns a corporation

(B) a corporation is not a human entity

(C) corporations are unfeeling and inhumane

(D) many individuals combine to make up a corporation

**15.** Which of the following can be inferred about a sole proprietorship?

(A) It could cease to exist upon the death of its owner.

(B) It is less inventive than a corporation.

(C) It has a hard time attracting qualified managers.

(D) It is difficult to establish and administer.

**Go on to the next page** ➡

**16.** Which of the following aspects of a corporation is most extensively discussed in paragraph 3?

(A) Determining how much stock to issue
(B) Appointing managers to run the business
(C) Acquiring the capital necessary to operate
(D) Deciding which types of assets to purchase

**17.** The phrase "run into" in line 21 is closest in meaning to

(A) collide with
(B) compete with
(C) attain
(D) approach

**18.** With which of the following statements would the author most likely agree?

(A) There is an increasing separation of stockholders and management in modern corporations.
(B) Managers are more highly motivated if they also own stock in the corporation.
(C) Stockholders are not usually very interested in how the corporation is managed.
(D) A smaller number of shareholders allows the firm to be managed more efficiently.

**19.** Which of the following is NOT mentioned as an important use of the capital raised by the corporation?

(A) The building of production facilities
(B) The acquisition of machinery
(C) The training of corporate managers
(D) The establishment of distribution outlets



Go on to the next page ➡

**20.** What is probably discussed in the paragraph that precedes the passage?

(A) Further advantages provided by the corporate form of business

(B) Characteristics of the single-owner form of business

(C) Reasons why the corporation has recently become popular

(D) Different types of multi-national business organizations

## Questions 21-30

Phillis Wheatley, ignored as a poet for almost two hundred years, was not only a talented writer, recognized in Europe more than in the United States, but she was also the first African American to publish a book, the first woman writer whose publication was promoted and nurtured by a community of women, and the first American woman author who for a while earned a living by means of her writing. She was also a slave and survived the horrific "middle passage" from Africa to North America.

Phillis Wheatley was born in West Africa, along the fertile lowlands of the Gambia River. But when she was seven or eight, she was captured by slave traders, transported to Boston, and on July 11, 1761, sold to John and Susanna Wheatley. Unlike most slave owners of the time, the Wheatleys permitted the young girl to learn to read her new language, and soon after, her poetic talent began to emerge. Her earliest published poem appeared when she was fourteen and relates how two men narrowly escaped being drowned off Cape Cod in Massachusetts. Much of her subsequent poetry also deals with mortality. Of her surviving fifty-five poems, for instance, nineteen are elegies, poems written in the memory of people who have passed away. Her last poem is an elegy written about herself and her career.

Wheatley's first book, simply entitled *Poems*, having been turned down for publication in Boston because of her race and sex, appeared in London in 1773. The following year she was granted her freedom, probably because a group of British women, her literary patrons, paid for her release from slavery. In 1778 Wheatley married John Peters, a free African American who managed a store and sometimes represented African Americans in the courts of law. But neither her writing nor her husband's work could protect their family from tragedy, and in 1784, she died after a difficult child-birth with her newborn infant in a shack on the edge of Boston.

Go on to the next page ➡

**21.** What is the main purpose of the passage?

(A) To analyze the main themes of Phillis Wheatley's poems
(B) To illustrate the cruelty of slavery in colonial America
(C) To describe Phillis Wheatley's life and work as a writer
(D) To show that Phillis Wheatley was one of America's most talented poets

**22.** The word "horrific" in line 6 is closest in meaning to

(A) long
(B) deserted
(C) liberal
(D) dreadful

**23.** Which of the following is NOT mentioned as one of Phillis Wheatley's accomplishments?

(A) She was the first African American to publish a book.
(B) She was the first female writer supported mainly by other women.
(C) She was the first slave who earned her freedom through her writing.
(D) She was the first professional woman writer in America.

**24.** The author implies in the first paragraph that Phillis Wheatley's

(A) writing has not received as much attention as it deserves
(B) interest in writing began when she was a child in Africa
(C) poetry was rejected by many contemporary women writers
(D) poems were better known in America than in Europe

**25.** It can be inferred from the second paragraph that

(A) Phillis Wheatley tried to escape from her captors
(B) many people in Boston opposed slavery
(C) Phillis Wheatley had a difficult time learning English
(D) few slaves at that time learned how to read

**Go on to the next page ➡**

**26.** The word "subsequent" in line 15 is closest in meaning to

(A) substantial
(B) later
(C) best
(D) misplaced

**27.** What appears to be one of the main themes of Phillis Wheatley's poetry?

(A) Love
(B) Race
(C) Death
(D) Religion

**28.** When was Phillis Wheatley's first volume of poetry published?

(A) 1773
(B) 1774
(C) 1778
(D) 1784

**29.** According to the author, how did Phillis Wheatley gain her freedom?

(A) Her friends purchased her liberty.
(B) Her masters recognized her talent.
(C) She married a white landowner.
(D) She refused to serve anymore as a slave.

**30.** What is true of Phillis Wheatley's final poem?

(A) It was simply called *Poems.*
(B) It concerned her own death.
(C) It was discovered after she had died.
(D) It was about her husband and newborn child.

## Questions 31-40

The world's volcanoes are classified into types based mainly upon how they have formed. This itself is a result of the types of materials that have erupted from them, the velocity at which the materials have been ejected, and the length of time over which the eruptions have occurred.

The most common type of volcano, the shield volcano, is a gently sloping dome gradually built up over time by thin layers of volcanic ash and a series of lava flows. These flows are relatively thin, rarely exceeding seven meters in thickness, and made from lava that flowed out slowly. Any fragmental materials such as volcanic rock and volcanic boulders thrown out by explosions are insignificant and have virtually no effect on the shape of the mountain. As a shield volcano grows, eruptions of lava gradually cease to originate from the volcano's central vent and instead lava flows out of secondary fissures on the slopes of the mountain. Eventually, the main column of lava is no longer capable of reaching the summit of the volcano, and all the eruptions come from the secondary vents. From then on the volcano increases in diameter but not in height.

The second type of volcano is created when several smaller lava domes unite as they grow in size, forming a compound volcano. The island of Hawaii, for example, has been formed by the union of five such lava domes. In a compound volcano, lava domes are built up by thick lava that flows down from the vent at the top of each dome; over time a compound volcano can grow to a tremendous size as its various vents build up its base. Some compound volcanoes have risen from thousands of meters below the sea's surface to form islands or island chains.

In contrast, the third type, a composite volcano, which is also sometimes called a "stratovolcano," develops a form dominated by rock fragments exploded from the topmost crater of a single volcano that are interspersed with the lava that flows from its central vent. Compared to the size of the entire mountain, which may rise more than 3,000 meters above its base, the crater that forms the central vent is quite small, hardly ever more than a few hundred meters in diameter. A volcano of this kind normally exhibits a steep slope and appears symmetrical when viewed from a distance. Mt. St. Helens in the United States, Mt. Vesuvius in Italy, and Mt. Fuji in Japan are perhaps the most famous examples of composite volcanoes.

Go on to the next page

**31.** What does the passage mainly discuss?

(A) The worldwide distribution of volcanoes
(B) The physical forms of volcanoes
(C) The dangers posed by volcanoes
(D) The creation of new volcanoes

**32.** What factor is NOT mentioned in paragraph 1 as playing a role in the formation of a volcano?

(A) How long a volcano has been active
(B) What kinds of materials a volcano has discharged
(C) The place a volcano has occurred
(D) How fast lava and rock have erupted

**33.** According to the passage, at some point a shield volcano will

(A) merge with adjacent lava domes
(B) be destroyed by explosions
(C) cease growing in height
(D) be subject to fragmentation

**34.** The word "rarely" in line 7 is closest in meaning to

(A) hardly
(B) periodically
(C) ordinarily
(D) seldom

**35.** What materials are unlikely to be present in a shield volcano?

(A) Lava flows
(B) Volcanic ash
(C) Large rocks
(D) Lava layers



Go on to the next page ➡

**36.** It can be inferred from the passage that which type of volcano may be most commonly seen in the Pacific Ocean?

(A) Shield volcanoes
(B) Stratovolcanoes
(C) Compound volcanoes
(D) Composite volcanoes

**37.** Rock fragments play a major role in the formation of

(A) shield volcanoes
(B) lava domes
(C) compound volcanoes
(D) composite volcanoes

**38.** The word "steep" in line 29 is closest in meaning to

(A) sharp
(B) slow
(C) beautiful
(D) gentle

**39.** Why does the author mention Mt. Vesuvius?

(A) To explain a famous volcano
(B) To imply the danger that volcanoes pose
(C) To suggest how beautiful volcanoes can be
(D) To illustrate a composite volcano

**40.** Which of the following best characterizes the organization of the passage?

(A) Cause and effect
(B) Chronological development
(C) An extended narrative
(D) A classification of types

**Go on to the next page ➡**

## Questions 41-50

The Great Plains of North America cover about a million square miles. The Plains' immense size and few natural barriers create almost inconceivable space that seems to reach in all directions. Persistent winds sweeping through this vastness meet little resistance.

Coping with the extremes of this environment was a skill that the Native Americans commonly called "Plains Indians" perfected, and it was only during unusually bitter winters, or when an accident of fate created a dangerous situation, that there was any real threat to the survival of their nomadic communities. In a sheltered wooded valley with the teepees tucked well back into a grove of cottonwoods and banked high with brush, a Plains Indian camp was secure against all but the most severe winter storms.

Since families were usually too small to offer adequate protection and tribes too large to be supported by the conditions of Plains' environment, the band was the basic unit to which a person belonged. It was a social entity consisting of a series of families united both politically and economically under the leadership of a chief and a council; it averaged about three hundred members. The security offered by the band was of essential economic importance in winter when unpredictable and often extremely harsh weather could make it impossible to hunt or travel.

The children of the Plains tribes were encouraged to follow the moral values that emphasized respect for tribal rules and elders and to avoid greed, egotism, and irresponsibility. The young men were taught that it was their duty to provide food and to protect the community, while young women were instructed to uphold a virtuous life of service to their parents, their future husbands, their children, and their tribe.

Go on to the next page ➡

**41.** What does the passage mainly discuss?

(A) The geography of the Great Plains
(B) The climate of the Great Plains
(C) The society of the Plains Indians
(D) The leadership of Plains Indian tribes

**42.** It can be concluded from paragraph 1 that the Great Plains are unusually

(A) moist
(B) windy
(C) fertile
(D) dry

**43.** What is most likely the main reason why the author describes in detail the physical characteristics of the Great Plains?

(A) Because they are unique to the North American continent.
(B) Because they affected the social structure of Plains Indian culture.
(C) Because they are subject to some of the world's harshest weather.
(D) Because they influenced the worldview of the Plains Indians.

**44.** According to the passage, where did the Plains Indians typically make their camps?

(A) On mountain slopes
(B) Next to rivers
(C) In open spaces
(D) Among trees

**45.** According to the passage, what presented the greatest danger to Plains Indians?

(A) Drought
(B) Winter
(C) Disease
(D) War

**Go on to the next page ➡**

**46.** According to the passage, what was the principal group in which Plains Indians were organized?

(A) The family
(B) The tribe
(C) The clan
(D) The band

**47.** The word "unpredictable" in line 17 is closest in meaning to

(A) unforeseeable
(B) unfamiliar
(C) furious
(D) frantic

**48.** The word "egotism" in line 20 is closest in meaning to

(A) sin
(B) selfishness
(C) disrespect
(D) violence

**49.** The word "their" in line 23 refers to

(A) young women
(B) parents
(C) future husbands
(D) children

**50.** It can be inferred from the author's discussion of Plains Indian children that

(A) males and females fought side-by-side during war
(B) women were also expected to hunt for food
(C) girls matured more quickly than boys
(D) male and female roles were quite different

**This is the end of the test.**

# Practice Test 3
# 第3回実戦問題

## Section 1—Listening Comprehension

Section 1 is designed to measure your ability to understand spoken English. This section has three parts: short conversations, long conversations, and talks. Each short conversation is followed by one question, and each long conversation and talk is followed by four questions. There are 50 questions in this section.

### Part A

Listen to the short conversations that follow. After each short conversation, choose the best answer to the question about that conversation.



Go on to the next page

088

**1.** What does the woman mean?

(A) She filed the application earlier in the morning.

(B) Her acceptance letter has not arrived yet.

(C) Her application to graduate school was successful.

(D) She decided not to apply to graduate school.

089

**2.** What did the man do while he was waiting for the woman?

(A) He wrote a note.

(B) He studied for a test.

(C) He prepared for a presentation.

(D) He outlined an essay.

090

**3.** What does the woman imply?

(A) Her performance has been canceled.

(B) She plans on going to a lecture later.

(C) The man is welcome to attend the play.

(D) She will leave the dorm soon.

091

**4.** What problem is the woman having?

(A) The research facilities she needs are seldom available.

(B) The biology department does not hire undergraduates.

(C) The biology laboratory is closed at night.

(D) The biology faculty are too busy to help the students.

**Go on to the next page**

092

**5.** What does the woman imply about Robert?

(A) He likes studying in the library.

(B) He took too many courses this term.

(C) He is not a very good student.

(D) He is taking a class in library research.

093

**6.** What does the woman mean?

(A) She is rather busy tomorrow.

(B) She is planning to go downtown.

(C) She can check his report the next day.

(D) She hopes the man will finish his research soon.

094

**7.** What can be inferred from the conversation?

(A) The man enjoys the woman's sense of humor.

(B) The woman will go to see a film later in the evening.

(C) The man does not intend to loan money to the woman.

(D) The woman has not seen the man for several months.

095

**8.** What problem are the speakers discussing?

(A) The professor speaks too softly.

(B) The professor's pronunciation is unclear.

(C) The professor's lectures are disorganized.

(D) The professor has poor handwriting.



Go on to the next page ➡

096

**9.** What can be inferred about the woman?

(A) She completes assignments at the last minute.

(B) She is an excellent researcher.

(C) She enjoys writing term papers.

(D) She plans to go to an all-night party.

097

**10.** What does the woman mean?

(A) She will try to check out the book later.

(B) Use of the self-study lab should not be required.

(C) Her pronunciation in French is already good enough.

(D) She will visit the self-study lab herself.

098

**11.** What will the speakers do this weekend?

(A) Invite the man's family for dinner

(B) Help the man's mother cook a meal

(C) Take a hike on the coast

(D) Visit the man's family

099

**12.** What does the man imply about Professor Salazar?

(A) His lectures are not very interesting.

(B) His lectures often run overtime.

(C) He often comes early to his lectures.

(D) He does not mind if students miss his lectures.

Go on to the next page ➡

100

**13.** What does the woman mean?

(A) The man should take a shower after playing tennis.
(B) The tennis team changed its practice schedule.
(C) The man will be lucky to win his tennis match.
(D) The weather may not be very good for tennis.

101

**14.** What does the woman imply about the man?

(A) His plans are unrealistic.
(B) He ought to take a short break from his reading.
(C) He should begin reading the class textbook.
(D) He studies more than he actually needs to.

102

**15.** What can be inferred from the conversation?

(A) The tickets for the concert were sold out.
(B) The woman paid for the man's concert ticket.
(C) The concert will start just before 8 o'clock.
(D) The man decided not to attend the concert.

103

**16.** What does the woman mean?

(A) The man needs to move to another seat right away.
(B) The man can sit there for the time being.
(C) She would like the man to meet her friend.
(D) She is unsure whether her friend is coming.



Go on to the next page

104

**17.** What does the man imply about the woman's research partner?

(A) He is not very reliable.

(B) He has a very good sense of humor.

(C) He can do just about anything.

(D) He is more of a leader than a follower.

105

**18.** What are the speakers complaining about?

(A) Their professor's lectures are not very clear.

(B) They do not know when their reading assignments are due.

(C) They did not receive a copy of the course syllabus.

(D) The articles they are reading are difficult to understand.

106

**19.** What does the woman imply?

(A) She will have to study especially hard this semester.

(B) She probably will not be able to persuade her parents.

(C) She does not really need to have a car on campus.

(D) She is worried that her grades may drop this term.

107

**20.** What does the woman mean?

(A) All of her applications have been submitted.

(B) She will be able to submit the last application soon.

(C) She has decided against going to graduate school.

(D) All of her professors wrote recommendations..

Go on to the next page

108

**21.** What does the man imply about the study group?

(A) It is much too difficult for him.

(B) It has no regular meeting place.

(C) It has too many members.

(D) It always meets at the same time.

109

**22.** What are the speakers discussing?

(A) The high fees to use the student recreation center

(B) The new campground that has been built

(C) The low cost of renting camping gear

(D) The sale of tents at a camping supply shop

110

**23.** What can be inferred from the conversation?

(A) The carpool was unsuccessful.

(B) The carpool will resume later in the year.

(C) The woman would like to join the carpool.

(D) The carpool was expensive to maintain.

111

**24.** What does the man tell the woman?

(A) His backpack is unusable.

(B) He will buy a new backpack this weekend.

(C) His backpack is not big enough.

(D) He will pay back the money next month.



Go on to the next page

112

**25.** What do the speakers imply about the cafeteria?

(A) Its prices are unreasonably high.

(B) Its food is not very delicious.

(C) It closes too early in the evening.

(D) It serves rather healthy meals.

113

**26.** Why is the woman upset?

(A) She will not be able to attend the dance.

(B) She does not have time to go to the laundromat.

(C) She does not know where the dance will be held.

(D) She cannot use the washing machine in her dorm.

114

**27.** What does the woman imply about the man?

(A) He is often late for appointments.

(B) He did rather well on the mid-term test.

(C) He needs to include more details in his writing.

(D) He is usually a very good student.

115

**28.** What problem do the speakers have?

(A) The woman forgot to reserve the dorm lounge.

(B) The man told John about the surprise party.

(C) The room they wanted to use is already taken.

(D) They made a mistake on the time of the party.

Go on to the next page

**29.** What does the man mean?

(A) He would like to have a different roommate.

(B) He thinks more students should live in the dormitory.

(C) He plans to live outside the university next year.

(D) He believes the housing office made a mistake.

117

**30.** What are the speakers planning to do?

(A) Visit an art exhibit

(B) Send some packages at the post office

(C) Buy some stationery supplies on sale

(D) Purchase some books at a bookstore

**This is the end of part A.**

**Go on to the next page**

**NO TEST MATERIAL ON THIS PAGE**

## Part B

Listen to the conversations that follow. After each conversation, choose the best answer to each of the four questions about that conversation.



Go on to the next page

119 120

## Questions 31-34

**31.** What can be inferred about the speakers?

(A) They are both enrolled in the same program.

(B) They started the university at the same time.

(C) They have not seen each other for quite a while.

(D) They both hope to graduate at the end of the term.

**32.** Where has the man been working?

(A) A government office

(B) A private company

(C) A university planning department

(D) An urban studies program

**33.** What was unusual about the man's internship?

(A) It lasted an entire year.

(B) He received money for doing it.

(C) It was unrelated to his major.

(D) He obtained it after he graduated.

**34.** How does the man feel about his internship experience?

(A) Nervous

(B) Regretful

(C) Frustrated

(D) Enthusiastic

Go on to the next page ➡

## Questions 35-38

**35.** Why did the woman go to talk to the man?

(A) She cannot get into the graduate program she wants to enter.

(B) She is having a difficult time finding a job.

(C) She does not know what she wants to do when she graduates.

(D She has been unable to complete all of the requirements for her major.

**36.** What field is the woman studying?

(A) Economics

(B) Mathematics

(C) Engineering

(D) Linguistics

**37.** What can be inferred about the woman?

(A) She seldom meets with her advisor.

(B) She is probably a very good student.

(C) She may decide to change her major again.

(D) She will not be able to graduate this spring.

**38.** What does the man suggest the woman do?

(A) Consult with an academic counseling office

(B) Contact as many potential employers as possible

(C) Concentrate more on her current courses

(D) Consider working and studying at the same time

**This is the end of part B.**

**Go on to the next page ➡**

**NO TEST MATERIAL ON THIS PAGE**

Go on to the next page ➡

## Part C

Listen to the talks and lectures that follow. After each talk or lecture, choose the best answer to the four questions about it.

【第1回】実戦問題
【第2回】実戦問題
【第3回】実戦問題
【第1回】実戦問題 解説
【第2回】実戦問題 解説
【第3回】実戦問題 解説

Go on to the next page

124 125

## Questions 39-42

**39.** Why did so many people suddenly move to California in 1848?

(A) Gold had become a more valuable commodity.

(B) People had more access to current information.

(C) Mining equipment was cheaper in price.

(D) More rapid forms of transportation were available.

**40.** How can the people who mined gold in North America best be described?

(A) They were an ethnically diverse group of people.

(B) They had little idea of how to mine gold effectively.

(C) They coordinated their activities carefully.

(D) They mainly worked for large mining corporations.

**41.** With which of the following statements would the professor most likely agree?

(A) Gold has been the source of many conflicts between nations.

(B) It is extremely difficult to measure the concept of wealth.

(C) There is a close relationship between freedom and creativity.

(D) Europe is more socially progressive than North America.

**42.** According to the professor, what was one result of the gold rush?

(A) The value of the dollar became based upon gold.

(B) California became the most populated state.

(C) The cross-continental railroad became profitable.

(D) American mining companies became international.

**Go on to the next page**

## Questions 43-46

**43.** What is the topic of the talk?

(A) An important Canadian poet

(B) The origin of Canadian poetry

(C) Themes of North American poetry

(D) One of Don Coles's best-known poems

**44.** According to the professor, how does Coles view the power of time?

(A) As an illusion

(B) As overwhelming

(C) As thoroughly reversible

(D) As temporarily controllable

**45.** What technique does Coles use to convey his view of time?

(A) Short sentences

(B) Lack of punctuation

(C) Repeated phrases

(D) Unconnected words

**46.** What does the professor imply about Coles's father?

(A) He worked hard to educate his son.

(B) He was also a successful writer.

(C) He was rarely involved in family affairs.

(D) He initially disapproved of his son's career.

Go on to the next page ➡

128 129

## Questions 47-50

**47.** What is the main topic of the talk?

(A) When lakes are formed

(B) Why lakes vanish

(C) Where lakes occur

(D) What function lakes have

**48.** What have the students in this class previously been studying?

(A) Storms

(B) Climate

(C) Earthquakes

(D) Oceans

**49.** According to the professor, what is the most common reason for the disappearance of a lake?

(A) Its outlet stream empties its water.

(B) Its water evaporates into air.

(C) Its basin gradually fills in.

(D) Its bottom is taken over by plants.

**50.** According to the professor, why do the basins of some lakes gradually fill in?

(A) An outlet stream becomes blocked.

(B) An earthquake changes the basin level.

(C) Sediment is deposited at the lake bottom.

(D) The amount of rainfall in an area decreases.

**This is the end of Section 1.**

**Stop work on Section 1 now.**

**Go on to the next page ➡**

# Section 2—Structure and Written Expression

**Time: 25 minutes**

Section 2 is designed to measure your knowledge of the grammar and usage of written English. This section has two parts: Structure and Written Expression.

## Structure

For each of the sentences that follow, choose the answer that best completes the sentence.

**Go on to the next page ➡**

**1.** Iron, ——, is also present in the crust.

(A) the main component of the Earth's core
(B) the core of the Earth's main component
(C) in the Earth's core the main component
(D) the component main of the Earth's core

**2.** The doctrine of the expanding universe is based on the observation that the light from all of the galaxies is red-shifted, —— that they are moving away from us.

(A) indicate
(B) indicates
(C) indicating
(D) indicated

**3.** Female oysters may discharge —— a million eggs during a single spawning season.

(A) as much as
(B) so many as
(C) so more than
(D) as many as

**4.** —— is the principal focus of organic chemistry.

(A) Analyze carbon compounds
(B) The analyzing of carbon compounds
(C) Carbon compound analyze
(D) Compounds that are carbon to analyze

**Go on to the next page ➡**

**5.** In Arctic latitudes the fur of the ermine is usually white, —— in warmer regions the fur on the back of the animal tends to be brown.

(A) while

(B) in spite of

(C) in contrast to

(D) wherever

**6.** —— study of the relationship between people and the furniture, tools, and machinery they use at work.

(A) It is ergonomics which

(B) Ergonomics

(C) That ergonomics is the

(D) Ergonomics is the

**7.** After being eaten, food passes through the alimentary canal where it is digested ——.

(A) as absorbed it is

(B) and also it is absorbed

(C) and being absorbed

(D) and absorbed

**8.** —— bird species have survived from the Miocene Age, but one that has is the Sandhill Crane.

(A) Few

(B) Any

(C) Many

(D) Most



Go on to the next page ➡

**9.** —— the most easily identified constellation in the winter sky of the Northern Hemisphere.

(A) Orion being

(B) Orion is

(C) It is Orion

(D) Orion which is

**10.** Evolutionary psychology —— all human emotions arise because they increase the chance of survival in some way.

(A) assuming that

(B) is assumed that

(C) assumes that

(D) which assumes that

**11.** Some scholars argue that the first Thanksgiving celebration was not that of the British colonists at the Plymouth Colony in Massachusetts in 1621, —— that of the Spanish settlers in St. Augustine, Florida in 1565.

(A) yet

(B) but

(C) instead

(D) however

**12.** Not unless one uses special instruments during a solar eclipse —— to view the chromosphere of the Sun.

(A) is it possible

(B) possible it is

(C) possible

(D) it is possible

**Go on to the next page ➡**

**13.** The larger the area of a heated surface, —— is the rate of evaporation.

(A) the great

(B) the greater

(C) greatest

(D) the greatest

**14.** The Sioux Indians were one of the first Native American tribes to win —— from the United States government for the loss of the natural resources on their tribal homelands.

(A) compensatory

(B) compensating

(C) compensation

(D) compensate

**15.** New York's Carnegie Hall, originally known as Music Hall, was renamed in 1891 because of Andrew Carnegie's large contribution to —— construction.

(A) their

(B) his

(C) one's

(D) its

Go on to the next page ➡

## Written Expression

For each of the sentences that follow, choose the underlined portion of the sentence (A, B, C, or D) that contains a grammar, usage, or word choice error.

Go on to the next page ➡

**16.** Carbohydrates serve as the source main of nutrition for herbivorous, or
A B C
plant-eating, animals.
D

**17.** Despite being excellent swimmers, penguins are one of the most
A B C
awkward animal on land.
D

**18.** William Seward, who purchase of Alaska in 1867 was ridiculed as
A B
Seward's Folly, is now credited with one of the most important land
C
acquisitions in American history.
D

**19.** It has now been widely confirmed that neutrons and protons are
A B
compose of smaller particles called quarks.
C D

**20.** When certain substances are kept at very low temperatures, electrical
A B
resistance complete disappears, resulting in superconductivity.
C D

**21.** Mammal embryos tend to develop in two stages, dividing into highly
A B
versatile cells such as brain stem cells in the first, and it produces highly
C
specific cells such as organ cells in the second.
D

**22.** Herring, an important commercial fish, it has been fished virtually to the
A B C D
point of extinction.

**23.** By the early 1980's, the consumer price index had climbed from a value
A B C
of 100 in 1967 to more than 300, raising more than 200 percent.
D

**24.** Beginning in the 1950's, the number of American composers began
A B
experimenting with non-musical sounds in their compositions.
C D

**25.** Economics can be defined as the study of how people choose in the
A B C
various possible uses of their scarce resources.
D

**26.** As their name indicates, Gulfport, Mississippi is a major shipping
A B
point for the entire Gulf of Mexico region.
C D

Go on to the next page ➡

**27.** The best known (A) of the saber-toothed cats, the Smilodon of California, was (B) much larger (C) than either the Asian tiger and (D) African lion.

**28.** Graphite, widely (A) used in pencils, it (B) is a form of carbon that is (C) soft enough to form a line on (D) paper.

**29.** The novels (A) of Mark Twain are (B) known for (C) their memorable characters, accurate dialect, and humor that is colorful (D).

**30.** The fast (A) land animal is (B) the cheetah, which can (C) achieve speeds (D) of more than 110 kilometers an hour.

**31.** When (A) South Dakota became a state in 1889, the city of Pierre was (B) established as its (C) capital there (D).

**32.** The turnip, though (A) not as widely (B) consumed as the potato or the radish, are (C) still one of the (D) most important root vegetables.

**33.** Environmental destruction (A) caused by pollution air (B) and water contamination costs major urban areas (C) millions of dollars in annual (D) clean-up costs.

**34.** Emily Dickinson, one of the most (A) famous 19th-century American poets, lived (B) almost her entirely (C) life in seclusion in (D) Amherst, Massachusetts.

**35.** During (A) the 1960's, a large shift occurred (B) in media as more people watched the news in (C) TV rather than reading it (D) in the newspaper.

**36.** Frank Lloyd Wright was influence (A) in not only the designing of individual (B) homes but also (C) the planning (D) of public facilities.

**37.** The principle of successful (A) weight loss for both men and women is for them (B) to consume fewer (C) calories than they expends. (D)

**38.** Although some (A) of Iowa's corn crop is consumed by (B) humans, much of itself (C) is used as animal feed. (D)

---

Go on to the next page ➡

**39.** The development of the electrical circuit led to the invention of the radio,
A B C
television, and the computer.
D

**40.** Through her experiments with radiation, Madame Curie was the first to
A B
identify the difference among a non-radioactive element and a radioactive
C D
isotope.

**This is the end of Section 2.**

**Stop work on Section 2 now.**

**Go on to the next page ➡**

**NO TEST MATERIAL ON THIS PAGE**

Go on to the next page

# Section 3—Reading Comprehension

**Time: 55 minutes**

Read the passages that follow. After each passage, respond to the questions by choosing the best answer to each question.



Go on to the next page ➡

## Questions 1-10

In the years before the Civil War, the Underground Railroad smuggled thousands of Black slaves from the South to freedom in the North. Although White abolitionists who opposed slavery contributed to this effort, the Underground Railroad was primarily run, maintained, and funded by African Americans. Black working-class men and women collected the bulk of the food and clothing and provided the shelter and transportation for the run-away slaves, and wealthier, better educated Blacks arranged for legal assistance and offered leadership and financial support.

Although the origins of the term are uncertain, by 1850 both those who participated in the Underground Railroad and those who sought to destroy it freely employed metaphors from the railroad business to describe its activities and operations. More important, Northerners and Southerners understood both its symbolic and real meaning. The number of African Americans who fled or were smuggled out of the South was never large enough to threaten the institutional stability of slavery. Yet the number actually freed was, in a way, less significant than the heroic and symbolic value of the fact that a metaphorical transportation system was in place to free slaves. In other words, the Underground Railroad was an indictment of the institution of slavery and the true character of the institutions that supported it.

Most of the slaves who reached freedom in the North actually initiated their own escapes. After their initial flight, however, fugitives needed guidance and assistance to keep their hard-won liberty. Although the effectiveness of the Black underground varied depending upon the time and place, there was an astonishingly large number of semi-autonomous networks that operated across the North and the upper South. They were especially active and efficient in Ohio, Pennsylvania, and New York, and surprisingly effective networks, often centered in local Black churches, existed in most northern and border states.

The most daring and best organized "station" was operated in the very shadow of the U.S. Capitol. Run by free Blacks from Washington, D.C., this underground network was remarkably successful in rescuing a huge number of slaves from plantations in Maryland and Virginia at considerable risk to its operators. It was one of the bravest and most noble ventures in American history.

Go on to the next page ➡

**1.** What is the passage mainly about?

(A) How the Underground Railroad helped slaves to escape

(B) The operation and support of the Underground Railroad

(C) The place where the Underground Railroad functioned most effectively

(D) Famous people who contributed to the Underground Railroad

**2.** The phrase "funded by" in line 4 is closest in meaning to

(A) led by

(B) founded by

(C) paid for by

(D) overseen by

**3.** All of the following are referred to in the passage as supporters of the Underground Railroad EXCEPT

(A) White abolitionists

(B) Black workers

(C) educated African Americans

(D) northern Catholics

**4.** According to the author, what was the main significance of the term "Underground Railroad"?

(A) Its symbolism

(B) Its accuracy

(C) Its secrecy

(D) Its deception

**5.** In paragraph 3, the author implies that

(A) many slaves had little desire to escape from their masters

(B) most northern governments officially supported slavery

(C) the Underground Railroad eventually caused the slave system to collapse

(D) most slaves had to undertake their own initial escapes



Go on to the next page ➡

**6.** The word "astonishingly" in line 22 is closest in meaning to

(A) amazingly
(B) increasingly
(C) slightly
(D) deceptively

**7.** According to the passage, what particular organizations played a significant role in the Underground Railroad?

(A) White law firms
(B) Black churches
(C) Local governments
(D) Northern newspapers

**8.** According to the passage, where was the Underground Railroad boldest and most efficient?

(A) New York
(B) Pennsylvania
(C) Maryland
(D) Washington, D.C.

**9.** In which paragraph does the author most clearly express an opinion?

(A) Paragraph 1
(B) Paragraph 2
(C) Paragraph 3
(D) Paragraph 4

**10.** With which of the following statements would the author most likely agree?

(A) The support of wealthy whites was crucial to the operation of the Underground Railroad.
(B) The Underground Railroad played a major role in starting the Civil War.
(C) The Underground Railroad seriously threatened the slavery system in the South.
(D) African Americans were mainly responsible for running the Underground Railroad.

**Go on to the next page ➡**

## Questions 11-20

When the early European immigrants arrived in North America in the late 16th century, they brought their dolls with them. It was not until 1858, however, that the first original North American doll was patented by Ludwig Greiner, a German-born toy-maker in Philadelphia. By 1862, several designers had developed dolls that could walk and say simple words or phrases, such as "mama" or "papa." The next two decades saw a flurry of activity by doll-makers to try to get them to perform actions typical of human children, like nursing, swimming, or consuming food. Even the famous inventor Thomas Edison became involved. In the early 1880's, he succeeded in reducing the size of the record player he had invented so one could fit inside the body of a doll, making it able to "speak." Other patents were issued for dolls that could wave their hands or wink.

During the first half of the 20th century, the emphasis among doll-makers was on developing new types of materials for the construction of dolls. Consumers demanded durability and realism, both in form and feel. Dolls modeled after newborn babies were popular in the 1920's, and in the 1930's the rising popularity of motion pictures led to the creation of portrait dolls, dolls made to resemble well-known people, especially movie stars. The late 1940's represented a watershed in the history of dolls. With the development of modern plastics, notably vinyl, the degree of realism doll manufacturers could attain increased dramatically. The close of the 1950's saw the introduction of the Barbie doll. Like the fashion dolls of the previous century, these dolls had huge wardrobes. Unlike their predecessors, however, these newer dolls were first and foremost meant to be played with, rather than being intended mainly as way of displaying clothing fashions.

Go on to the next page ➡

**11.** What does the passage mainly discuss?

(A) The origin of dolls in American life
(B) The uses of dolls in the United States
(C) The development of dolls in American society
(D) Materials used in making dolls in the United States

**12.** Which of the following is NOT mentioned in the passage as an example of human behaviors performed by dolls during the 1800's?

(A) Eating
(B) Swimming
(C) Crying
(D) Speaking

**13.** Which aspect of dolls does paragraph 1 mainly discuss?

(A) Function
(B) Composition
(C) Usage
(D) Realism

**14.** People who purchased dolls in the early 1900's were greatly concerned that a doll should

(A) be relatively inexpensive
(B) appear as human as possible
(C) have an educational use
(D) exhibit a wide range of abilities

**15.** Why does the author mention the famous inventor Thomas Edison?

(A) To explain the reason why dolls were becoming increasingly smaller
(B) To show that there had previously been little interest in producing dolls
(C) To illustrate how important the manufacture of dolls had become
(D) To reveal a well-known inventor's unexpected fondness for dolls

**Go on to the next page ➡**

**16.** What can be inferred about many dolls in the 1930's?

(A) They resembled film actors and actresses.
(B) They looked like newborn babies.
(C) They were extremely small in size.
(D) They were made of new lightweight materials.

**17.** According to the passage, the biggest breakthrough in doll construction occurred during

(A) the 1920's
(B) the 1930's
(C) the 1940's
(D) the 1950's

**18.** The word "dramatically" in line 20 is closest in meaning to

(A) progressively
(B) instantaneously
(C) marginally
(D) radically

**19.** The phrase "first and foremost" in line 22 is closest in meaning to

(A) above all
(B) at the beginning
(C) practically speaking
(D) in many respects

**20.** Compared to the fashion dolls of the late 19th century, Barbie dolls were

(A) furnished with more extensive wardrobes
(B) primarily meant to display the newest fashions
(C) popular with both children and adults
(D) mainly intended to be used as toys



Go on to the next page ➡

## Questions 21-30

Uranus and Neptune, rather similar in size and make-up, lie beyond Jupiter and Saturn towards the outer edge of the Solar System. They are much smaller than these two giant planets, but they are still huge bodies in comparison with the inner planets nearer the Sun: Mercury, Venus, Earth, and Mars. Like Jupiter and Saturn, both Uranus and Neptune are gaseous and dense.

Uranus is composed of hydrogen, helium, substantial amounts of water, and probably some methane and ammonia. Quite likely it is the trace amounts of methane in its upper atmosphere that give it a blue-green color. Underneath the thick clouds over the planet's surface, there may well be an immense ocean of water that, though it is heated to several thousand degrees Kelvin, does not boil away because of the intense pressure from the atmosphere above it. The core of the planet is most likely rock and metal.

One unusual feature of Uranus is that in contrast to most other planets its rotational axis is tilted, and the planet lies on its side with its north pole pointing slightly below the plane. During the course of its 84-year orbit around the Sun, Uranus points first one pole toward the Sun, then its equator, and then the other pole. Many astronomers believe that a catastrophic collision between Uranus and another body, perhaps a large comet, may have knocked the planet on its side. Another unusual feature is that it rotates in retrograde, or clockwise, motion about once every 17 hours. The planet has 15 known satellites, which are composed mostly of ice and are heavily cratered. Like Saturn, Uranus has a system of narrow, circular, sharp-edged rings, but instead of being bright and icy they are made of some unusually dark material; moreover, in some places the rings are so thin that they disappear.

Neptune is even more of a mystery than Uranus. Little was known about it at all until the spacecraft Voyager 2 flew by in 1989. The planet's mass is comparable to that of Uranus, and it has a similar composition. Its thick atmosphere of hydrogen, helium, and some methane gives it a bluish color. Like Uranus, Neptune rotates rapidly, once every 16.1 hours; however, the planet's high temperature suggests that Neptune by contrast has an internal heat source.

Go on to the next page

**21.** What is the main topic of the passage?

(A) The contrast between Uranus and Neptune
(B) Outer planets of the Solar System
(C) The physical make-up of Uranus
(D) Features of Uranus and Neptune

**22.** The word "they" in line 3 refers to

(A) Uranus and Neptune
(B) Jupiter and Saturn
(C) two giant planets
(D) inner planets

**23.** In what way is Uranus similar to the Earth?

(A) They are roughly the same size.
(B) They have comparable atmospheres.
(C) They are both probably covered by seas.
(D) They each rotate once every 24 hours.

**24.** According to the passage, why does Uranus appear to be blue-green in color?

(A) Because of its high temperature
(B) Because of the methane in its atmosphere
(C) Because of its thick cloud cover
(D) Because of the metal found in its soil

**25.** According to the passage, Uranus is composed of all of the following EXCEPT

(A) hydrogen
(B) ammonia
(C) lava
(D) metal

Go on to the next page ➡

**26.** The word "intense" in line 11 is closest in meaning to

(A) faint

(B) direct

(C) variable

(D) high

**27.** What does paragraph 3 mainly discuss?

(A) The manner in which Uranus spins

(B) The collision between Uranus and an asteroid

(C) The moons of Uranus

(D) The composition of Uranus's ring

**28.** What can be inferred about the spacecraft Voyager 2?

(A) It passed close by the planet Uranus.

(B) It provided important information about Neptune.

(C) It made the first accurate measurement of Neptune's rotation.

(D) It used Uranus's gravity to swing around to Neptune.

**29.** According to paragraph 4, how does Neptune differ from Uranus?

(A) It has a denser mass.

(B) It has a thicker atmosphere.

(C) It generates its own heat.

(D) It rotates more slowly.

**30.** What does the paragraph preceding the passage probably discuss?

(A) The make-up of Uranus and Neptune

(B) Mercury, Venus, Earth, and Mars

(C) The size of the Solar System

(D) Jupiter and Saturn

**Go on to the next page ➡**

## Questions 31-40

Most of the artwork produced by the American painter Jacob Lawrence depicted the lives of African Americans in the United States during the middle of the 20th century. His paintings portray contemporary Black history, culture, and significant events or people. His style can be thought of as expressive and direct, made more so by the bold colors he chose to employ. The most interesting feature of Lawrence's painting is the narrative format he used. Rather than confining himself to a single painting, his signature mark was creating a series of paintings related to a central theme. These multiple images were often accompanied by relevant text researched by the artist.

When Lawrence was nine, his family moved to Harlem in New York City, whose museums and art centers provided him with his first real exposure to art and a chance to develop his emerging artistic talents. By the time he was fifteen, he was studying under the leading African American artist of the day, Charles Alston, at the Harlem Art Workshop. Lawrence then attended the prestigious American Artists School on a two-year scholarship, where he first exhibited his Toussaint L'Ouverture series. Soon after he painted his Frederick Douglass and Harriet Tubman series, he started what would eventually become his most celebrated work, "The Migration of the Negro," a monumental series comprising 60 paintings that chronicle the exodus of southern Blacks to the urban North after World War I. The themes of subsequent series included hospitals, theater, Nigeria, and Hiroshima. In addition to those narrative series for which he is best known, throughout his career he also painted single works, whose subjects ranged from pool parlors to jazz musicians to self portraits. An image of Jesse Jackson painted by Lawrence became the cover of *Time* magazine in 1970.

**Go on to the next page ➡**

**31.** What topic does the passage mainly discuss?

(A) The development of American modernism
(B) Twentieth-Century African American artists
(C) The struggles of Jacob Lawrence
(D) The life and work of a notable American artist

**32.** How can the style of Jacob Lawrence's paintings best be described?

(A) Assertive
(B) Ambiguous
(C) Subdued
(D) Sparse

**33.** According to paragraph 1, what was the distinctive feature of Jacob Lawrence as a painter?

(A) He always based his paintings upon a written text.
(B) He preferred to paint using shades of black and white.
(C) He composed multiple paintings around a single theme.
(D) He mainly used events in his own life to illustrate his paintings.

**34.** The word "relevant" in line 9 is closest in meaning to

(A) written
(B) related
(C) personal
(D) visual

**35.** It can be inferred that the author mentions Charles Alston because

(A) he was an important influence on Jacob Lawrence's art
(B) he was the subject of a Jacob Lawrence painting
(C) he helped Jacob Lawrence win a scholarship
(D) he gave Jacob Lawrence significant financial support

**Go on to the next page ➡**

**36.** Moving to Harlem was important for the young Jacob Lawrence because it was the first time that he

(A) lived among African Americans
(B) encountered serious artwork
(C) was able to attend school
(D) attempted to draw and paint

**37.** Which of Lawrence's works apparently received the greatest critical acclaim?

(A) His Toussaint L'Ouverture
(B) The Harriet Tubman series
(C) The Migration of the Negro
(D) His portrait of Jesse Jackson

**38.** The word "eventually" in line 17 is closest in meaning to

(A) in reality
(B) in time
(C) unexpectedly
(D) potentially

**39.** Which of the following can be inferred from the passage about the single works of Jacob Lawrence?

(A) They were primarily concerned with foreign themes.
(B) They were mostly commissioned by famous people.
(C) They were mainly painted near the end of his life.
(D) They were secondary to his multiple image paintings.



Go on to the next page ➡

**40.** All of the following are mentioned as subjects of Lawrence's paintings EXCEPT

(A) hospitals

(B) jazz musicians

(C) landscapes

(D) himself

Go on to the next page ➡

## Questions 41-50

There are more than 26,000 species of crustaceans, ranging from crabs to sea lice and barnacles to krill. They can be found in almost every type of habitat except the most arid of deserts. The vast majority, however, are found in the sea, where they live from the surface layers all the way down to the greatest depths of the ocean. Crustaceans exhibit an almost infinite variety of colors and patterns. Some of the smaller varieties of plankton have completely transparent bodies with little or no pigment. On the other hand, deep-sea shrimps are often a uniformly brilliant red. Some marine crustaceans, like particular kinds of krill, are self-luminescent, emitting their own light; land and freshwater crustaceans may become luminous if infected with bright-colored bacteria but are unable to produce the light by themselves.

Crustaceans typically have five pairs of appendages protruding from their heads, the function of which varies depending on the species. In general, the first two are primarily sensory antennae, though they may also assist in locomotion or feeding. The third set is the mandibles used to chew food. The latter two pairs are mainly used to set up feeding currents designed to propel food toward the mandibles.

No special hearing organ, or ear, has been found among the various species of crustaceans, but numerous hollow, hair-like bristles, supplied with nerves, are present on the surface of the body and the appendages. These move when touched, making it possible for the organism to respond to and discern vibrations, including sound.



Go on to the next page

**41.** What does the passage mainly discuss?

(A) The types of crustaceans
(B) The evolution of crustaceans
(C) Characteristics of crustaceans
(D) Origins of crustaceans

**42.** It can be inferred from the passage that crustaceans would NOT likely be found

(A) at the lower levels of the ocean
(B) in places with very limited rainfall
(C) in conditions of high humidity
(D) at high mountain elevations

**43.** The word "exhibit" in line 5 is closest in meaning to

(A) perform
(B) display
(C) proclaim
(D) distinguish

**44.** According to paragraph 1, some varieties of plankton are

(A) devoid of color
(B) found only near the surface
(C) consumed by sea shrimps
(D) extremely numerous

**45.** Which of the following is true of self-luminescent crustaceans?

(A) They are present in nearly every environment.
(B) They usually live only in salt water.
(C) They emit a bright red glow.
(D) They are often infected by bacteria.

**Go on to the next page ➡**

**46.** The main function of the first two pairs of crustacean appendages is to allow the organism to

(A) perceive its surroundings
(B) move from one place to another
(C) digest its food
(D) gather essential nutrients

**47.** The word "These" in line 20 refers to

(A) species of crustaceans
(B) hair-like bristles
(C) nerves
(D) appendages

**48.** The word "discern" in line 21 is closest in meaning to

(A) detect
(B) resemble
(C) avoid
(D) calculate

**49.** Which of the following is true about a crustacean's sense of hearing?

(A) It can only hear loud noises.
(B) It responds primarily to chemical stimuli.
(C) It utilizes no specific hearing organ.
(D) It functions better under water than on land.

**50.** What type of crustacean is NOT mentioned in the passage?

(A) Crabs
(B) Lobsters
(C) Krill
(D) Shrimp

**This is the end of the test.**

# Practice Test 1
# 第1回実戦問題
## 解説

# 【第 1 回】実戦問題　正答一覧

## Listening Comprehension

| Part A | | Part B | |
|---|---|---|---|
| 1 | B | 31 | D |
| 2 | D | 32 | B |
| 3 | C | 33 | C |
| 4 | A | 34 | A |
| 5 | B | 35 | D |
| 6 | C | 36 | B |
| 7 | B | 37 | A |
| 8 | C | 38 | C |
| 9 | D | **Part C** | |
| 10 | A | 39 | A |
| 11 | C | 40 | C |
| 12 | B | 41 | A |
| 13 | C | 42 | B |
| 14 | D | 43 | D |
| 15 | A | 44 | B |
| 16 | D | 45 | D |
| 17 | B | 46 | A |
| 18 | C | 47 | D |
| 19 | A | 48 | C |
| 20 | D | 49 | C |
| 21 | B | 50 | B |
| 22 | A | | |
| 23 | D | | |
| 24 | B | | |
| 25 | C | | |
| 26 | A | | |
| 27 | C | | |
| 28 | D | | |
| 29 | A | | |
| 30 | D | | |

## Structure and Written Expression

| Structure | | Written Expression | |
|---|---|---|---|
| 1 | D | | |
| 2 | C | 16 | B |
| 3 | B | 17 | A |
| 4 | A | 18 | C |
| 5 | C | 19 | B |
| 6 | A | 20 | B |
| 7 | D | 21 | B |
| 8 | D | 22 | B |
| 9 | C | 23 | D |
| 10 | A | 24 | A |
| 11 | B | 25 | C |
| 12 | A | 26 | D |
| 13 | D | 27 | A |
| 14 | C | 28 | A |
| 15 | B | 29 | D |
| | | 30 | C |
| | | 31 | A |
| | | 32 | A |
| | | 33 | C |
| | | 34 | A |
| | | 35 | C |
| | | 36 | B |
| | | 37 | B |
| | | 38 | B |
| | | 39 | A |
| | | 40 | B |

## Reading Comprehension

| | | | |
|---|---|---|---|
| 1 | D | 26 | B |
| 2 | C | 27 | D |
| 3 | B | 28 | A |
| 4 | B | 29 | C |
| 5 | C | 30 | D |
| 6 | A | 31 | A |
| 7 | B | 32 | B |
| 8 | D | 33 | C |
| 9 | A | 34 | A |
| 10 | B | 35 | D |
| 11 | C | 36 | D |
| 12 | A | 37 | B |
| 13 | C | 38 | A |
| 14 | A | 39 | B |
| 15 | C | 40 | C |
| 16 | C | 41 | D |
| 17 | C | 42 | A |
| 18 | A | 43 | D |
| 19 | A | 44 | D |
| 20 | B | 45 | C |
| 21 | C | 46 | B |
| 22 | B | 47 | D |
| 23 | D | 48 | B |
| 24 | D | 49 | D |
| 25 | A | 50 | A |

# Section 1—Listening Comprehension Part A

## 1. 翌日の予定についての学生同士の会話　正答：B

002

**M** Tomorrow Richard and I are going to go to the baseball game, and we've got a couple of extra tickets. Would you and your roommate care to join us?

**M:** 明日，リチャードと一緒に野球の試合に行くんだけど，チケットが何枚か余ってるんだ。きみもルームメイトと一緒に来る？

**W** You bet. I'll give her a call right now. She's crazy about baseball.

**W:** もちろん。今すぐ彼女に電話するわ。彼女，野球が大好きなの。

What does the woman mean?

女性は何と言っていますか。

(A) She would like to bet on the game.
(B) She will go to the game tomorrow.
(C) She also bought some lottery tickets.
(D) She is surprised at what the man said.

(A) 試合で賭けをしたい。
(B) 明日試合を見に行く。
(C) 宝くじも何枚か買った。
(D) 男性の言ったことに驚いた。

Would you and your roommate care to join us? と，女性と彼女のルームメイトを野球に誘う男性に対して，女性は You bet. と応じている。これは「もちろん，きっと」という意味の口語表現。よって，(B) が正答。bet を字義どおり「お金を賭ける」ととると，(A) を選んでしまう。最後の発言での女性のイントネーションは感情を表しているが，喜びであり，驚きではないので (D) は誤り。

ボキャブラリー □ **You bet.**「もちろん，きっと」　□ **be crazy about ...**「～に熱をあげている」

## 2. 教授についての学生同士の会話　正答：D

003

**M** Did you hear the news about Professor Collins?

**M:** コリンズ教授のことは聞いた？

**W** Yes. I was really surprised to find out that she was leaving the computer science department to take a job in private industry.

**W:** ええ。彼女が民間企業で仕事をするためにコンピュータ学科を辞めると知って，とても驚いたわ。

What does the woman say about Professor Collins?

女性はコリンズ教授について何と言っていますか。

(A) She appeared on a news program.
(B) She just joined the science faculty.
(C) She had a problem with her computer.
(D) She is quitting her position at the university.

(A) ニュース番組に出演した。
(B) 理学部に加わったばかりである。
(C) コンピュータに問題がある。
(D) 大学の職を辞める。

大学教授が leaving「辞める」とあるので，大学を去る予定とわかる。これを quitting と言い換えている (D) が正答。computer science department からの誤った連想で (B) や (C) を選ばないように注意。なお，アメリカの大学などでは，研究者が大学と民間を行き来することは珍しくない。

ボキャブラリー □ **private industry**「民間企業」　□ **faculty**「学部，（学部の）教職員」

## 3. 明日の天気についての学生同士の会話　正答：C

004

| | |
|---|---|
| **M** Did you happen to hear what tomorrow's weather will be like? | **M:** 明日の天気はどうなるか知ってる？ |
| **W** Do you really want to know? It's bad. According to the TV, same as today: very hot and very muggy. | **W:** 本当に知りたい？　よくないわ。テレビによれば，今日と同じですごく蒸し暑いって。 |

What are the speakers discussing?
話者らは何について話していますか。

(A) What they will do tomorrow　(A) 明日何をするか
(B) The schedule of TV programs　(B) テレビ番組表
(C) The weather forecast　(C) 天気予報
(D) A bad accident on the news　(D) ニュースで報じられたひどい事故

tomorrow's weather, very hot and very muggy などのキーワードが聞き取れれば，2人が天気について話しているとわかる。(C) が正答。tomorrow, bad, TV などの断片的な聞き取りで誤った選択肢にひっかからないように。

ボキャブラリー □ **muggy**「蒸し暑い」

## 4. 学費ローンについての学生と大学職員の会話　正答：A

005

| | |
|---|---|
| **M** I'd like to apply for a student loan. I'm a full-time student, and I'm afraid I just don't have enough money to cover all of my housing and tuition costs. | **M:** 学費ローンに申し込みたいのですが。私は正規の学生なのですが，住居費と授業料をまかなうのに十分なお金がないのです。 |
| **W** All right. Please fill out these forms, and I'll be with you in a moment. I'm not sure how much money is left this year, but we'll try to help you the best we can. | **W:** わかりました。こちらの用紙に記入して，少々お待ちください。今年度の予算がどのくらい残っているかわかりませんが，できる限りのお手伝いをしましょう。 |

What does the woman ask the man to do?
女性は男性に何をするように求めていますか。

(A) Complete some documents　(A) 書類に記入する
(B) Come back later　(B) 後でまた来る
(C) Re-apply next year　(C) 来年に再申請する
(D) Estimate how much money he needs　(D) 必要な金額を算出する

女性職員が学生に Please fill out these forms「こちらの用紙に記入してください」と指示している。fill out は書類などの記入欄に「書き込む」こと。よって，この言い換えである (A) が正答。fill out は complete「～を仕上げる」, form は document と同義表現。how much money を部分的に繰り返している (D) を選ばないようにしよう。

ボキャブラリー □ **student loan**「学費ローン」
□ **full-time student**「正規学生」
＊ part-time student は，仕事などをしながら通学する学生のこと。
□ **housing and tuition costs**「住居費と授業料」

## 5. 今夜の予定についての学生同士の会話　正答：B

006

**M** Thanks for inviting me to your party, but I've got to work at my part-time job tonight. How late do you imagine the party will last?

**W** Well, it's just a few close friends, but you know us. Tomorrow's Saturday, and nobody has class. It's anybody's guess when the party will break up. Why don't you give me a call after you get off work?

**M:** パーティーに誘ってくれてありがとう。でも，今夜はバイトがあるんだ。どれくらい遅くまでやってると思う？

**W:** そうね，何人か仲のよい友人だけなんだけど，まあ予測がつくでしょ。明日は土曜日で，みんな授業はないし。パーティーがいつ終わるかなんてだれにもわからないわ。仕事が終わったら電話してみて。

What does the woman mean?

(A) The party will end relatively early.
(B) The man can probably attend the party later.
(C) Many people have been invited to the party.
(D) Saturday evening is the best time for a party.

女性は何と言っていますか。

(A) パーティーは比較的早く終わる。
(B) 男性はおそらく後からパーティーに参加できる。
(C) 大勢の人をパーティーに招いた。
(D) 土曜日の夜はパーティーをするのに最適である。

Tomorrow's Saturday, and nobody has class. It's anybody's guess when the party will break up. と，女性はパーティーが遅くまで続くとほのめかしている。また，最後に男性に Why don't you give me a call after you get off work? と言っているのは，男性のアルバイトが終わった後でもパーティーがまだ続いているはずだから。よって，(B) が正答。You know us. は文脈から「私たち（がパーティー好きだということ）を知っているでしょう」という意味。(A) (C) は会話の内容に反する。またパーティーがあるのは今夜（金曜日）なので (D) は誤り。

ボキャブラリー □ **last**「続く」 □ **anybody's guess**「だれにもわからないこと」
□ **break up**「解散する」 □ **Why don't you ...?**「～しませんか」

## 6. 交換留学プログラムについての学生同士の会話　正答：C

007

**W** Is that a German textbook? What do you need that for?

**M** I'm going there next year on the year-abroad exchange program.

**W:** それってドイツ語のテキスト？　何のために必要なの？

**M:** 来年，1年間の交換留学プログラムでドイツに行くんだ。

What can be inferred about the man?

(A) He is finished reading the book.
(B) He needs to exchange the text.
(C) He is studying a foreign language.
(D) He will graduate later in the year.

男性について何が推測できますか。

(A) その本を読み終えた。
(B) テキストを交換する必要がある。
(C) 外国語を勉強している。
(D) 今年の後半に卒業する。

女性の質問から，男性がドイツ語の教科書を読んでいるとわかる。ドイツ語を a foreign language と言い換えている (C) が正答。text, exchange, year などの繰り返しから (A) (B) (D) を選ばないようにしよう。

ボキャブラリー □ **year-abroad exchange program**「（大学の提供する）１年間の交換留学プログラム」

## 7. 成績についての学生同士の会話　正答：B

008

**M** I know Professor Robertson is really a hard grader, so how'd you end up doing in his Modern Literature class?

**W** Don't ask. The class was great, and I learned a lot, but he only gave me a C.

M: ロバートソン教授が成績にすごく厳しいのは知っているけど，彼の「近代文学」の成績は結局どうだったの？

W: 聞かないで。クラスはよかったし，とても勉強になったけど，彼，Cしかくれなかったの。

What seems to be true about Professor Robertson?

(A) His lectures are hard to follow.
(B) His grading policy is strict.
(C) His course is becoming popular.
(D) His class is rather dull.

ロバートソン教授について正しいと思われるのは何ですか。

(A) 授業についていくのがたいへんである。
(B) 成績のつけ方が厳しい。
(C) 人気授業になりつつある。
(D) 授業がかなりつまらない。

a hard grader は，成績評価が厳しいということ。これを grading policy is strict と言い換えている (B) が正答。how'd は how did の省略形。

ボキャブラリー □ **end up *doing* ...**「～することで終わる，結局～する」
□ **dull**「退屈な，つまらない」

## 8. 遅刻理由についての学生同士の会話　正答：C

009

**M** Jessica, I noticed you were late coming to sociology class this morning. What happened?

**W** Same as usual. I got up with plenty of time, ate breakfast, and then my car wouldn't start again. I've just about had it with that piece of trash.

M: ジェシカ，けさ，社会学の授業に遅れて来ただろ。どうしたの？

W: いつもどおりよ。余裕を持って起きて，朝食を食べて，そうしたら車のエンジンがまたかからなかったの。あのがらくたにはもううんざり。

What does the woman mean?

(A) She feels about the same as usual today.
(B) She forgot to take out the trash this morning.
(C) She is extremely frustrated with her car.
(D) She does not like her sociology class.

女性は何と言っていますか。

(A) 今日はいつもと同じ気分である。
(B) けさゴミを出すのを忘れた。
(C) 自分の車にうんざりしている。
(D) 社会学の授業が好きではない。

女性が最後に I've just about had it with that piece of trash. と言っているが，have it with ... は「〜にうんざりする，〜に耐えられない」という意味の口語表現。よって，これを言い換えた be frustrated with ... を含む (C) が正答。that piece of trash は，ここではエンジンがかからない車のこと。これを字義どおりにとると take out the trash「ゴミを出す」を含む (B) にひっかかる。same as usual，sociology class の断片的な聞き取りで (A) (D) を選ばないように。

ボキャブラリー ☐ **sociology**「社会学」 ☐ **have it with ...**「〜にうんざりする」
☐ **trash**「がらくた」

## 9. チケット購入についての学生同士の会話 正答：D

010

**W** Hank, some bad news: I couldn't get your concert tickets. I went over to the auditorium box office the first thing this morning, but the seats were all sold out.

**M** You've got to be kidding! They just went on sale the day before yesterday.

**W:** ハンク，悪い知らせなんだけど…。コンサートのチケットが取れなかったの。けさ一番に講堂のチケット売場に行ったんだけど，席はもう全部売り切れだったわ。

**M:** まさか！　おととい売り出したばかりだよ。

Why is the man upset?

(A) He does not like the seat he has been assigned.
(B) He will not be able to attend the lecture.
(C) The woman forgot to reserve the seats.
(D) The woman could not obtain the concert tickets.

男性はなぜ怒っているのですか。

(A) 指定された座席が気に入らない。
(B) 講義に出席できない。
(C) 女性が席を予約するのを忘れた。
(D) 女性がコンサートのチケットを入手できなかった。

女性の some bad news, the seats were all sold out から，「チケットがとれなかった」とわかる。よって (D) が正答。You've got to be kidding! は，相手の発言に対して「冗談でしょう！」「まさか，とんでもない！」と応じる口語表現。

ボキャブラリー ☐ **auditorium**「講堂」 ☐ **box office**「チケット売場」
☐ **You've got to be kidding!**「まさか，冗談でしょう！」
☐ **on sale**「売りに出て」

## 10. 夏の予定についての学生同士の会話 正答：A

011

**M** I'm still hoping you'll go on tour with our orchestra this summer. Any news back yet from that brokerage house you applied to for your summer internship?

**W** You haven't heard? They offered me a chance to work at their head office in New York. I'm leaving at the beginning of next week.

**M:** やっぱり今年の夏，きみもうちのオーケストラの公演旅行に一緒に行けるといいんだけれど。夏のインターンシップを申し込んだ証券会社からは何か連絡あった？

**W:** 聞いてない？　ニューヨークの本社で働くチャンスをもらったのよ。来週初めに発つわ。

What can be inferred from the conversation? この会話から何が推測できますか。

(A) The woman will not tour with the orchestra.
(B) The internship is not available this year.
(C) A new office will be opened in New York.
(D) The woman does not play a musical instrument.

(A) 女性はオーケストラの公演旅行に同行しない。
(B) インターンシップは今年は利用できない。
(C) 新しい事務所がニューヨークに開く。
(D) 女性は楽器を弾かない。

男性の I'm still hoping you'll go on tour with our orchestra this summer. に対し，女性は I'm leaving at the beginning of next week. と，すぐにニューヨークに発つと告げている。よって (A) が正答。(B) の not available，(C) の new office，(D) の musical instrument についてはいずれも会話で述べていない。

ボキャブラリー □ **brokerage house**「証券会社」 □ **apply for ...**「～を申し込む」
□ **internship**「実習訓練（期間）」 □ **available**「利用できる，空きがある」

## 11. 成績についての学生同士の会話 正答：C

012

**W** Did you hear that Karen got an A in Advanced Math?
**M** Karen? You've got to be joking.

**W:** カレンが高等数学のクラスでAを取ったって聞いた？
**M:** カレンが？ 冗談だろ。

What does the man imply about Karen? 男性はカレンについて何を示唆していますか。

(A) She has a good sense of humor.
(B) She has not contacted him for a while.
(C) She usually does not get such good grades.
(D) She enjoys studying mathematics.

(A) ユーモアのセンスがある。
(B) しばらく男性と連絡を取っていない。
(C) 普段はそんなに好成績をとらない。
(D) 数学の勉強を楽しんでいる。

男性の応答が驚きを表していることに注意。ここから，カレンの普段の成績があまりよくないとわかる。よって，(C) が正答。have got to *do* は口語表現で，must と同義。Did you hear ... を Did you hear from ... と勘違いすると，(B) を選んでしまう。また，kidding からの誤った連想で，(A) を選ばないように。

ボキャブラリー □ **advanced math [mathematics]**「高等数学」

## 12. 試験勉強についての学生同士の会話 正答：B

013

**W** Would you like to get together later and review for tomorrow's mid-term exam in psychology?
**M** Would I? You bet. I need all the help I can get.

**W:** 後で集まって一緒に，明日の心理学の中間テストの勉強をしない？
**M:** 勉強しないかって？ そりゃ，もちろん。とにかく助けが必要なんだ。

What does the man mean?

(A) He cannot meet the woman until tomorrow.
(B) He finds his psychology course challenging.
(C) He is thinking of dropping the class.
(D) He does not have time to study for the test.

男性は何と言っていますか。

(A) 明日まで女性に会えない。
(B) 心理学の授業は難しいと思っている。
(C) その授業を取るのをやめようと思っている。
(D) テストの勉強をする時間がない。

男性の Would I? は修辞的な疑問文で，ここでは「もちろん」という意味を表す。また，You bet. は，「もちろん，確かに」という意味の口語表現。男性が，テストのために I need all the help I can get. と言っていることから，これまであまり勉強していないと推測できる。よって，(B) が正答。アメリカ英語では，Thank you. への応答として「どういたしまして」の意味で You bet. が使われる。

ボキャブラリー □ **mid-term exam**「中間試験」 □ **challenging**「努力を要する」
□ **drop**「（学期途中で登録科目を）放棄する」

## 13. 春休みの予定についての学生同士の会話 正答：C

014

**W** For spring break, several of us have decided to hang out on a beach in California and go surfing. You want to come?

**M** I'd love to, but I've got to turn in my honor's thesis by March 25th. I won't even be able to visit my family this year.

**W:** 春休みは，私たち数人でカリフォルニアのビーチに遊びに行って，サーフィンすることにしたの。あなたも来る？

**M:** ぜひそうしたいところだけど，3月25日までに優等学位論文を提出しなければならないんだ。今年は実家にも帰れそうにないよ。

What will the man probably do during spring break?

(A) Take a trip with his friends
(B) Visit his family in California
(C) Work on an important paper
(D) Go surfing with the woman

男性はおそらく春休みに何をしますか。

(A) 友人と旅行に行く
(B) カリフォルニアの家族を訪れる
(C) 重要な論文に取り組む
(D) 女性とサーフィンに行く

honor's thesis とは，卒業時に優等学位（magna cum laude など）を得るために書く卒業論文のこと。これを an important paper と言い換えている (C) が正答。visit his family, go surfing などの部分的な繰り返しにひっかからないように。なお，アメリカの大学では，spring break には学生同士でリゾート地などに旅行に出かける習慣がある。日本の大学の夏休みに近い感覚。

ボキャブラリー □ **hang out**「ぶらぶらして時間を過ごす」 □ **turn in ...**「～を提出する」

## 14. カフェテリアについての学生同士の会話 正答：D

015

**W** I really recommend the chocolate cake at the student cafe.

**M** Yes, I've tried it. It is out of this world.

**W:** カフェテリアのチョコレートケーキは本当にお勧めよ。

**M:** ああ，食べてみたよ。あれは天下一品だね。

What do the speakers mean?

(A) They both like drinking coffee.
(B) The cafeteria is out of cake.
(C) Most students do not go to the cafe.
(D) They agree the cake is excellent.

話者らは何と言っていますか。

(A) 2人ともコーヒーを飲むのが好きだ。
(B) カフェテリアはケーキを切らしている。
(C) ほとんどの学生はカフェに行かない。
(D) 2人ともそのケーキがおいしいと同意している。

女性がカフェのチョコレートケーキを勧めたのに対して，男性も It is out of this world. と言っているので，2人ともそのケーキがおいしいと思っているとわかる。out of this world. は「(この世の物とは思えないほど)すばらしい」という意味の口語表現。よって (D) が正答となる。(B) の out of ... は「〜が不足している」の意味。

ボキャブラリー □ **recommend**「〜を勧める」 □ **excellent**「すばらしい」

## 15. 教職課程についての学生同士の会話 正答：A

016

**W** Carl, I remember you told me you wanted to work with young kids after you graduated. Are you still enrolled in the teacher certification program?

**M** Sure am. In fact, I'm on my way to the university day-care center right now. I work there two days a week helping them evaluate their program as part of my student teaching assignment. Then, three days a week I go to the local elementary school.

**W:** カール，あなたは卒業したら小さい子どもと働きたいって言ってたわよね。まだ教職課程を取っているの？

**M:** もちろんさ。実は今も大学の託児所に行く途中なんだ。教職実習の一環として週2回，プログラムの評価を手伝いに行ってるんだ。それに，週3日は地元の小学校に行っているよ。

What can be inferred about the man?

(A) He is preparing to become a teacher.
(B) His children are enrolled in a day-care center.
(C) His teacher gave him a high evaluation.
(D) He just received his teaching credential.

男性について何が推測できますか。

(A) 教師になる準備をしている。
(B) 自分の子どもが託児所に入っている。
(C) 自分の先生が高い評価をくれた。
(D) 教職の資格を取ったばかりである。

女性が the teacher certification program「教職課程」を取っているかと尋ねると，男性は Sure am.「もちろん，そのとおり」と肯定している。また the university day-care center，my student teaching assignment，the local elementary school などのキーワードから，男性が教職資格を取ろうとしていることが推測できる。よって，正答は (A)。day-care center，evaluate，credential などの断片的な聞き取りだけだと，誤った選択肢にひっかかってしまう。

ボキャブラリー □ **be enrolled in ...**「〜に登録している」
□ **teacher certification**「教員資格」 □ **day-care center**「託児所」

## 16. 今夜の予定についての学生同士の会話　正答：D

017

**M** Can I give you a ride to the dance tonight?

**W** I thought you had to finish your art project.

M: 今夜のダンスパーティー，車で送っていこうか？

W: あなたは美術の宿題を終わらせなければいけないと思ったんだけど。

What had the woman assumed?

(A) Art would give her a ride to the dance.
(B) The man does not like dancing.
(C) The report was not about art.
(D) The man had an assignment to complete.

女性は何を想定していましたか。

(A) アートが車でダンスパーティーに送ってくれる。
(B) 男性はダンスが好きではない。
(C) レポートは美術についてではなかった。
(D) 男性には仕上げなければならない宿題がある。

女性が男性に対して，I thought you had to finish your art project. と答えていることから，男性には art の宿題があることがわかる。この art project を an assignment と言い換えている (D) が正答となる。(A) の Art は，男性名 Arthur のニックネーム。

ボキャブラリー □ **give ... a ride**「(人を車に) 乗せてやる」 □ **project**「学習課題，研究計画」

## 17. 寮生活についての学生同士の会話　正答：B

018

**M** Yesterday's dorm meeting was a total waste of time. I imagine very few people had any idea why we had to be there.

**W** Well, what do you expect when nobody bothers to prepare an agenda in advance?

M: 昨日の寮のミーティングはまったく時間の無駄だったよ。なぜ出席する必要があるのかわかった人なんかいなかっただろうよ。

W: そうね。だれもあらかじめ議題を用意してないんだもの，どうしようもないわね。

What was the problem with the meeting?

(A) It was attended by few people.
(B) Its purpose was unclear.
(C) It went on longer than expected.
(D) It was called on short notice.

ミーティングの何が問題でしたか。

(A) ほとんど出席者がいなかった。
(B) 目的がはっきりしなかった。
(C) 予想以上に時間がかかった。
(D) 急な連絡で集められた。

だれも agenda「協議事項，検討事項」を事前に考えてこなかったので very few people had any idea why we had to be there であったと述べている。よって，(B) が正答。few が a を伴わないため，準否定語であることに注意。bother to *do* は，「わざわざ～する」という意味。女性の what do you expect ...? は修辞的疑問文で，「何を期待できるのか？（何も期待できないだろう）」という意味。(D) の on short notice は「直前の連絡で」という意味。

ボキャブラリー □ **dorm meeting**「寮のミーティング」 □ **agenda**「協議事項」
□ **in advance**「前もって」

## 18. 宿題についての学生同士の会話　正答：C

019

**W** Walt, I know you're really busy, but I sure could use some help on these calculus equations. I don't have a clue about what's going on in this unit.

**M** No problem. How does after dinner sound?

W: ウォルト，すごく忙しいとは思うんだけど，この微分方程式の問題を手伝ってもらえるとありがたいんだけど。この部分がどうなっているのかさっぱりわからないの。

M: いいよ。夕食の後でどう？

What does the man mean?

(A) He probably will not have time to help the woman.
(B) He would like the woman to join him for dinner.
(C) He will give the woman a hand this evening.
(D) He cannot solve the woman's problem.

男性は何と言っていますか。

(A) 女性を手伝う時間はおそらくない。
(B) 女性に夕食に付き合ってもらいたい。
(C) 今夜女性を手伝う。
(D) 女性の問題を解決できない。

女性が「忙しいとは思うけど…」と遠慮がちに宿題の助けを求めると，男性は No problem.「もちろんいいよ」と快諾している。よって，(C) が正答。give ... a hand で「～を手伝う」。会話中の after dinner を選択肢は this evening と言い換えている。help, dinner, problem などの単語の繰り返しだけで (A) (B) (D) を選ばないように。

ボキャブラリー □ **calculus**「微積分」 □ **equation**「方程式，等式」 □ **clue**「ヒント，手がかり」 □ **How does [do] ... sound?**「～はどうですか」

## 19. ジョギングについての男性と女性の会話　正答：A

020

**M** Patty, I'm not sure I want to go running. I'm a little sore and kind of tired today. Besides, I heard it's going to rain.

**W** Oh, Grant. Remember the promise we made to each other to jog every day to get in shape. You'll use any excuse to escape some healthy exertion.

M: パティ，あまり走りたい気にならないんだ。今日は少し体が痛いし，なんだか疲れてるんだよ。それに，雨が降るって聞いたよ。

W: もう，グラント。毎日走って体力をつけるってお互いに約束したでしょ。あなたって，運動から逃げるためにはどんな言い訳でもするわね。

What does the woman imply about the man?

(A) He often tries to avoid exercise.
(B) He stayed up too late last night.
(C) He should go jogging by himself.
(D) He ought to get a health check-up.

女性は男性について何を示唆していますか。

(A) 運動を避けようとすることがよくある。
(B) 昨夜遅くまで夜ふかしした。
(C) ひとりでジョギングに行くべきだ。
(D) 健康診断を受けるべきだ。

男性がジョキングから逃れようと言い訳を並べると，女性は You'll use any excuse to escape some healthy exertion.「運動から逃げるためにはどんな言い訳でもするわね」とあきれている。ここから男性はいつも運動をさぼろうとしていると推測できるので，(A) が正答。kind of tired からの誤った連想で (B) を選んだり，a little sore から (D) を選んだりしないように。

ボキャブラリー □ **get in shape**「体力をつける」 □ **excuse**「言い訳」 □ **exertion**「努力」

## 20. クリーニングについての学生同士の会話　正答：D

021

**W** Oh no! I just noticed a stain on this dress, and I wanted to wear it to the concert tonight. Do you know any place in town that does same-day dry cleaning?

**W:** あら，いやだ。このドレス，染みが付いているわ。今夜，コンサートに着ていこうと思っていたのに。どこか即日仕上げのクリーニングをやってる店を知らない？

**M** There was a place over by the park, but I think they went out of business earlier this year.

**M:** 公園の近くに1軒あったんだけど，そこは今年初めに店をたたんだよ。

What can be inferred from the conversation?

この会話から何が推測できますか。

(A) There is a new dry cleaner near the park.
(B) The paint store has gone out of business.
(C) The man will not have time to attend the concert.
(D) The woman may not be able to wear the dress she wanted to.

(A) 公園の近くに新しいクリーニング店がある。
(B) ペンキ屋は店をたたんだ。
(C) 男性はコンサートに行く時間がないだろう。
(D) 女性は，着たかったドレスが着れないかもしれない。

着たかったドレスに染みがあり，これをクリーニングできる店がないのだから，女性はこのドレスを着ることができないかもしれない。よって，正答は (D)。stain からの誤った連想で (B) を選ばないように。dry cleaner，the park，concert などの断片的な聞き取りでは (A) や (C) にひっかかってしまう。

ボキャブラリー □ **stain**「しみ，よごれ」 □ **same-day**「同日付けの，即日仕上げの」
□ **go out of business**「倒産する，店をたたむ」

## 21. 夕食についての学生同士の会話　正答：B

022

**W** I'm heading over to the cafeteria for dinner. Would you care to join me? Or better yet, why don't we go downtown and grab a pizza or something?

**W:** カフェテリアに夕食を食べに行くところなの。一緒に行く？　それか，いっそのこと，町に出てピザか何か食べない？

**M** That sounds good to me. I haven't been off campus for almost two weeks. It'll be nice to get some decent food for a change.

**M:** それはいいね。もう2週間近く学外に出ていないんだ。たまにはまともなものを食べるのもいいね。

What does the man imply?

男性は何を示唆していますか。

(A) He has been eating out a lot recently.
(B) He does not like the cafeteria's food.
(C) He is too busy to go off campus tonight.
(D) He does not want to go downtown.

(A) 最近よく外食している。
(B) カフェテリアの料理が好きではない。
(C) 忙しくて今夜は学外に出られない。
(D) 町には行きたくない。

男性は最後に，学外に食事に出ることを get some decent food for a change「たまにはきちんとしたものを食べる」と述べている。ここから，普段食べているカフェテリアの食事が decent（きちんとした）ではない，つまりまずいと思っていると推測できる。よって，(B) が正答。

**ボキャブラリー** □ **head (over) to ...**「～に向かう」 □ **off campus**「学外に」
□ **decent**「まともな」 □ **for a change**「気分転換に」

## 22. 校内書店についての学生同士の会話　正答：A

023

| | |
|---|---|
| **M** It's so inconvenient that the college bookstore doesn't accept credit cards. That's how I make almost all of my purchases. | **M:** 校内の書店でクレジットカードが使えないのはすごく不便だね。ぼくはたいていの買物はカードで済ませているのに。 |
| **W** Oh, no. In that case I guess I'll have to put off buying the books I need until I have a chance to go to the bank and make a withdrawal. | **W:** 困ったわ。それじゃ，銀行に行って現金を引き出してからでないと，必要な本が買えそうにないわ。 |

What can be inferred about the woman?　女性について何が推測できますか。

(A) She was planning on using a credit card.　(A) クレジットカードを使おうと思っていた。
(B) She just went to the bank this morning.　(B) けさ銀行に行ったばかりである。
(C) She is not taking classes this term.　(C) 今学期は授業を取っていない。
(D) She has already purchased what she needed.　(D) すでに必要なものは購入した。

校内の書店ではクレジットカードが使えない，と男性が述べている。銀行で現金をおろさなければ買い物ができないということは，女性はカードを使うつもりで，現金を用意していないということ。よって，(A) が正答。bank，purchase，need などの断片的な聞き取りで (B) (C) (D) を選ばないように。

**ボキャブラリー** □ **purchase**「買い物（をする）」 □ **withdrawal**「預金の引き出し」

## 23. 図書館での学生同士の会話　正答：D

024

| | |
|---|---|
| **M** Excuse me, is this seat taken? | **M:** すみません。この席は使用中ですか。 |
| **W** I'm afraid it is. My friend just went over to the periodicals desk for a minute. | **W:** 悪いけど，ええ。友人がちょっと雑誌の貸出カウンターに行っているの。 |

What will the man likely do next?　男性はおそらく次に何をしますか。

(A) Take a seat next to the woman　(A) 女性の隣に席を取る
(B) Read a periodical　(B) 雑誌を読む
(C) Check out a book　(C) 本を借り出す
(D) Look for another place to sit down　(D) 別に座る場所を探す

男性が空いている席を探している。よって，正答は (D)。I'm afraid ... は，「(好ましくないことを）思う」という意味。 take a seat, periodical などの部分的な繰り返しで (A) や (B) を選ばないように。

ボキャブラリー □ **periodical**「(学会誌，専門誌などの）定期刊行物」
□ **check out**「(本などを）借り出す」

## 24. 寮生活についての学生同士の会話　正答：B

025

W: I understand we're getting a new piano for our dorm lounge.
M: That's great! The old one doesn't stay in tune for more than a week.

W: 寮のラウンジに新しいピアノを買うことになっているらしいよ。
M: それはよかった！　古いのは調律しても1週間ともたないから。

What does the man mean?

(A) Some dorm members cannot sing in tune.
(B) The dorm really needs a new piano.
(C) The piano will not be delivered for another week.
(D) Dorm students should not play the piano so much.

男性は何と言っていますか。

(A) 寮のメンバーには音痴の人がいる。
(B) 寮には新しいピアノがぜひ必要だ。
(C) ピアノはあと 1 週間は届かない。
(D) 寮の学生はそんなにピアノを弾くべきではない。

寮で新しいピアノを買う予定だと女性が男性に知らせると，男性は That's great! と喜んでいる。ここから，男性も寮に新しいピアノが必要と考えていることがわかるので，(B) が正答。I understand ... はここでは「～と聞き及んでいる」という意味。(A) の in tune は部分的な重複によるひっかけ。

ボキャブラリー □ **in tune**「正しい音程で」

## 25. 期末試験についての学生同士の会話　正答：C

026

W: So, Gary, I know you put a lot of time and effort into studying for your accounting final. How'd you do?
M: I wasn't able to answer all of the questions because I had trouble finishing some of the calculations. I think I answered enough to keep from failing, though.

W: それでゲイリー，会計学の期末試験の勉強に相当な時間と労力をつぎ込んでいたことは知っているけど，結果はどうだったの？
M: 計算でいくつか手間取って，全問は解答できなかったんだ。まあ落第にならない程度には解答したと思うけど。

What does the man imply?

(A) He will likely fail the course he is taking.
(B) He should have studied more than he did.
(C) He could not complete all of the exam questions.
(D) He found his calculator was broken.

男性は何を示唆していますか。

(A) 受講中のコースを落としそうである。
(B) もっと勉強しておくべきだった。
(C) 試験問題を全問解き終えられなかった。
(D) 計算機が壊れていることがわかった。

男性は I wasn't able to answer all of the questions「全問解き終えることができなかった」と述べている。よって，(C) が正答。fail，study，calculate などの単語の繰り返しだけで (A) や (D) を選ばないように注意。

ボキャブラリー □ **accounting**「会計（学）」 □ **final**「期末試験」 □ **calculation**「計算」 □ **fail**「落第する」

## 26. グループ発表についての学生同士の会話　正答：A

027

**W** I'm really sorry, Jeff. I overslept again. And I know we were supposed to give our group presentation this morning.

**M** Yeah, and you didn't bother to come to our practice session last night, either. You know, we're really lucky Professor Beck allowed us to reschedule our group presentation for the next class.

**W:** ごめんなさい，ジェフ。また寝過ごしちゃったの。今日の午前中に私たちがグループ発表をすることになっていたのはわかっているんだけど。

**M:** そうだよ，それに昨夜の事前練習にも来なかったじゃないか。いいかい，ぼくたちのグループ発表をベック教授が次回のクラスに変更してくれて助かったんだよ。

What can be inferred about the woman?

(A) She is somewhat irresponsible.
(B) She already gave her class presentation.
(C) She completed the preparation last night.
(D) She will ask the professor to change the schedule.

女性について何が推測できますか。

(A) いささか無責任なところがある。
(B) すでに授業での発表を終えた。
(C) 昨晩に準備を済ませた。
(D) 教授に予定の変更を依頼するつもりだ。

女性は，前日の練習に参加しなかったうえに，発表の日にも寝過ごして遅刻している。このことから，彼女が責任感に乏しいと判断できるので，(A) が正答。presentation，last night，schedule などの単語の繰り返しだけで (B) (C) (D) を選ばないように。

ボキャブラリー □ **not bother to *do***「（億劫がって）～しようとしない」
□ **session**「集まり，打ち合わせ」

## 27. 教科書についての学生同士の会話　正答：C

028

**M** You spent over $500 for textbooks at the campus bookstore! Why didn't you go to Steve's Used Books? They're much cheaper there.

**W** I know Steve's is cheaper, but those used texts are already written in. I like to do my own highlighting.

**M:** 大学の書店で教科書に500ドル以上も使ったって！　スティーヴ古書店に行けばよかったのに。あっちのほうがずっと安いよ。

**W:** スティーヴ書店のほうが安いのは知ってるわ。でも，古本って書き込みがあるでしょ。私，マーキングは自分でしたいのよ。

What does the woman mean?

(A) She regrets not shopping at Steve's.
(B) She could not afford to buy her textbooks.
(C) She prefers to use new textbooks.
(D) She thinks Steve's is also expensive.

女性は何と言っていますか。

(A) スティーヴ書店で買わなかったことを後悔している。
(B) 教科書を買う余裕がなかった。
(C) 新しい教科書のほうがよい。
(D) スティーヴ書店も値段が高いと思う。

古本は安いけれども，他人の書き込みがあり，自分で書き込むには使いづらい，と女性は述べている。ここから，女性が新しい教科書を好んでいることがわかる。よって，正答は (C)。なお，アメリカの大学では，一科目に複数冊の教科書があり，その値段もばかにならない。そこで，たいていキャンパスの近くに教科書の古本を扱う書店がある。

ボキャブラリー □ **used**「中古の」 □ **highlight**「～に蛍光マーカーでマークする」
□ **afford**「(経済的・時間的な) 余裕がある」

## 28. 移動手段についての学生同士の会話 正答：D

029

W I'm really in a hurry. Is there any chance you could give me a lift over to the student union? My play rehearsal starts in five minutes.

M I'd love to, Marsha, but my schedule is really tight this morning.

W: すごく急いでいるの。学生会館まで車に乗せていってもらえない？ 劇のリハーサルがあと5分で始まるよ。

M: マーシャ，そうしてあげたいところなんだけど，けさはすごく忙しいんだ。

What does the man mean?

(A) He would love to see the woman's rehearsal.
(B) He does not know his schedule for the day.
(C) He hopes he can meet the woman later.
(D) He does not have time to give the woman a ride.

男性は何と言っていますか。

(A) 女性のリハーサルをぜひ見たい。
(B) その日の自分のスケジュールがわからない。
(C) 後で女性に会えればよいと思っている。
(D) 女性を車で送っていく時間がない。

急いでいるので車で送ってほしいと頼む女性に対して，男性は my schedule is really tight this morning と言って断っている。よって，(D) が正答。lift と ride は同義語で，《give ＋人＋ a ride [lift]》で「～を車に乗せてやる」という意味。tight は「(予定が) つまった，余裕がない」ということ。ちなみに「ハードスケジュール」は和製英語で，tight schedule と言うのが適切。

ボキャブラリー □ **student union**「学生会館」

## 29. 通学についての学生同士の会話　正答：A

030

W Why are so many students late for class this evening? Usually everybody is on time.

M Apparently, the bus drivers walked off the job this afternoon, so everyone had to either walk or drive. That's why the parking lot was almost full.

W: どうして今夜はこんなに大勢の学生がクラスに遅刻しているの？　いつもはみんな遅れないのに。

M: どうやらバスの運転手が午後に仕事をボイコットしたらしい。だから，みんな徒歩や自分の車で来るしかないのさ。そんなわけで駐車場はほとんど満車さ。

Why were the students late for class?

(A) The bus drivers went on strike.
(B) There were no open parking spaces.
(C) There was a bus accident.
(D) They had to work overtime.

なぜ学生たちは授業に遅刻したのですか。

(A) バスの運転手がストライキをした。
(B) 駐車スペースが空いていなかった。
(C) バスの事故があった。
(D) 残業しなければならなかった。

walk off「～を放棄する」を，go on strike と言い換えている (A) が正答。late for class，on time などから誤った連想で (D) の work overtime を選ばないように。

ボキャブラリー □ **on time**「時間どおりに，遅れずに」 □ **parking lot**「駐車場」
□ **work overtime**「残業する」

## 30. 就職活動についての学生同士の会話　正答：D

031

W John, how's your job search coming along?

M Couldn't be better. I've already got offers from three companies. Now I just need to decide which one to take.

W: ジョン，就職活動の進み具合はどう？

M: 絶好調だよ。もう3社から内定をもらってるんだ。あとはどこにするか決めるだけさ。

What does the man mean?

(A) He needs to continue searching for work.
(B) He hopes he can find a better job.
(C) He did not receive any job offers.
(D) He has to choose which company to work for.

男性は何と言っていますか。

(A) 就職活動を続ける必要がある。
(B) もっとよい仕事を見つけたい。
(C) まだひとつも内定をもらっていない。
(D) どの会社で働くか決めなければならない。

decide which one to take を choose which company to work for と言い換えている (D) が正答。search for work，better job，job offer などの繰り返しから (A) (B) (C) を選ばないように。

ボキャブラリー □ **job search**「就職活動」 □ **come along**「（物事が）進む，はかどる」
□ **job offer**「内定」

## Questions 31-34 *Long Conversation 1*

033 学生同士の会話。男性のルームメイトが転居することになり，女性に新しいルームメイトを紹介してもらえないかと頼んでいる。

| | |
|---|---|
| **Listen to the following conversation between two students.** | **2人の学生による次の会話を聞きなさい。** |
| M Carol, could I talk to you for a minute? | M: キャロル，ちょっといいかな。 |
| W Sure, Jake. What is it? | W: もちろんよ，ジェイク。どうしたの？ |
| M Probably you heard that Linda decided to move out of our place at the end of this month. | M: リンダが今月末にぼくらのところを出ていくことにしたのは，たぶん聞いているよね。 |
| W Yeah, she told me. Q32 Her parents asked her to move back home and, given her financial situation, she jumped at the chance. So what's this got to do with me? You and Kevin thinking about asking me to move in with you to take Linda's place or something? | W: ええ，彼女から聞いているわ。Q32 彼女の両親が家に戻ってくるように言ったんでしょ。彼女は自分の経済状態を考えて，そのチャンスに飛びついたのよね。で，それが私に何か関係があるの？ あなたとケビンは，リンダの代わりに私に入居するように頼むつもりなのかしら。 |
| M To be honest, that'd be great. Q33 But I know how much you like living on campus, especially with all the time you spend studying late in the library. No, the reason I mention it is that I thought Q31 maybe you might know someone who's looking for a place to live. | M: 正直なところ，そうしてくれたらいいんだけどね。Q33 でも，きみがキャンパス内に住むのがすごく好きなことはわかっているよ。特にいつも遅くまで図書館で勉強していることを思えばね。いや，この話をしたのは，Q31 きみならだれか住む場所を探している人を知ってるんじゃないかと思ったからなんだ。 |
| W As a matter of fact, I do. Jennifer Perez decided not to renew her dorm contract next term. You know her, right? Q34 I think she'd make a great roommate for you and Kevin. Here. Let me write down her phone number for you. | W: ええ，実は知っているわ。ジェニファー・ペレズが来学期の寮の契約を更新しないことにしたの。彼女，知ってるでしょ？ Q34 彼女ならあなたとケビンにぴったりのルームメイトになると思うけど。じゃあ，彼女の電話番号を書いておくわね。 |

## 31. 正答：D

034 What does the man want the woman to do? 男性は女性に何をしてほしいと思っていますか。

(A) Meet him later to study in the library (A) 図書館で勉強するために後で自分と落ち合う
(B) Help him look for a new place to live (B) 自分が新しく住む場所を探すのを手伝う
(C) Recommend a reliable moving company (C) 信頼できる引っ越し業者を推薦する
(D) Suggest someone to move in with him (D) 自分と同居してくれる人を教える

男性は女性に maybe you might know someone who's looking for a place to live「きみなら住むところを探している人を知っているんじゃないか」と言っている。形は平叙文だが，文脈上，頼み事をしているとわかる。よって，この言い換えとなっている (D) が正答。また，最後で，女性が I think she'd make a great roommate for you and Kevin. と言って友人を紹介しようとしているところからも，男性がルームメイトを探しているとわかる。なお，make a great roommate の make は「～を作る」ではなく，「～になる」という意味。

## 32. 正答：B

034 Why is Linda moving? リンダはなぜ引っ越すのですか。

(A) She does not get along with her roommates.
(B) She can save money by living with her parents.
(C) She wants to live in an apartment closer to campus.
(D) She is not happy with the place she lives now.

(A) ルームメイトとうまくいっていない。
(B) 両親と一緒に暮らすことでお金を節約できる。
(C) もっとキャンパスに近いアパートに住みたい。
(D) 今住んでいる場所に満足していない。

リンダが引っ越す理由は，女性の Her parents ... the chance. からわかる。この一文をまとめて言い換えている (B) が正答。この文を聞き逃すと，引っ越しの理由としてもっともらしい (A) (C) (D) にひっかかってしまう。

## 33. 正答：C

034 What can be inferred about the dormitory? 寮について何が推測できますか。

(A) It is noisy. (A) うるさい。
(B) It is expensive. (B) 費用が高い。
(C) It is convenient. (C) 便利である。
(D) It is crowded. (D) 混雑している。

男性は，living on campus「キャンパス内に住む」ことは，studying late in the library「遅くまで図書館で勉強する」のに便利であると示唆している。よって，(C) が正答。

## 34. 正答：A

034

What will the man probably do next?

(A) Give Jennifer a call
(B) Ask Linda not to leave
(C) Speak with his parents
(D) Look at the dorm contract

男性はおそらく次に何をしますか。

(A) ジェニファーに電話をする
(B) リンダに留まるように頼む
(C) 自分の両親と話す
(D) 寮の契約に目を通す

女性が最後に ... Let me write down her phone number for you.「電話番号を書いておくわね」と言って，部屋を探しているジェニファーの電話番号を渡しているので，男性は彼女に電話するだろうと推測できる。よって，(A) が正答。このように会話後の行動や予定を問う設問の根拠は会話の最後にあることが多い。

---

ボキャブラリー
- □ **given**「～を考慮して」
- □ **financial situation**「経済状況」
- □ **to be honest**「正直に言えば」
- □ **on campus**「キャンパス内で」
- □ **as a matter of fact**「実際のところ」
- □ **get along with ...**「～と仲よくやる」

## Questions 35-38　*Long Conversation 2*

035 教授と学生の会話。学生は，レポートを書くにあたって資料が見つからない，と教授に相談している。教授は，学生の考えるテーマとレポート作成の手順についてアドバイスしている。

**Listen to the following conversation between a professor and a student.**

教授と男性による次の会話を聞きなさい。

**M** Dr. Jenkins, do you have a moment?

M: ジェンキンズ先生，ちょっとよろしいですか。

**W** Sure, Mike. Come on in. What's on your mind?

W: どうぞ，マイク。入ってください。どうしましたか。

**M** Q35 I'm having trouble with my term paper. I'm really interested in the role women played during Q36 westward expansion. So I started out trying to find information on what women did in Q36 wagon trains that crossed the Great Plains during the 19th century. Q37 But even though I've spent a lot of time in the library looking for books and searching various databases, I can't really find much.

M: Q35 期末レポートのことで困っています。ぼくは Q36 西部開拓時代に女性が果たした役割についてとても興味を持っています。そこで，Q36 19世紀にグレート・プレーンズを横断した幌馬車隊で女性が何をしていたのかについて，資料を探し始めました。Q37 でも，図書館でずいぶん時間をかけて本を探したり，いろいろなデータベースをあたってみたりしたのですが，それほど資料を集められなかったんです。

**W** I'm kind of surprised, Mike. Usually the students in my history classes have the opposite problem. They choose topics that are too broad, and then they can't really focus or write well about them. In your case, though, you need to broaden your topic. Maybe you should focus on something like the role of women in Q36 frontier life. Depending upon your sources, you can then narrow your focus to, say, Q36 the Midwest in the 1850's, or even a particular state such as Iowa.

W: それはちょっと驚きですね，マイク。私の歴史学のクラスの学生は普通，それと逆の問題にぶつかるんですよ。広すぎるテーマを選んでしまって，焦点が絞れなかったり，うまくまとめられなかったり。でも，あなたの場合はトピックを広げる必要がありそうですね。たぶん，Q36 開拓生活における女性の役割といった事柄に焦点を当てるのがよいでしょうね。そうすれば，集めた資料に応じて，Q36 1850年代の中西部とか，あるいは，さらにアイオワ州など特定の州といった具合にテーマを絞り込むことができますから。

**M** All right, that's beginning to make sense. You're saying I should open my topic up a little, like to frontier women, and then depending upon what resource materials I find, focus on something specific.

M: なるほど，だんだんわかってきました。開拓時代の女性などのようにトピックを少し広げて，それから自分の集めた資料に基づいて，特定の事柄に焦点を絞ればよいとおっしゃるわけですね。

**W** That's exactly right. Also, once you start making some progress in writing, Q38 don't be afraid to drop in and see me during my office hours. I'd be happy to give you some feedback on your organization, introduction and conclusion, and so on.

W: そのとおりです。それと，少し書き進めたら，Q38 気軽にオフィスアワーに立ち寄ってください。構成や導入，結論などについて，喜んでアドバイスしますから。

## 35.

正答：D

036

Why is the man talking to the woman?

(A) To discuss a presentation topic
(B) To ask about a missed assignment
(C) To request an introduction
(D) To receive help on an essay

なぜ男性は女性に話をしているのですか。

(A) 発表の主題について相談するため
(B) 提出しそこねた課題について質問するため
(C) 紹介をお願いするため
(D) レポートについて助言を求めるため

女性のオフィスに入室してすぐに，男性は I'm having trouble with my term paper.「期末レポートのことで困っています」と来意を告げている。よって，term paper を essay と言い換えている (D) が正答。ほかにも topic，focus，sources，resource materials，writing，organization, introduction and conclusion，など，レポートについての相談であることを示すキーワードが複数，聞き取れるはず。

## 36.

正答：B

036

What subject is the man studying?

(A) American literature
(B) United States history
(C) Modern economics
(D) Contemporary sociology

この学生が学んでいる課目は何ですか。

(A) アメリカ文学
(B) アメリカ史
(C) 近代経済学
(D) 現代社会学

westward expansion，wagon trains that crossed the Great Plains during the 19th century，frontier life，the Midwest in the 1850's などの表現から，男性がアメリカ史のレポートに取り組んでいるのは明らか。よって，(B) が正答。また，女性が my history classes と言っていることからも，歴史であるとわかる。解答の根拠が何度も繰り返されているので，比較的解答しやすい。

## 37.

正答：A

036

What initial problem did the man have in researching his topic?

(A) He could not find many sources.
(B) He did not know what to focus on.
(C) He chose a theme that was too broad.
(D) He could not use the library databases.

男性が自分のトピックについて調べていて最初にぶつかった問題は何ですか。

(A) 多くの資料を見つけられなかった。
(B) 何に焦点を当てればよいかわからなかった。
(C) 広すぎるテーマを選んでしまった。
(D) 図書館のデータベースを使えなかった。

会話の前半で，男性は ... I can't really find much と言っているが，この much はレポートに使える資料のこと。これを many sources と言い換えている，(A) が正答。

## 38. 正答：C

036

What final suggestion does the woman make to the man?

女性は男性に対して最後に何を提案していますか。

(A) He should start writing as soon as possible.
(B) He should ask the library staff for help.
(C) He should come back and see her again later.
(D) He should focus on the organization of his essay.

(A) できるだけ早く書き始める。
(B) 図書館の職員に相談する。
(C) 後でもう一度自分に会いにくる。
(D) 論文の構成に焦点を当てる。

設問に final suggestion とあるので，最後の発言を思い出せばよい。女性は don't be afraid to drop in and see me during my office hours と言っている。drop in とは「立ち寄る」という意味の口語表現。これを come back and see と言い換えている (C) が正答となる。writing や organization の繰り返しで (A) (B) (D) を選ばないように。

---

ボキャブラリー
- □ **term paper**「学期末レポート」
- □ **westward expansion**「西部開拓」
- □ **wagon train**「幌馬車隊」
- □ **Great Plains**「グレートプレーンズ（ロッキー山脈東方の大草原地帯）」
- □ **frontier life**「開拓者の生活」
- □ **Midwest**「中西部」
- □ **make sense**「（なるほどと）わかる，道理にかなう」
- □ **specific**「特定の」
- □ **drop in**「立ち寄る」
- □ **feedback**「意見，アドバイス」
- □ **organization**「構成」

## Questions 39-42

*Introduction to Chemistry*

038

1 化学の概説についての講義。
2 化学は物質の改良や開発など，生活に重大な影響を及ぼす学問である。
3 化学は「物質が被る変化」に関する学問であるために，革新をもたらすことができる。一般に研究はグループで行う。
4 最後に，テストを行うと告げる。

**Listen to part of a talk in an Introduction to Chemistry class.**

**化学概論の授業での講義の一部を聞きなさい。**

1 Today, I'd like to start my lecture with Q39 some general remarks about the field of chemistry, because when you plunge into experiments and particular problems, it's easy to lose perspective about the overall field and what chemistry means, practically speaking, in today's world.

パラグラフ1 今日は授業を始めるにあたって，Q39 まず化学という分野について一般的な事柄を少し述べておきたいと思います。というのも，みなさんが実験や特定の問題にのめり込むと，化学という分野全般についての見通しや，化学が特に現代世界で実際どのような意味を持っているのかといったことを見失いがちになるからです。

2 To begin, I'd like to make the point that of all of the sciences, one could argue that Q40 chemistry has had the greatest impact on our standard of living. Yes, I know that the green revolution in agriculture—namely, research in botany—has been important in increasing our food supply, but Q40 when one looks at the entire range of contributions made to our daily life, it's hard to find a science more dramatic in its effect than chemistry. Chemistry has been used to make stronger metals, to improve the soil, and to destroy life-threatening bacteria. It has also led to the development of substances that we wear and use every day, such as nylon, rubber and plastics. Q40 In my opinion, it is basically impossible to overestimate the effect that chemistry has had on contemporary human beings.

パラグラフ2 まず初めに，あらゆる学問分野の中でも，Q40 化学が生活水準にもっとも大きな影響を及ぼしてきたと言えるという点を指摘しておきたいと思います。なるほど，農業における緑の革命，つまり植物学の研究が食料供給を増大させるうえで重要であったことはわかります。しかし，Q40 私たちの日常生活に対する全般的な貢献度から言えば，化学ほどめざましい影響力を持つ学問分野は見当たりません。化学は，より丈夫な金属を作ったり，土壌を改良したり，生命を脅かすバクテリアを駆除するのに用いられてきました。また，化学によって，ナイロン，ゴム，プラスチックなど，私たちが毎日身につけ，使う物質が開発されました。Q40 私が思うには，化学が現代の人間に与えてきた影響を評価しすぎるということはまずありえないのです。

3 Now, as you know, chemistry is the study of matter and the changes that matter undergoes. Q41 The "changes that matter undergoes" is the key phrase to

パラグラフ3 さて，みなさんもご存じのように化学は，物質と，物質が被る変化に関する学問です。Q41 この「物質が被る変化」というのが，現代の研究の特徴を表すキー

| | | |
|---|---|---|
| | describe contemporary research. It is in chemical reactions and recombinations that innovations are made. However, the process by which these innovations come about is worth discussing. It's not a matter of some lonely or mad scientist alone in his lab at night, Q42 because chemists typically work in groups or teams. They share information, analyze problems together, and coordinate their research activities in the laboratory. | フレーズです。技術革新がもたらされるのは，化学反応と再化合においてです。しかし，こうした革新がなされる過程は一考に値します。これは，夜中に実験室にこもる孤独な，あるいは狂気じみた化学者がひとりで成し遂げるようなことではありません。Q42 というのも，化学者は本来グループやチームで研究を行うからです。彼らは情報を共有し，ともに問題を分析し，また実験室での研究活動を共同で行います。 |
| 4 | All right. I'm sure you all did the reading I assigned for today, but I'd like you to clear the books and papers off of your desks. I'm going to give you a short quiz to check your comprehension. | パラグラフ 4 このぐらいでいいでしょう。今日の授業のために出しておいた課題はみなさん目を通してきたと思いますが，机の上の本やノートはしまってください。みなさんの理解を測るために小テストを行います。 |

## 39.

正答：A

039

What is the main purpose of the talk?

(A) To give an overview of contemporary chemistry
(B) To describe changes to the field of chemistry
(C) To identify problems facing modern chemistry
(D) To explain how to conduct research in chemistry

この講義の主な目的は何ですか。

(A) 現代の化学について概観すること
(B) 化学という分野での種々の変化を説明すること
(C) 現代化学が直面している問題を指摘すること
(D) 化学研究をどう行うかを説明すること

この講義がいわゆる概論・入門レベルであることは，指示文にある Introduction to Chemistry class という表現から明らか。また講義の冒頭 1 でも，some general remarks about the field of chemistry「化学という分野について一般的な事柄」とある。よって，これらを overview「概観」と言い換えている (A) が正答。

## 40.

正答：C

🔊039 What point does the professor make about the field of chemistry compared to other sciences?

(A) It is the oldest.
(B) It is theoretically the most challenging.
(C) It has the greatest effect on human life.
(D) It requires the most sophisticated research.

教授は，化学について他の科学と比べてどのような指摘をしていますか。

(A) もっとも古い。
(B) 理論面でもっともやりがいがある。
(C) 人間生活にもっとも大きな影響を与える。
(D) もっとも複雑な研究を必要とする。

教授は 2 の To begin ... 以下の部分で，the greatest impact ..., the entire range of contributions ..., its effect ..., the effect ... と繰り返し，化学の「影響」の大きさを強調している。よって，(C) が正答となる。

## 41.

正答：A

🔊039 What aspect of chemical investigation does the professor say is most crucial?

(A) Chemical change
(B) Elemental analysis
(C) Physical make-up
(D) Atomic composition

教授は，化学研究のどの側面がもっとも重要であると述べていますか。

(A) 化学変化
(B) 元素分析
(C) 物質の構造
(D) 原子の組成

教授は 3 で The "changes that matter undergoes" is the key phrase to describe contemporary research. と述べて，「化学変化」の重要性を指摘している。(A) が正答となる。ここで，the key phrase が設問の most crucial「もっとも重要な」と同義的に対応していることに留意。また，この後で It is in chemical reactions and recombinations that innovations are made. と述べているが，chemical reactions and recombinations は the changes that matter undergoes の言い換えであり，It ... that の強調構文によって強調されている。このように，反復や強調がある箇所は設問の対象となりやすいので注意。

## 42.

正答：B

🔊039 According to the professor, how is most research conducted in chemistry?

(A) By individuals
(B) By teams
(C) By academic researchers
(D) By corporate laboratories

教授によれば，化学では大半の研究はどのように行われますか。

(A) 個人によって
(B) チームによって
(C) 大学の研究者によって
(D) 企業の研究所によって

教授は 3 で However ... と学生の注意を喚起した後に，... chemists typically work in groups or teams. と説明している。よって，(B) が正答。直前の some lonely or mad scientist alone と groups or teams が対照をなしていることに留意。また，It's not ...「〜ではなくて」と否定表現が聞こえたら，次に「〜である」と肯定の答えがくると予測できる。

ボキャブラリー □ **remark**「意見，注意」
□ **field**「分野」
□ **plunge into ...**「～にのめり込む」
□ **perspective**「展望，見通し」
□ **practically speaking**「実際は，実質的に」
□ **impact**「影響，衝撃」
□ **green revolution**「緑の革命」
□ **namely**「すなわち」
□ **botany**「植物学」
□ **recombination**「再結合，組み換え」
□ **sophisticated**「複雑な」
□ **elemental**「元素の」
□ **make-up**「構造」
□ **atomic**「原子の」
□ **composition**「組成，構成」

## Questions 43-46 *Pre-Columbian Peoples*

040

1 コロンブス以前の北米の民族についての講義。アメリカ先住民はアジアからベーリング海峡経由で３万年かけて移住してきた。
2 これら先住民は辺境の地シベリアで暮らし，大文明から隔絶されていた。
3 彼らは家畜も，トウモロコシと豆以外の穀物も持っていなかった。
4 彼らは多くの異なる部族であり，互いに関連のない言語を話した。

**Listen to part of a talk in an American history class. The class has been studying the Pre-Columbian peoples of North America.**

**アメリカ史の授業での講義の一部を聞きなさい。この授業では，コロンブス到来前の北アメリカの民族について学んでいます。**

1 One of the things we should remember when studying peoples of the Americas, both European and so-called "native," is that all are immigrants. The ancestors of all of the people who were to become Native Americans crossed into the New World from Asia via the land bridge across the Bering Strait. Okay, I know there are some theories about Native Americans arriving in the New World via Europe, but, Q44 in my opinion, these theories are still highly speculative. So the ancestors of all of the Pre-Columbian inhabitants of America—that is, the indigenous peoples who were here in the 15th century before the first white Europeans arrived—crossed over from Siberia. Q43 The first immigrants probably arrived 33,000 years ago. They came over slowly, on foot and over time, in small groups, between 33,000 and 5,000 years ago—over a span of 30,000 years, more or less. Now, let me offer some perspective and information on these early peoples.

パラグラフ１ 南北アメリカ大陸の諸民族，つまりヨーロッパ系と，いわゆる「先住民」について学ぶ際に，私たちが忘れてならないのは，全民族が移民なのだということです。アメリカ先住民となったすべての人々の先祖は，アジアからベーリング海峡にかかる陸橋を渡って新世界へやってきたということです。もちろん，アメリカ先住民がヨーロッパから新世界へやってきたとする説があることは承知しています。でも，Q44 私の考えでは，こうした説はいまだきわめて不確かなものです。ですから，アメリカのコロンブス到来前のすべての先住民，つまりヨーロッパの白人が最初にやって来る前，15世紀にここに住んでいた原住民の祖先は，シベリアから渡来してきたのです。Q43 最初の移住者はおそらく，３万３千年前に到達しました。彼らは，３万３千年前から５千年前にかけて，おおよそ３万年かけて，徒歩で，小集団で，ゆっくりと渡ってきたわけです。では，こうした初期の種族について少し解説しましょう。

2 Q45 First, the tip of Siberia was a bleak and isolated region. Deserts, vast distances, and mountain ranges cut these people off from the civilizations that were developing elsewhere in Asia, the Middle East and the Mediterranean. The news of a discovery or invention made in one of the centers of civilization—in China, India, or Asia Minor—spread widely in a thousand

パラグラフ２ Q45 第一に，シベリアの先端は荒涼とした辺境の地でした。砂漠，途方もない距離，山脈などのために，これらの種族はアジアや中東，地中海など他の土地で発達しつつあった文明から隔絶していました。中国，インド，あるいは小アジアといった文明の中心地でなされた発見や発明の知らせは，千年の時をかけて広まっていきましたが，おそらくシベリアに居住する人々

years, but it probably never reached the inhabitants of Siberia.

にまで届くことはなかったのです。

3 A second point about these peoples. They had no livestock or beasts of burden as in the Old World, except for dogs. They had no cattle, no sheep, no goats, no pigs, no camels, and no horses. Though we associate horses with Native Americans, they didn't have any until after the Spanish arrived. Dogs guarded their camps and carried small bundles on their backs. Also, the early Americans had none of the domesticated grains, tubers or fruits that were developed in the Old World. The only early crops that were cultivated were corn—a primitive form of corn called maize—and beans. So this entire new continent was more or less on its own.

パラグラフ3 こうした種族に関する第二の点はこうです。彼らは犬のほかには，旧世界のように家畜や荷物を運ぶ動物を飼っていませんでした。畜牛も，羊も，ヤギも，豚も，ラクダも，馬もいなかったのです。私たちは馬とアメリカ先住民を結び付けて考えますが，スペイン人がやってくるまで彼らは馬を飼っていなかったのです。犬は集落を守り，ちょっとした荷物を背中にのせて運んでいました。また，古代アメリカ先住民たちは，旧世界で広まっていた穀物，イモ，果物も栽培していませんでした。唯一栽培されていたのはトウモロコシ，と言ってもメイズと呼ばれるトウモロコシの原種と，豆だけでした。ですから，新大陸全体は事実上，孤立していたわけです。

4 Lastly, it's important to remember of the Pre-Columbians, that during thousands of years, Q46 many different peoples crossed over. They were physically different, culturally different, and linguistically different from each other. This is one of the reasons for the profusion of different Native American languages that are largely unrelated to each other.

パラグラフ4 最後に，コロンブス以前の時代に関しては，何千年もの間に，Q46 多くの異なる種族が渡来したということを忘れてはなりません。彼らは身体的にも，文化的にも，言語的にも互いに異なっていました。アメリカ先住民の間に，互いにほとんど関連のない言語が多数あるのはこれが一因です。

## 43.

正答：D

041 According to the professor, when did the first peoples arrive in America?

(A) About 3,000 years ago
(B) About 13,000 years ago
(C) About 30,000 years ago
(D) About 33,000 years ago

教授によれば，アメリカ大陸に最初の種族が渡って来たのはいつですか。

(A) 約３千年前
(B) 約１万３千年前
(C) 約３万年前
(D) 約３万３千年前

1 の最後で，The first immigrants probably arrived 33,000 years ago. とある。この渡来の時期はさらに直後で，between 33,000 and 5,000 years ago と繰り返されている。よって，(D) が正答。

## 44. 正答：B

041

How does the professor regard the theory that early peoples may have crossed from Europe to America?

(A) With enthusiasm
(B) With skepticism
(C) With curiosity
(D) With surprise

初期の種族がヨーロッパからアメリカへ渡来したかもしれないとする説に対する教授の態度はどのようなものですか。

(A) 熱狂
(B) 懐疑
(C) 好奇心
(D) 驚き

アメリカ先住民のヨーロッパ起源説について教授は 1 で，in my opinion, these theories are still highly speculative. と述べている。speculative とは「推論的」つまり「根拠がない」ということ。よって，(B) が正答となる。

## 45. 正答：D

041

What does the professor's description of Siberia suggest about the various peoples there?

(A) They may have communicated with each other.
(B) They benefited from discoveries elsewhere in Asia.
(C) They shared common ancestors.
(D) They were unusually isolated and cut off.

シベリアに関する教授の説明は，そこに住んでいたさまざまな種族について何を指摘していますか。

(A) お互いに交流していたと考えられる。
(B) アジアのその他の地域でなされた発見の恩恵を受けた。
(C) 共通の祖先を持っていた。
(D) きわめて孤立し，隔絶していた。

2 のシベリアに関する説明の中で教授は，isolated region「孤立した地域」，cut ... off from the civilizations「他の文明から隔絶させた」，The news of a discovery or invention ... never reached「発明や発見の知らせも届かなかった」と，シベリアが孤立していたことを繰り返し強調している。よって，正答は (D)。

## 46. 正答：A

041

What does the professor conclude about Native American groups?

(A) They were extremely diverse in character.
(B) They were culturally very inventive.
(C) Their languages were closely related.
(D) Their physical appearance was surprisingly similar.

教授はアメリカ先住民についてどのように結論づけていますか。

(A) きわめて多様な特徴を持っていた。
(B) 文化的に非常に創意に富んでいた。
(C) 諸言語が密接に関連していた。
(D) 驚くほど容姿が似ていた。

結論なので最後の部分を思い出す。教授は Lastly, it's important to remember と述べて学生の注意を喚起し，many different peoples, physically different, culturally different, linguistically different と，先住アメリカ人諸部族間の違い，すなわち多様性を繰り返し強調している。よって，(A) が正答となる。

ボキャブラリー
- □ **Pre-Columbian**「コロンブス以前の」
- □ **ancestor**「祖先」
- □ **Native American**「アメリカ先住民」
- □ **New World**「新世界：アメリカ（⇔ **Old World**：旧世界：ヨーロッパ）」
- □ **speculative**「不確かな」
- □ **indigenous**「土着の，現地の」
- □ **bleak**「荒涼とした，寒冷な」
- □ **livestock**「家畜」
- □ **domesticate**「～を栽培する」
- □ **skepticism**「懐疑（主義）」

## Questions 47-50 *Amphibians*

042

1 両生類に関する生物学の講義。
2 両生類は硬骨魚が進化して陸生生物化した。
3 これまでに5000種の両生類が確認され，さらに毎年500種が新たに発見されている。
4 しかし，環境破壊により，多くの種が絶滅の危機に瀕している。

**Listen to part of a talk in a biology class.**

**生物学の授業での講義の一部を聞きなさい。**

1 First, I hope you all had a good break. Now that mid-term exams are behind us, we're going to begin the second part of this course. We're going to turn our attention from the early creatures in the sea to early life on land. So today, I'd like to turn our attention to those special transitional creatures: amphibians.

パラグラフ1 まずは，みなさん，よい休暇だったでしょうか。中間試験もすでに終わったことですし，本コースの後半に進みたいと思います。海中の古代生物から，陸上の古代生物へと検討を進めたいと思いますが，今日は，これらの中間的な特別な生物，両生類に注目したいと思います。

2 When amphibians first appeared, Earth's land area was essentially one giant landmass inhabited by plants and insects. It was amphibians, as you know, that were the first vertebrates to make the transition from water to land. We don't fully understand the why or how of this transition, but somehow, a type of bony fish gradually evolved into a creature that had four legs and could move about without the support of water; it could also breathe atmospheric oxygen rather than oxygen dissolved in water. Q47 The significance of amphibian evolution cannot be overstated: after all, it was these traits that laid the foundation for the development of all other types of land animals, including reptiles, birds and mammals. Without amphibians, our other forms of land animals would not have evolved as we know them today.

パラグラフ2 両生類が初めて出現したとき，地球の陸地は実質的に，植物や昆虫が生息するひとつの巨大な大陸でした。みなさんもご存じのように，水中から陸地へ移り棲んだ最初の脊椎動物は両生類でした。この移動がなぜ，どのように起こったのか十分にはわかっていませんが，何らかの形である種の硬骨魚が徐々に進化して，四肢を持ち，水がなくても動き回れる生物へと進化したのです。また，この生物は，水中に溶解した酸素の代わりに，大気中の酸素で呼吸することができました。Q47 両生類の進化の重要性を強調しすぎるということはありません。というのも，爬虫類，鳥類，哺乳類など他のすべての種類の陸生動物の発達の基礎になったのは，こうした両生類の持つ特質なのですから。もし両生類が存在していなかったなら，今日わたしたちが知っている他の陸生の生物も，進化していなかったことでしょう。

3 Q48 So far scientists have identified nearly 5,000 species of amphibians—more than the number of mammals. What's really interesting about research in amphibians—and one of the reasons why I personally have chosen to specialize in this type of animal—is that

パラグラフ3 Q48 これまでに学者たちは約5000種の両生類を確認していますが，この数は哺乳類よりも多いものです。両生類の研究で非常に興味深いのは，これはまた私個人が両生類を研究対象に選んだ理由のひとつでもあるのですが，年々つぎつぎと

more and more species are being discovered every year. Q49 In fact, the number of new species being discovered and described each year is about 10 percent of Q48 the currently known 5,000 species. If you do the math, this comes out to an additional 500 species being identified by zoologists every year.

新種が発見されている点です。Q49 実際，毎年新たに発見され，記録される新種の数は，Q48 現在知られている5000種の約10％です。これは計算してみれば，動物学者によって毎年新たに500種が確認されていることになります。

4 Even as the number of newly identified amphibian species grows, however, many other species are dying off. Because the amphibian life cycle is both aquatic and terrestrial—that is, it depends upon both water and land— Q50 amphibians are particularly vulnerable to environmental destruction. In water, for example, amphibians are particularly sensitive to poisons and pollution since their skin is thin and permeable. When water changes temperature or is contaminated, they die.

パラグラフ4 ところが，新たに確認される両生類の種は増えていても，他の多くの種が絶滅しつつあります。両生類の生活環境は水陸両方，つまり水と土の両方に依存しているので，Q50 両生類は環境破壊の被害を特に受けやすいのです。例えば，水中では，両生類は皮膚が薄く透水性であるため，有害物や汚濁に特に影響を受けやすいのです。水温が変わったり汚染されたりすると，死んでしまうのです。

## 47.

正答：D

043

What was particularly important about the early amphibians?

初期の両生類について特に重要なことは何ですか。

(A) They were the first creatures to lay eggs.
(B) They were able to breathe both under water and on land.
(C) They were the first creatures with hard backbones.
(D) They were the organisms from which land creatures evolved.

(A) 卵を生む最初の生物だった。
(B) 水中と陸上の両方で呼吸できた。
(C) 堅い背骨を有する最初の生物だった。
(D) 陸生動物が進化する元になった生物だった。

2 で教授は，The significance of amphibian evolution cannot be overstated:「両生類の進化は重要である」と指摘し，すぐに it was these traits that laid the foundation for the development of all other types of land animals「他のすべての陸生動物の進化の元となった」と，It ... that 強調構文で理由を説明している。これを言い換えている (D) が正答。

## 48. 正答：C

🔊 043

According to the professor, how many species of amphibians have been identified?

教授によれば，今までに何種類の両生類が確認されましたか。

(A) 1,500
(B) 3,000
(C) 5,000
(D) 7,500

(A) 1,500 種
(B) 3,000 種
(C) 5,000 種
(D) 7,500 種

> 発見されている両生類の数は，3 で So far ... nearly 5,000 species of amphibians, the currently known 5,000 species と繰り返されている。よって，(C) が正答。So far は「現在までのところ」という意味。

## 49. 正答：C

🔊 043

Approximately how many new species of amphibians are discovered every year?

毎年新たに発見される両生類の数はおよそどのくらいですか。

(A) 50
(B) 150
(C) 500
(D) 850

(A) 50 種
(B) 150 種
(C) 500 種
(D) 850 種

> 前問と混同しないように注意。ここでは 1 年間の発見数が問われている。教授はまず about 10 percent of the currently known 5,000 species と言い，これを do the math「計算する」ことで，さらに 500 species being identified by zoologists every year と説明している。よって，(C) が正答。

## 50. 正答：B

🔊 043

According to the professor, why are large numbers of amphibians dying off?

教授によれば，数多くの両生類が絶滅しつつあるのはなぜですか。

(A) Changes in weather patterns
(B) Environmental pollution
(C) Loss of habitat
(D) Emergence of new diseases

(A) 気候パターンの変化
(B) 環境汚染
(C) 生息地の減少
(D) 新種の病気の出現

> 4 で両生類の多くが絶滅する原因として，environmental destruction, pollution, contaminated と，環境破壊を表す表現が繰り返され，強調されている。よって，(B) が正答となる。水温変化への言及はあるが，(A) の直接的な指摘はない。

ボキャブラリー
□ **amphibian**「両生類，両生動物」
□ **landmass**「大陸，広大な土地」
□ **vertebrate**「脊椎動物」
□ **bony fish**「硬骨魚」
□ **oxygen**「酸素」
□ **dissolve**「溶解する」
□ **trait**「特質」
□ **reptile**「爬虫動物」
□ **mammal**「哺乳動物」
□ **zoologist**「動物学者」
□ **aquatic**「水の」
□ **terrestrial**「陸の」
□ **vulnerable**「傷つきやすい」
□ **permeable**「透水性の」
□ **contaminate**「～を汚染する」

# Section 2—Structure and Written Expression

## Structure

### 1.

正答：D

**The lowest** possible temperature is called absolute zero.

考えられるもっとも低い温度は絶対零度と呼ばれる。

文意から，空所には最上級が最適である。(D) が正答。形容詞の最上級が名詞を修飾する場合（限定用法）には，通例，定冠詞 the を伴う。

ボキャブラリー □ **absolute zero**「絶対零度」

### 2.

正答：C

**During** the Neolithic Period, humans learned to make pottery, which enabled them to more easily and efficiently store food and water.

新石器時代に人間は陶器を作るようになり，これによって食料や水をいっそう容易に，かつ効率よく貯蔵できるようになった。

the Neolithic Period「新石器時代」のように特定の期間をとる前置詞は (C) During「～の間」が適切。なお，不特定の期間の場合は for を用いる。(D) between も「～の間」と訳されるが，between *A* and *B* の形で「２者の間」に限られる。

ボキャブラリー □ **the Neolithic Period**「新石器時代」 □ **pottery**「陶器類」

### 3.

正答：B

Parkinson's disease, **seen mainly** in people over the age of fifty, is a degenerative disease of the brain affecting muscular control.

パーキンソン病は主として 50 歳以上の人に見られ，筋肉の制御に支障をきたす退行性の脳疾患である。

正答 (B) は分詞構文の挿入で，ここでは形容詞的に主語 Parkinson's disease を補足的に修飾している。(A) that を関係詞としてカンマの後に挿入するのは不可。(C) は完全文なので，主語が重複することになり，接続詞なしで他の文中に挿入できない。(D) は be 動詞を補って which is seen mainly の形なら可。

ボキャブラリー □ **Parkinson's disease**「パーキンソン病」 □ **degenerative**「退行性の」

### 4.

正答：A

**Most of the** small businesses operating in North America are sole proprietorships, meaning they are owned by one person.

北米で営業する小企業の大半は個人事業，つまり個人によって所有されている。

most は「たいていの」という意味の形容詞では通例無冠詞なので，(C) は誤り。(D) の almost は副詞なので名詞 businesses を修飾できない。most が代名詞となっている (A) (B) に絞られるが，one of ..., any of ..., none of ... などと同様，most of ... に続く語は限定されていなければならない。よって，定冠詞 the を伴う (A) が正答。

ボキャブラリー □ **proprietorship**「所有権，所有（していること）」

## 5.

正答：C

Tarragon, a bushy herb with narrow leaves, contains an aromatic oil which makes it an excellent spice for flavoring salads, pickles, and **tartar sauce**.

タラゴンは細い葉をもつハーブ草だが，芳香性の油を含んでいるので，サラダ，ピクルス，タルタルソースの味付けをするのに適したスパイスである。

*A* and *B* や *A*, *B*, and *C* の形で並列される語や句は文法的に等しくなければならないので，salads，pickles に合わせて，同じく名詞の (C) を入れるのが正しい。(D) は定冠詞 the が不要。

ボキャブラリー □ **bushy herb**「ハーブ草」 □ **flavor**「味（を付ける）」

## 6.

正答：A

Robert Penn Warren, **who eventually became America's first poet laureate**, was originally a member of the Fugitive Group of young Southern writers.

ロバート・ペン・ウォレンは後にアメリカ初の桂冠詩人となったが，元々は南部の若い作家たちから成るフュージティブ派の一員だった。

空所は，主語 Robert Penn Warren と述語動詞 was ... から成る文の挿入部分。(B) (C) は節であり，従位接続詞なしに挿入できない。(D) も挿入するには関係代名詞 who が必要。正答の (A) は関係代名詞 who を伴っているので，主語 Robert Penn Warren を修飾する形容詞節として正しく挿入できる。

ボキャブラリー □ **laureate**「桂冠詩人」

## 7.

正答：D

The auditory canal, a tube leading to the outer ear opening, is found only in animals having eardrums inside **their** skulls.

耳道とは外耳口に通じる管で，頭骨内に鼓膜を持つ動物のみに見られる。

選択肢に代名詞が並んでいるので，文脈に留意し，数と格が対応するものを選択する。ここでは skulls は「animals の頭骨」なので，複数形・所有格の (D) が正答となる。

ボキャブラリー □ **auditory**「聴覚（器）の」 □ **eardrum**「鼓膜」 □ **skull**「頭蓋骨」

## 8.

正答：D

**To be defined** as overweight, an adult male or female should have a body weight 10 to 20 percent greater than other adults of the same size and sex.

「太りすぎ」とされるのは，成人男女が，同体格，同性の他の成人に比べて 10 ～ 20 パーセント体重が多い場合である。

文脈から判断して，空所部分は「～するためには」という目的を表す to 不定詞の副詞用法が入るべきである。よって，(D) が正答となる。define「～を定義する」は他動詞なので，目的語となる名詞を含んでいない (B) (C) は誤り。

ボキャブラリー □ **overweight**「太りすぎの」

## 9.

正答：C

Volcanic soils, **deposited by eruptions**, are often some of the richest and most fertile.

火山性土は，噴火によって堆積されるが，しばしば非常に豊かで肥えている。

選択肢中，カンマにはさまれた空所に挿入できるのは分詞構文の (C) のみ。独立した節である (B) (D) を挿入するためには従位接続詞が必要である。

ボキャブラリー □ **volcanic**「火山の」 □ **eruption**「噴火」 □ **fertile**「肥沃な」

## 10.

正答：A

Research suggests that bears that attack humans are rarely hunting for food **but** rather defending their cubs or their territory.

研究によれば，人間を襲ってくる熊はたいがい，餌を求めているのではなく，自分の子や縄張りを守ろうとしている。

not *A* but (rather) *B* で「A ではなく（むしろ）B」という意味。よって，(A) が正答。ここでは否定語 not の代わりに，準否定語の rarely「めったに〜ない」が使われている。(B) (C) も but と同じく「しかし」と訳されるが，yet は not と相関的に使われることはない。however は接続副詞で，語・句・節同士の接続には使えない。また，文中に挿入する際は，前後にカンマが必要。

ボキャブラリー □ **rarely**「めったに〜ない」 □ **territory**「縄張り，領地」

## 11.

正答：B

Founded in 1565 by the Spanish explorer and admiral Pedro Menéndez de Avilés, St. Augustine, Florida is **the oldest** continually inhabited city in the United States.

1565 年にスペイン人探検家で海軍提督のペドロ・メネンデス・デ・アビレスによって建設されたフロリダ州セントオーガスティンは，今日まで現存している合衆国最古の都市である。

選択肢には形容詞 old の原級，比較級，最上級が含まれるが，文脈上ここでは最上級が適切。よって，(B) が正答となる。形容詞の最上級は，限定用法（名詞を修飾する）では通例，the が付く。叙述用法（補語になる）ではしばしば省略される。

ボキャブラリー □ **explorer**「探検家」 □ **inhabit**「〜に居住する」

## 12.

正答：A

The telegraph, **the first electric communication device produced by humans**, was used to establish the first direct link between the West and East coasts of the United States in 1861.

電報は，人間が作った最初の電気的な通信手段であり，合衆国の西海岸と東海岸を直結する初の手段として 1861 年に採用された。

The telegraph ... was used で受動態の文が成立しているので，空所には文型を乱さない挿入句または挿入節が入る。(B) (C) はいずれも完全文なので，従位接続詞なしには挿入できない。(D) は関係詞節として挿入可能だが，節内の語順が誤り。正答 (A) を入れると，主語 The telegraph と the first electric communication device とが同格になる。produced ... は述語動詞ではなく，過去分詞の形容詞用法で，後ろから device を修飾する。

ボキャブラリー □ **telegraph**「電報」 □ **establish**「〜を確立する」

## 13.

正答：D

**Among** the many important functions of the liver are the producing of proteins and the cleaning of the blood.

肝臓が果たしている数多くの重要な機能には，タンパク質の生成や血液の浄化が含まれる。

「～の間の，～の中で」という意味の前置詞には between と among があるが，通例，between は「2つのもの」，among は「3つ以上のもの」の場合に用いる。空所の後に3つ以上を表す many important functions ... が続くので，(D) が正答。

ボキャブラリー □ **liver**「肝臓」

## 14.

正答：C

Residents of the District of Columbia **elect a mayor** and members of a city council, as well as one non-voting delegate to the Congress of the United States.

コロンビア特別区の住民は，投票権を持たない合衆国議会議員1名，および市長と市会議員を選出する。

主語 Residents に対応する述語動詞が欠落しているので，動詞 elect を含む (C) が正答となる。*A* as well as *B* は「B だけでなく A も」という意味の表現。ちなみに District of Columbia は首都 Washington, D.C. のことで，行政上どの州にも属さない連邦議会直轄地。

ボキャブラリー □ **city council**「市議会」 □ **delegate**「代議員，代理人」

## 15.

正答：B

It is the arrangement of the electrons, **different for each element**, which determines the formation of a compound.

化合物の構造を決定するのは，元素によって異なる電子の配置である。

the arrangement of the electrons を修飾する挿入部分として適切な選択肢を選ぶ。(A) (C) は節なので，接続詞や関係副詞なしに挿入できない。また，(D) は that を含むが，関係詞 that は which とは異なり，カンマの後にくる用法（非限定用法）はない。よって，正答は (B)。different の前に which is を補うとわかりやすい。なお，この文は It is ... which の強調構文である。

ボキャブラリー □ **electron**「電子」 □ **compound**「化合物」

## 16. itを削除する　正答：B

The triode, invented by the American engineer Lee De Forest, **was** used in amplifiers until it was superseded by the transistor during the 1950's.

三極真空管はアメリカ人技師リー・デ・フォレストによって発明され，1950年代にトランジスタに取って代わられるまで，アンプに使用された。

The triodeとwas used ...はこの文の主語と述語動詞である。よって，主語として重複している(B) itを削除する。カンマに囲まれたinvented ... Lee De Forestは分詞構文の挿入なので，省いて考えると文構造がわかりやすい。

ボキャブラリー □ **triode**「三極管」 □ **amplifier**「アンプ」 □ **supersede**「～に取って代わる」

## 17. estimationをestimatedにする　正答：A

It is **estimated** that there are about 1 billion bicycles in use throughout the world, compared to about 1.5 billion automobiles.

世界中で約10億台の自転車が使用されていると推定されるのに対し，自動車は約15億台である。

文頭のItが形式主語，that節が真主語で，Itはthat以下を指す。(A) estimationは名詞で「推定，推算」だが，that節は「推定」ではなく「推定される内容」である。よって，estimatedと過去分詞に直して受動態とするのが正しい。

ボキャブラリー □ **estimate**「推定する」

## 18. thoseをoneにする　正答：C

Asset stripping is the sale or exploitation of the assets of a business, often **one** that has been intentionally acquired for that purpose.

資産剥奪とは会社の資産を売却または奪取することであり，これを目的として意図的に会社が吸収される場合も多い。

主格の関係詞の先行詞と関係詞節中の動詞とは，数が対応していなければならない。(C) those直後の関係代名詞節の動詞はhas beenなので，先行詞も単数扱いの名詞とする。よって，oneと直すのが正しい。

ボキャブラリー □ **exploitation**「搾取，開発」 □ **asset**「資産」 □ **acquire**「(企業を) 吸収する」

## 19. returningをreturnedにする　正答：B

The Esch-Cummins Act of 1920, also known as the Railroad Transportation Act, **returned** the railroads to private operation.

1920年制定のエッシュ・カミンズ法は，鉄道運輸法としても知られており，鉄道を民営に戻した。

この文には述語動詞が欠けている。主語The Esch-Cummins Act of 1920に対応するように(B) returningをreturnedに直して述語動詞とすると，正しい文構造となる。also以下カンマに囲まれた部分は主語を修飾する分詞構文なので，省いて考えるとThe Esch-Cummins Actとreturnedの主述関係がはっきりする。

ボキャブラリー □ **act**「制定法，条例」 □ **private operation**「民間事業」

## 20.
**is** を **are** にする　正答：B

The planet Uranus has at least ten rings, which **are** composed mainly of jagged rocks and icy boulders.

天王星には少なくとも10個の環があるが，これらは主にゴツゴツした岩石と氷の固まりでできている。

主格の関係詞 which の先行詞と，which 節の動詞の間には《主語＋述語動詞》の関係が成立し，数が対応しなければならない。ここでは which の先行詞は ten rings と複数形なので，(B) is (composed) を are (composed) と直すのが正しい。

ボキャブラリー □ **Uranus**「天王星」 □ **jagged**「ゴツゴツした」 □ **boulder**「巨礫，丸石」

## 21.
**including** を **and** にする　正答：B

The fathom, a unit of measurement once used both at sea **and** on land, approximates the distance between an adult man's outstretched hands.

ファゾムはかつて海洋，陸上の両方で用いられていた計測単位であり，おおむね成人の伸ばした両手の間の長さである。

both *A* and *B*「A と B の両方」という定型表現を作るために，(B) including を and とするのが正しい。both *A* and *B*，either *A* or *B* など2語以上の決まった組み合わせで接続詞の働きをする句を相関接続詞と呼ぶ。なお，including は「～を含めて」という意味の前置詞。

ボキャブラリー □ **approximate**「（数量的に）～に近い」 □ **outstretch**「～を伸ばす」

## 22.
**require** を **requires** にする　正答：B

Heavy industry, such as that involving the manufacture of steel, petroleum and rubber, **requires** high capitalization and the production of large quantities of materials.

鉄，石油，ゴムの製造などの重工業は，巨額の資本投下と原料の大量生産とを必要とする。

主語 Heavy industry は不可算名詞なので，これに対応するように述語動詞の (B) require にも三人称単数の -s を付して requires とする。不可算名詞は単数扱いである。such as から rubber までは Heavy industry を修飾する挿入句なので，省いて考えると文型がわかりやすい。

ボキャブラリー □ **petroleum**「石油」 □ **capitalization**「資本化，資本総額」

## 23.
**power** を **powerful** にする　正答：D

Although the paintings of Morris Louis do not feature recognizable people, landscapes, or objects, their form and energy have a **powerful** effect on the viewer.

モリス・ルイスの絵は人物，風景，静物を明瞭に描くものではないが，その形式と力強さは見る者に強い印象を与える。

(D) power は続く名詞 effect を修飾すべき語なので，powerful と形容詞に直すのが正しい。なお，have an effect on ...「～に影響を与える」は頻出の重要表現。

ボキャブラリー □ **feature**「～を特徴とする；特徴」

## 24. Much を Many にする　正答：A

**Many** different micro-organisms can be classified as germs since they cause disease.

多くの微生物は，病気を発症させることから病原菌として分類される。

micro-organisms「微生物」は可算名詞の複数形なので，それを修飾する (A) Much は Many と直すのが正しい。much が修飾するのは不可算名詞。

ボキャブラリー □ **micro-organism**「微生物」 □ **germ**「細菌，病原菌」

## 25. and を or にする　正答：C

An audit may be conducted by either a member of the organization as an internal audit **or** an outsider as an independent audit.

会計監査は，内部監査として組織内の者によって行われても，もしくは独立監査として外部の者によって行われてもよい。

either と組み合わせて用いられる接続詞は (C) and ではなく or である。この either *A* or *B* や both *A* and *B* など，前後 2 つの要素が組になって接続詞の働きをするものを相関接続詞と呼ぶ。

ボキャブラリー □ **audit**「会計監査」 □ **outsider**「部外者，外部の者」

## 26. there を削除する　正答：D

The city of Long Beach is home to the largest commercial port **in California**.

ロングビーチ市にはカリフォルニアで最大の商業港がある。

in California「カリフォルニアで」という副詞句と，(D) there「そこで」という副詞が重複しているので，後者を削除する。

ボキャブラリー □ **commercial port**「商業港」

## 27. significantly を significant にする　正答：A

The most **significant** provider of retirement income in the United States is the Social Security Administration, which oversees a non-voluntary pension plan.

合衆国でもっとも重要な退職金支払い者は社会保障庁であり，この団体は強制加入の年金制度を監督する。

(A) significantly は副詞であり，続く名詞 provider を修飾できない。significant と形容詞にするのが正しい。

ボキャブラリー □ **non-voluntary**「強制の」

## 28. 語順を conservative writer にする　正答：A

William Buckley, a **conservative writer** and editor, founded *The National Review* in 1955 as a forum for his right-wing political views.

保守的な著述家，編集者であるウィリアム・バクレーは 1955 年，自らの右派的な政治見解を論じる場として『ナショナルレビュー』誌を創刊した。

(A) conservative「保守的な」は形容詞なので，通例，修飾する名詞の前に置く。よって，conservative writer と直すのが正しい。

ボキャブラリー □ **conservative**「保守的な」 □ **forum**「討論欄［会］」 □ **right-wing**「右派の」

## 29. transportation of the public を public transportation にする　正答：D

In the mid-19th century, the industrial revolution marked the beginning of mass production, technological innovation, and **public transportation**.

19 世紀中ごろになると，産業革命により大量生産，技術革新，公共交通機関が始まった。

*A* and *B* や *A*, *B*, and *C* などの形で並列される語や句は文法的に等しくなければならない。よって，mass production《形容詞＋名詞》，technological innovation《形容詞＋名詞》に合わせて，(D) を public transportation《形容詞＋名詞》と直すのが正しい。

ボキャブラリー □ **industrial revolution**「産業革命」 □ **mass production**「大量生産」 □ **innovation**「革新」

## 30. there を where または in which にする　正答：C

An amphibian must spend part of its life cycle in the water, **where ［in which］** its eggs are laid and fertilized.

両生類は生涯の一時期を必ず水中で過ごし，そこで産卵と受精が行われる。

この文には An amphibian must spend ... と its eggs are laid ... という 2 つの節が含まれるが，間にある (C) there は副詞であり，節同士を接続できない。よって，関係副詞の where を用いるのが正しい。where 以下は，the water を修飾する形容詞節となる。where と同義になる in which としてもよい。

ボキャブラリー □ **amphibian**「両生類」 □ **fertilize**「～を受精させる，肥沃にする」

## 31. the great を the greatest または a great にする　正答：A

Regarded as **the greatest [a great]** American playwright, Tennessee Williams wrote about the consequences of intense passion and pain as well as the gradual deterioration of Southern gentility.

アメリカでもっともすぐれた劇作家と見なされているテネシー・ウィリアムズは，南部上流階級のゆるやかな衰退，そして激しい情熱と苦痛の結末を描き出した。

(A) the great は「その偉大な～」という意味で，ここでは意味が通じない。the greatest と最上級にするか，不定冠詞を用いて a great とするのが正しい。

ボキャブラリー □ **playwright**「脚本家」 □ **deterioration**「衰退」 □ **gentility**「上流階級」

## 32. occur を occurs にする　正答：A

Hibernation is a state which **occurs** in some mammals, such as bats and gophers, during which the animals' heart rate and respiration slow down.

冬眠とは，コウモリやホリネズミなど，一部のほ乳類に生じる状態であり，この間，動物の心拍や呼吸は低下する。

文の主語と述語動詞の間だけでなく，主格の関係詞節中でも，主語と動詞は一致しなければならない。ここでは which の先行詞が a state と単数なので，これに合わせて (A) occur には三単現の -s を付し，occurs とする。

ボキャブラリー □ **hibernation**「冬眠」 □ **mammal**「哺乳動物」

## 33. instead を instead of にする　正答：C

Collectivist societies place emphasis on the optimal performance of the group **instead of** the outstanding achievements of the individual.

集団主義社会は，個人の卓越した業績ではなく，集団の最上の業績を重視する。

(C) instead「その代わりとして，それよりも」は副詞なので，このままでは後に名詞をとることはできない。instead of ...「～の代わりに」と群前置詞的に使わなければならない。

ボキャブラリー □ **emphasis**「強調」

## 34. characteristic を characteristics にする　正答：A

One of the distinguishing **characteristics** of the Hudson River School of Painting was its focus on vast landscapes, especially mountains and rivers.

ハドソン・リバー派の絵画の際立った特徴のひとつは，雄大な風景，特に山や河を数多く描いたことだ。

「～の中のひとつ」は《one of the ＋可算名詞の複数形》で表す。よって，(A) characteristic は characteristics とするのが正しい。主語は characteristics ではなく one なので，述語動詞は was で問題ない。

ボキャブラリー □ **characteristic**「特質」 □ **landscape**「景色」

## 35. society を social にする　正答：C

The phrase "The Roaring Twenties" was employed to characterize the **social**, artistic, and cultural dynamism of the 1920's.

「狂乱の 20 年代」という句は，1920 年代の社会的，芸術的，文化的な躍動感を表すために用いられた。

等位接続詞 and で並列される語や句は文法的に等しくなければならない。これは $A$，$B$，and $C$ のように 3 語以上の並列でも同様。よって，ここでは artistic, and cultural という形容詞の並びに合わせて，名詞の (C) society も social と形容詞にするのが正しい。

ボキャブラリー □ **employ**「～を用いる」

## 36. it を削除する 正答：B

The most significant accomplishment of Eli Whitney, famous for his invention of the cotton gin, **was** actually his achievement of producing equipment with interchangeable parts.

綿繰り機械の発明で知られるエリー・ホイットニーのもっとも重要な業績は，実は，部品交換ができる機械を製造するのに成功したことだ。

カンマではさまれた挿入句を除くと，The most significant accomplishment ... it was ... と，主語が重複しているのがわかる。よって不要な (B) it を削除するのが正しい。

**ボキャブラリー** □ **accomplishment**「業績」 □ **invention**「発明」 □ **equipment**「機器」

## 37. which を whose にする 正答：B

Charles Monroe Schultz was an American artist **whose** *Peanuts* cartoons brought him worldwide fame.

チャールズ・モンロー・シュルツはアメリカ人アーチストであり，『ピーナッツ』という漫画で世界的に有名になった。

先行詞 an American artist と *Peanuts* cartoons は作者とその作品という関係なので，関係詞 (B) which は所有格の whose を用いるのが正しい。whose は《and ＋代名詞所有格（his, her, their など）》という意味。

**ボキャブラリー** □ **fame**「名声」

## 38. those を that にする 正答：B

The market price of palladium, like **that** of gold or silver, is determined by a combination of factors including current supply, future production, and projected demand.

パラジウムの市場価格は，金や銀の市場価格と同じように，現在の供給量，今後の生産量，予想される需要など，さまざまな要素がからんで決まる。

比較の前置詞 like を用いて比べているのは，palladium の the market price と gold or silver の「それ」である。the market price が単数扱いなので，これに合わせて後の代名詞 (B) those も単数の that とするのが正しい。

**ボキャブラリー** □ **supply**「供給」 □ **demand**「需要」

## 39. With を By にする 正答：A

**By** requiring that dogs be vaccinated while they are young, public health officials have been able to bring rabies and other canine diseases under control.

犬が幼いうちに予防接種を受けさせるよう義務づけることによって，公衆衛生当局は，狂犬病などのイヌの病気を抑え込むことができている。

前置詞 (A) With は，後に道具や手段を意味する名詞をとって「〜を用いて」を意味する。しかし，requiring は道具ではなく行為なので By を用いて「〜することによって」とするのが正しい。

**ボキャブラリー** □ **vaccinate**「〜にワクチンを接種する」 □ **public health**「公衆衛生」 □ **rabies**「狂犬病」 □ **canine**「イヌの」

## 40. plays を played にする　正答：B

For half a century the logging of timber **played** an important role in Michigan's economy, though its influence is now negligible.

半世紀にわたって，材木の伐採はミシガン州の経済にとって大きな役割を果たしてきたが，その影響は今ではわずかにすぎない。

For half a century「半世紀にわたって」という過去を表す副詞句があるので，述語動詞(B) plays の時制は過去形 played にするのが適切。接続詞 though をはさんで前後の節が現在（now）と過去の対比対照になっていることにも留意。

ボキャブラリー □ **timber**「材木」 □ **negligible**「取るに足らない」

## Questions 1-10

*Joseph Pulitzer*

1 ピューリッツァー賞で知られるジョセフ・ピューリッツァーはアメリカに移民してきた。
2 いろいろな職に就いた後，彼はドイツ語新聞の経営者の目に留まり，記者として精力的に働いた。
3 1871 年の半ばに冗談からピューリッツァーは共和党の候補者に選ばれて州議会選挙で当選し，その後ミズーリ州の上院議員として長年活動した。

1 Joseph Pulitzer is now mainly known for the writing prizes which bear his name, but Q8 he exemplified "the American Dream": the notion that anyone could, through diligence and perseverance, become a success regardless of national origin or background. As a teenager, Pulitzer immigrated from Hungary and fought for the Union during the Civil War.

パラグラフ 1 ジョセフ・ピューリッツァーは今日，彼の名を冠した評説賞で主に知られているが，Q8 アメリカン・ドリーム，すなわち，出身国や背景に関係なく，だれでも勤勉と忍耐によって成功できるという考えを体現していた。ピューリッツァーは十代でハンガリーから移民し，南北戦争中は北部諸州のために戦った。

2 After the war, Q2 Pulitzer, who could speak German and French, moved to Missouri, drawn by the growing German community there. At first, like many others, he struggled to make ends meet, performing a range of Q1 **menial** tasks and working as a waiter, a taxi driver, and even a caretaker of mules. Finally, in 1868 he landed an office job with a railroad company. The young Pulitzer impressed the company's lawyers so much that they encouraged him to become an attorney himself. In a quick rise that would Q4 **foreshadow** his future success, he completed his studies within a year and was admitted to the bar to practice law. But Q3 due to his youth, odd appearance, worn clothes, and imperfect English, Pulitzer attracted few clients. He did, however, manage to come to the attention of Carl Schurz, chief reporter and co-owner of the influential German-language newspaper in the community, who admired Pulitzer's intensity and his affinity for hard work.

パラグラフ 2 南北戦争後，Q2 ドイツ語とフランス語が話せたピューリッツァーはミズーリ州で大きくなりつつあったドイツ系コミュニティに引きつけられて，そこに移った。当初は彼も，他の多くの人と同じように生計を立てるのに苦労し，いろいろと Q1 雑多な仕事を手がけ，ウェイター，タクシー運転手，さらにはラバの世話係までして働いた。ようやく 1868 年に，彼は鉄道会社の事務職に就いた。会社の弁護士たちは若きピューリッツァーにたいへん感心し，弁護士になるよう勧めた。彼の将来の成功は早い出世が Q4 示していた。彼は 1 年もたたないうちに弁護士の資格を取って開業した。だが，Q3 若さ，風変わりな外見，みずぼらしい身なり，そして不完全な英語ゆえに，ピューリッツァーにはほとんど顧客がつかなかった。だが，彼はどうにか，ドイツ系コミュニティで影響力を持つ独語新聞の主任記者兼共同経営者であったカール・シュルツの目に留まった。シュルツは，ピューリッツァーが仕事熱心で，勤勉なことに感心していたのだった。

3 When Schurz was elected to the United States Senate, he was forced to devote more of his time and effort to politics. Consequently, the newspaper needed to

パラグラフ 3 合衆国の上院議員に選出されると，シュルツはより多くの時間と労力を政治に割かざるを得なくなった。その結果，新聞社は彼の職務の一部を肩代わりする新

hire a new reporter to take over some of his duties. Pulitzer was the choice, and he proved to be Q6 **indefatigable**, often working late in the night. He was such a prolific writer and showed such a mastery of his job that within the year he was promoted to help run the newspaper. Assigned to cover the Missouri state legislature, he made himself well known as a critic of the Democrats who controlled the legislature. Q5 In 1871, Pulitzer was chosen partly as a joke by the Republican party to run as a candidate in the upcoming election for the state legislature. The Republicans felt they had no chance of winning the election, but they relished the thought of the relentless Pulitzer campaigning against the Democrats. Pulitzer surprised everyone by winning an improbable victory in the general election. Q7 At age 21, he was four years too young to officially assume his seat in the state senate; nonetheless, no one objected to his participating, and Q10 Pulitzer went on to exert his influence for many years, politically as well as journalistically.

しい記者を雇わなければならなくなった。ピューリッツァーが選ばれ，彼は Q6 疲れ知らずで，夜遅くまで働くことも多かった。彼は健筆家で，たいへん仕事ができたので，その年のうちに昇進し，新聞社の経営を助けるようになった。ミズーリ州議会の担当となった際には，彼は，議会を支配していた民主党員の批判者として，広く知られるようになった。Q5 1871 年にピューリッツァーは，共和党から半ば冗談で候補者に選出され，来たるべき州議会選挙に立候補した。共和党員たちは，この選挙で自分たちに勝算はないと考えていたが，粘り強いピューリッツァーが民主党員に対して選挙戦を闘う姿を想像して楽しんでいたのだ。だれもが驚いたことに，ピューリッツァーは本選挙で，あり得ないはずの当選を果たした。Q7 21 歳だった彼は，正式に州の上院議員になるには 4 歳若かった。それにもかかわらず，だれも彼の就任に反対せず，Q10 ピューリッツァーは政治家としてもジャーナリストとしても，長年にわたって影響を与え続けたのだった。

## 1.

正答：D

The word “menial” in line 8 is closest in meaning to

(A) extraordinary
(B) challenging
(C) profitable
(D) humble

8 行目の “menial” にもっとも近い意味を持つのは

(A) 並外れた
(B) やりがいのある
(C) もうかる
(D) つつましやかな

he struggled to make ends meet という先行する文脈から menial の意味はある程度推測できるだろう。生活が苦しいということは，仕事も小さなものであるはず。また a waiter, a taxi driver, a caretaker of mules と，その具体的な内容も列挙されている。よって，(D) が正答。humble には「謙虚な，控えめな，地味な」以外に，「卑しい，粗末な，みすぼらしい」という意味がある。

## 2.

**正答：C**

According to the passage, Pulitzer moved to Missouri because of

(A) a particularly good job offer
(B) the chance to purchase land
(C) the presence of European immigrants
(D) the recommendation of a famous journalist

パッセージによれば，ピューリッツァーがミズーリ州に移った理由は

(A) たいへんよい仕事のオファー
(B) 土地を購入する機会
(C) ヨーロッパ系移民の存在
(D) ある著名な新聞記者による勧め

設問の Pulitzer moved to Missouri に相当する表現を検索すると，2 に Pulitzer, ... moved to Missouri, drawn by the growing German community there とある。よって，下線部を言い換えている (C) が正答。ピューリッツァー自身がヨーロッパ系移民であることは，1 の Pulitzer immigrated from Hungary や，2 の imperfect English からも推測できる。

## 3.

**正答：B**

Why was Pulitzer unsuccessful as a lawyer?

(A) He failed to pass the bar exam.
(B) He did not look like a lawyer.
(C) No law firms would hire him.
(D) He was unfamiliar with Missouri law.

なぜピューリッツァーは弁護士として成功しなかったのですか。

(A) 彼は司法試験に合格できなかった。
(B) 彼の外見は弁護士らしく見えなかった。
(C) 彼を雇う法律事務所がなかった。
(D) 彼はミズーリ州法をよく知らなかった。

ピューリッツァーの弁護士時代については 2 に説明がある。Pulitzer attracted few clients とあまり顧客がつかなかったことが指摘されており，その理由として due to his youth, odd appearance, worn clothes, and imperfect English，すなわち，若さ，外見，身なり，英語力の 4 点が挙げられている。よって，これらをまとめて言い換えている (B) が正答。due to ... は because of ..., owing to ... と同じように，理由，原因を導く群前置詞。

## 4.

**正答：B**

The word “foreshadow” in line 12 is closest in meaning to

(A) prevent
(B) predict
(C) aid
(D) justify

12 行目の “foreshadow” にもっとも近い意味を持つのは

(A) ～を防ぐ
(B) ～を予測する
(C) ～を助ける
(D) ～を正当化する

語源の知識で選択肢の絞り込みが可能。(B) が正答。foreshadow の fore- には「前もって，先～，予～」という意味がある。forethought「見通し」，foresee「～を予見する」など。同様に predict の pre- は「あらかじめ，～以前の，～の前部にある」という意味の接頭辞。preconception「先入観」，precondition「前提条件」など。

## 5.

正答：C

It can be inferred from the passage that Pulitzer's success in winning election to the state senate was

パッセージから推測すると，ピューリッツァーが州上院選挙に勝ったことは

(A) regretful
(B) misguided
(C) ironic
(D) futile

(A) 残念なことだった
(B) 間違いだった
(C) 皮肉なことだった
(D) 無駄なことだった

設問の election to the state senate に相当する表現を検索すると，3 に In 1871, Pulitzer was chosen partly as a joke by the Republican party ..., また続いて，共和党の大方の予想に反して，ピューリッツァーが当選したとある。よって，(C) が正答。

## 6.

正答：A

The word "indefatigable" in line 21 is closest in meaning to

21 行目の "indefatigable" にもっとも近い意味を持つのは

(A) tireless
(B) reliable
(C) exemplary
(D) adept

(A) 疲れ知らずの
(B) 頼れる
(C) 模範的な
(D) 熟達した

indefatigable は, fatigue「疲労」に, 否定の接頭辞 in- と, 可能性の接尾辞 -able が伴った形。ここから「疲れない」という意味だと推測できる。続く often working late in the night からも, ある程度意味が推測できる。よって, (A) が正答。tireless も tire「疲れ」に,「〜のない」という意味の接尾辞 -less が付いた語。

## 7.

正答：B

It can be inferred from the passage that the minimum age to serve in the Missouri state legislature was

パッセージから推測すると，ミズーリ州議会で働くことができる最低年齢は

(A) 21
(B) 25
(C) 30
(D) 35

(A) 21 歳
(B) 25 歳
(C) 30 歳
(D) 35 歳

設問の the minimum age to serve in the Missouri state legislature に相当する表現を検索すると，3 に At age 21, he was four years too young to officially assume his seat in the state senate とある。下線部に 21 歳で「4 歳早い」とあるので，21 + 4 = 25 から，(B) が正答。

## 8. 正答：D

Which of the following generalizations is supported by the passage?

(A) Politics and journalism do not mix.
(B) America attracted many immigrants during the 18th century.
(C) German immigrants greatly influenced American history.
(D) Anyone could succeed if he or she works hard enough.

このパッセージによって裏付けられている一般論は次のどれですか。

(A) 政治とジャーナリズムは相容れない。
(B) 18 世紀のアメリカは多くの移民を引きつけた。
(C) ドイツ系移民はアメリカ史に大きな影響を及ぼした。
(D) だれでも一生懸命働けば成功できる。

このパッセージの主題がピューリッツァーであるのは明らか。しかし，1 の he exemplified “the American Dream” からわかるように，彼はあくまでも「アメリカン・ドリーム」の体現者の一例として取り上げられている。ここでは「アメリカン・ドリーム」は，the notion that anyone could, through diligence and perseverance, become a success regardless of national origin or background と説明されているので，これを言い換えている (D) が正答。

## 9. 正答：A

The author organizes the discussion according to what principle?

(A) Chronology
(B) Comparison
(C) Classification
(D) Contrast

筆者はどの原則によってこの論を構成していますか。

(A) 時系列
(B) 比較
(C) 分類
(D) 対比

このパッセージがピューリッツァーについての伝記的な記述であるのは明らか。now, As a teenager, the Civil War, After the war, At first, Finally, in 1868, The young Pulitzer, within a year, In 1871, At age 21 ... など，時間的経緯，時代，順番を表す表現が複数確認できる。よって，(A) が正答。

## 10. 　正答：B

A paragraph following the passage would most likely discuss
(A) a change in the Missouri legislature's age requirements
(B) Pulitzer's accomplishments in his subsequent career
(C) Pulitzer's campaign in the upcoming senate election
(D) Missouri's increasing influence on national politics

このパッセージに続くパラグラフがおそらく論じるのは
(A) ミズーリ州議会の年齢制限の変更
(B) ピューリッツァーのその後の仕事における業績
(C) 来たる上院選挙におけるピューリッツァーの選挙戦
(D) 国政において増大するミズーリ州の影響力

パッセージの最後に Pulitzer went on to exert his influence for many years, politically as well as journalistically. とあるが，具体的な政治，報道における活躍は言及されていない。これらについてはこの後で説明されると推測できる。よって，(B) が正答。

---

ボキャブラリー
- □ **exemplify**「～のよい例となる」
- □ **notion**「概念」
- □ **diligence**「勤勉」
- □ **perseverance**「忍耐」
- □ **immigrate**「移住してくる」
- □ **the Civil War**「アメリカ南北戦争」
- □ **make ends meet**「（金銭的に）やりくりする」
- □ **menial**「つまらない」
- □ **attorney**「弁護士」
- □ **foreshadow**「～を予示する，徴候を示す」
- □ **affinity**「好きなこと，親近感」
- □ **Senate**「上院」
- □ **indefatigable**「疲れ知らずの」
- □ **prolific**「多作の」
- □ **mastery**「優越，卓越」
- □ **Democrat**「民主党員」
- □ **legislature**「議会」
- □ **Republican party**「共和党」
- □ **relish**「～を楽しむ，たしなむ」
- □ **campaign**「（選挙）運動をする」
- □ **improbable**「あり得ない」
- □ **exert**「（影響力を）働かせる」

## Questions 11-20 *Electrical Lighting*

1 エジソンによる電球の発明以来，電気照明は世界を変えるうえで大きな役割を果たした。
2 最初の電灯である白熱灯は，フィラメントを熱して発光する仕組みで，のちにいくつかの改良が加えられた。
3 19 世紀後半に蒸気放電管であるネオン管が発明され，広告に利用された。
4 さらに 1930 年代に蛍光灯が実用化された。

1 Q12 Electrical lighting played a major role in transforming the world in the 20th century because it allowed humans to basically transcend the limitations of the natural lighting of the Sun and to continue their activities at night. Q11 The history of the electric light bulb, since its "first invention" by Thomas Edison in 1879, has been one of slow and steady progress as gradually technology has given humans Q19 more light for less cost, becoming cheaper but brighter, decade after decade.

パラグラフ 1 Q12 電気による照明は，20 世紀の世界を変えるうえで大きな役割を果たした。なぜなら，これによって人間は太陽の自然光の限界を超え，夜にも活動を続けられるようになったからである。Q11 電球の歴史は，1879 年のトーマス・エジソンによる「最初の発明」以来，ゆっくりとだが着実に発展し，技術は人々に Q19 より多くの光を，より安いコストでもたらし，電球は時代とともに，より安く，より明るくなった。

2 The first light was the incandescent lamp, which radiates light from a thread or filament heated by passing an electric current through it until it glows. Q13 Although Sir Joseph Wilson Swan in England fabricated an incandescent lamp one year prior to Edison, Edison constructed a complete lighting system and thus was given credit for the bulb's invention. Among the Q14 **subsequent** improvements to Edison's bulb were replacing the original carbon filaments with tungsten filaments for longer life, coiling them for improved efficiency, and frosting the interior of the glass bulb to soften its light.

パラグラフ 2 最初の電灯は白熱灯だった。白熱灯は，電流が通ることで細線またはフィラメントが白熱するほど熱せられ，それにより発光する。Q13 イギリスのジョゼフ・ウィルソン・スワン卿は，エジソンより 1 年早く白熱灯を作っていたが，エジソンは完全な照明装置を作り上げたことにより，白熱灯の発明という功績が認められた。エジソンの電球に Q14 その後加えられた改良には，初期型の炭素フィラメントからさらに寿命の長いタングステンフィラメントへの交換，効率を上げるためのフィラメントのコイル化，光を和らげるためのガラス球内面の白色化が含まれる。

3 In the late 19th century, French physicist Georges Claude discovered that a vapor tube filled with neon gas under low pressure produces intense orange-red light. He also found that additional colors could be produced by adding small amounts of other substances to a tube containing neon gas, gaseous sodium,

パラグラフ 3 19 世紀後半には，フランス人の物理学者ジョルジュ・クロードが，低圧のネオンガスで満たされた蒸気放電管が強い赤橙色の光を発することを発見した。彼はまた，ネオンガス，ナトリウムガス，または水銀が入った管に他の物質を少量加えると，他の色も作り出せることも発見した。その当時すでに Q15 クロードは，自分の発

| | |
|---|---|
| or mercury. Even at that time Q15 Claude recognized the value of his invention for commercial signs. **Neon signs became popular for this reason in the 1920's, and they are still used in the same way today.** | 明品の広告利用の価値を認識していた。ネオンサインは，この用途ゆえに，1920年代に普及し，現在でも同じように使われている。 |
| 4 Q16 During the 1930's, fluorescent lamps first came into use. These long tubes contain mercury vapor that fluoresces, **or glows, when Q18 subjected to the radiation of the mercury discharge.** Q17 Fluorescent lamps, which are far more efficient and longer-lived than incandescent lamps, were the first vapor-tube lamps to be used indoors. | パラグラフ4 Q16 1930年代には蛍光灯が初めて実用化された。蛍光灯の長い管には水銀蒸気が入っており，これが水銀放電の発光に Q18 さらされると蛍光発光，つまり白熱する。Q17 蛍光灯は白熱電球よりも効率がよく，寿命も長いので，屋内用の最初の蒸気放電灯となった。 |

## 11.

正答：C

What is the main purpose of the passage?

(A) To identify the inventor of the first light bulb
(B) To analyze the influence of the light bulb on human society
(C) To outline the technological evolution of the light bulb
(D) To compare the shortcomings of various kinds of light bulbs

このパッセージの主な目的は何ですか。

(A) 最初の電球の発明家がだれであるか明らかにすること
(B) 電球の人間社会に対する影響を分析すること
(C) 電球の技術的発達の概略を述べること
(D) さまざまな種類の電球の欠点を比較すること

1 の The history of the electric light bulb, since its "first invention" by Thomas Edison in 1879 ... から，このパッセージが「エジソン」以来の「電球の発達」についてのものであることは明らか。2 3 4 では時代を追って順次,「白熱灯」「蒸気放電管」「蛍光灯」について解説している。よって，(C) がもっとも適切。(A) は，エジソンをはじめスワン卿，クロードと発明家の名前は挙がっているが，焦点は発明家ではなくその発明品にあるので誤り。

## 12. 正答：A

Which of the following statements can be inferred from the first paragraph?

(A) The development of electrical lights significantly influenced modern society.
(B) The technology of electrical lighting was advanced by sudden breakthroughs.
(C) Electrical lighting has changed the biological rhythms of humans.
(D) Electric lights were reluctantly accepted by many people.

第1パラグラフから推測できるのは次のどの記述ですか。

(A) 電灯の発達は近代社会に多大な影響を与えた。
(B) 電灯の技術は突然の飛躍的進歩によって発達した。
(C) 電灯は人間の生物学的リズムを変えた。
(D) 電灯は多くの人々にいやいや受け入れられた。

1 に Electrical lighting played a major role in transforming the world in the 20th century とあるので，電灯が社会に大きな影響を及ぼしたことは容易に推測できる。よって，(A) が正答。play a role in ... は「～において役割を果たす」という意味。

## 13. 正答：C

In the second paragraph, what do we learn about the invention of electric lighting?

(A) Thomas Edison invented the first light bulb.
(B) The first light systems used tungsten filaments.
(C) A British inventor created the first electric lamp.
(D) The first electrical lights had soft tones.

第2段落では，電灯の発明について何がわかりますか。

(A) トーマス・エジソンは最初の電球を発明した。
(B) 最初の照明装置はタングステンフィラメントを使用していた。
(C) イギリスの発明家が最初の電灯を作った。
(D) 最初の電灯はやわらかな色調だった。

2 の Although Sir Joseph Wilson Swan in England fabricated an incandescent lamp one year prior to Edison で，電球を最初に作ったのはエジソンではなくスワン卿だったとある。よって，(A) ではなく，(C) が正答。Sir Joseph Wilson Swan in England が A British inventor，fabricated が created と言い換えられていることに留意。(B)(D) はいずれも the subsequent improvements to Edison's bulb「エジソンの電球にその後加えられた改良」の事例であり，(B)The first light systems，(D)The first electrical lights の特性ではない。

## 14. 正答：A

The word "subsequent" in line 11 is closest in meaning to

(A) later
(B) unexpected
(C) innovative
(D) expensive

11行目の "subsequent" にもっとも近い意味を持つのは

(A) あとで
(B) 思いがけない
(C) 革新的な
(D) 高価な

subsequent は sub「下に」＋ seque「続く」から成り「続いて起こる，その後の，すぐ次の」の意味の形容詞。よって，(A) が正答。

## 15.　正答：C

What is most likely the main use of the neon light?

(A) Street lighting
(B) Indoor lighting
(C) Advertising
(D) Heating

ネオン灯の主な用途は，おそらく何ですか。

(A) 街灯
(B) 屋内の照明
(C) 広告
(D) 暖房

> ネオン灯については 3 に言及があり，... the value of his invention for commercial signs. とある。ここで his invention とはネオン灯のこと。よって，下線部を言い換えている (C) が正答。

## 16.　正答：C

What type of gas is contained in fluorescent lights?

(A) Neon
(B) Sodium
(C) Mercury
(D) Fluoride

蛍光灯に含まれているガスの種類はどれですか。

(A) ネオン
(B) ナトリウム
(C) 水銀
(D) フッ素

> 設問の contained in fluorescent lights に相当する表現を検索すると，4 に During the 1930's, fluorescent lamps first came into use. These long tubes contain mercury vapor ... とある。よって，(C) が正答。

## 17.　正答：C

According to the passage, what was the first vapor-tube lamp to be used inside buildings?

(A) The incandescent bulb
(B) The neon lamp
(C) The fluorescent light
(D) The carbon filament lamp

パッセージによれば，屋内で使用された最初の蒸気放電灯は何でしたか。

(A) 白熱球
(B) ネオン灯
(C) 蛍光灯
(D) 炭素フィラメント電球

> 設問の the first vapor-tube lamp to be used inside buildings に相当する表現を検索すると，4 に Fluorescent lamps ... were the first vapor-tube lamps to be used indoors. とある。よって，(C) が正答。

## 18.　正答：A

The phrase "subjected to" in line 23 is closest in meaning to

(A) exposed to
(B) condensed by
(C) dissolved by
(D) fused to

23 行目の "subjected to" にもっとも近い意味を持つのは

(A) ～にさらされる
(B) ～によって凝縮される
(C) ～によって溶解される
(D) ～と融合させる

subject は，subject *A* to *B* で「A を B にさらす，A に B を課す」という意味。ここでは受動態で subjected to ...「〜にさらされる」となる。よって，(A) がもっとも近い。expose は「〜をさらす」という意味。

## 19.

正答：A

Where in the passage does the author refer to the relationship between the development of lighting and its price?

(A) Paragraph 1
(B) Paragraph 2
(C) Paragraph 3
(D) Paragraph 4

このパッセージのどこで筆者は，電気照明の進歩とその価格の関係について言及していますか。

(A) パラグラフ 1
(B) パラグラフ 2
(C) パラグラフ 3
(D) パラグラフ 4

1 の最後の文に，more light for less cost, becoming cheaper but brighter と，技術の発展に伴うコストダウンに関する記述がある。よって，(A) が正答。

## 20.

正答：B

The tone of the passage could best be described as

(A) cynical
(B) neutral
(C) anxious
(D) skeptical

このパッセージの論調を表すのにもっとも適切な表現は

(A) 皮肉的
(B) 中立的
(C) 不安げ
(D) 懐疑的

このパッセージは，電球の歴史を時系列に沿って客観的に説明しており，筆者の主観的な意見や批判などを直接，間接に表す表現は一切見られない。よって，(B) が正答。

---

ボキャブラリー
- □ **transcend**「(限界を) 超える」
- □ **light bulb**「電球」
- □ **incandescent lamp**「白熱灯」
- □ **radiate**「〜を照らす，放射する」
- □ **glow**「熱して輝く，ほてる」
- □ **give credit for ...**「〜を手柄とする」
- □ **frost**「白くする，つや消しにする」
- □ **vapor**「蒸気」
- □ **sodium**「ナトリウム」
- □ **mercury**「水銀」
- □ **fluorescent**「蛍光灯」

# Questions 21-30 *Blues*

| | |
|---|---|
| 1 | ブルースという音楽は定義しがたいものの，ポピュラー音楽に大きな影響を与えた。 |
| 2 | ブルースシンガーたちは生きていくうえでのさまざまな問題を歌にし，人間的な逆境と戦った。 |

1 Q21 The music called "the blues" is difficult to define. Some people think of the blues as a type of music that embodies a particular feeling (the blues); others regard it primarily as a musical genre characterized by a special blues scale which contains twelve bars and three chords in a particular order. The blues also involves particular characteristics of voice and movement and could be described as poetry set to dance music. Whatever the Q23 **exact** definition, Q22 its influence on jazz, gospel music, theater music, rock, and almost every subsequent form of popular music in the 20th century was incalculable.

パラグラフ1 Q21 「ブルース」と呼ばれる音楽は，定義しがたい。それをある特定のフィーリング（ブルーな気持ち）を表現したものと考えている人もいれば，それを主に，独特のブルース音階を特徴とするひとつの音楽的形式，すなわち一定の順序で進行する12小節と3つのコードから成る形式と見なす人もいる。ブルースにはまた，独特の歌声と動きが伴っており，ダンス音楽と一体化した詩であると言うこともできる。Q23 その正確な定義がなんであれ，Q22 ジャズ，ゴスペル，劇場音楽，ロック，そして20世紀のその後のほとんどすべてのポピュラー音楽にブルースが与えた影響は測り知れない。

2 The blues cannot be traced to a specific composer or particular date, but as an identifiable form of music Q24 it originated in the Mississippi Delta region of Louisiana towards the end of the 19th century. The earliest appearance of printed music Q28 **recognizable** as the blues was the publication of W.C. Handy's "the Memphis Blues" in 1912, and Handy himself said Q24 he had first heard the blues along the lower Mississippi River in 1890. Q26 Early blues singers composed their own songs, accompanying themselves on a piano or a guitar. Q26 They played solo, inventing verses and borrowing also from other singers, and Q25 they were probably the first American artists to express the feelings of social and personal alienation from modern life, and to rise above Q30 **them** through their art. By singing about frustration, mistreatment, or misfortune, and often by overcoming it with irony, blues singers helped themselves and

パラグラフ2 ブルースの起源を特定の作曲家や日付にさかのぼることはできないが，明確な音楽形式としてのブルースは，19世紀末に Q24 ルイジアナ州のミシシッピ川下流域で始まった。ブルースとして Q28 認められる譜面が初めて登場したのは，W.C. ハンディの「メンフィス・ブルース」が発行された1912年だが，ハンディ本人は Q24 1890年にミシシッピ川下流域で初めてブルースを聞いた，と言っている。Q26 初期のブルースシンガーは自ら作曲し，ピアノやギターの伴奏を伴った。Q26 彼らはソロで演奏し，自ら作詞をしたり他のシンガーから歌詞を借りたりした。Q25 彼らは，現代的な生活からの社会的，個人的な疎外感を表現し，Q30 こうした感覚を芸術によって乗り越えようとしたおそらく最初のアメリカ人アーティストだった。ブルースシンガーたちは失望，虐待，あるいは不幸を歌い，しばしばそれを皮肉で乗り越えることで，Q27 浮気をしている恋人，無知な主人，ひねくれた店員，警察の暴行，乏しい給料，失業，

their listeners to Q27 deal with the problems of life, whether frustrated and angered by cheating lovers, ignorant bosses, crooked shopkeepers, police brutality, inadequate pay, unemployment, or racism. **Blues singers fought human adversity by asserting human creativity, by turning life into art through ironic rebuttal, by linking themselves through their traditional art to others in the community, and by holding out a future hope for freedom and better times down the road.** Q29 Blues lyrics represent an oral poetry of considerable merit, perhaps one of the finest genres of home-grown poetry in the English language.

あるいは人種差別のゆえに絶望しているのであれ，怒っているのであれ，自分とそれを聴く人たちが人生のさまざまな問題に向き合えるようにしたのだ。ブルースシンガーは人間の創造性を主張し，皮肉混じりの反証によって人生を芸術に変え，伝統音楽を通じて地域社会の仲間と結びつき，自由ともっとよい時期がそのうちやってくるという将来への希望を持つことによって，人間的な逆境と戦ったのである。Q29 ブルースの歌詞は，すぐれた口誦詩を代表するものであり，おそらくは，アメリカで生まれた英語詩の形式の中でもっともすぐれたもののひとつである。

## 21.

正答：C

What is the main purpose of the first paragraph?

第1パラグラフの主な目的は何ですか。

(A) To summarize the history of the blues
(B) To describe the origin of the blues
(C) To offer a general definition of the blues
(D) To contrast different styles of blues

(A) ブルースの歴史を要約すること
(B) ブルースの起源を述べること
(C) ブルースの一般的な定義を提示すること
(D) ブルースの異なるスタイルを対比すること

第1行目の The music called "the blues" is difficult to define. からわかるように，1 はブルースの「定義」について検討している。よって，(C) が正答。

## 22.

正答：B

In paragraph 1, the author implies that

第1パラグラフで筆者が示唆しているのは

(A) blues in its purest form is an instrumental music
(B) blues affected many types of modern music
(C) blues has yet to be fully appreciated as music
(D) blues is an exclusively African American music

(A) もっとも純粋な形のブルースはインストゥルメンタル・ミュージックであること
(B) ブルースは現代の多くの種類の音楽に影響を与えたこと
(C) ブルースはいまだ音楽として十分に評価されていないこと
(D) ブルースはもっぱらアメリカ黒人の音楽であること

1 に its influence on jazz, gospel music, theater music, rock, and almost every subsequent form of popular music in the 20th century was incalculable とあり，ブルースがさまざまなジャンルの音楽に影響を及ぼしたとわかる。よって，この部分をまとめている (B) が正答。

## 23. 正答：D

The word "exact" in line 6 is closest in meaning to

(A) general
(B) required
(C) contemporary
(D) precise

6行目の "exact" にもっとも近い意味を持つのは

(A) 一般的な
(B) 必要とされる
(C) 現代的な
(D) 正確な

exact は，描写や知識などが，誤りがなく「正確・的確な」。同様に，細かい点に至るまで正確であることを表す語は (D) precise である。(A) general はこれとは反義的で，「一般的な，概括的な」という意味。

## 24. 正答：D

According to the author, where did the blues begin?

(A) Memphis
(B) St. Louis
(C) Large eastern cities
(D) The southern Mississippi River

筆者によれば，ブルースはどこで始まりましたか。

(A) メンフィス
(B) セントルイス
(C) 東部の大都市
(D) ミシシッピ川の南部

設問の the blues begin に相当する表現を検索すると，2 に it originated in the Mississippi Delta region of Louisiana とある。さらに he had first heard the blues along the lower Mississippi River in 1890. と同様の言及がある。よって，下線部と同義の (D) が正答。

## 25. 正答：A

According to the passage, what was distinct to early American blues singers?

(A) They reflected a modern sense of social isolation.
(B) They produced songs of vigorous political protest.
(C) They performed in collaborations with other artists.
(D) They received adequate compensation for their work.

パッセージによれば，初期のアメリカ人ブルースシンガーの特徴は何でしたか。

(A) 社会的疎外に対する現代的な感覚を反映していた。
(B) 力強い政治的抗議の歌を生み出した。
(C) 他のアーティストたちと共同で演奏した。
(D) 自分たちの作品に対して十分な報酬を受け取った。

2 に they were probably the first American artists to express the feelings of social and personal alienation from modern life とある。よって，下線部を言い換えている (A) が正答。

## 26. 正答：B

What can be inferred about early blues singers from paragraph 2?

(A) They usually copyrighted their music.
(B) They played individually.
(C) They used many different instruments.
(D) They performed before large audiences.

初期のブルース歌手について，第2パラグラフからどんなことが推測できますか。

(A) 通常は作曲の著作権を確保した。
(B) ひとりで演奏した。
(C) 多くの楽器を用いた。
(D) 大観衆の前で演奏した。

> 2 で，"early blues singers" に相当する表現を検索すると，Early blues singers composed their own songs, They played solo とあり，初期のブルース奏者が，単独で音楽活動を行っていたことがわかる。よって，solo を同義の individually で言い換えている (B) が正答。

## 27. 正答：D

Which of the following is NOT mentioned as a topic of blues songs?

(A) Lack of money
(B) The difficulty in finding a job
(C) The frustrations of love
(D) Respect for authority

ブルースの曲の題材として挙げられていないのは次のどれですか。

(A) お金がないこと
(B) 仕事を見つけることの難しさ
(C) 恋愛の苦しみ
(D) 権威に対する尊敬

> 曲の題材については 2 に言及がある。deal with the problems of life, whether frustrated and angered by cheating lovers, ignorant bosses, crooked shopkeepers, police brutality, inadequate pay, unemployment, or racism にブルース曲のテーマが間接的に示されている。下線部は選択肢 (A) (B) (C) に対応しているので，言及のない (D) が正答となる。

## 28. 正答：A

The word "recognizable" in line 12 is closest in meaning to

(A) identifiable
(B) achievable
(C) released
(D) disputed

12 行目の "recognizable" にもっとも近い意味を持つのは

(A) 識別できる
(B) 達成できる
(C) 解放された
(D) 議論されている

> recognizable は「認識できる」という意味の形容詞。よって，(A) が正答。recognize「認識する」＋ able「できる」，identify「識別する」＋ able「できる」と語源的に同じ構造を持っていることに留意。

## 29. 正答：C

The author mentions English language poetry because
筆者が英語の詩に言及している理由は

(A) the blues was widely recognized by literary critics
(A) ブルースが文芸批評家によって広く認められていたから

(B) blues songs were often written down and published as poems
(B) ブルースの曲がしばしば書き留められ，詩として出版されたから

(C) blues lyrics can be regarded as a form of sung poetry
(C) ブルースの歌詞を口誦詩と見なすことができるから

(D) the blues was based in part upon rural English verse
(D) ブルースの一部が地方の英語詩に基づいているから

設問の English language poetry に相当する表現を検索すると，**2** に Blues lyrics represent an oral poetry of considerable merit, perhaps one of the finest genres of home-grown poetry in the English language. とある。よって，下線部を言い換えている (C) が正答。oral「発話される」と，選択肢の sung「歌われる」が同義的であることに留意。

## 30. 正答：D

The word "them" in line 18 refers to
18 行目の "them" が指し示しているのは

(A) early blues singers
(A) 初期のブルース歌手

(B) verses
(B) 詩句

(C) other singers
(C) 他の歌手ら

(D) the feelings
(D) フィーリング

them は複数形なので直前部をさかのぼって，複数形名詞を検索すると，They, verses, other singers, the first American artists, the feelings が見つかる。この中で，rise above ... through their art「芸術によって乗り越える」対象として適切なのは，the feelings である。よって，(D) が正答。

---

**ボキャブラリー**
- ☐ **embody**「〜を体現する，組み入れる」
- ☐ **genre**「ジャンル」
- ☐ **bar**「（音楽の）小節」
- ☐ **chord**「コード」
- ☐ **incalculable**「数え切れない」
- ☐ **alienation**「孤立，疎外」
- ☐ **brutality**「野蛮，残忍」
- ☐ **adversity**「逆境，困難」
- ☐ **assert**「〜を示す，肯定する」
- ☐ **rebuttal**「反証」
- ☐ **down the road**「将来に」
- ☐ **oral**「口の，口述の」

## Questions 31-40 *Leaf Structure*

1 「葉」は根，茎とともに植物を構成する３器官のひとつで，光合成を行い，養分を作り出す。
2 葉はたいていは薄く平らで，葉緑素のため緑色である。葉はおのおのが効率よく光を受けるよう，一定の規則の元に配列されている。

1 Q35 The leaf is one of the three types of organs that collectively make up a typical plant found on land. The other two are Q34 the roots, which serve to anchor the plant and absorb water, and the stem, **which supports the leaves and bears water and other materials, such as minerals and other nutrients, to and from** Q32 **them.** Q38 The leaf is the plant's photosynthetic organ, the place where light is used to manufacture the food necessary for the plant to live. **In its strictest sense, the term "leaf" is applied only to the photosynthetic organs of vascular plants, which have specialized systems to** Q33 **conduct food, water, and other materials. In a loose sense, however,** Q36 the term is sometimes informally used to refer to the leaf-like structures of mosses and some liverworts. **These structures do indeed carry on photosynthesis, but since they do not possess a vascular system,** Q36 they are more properly classified as something other than leaves.

パラグラフ１ Q35 葉は，陸に生えている一般的な植物を構成している３種類の器官のひとつである。他の２つは，Q34 植物を固着させて水を吸収する根と，葉を支え，水と無機物や他の養分などの物質を Q32 葉から出し入れする茎である。Q38 葉は植物の光合成器官であり，そこでは植物が生きていくのに必要な養分が光を使って作り出される。きわめて厳密に言えば，「葉」という語は維管束植物，すなわち養分，水，その他の物質を Q33 運ぶのに特化した組織を持つ植物の光合成組織に対してのみ用いられる。だが，大雑把な意味では，Q36 コケ類やある種のタイコウ類の葉状体を指すのにも，しばしば略式に使われる。これらの組織は実際に光合成を行うが，維管束系を持っていないため，Q36 葉とは異なるものとして分類するほうが適切である。

2 **To perform their photosynthetic function, true leaves are typically thin and flat in order to maximize the amount of surface area available to absorb light and to facilitate the exchange of gases with the atmosphere.** Q37 They are usually green because the color of the major photosynthetic element, chlorophyll, is green. **A typical leaf consists of a flattened surface and an internal stalk. The arrangement of leaves on a stem is not random:** Q40 the most important principle of leaf arrangement is that the leaves are Q39 **oriented** so that each leaf is exposed to the light with a minimum of interference from neighboring leaves.

パラグラフ２ 光合成を行えるように，本当の葉は，光の吸収に使える表面積を最大にし，外気とガスの交換を促進するため，だいたいは薄く平らである。Q37 葉は，主要な光合成要素である葉緑素が緑色なので，たいてい緑色をしている。葉は一般的に，平らな表面と内部の茎で成り立っている。茎に葉が生える配列は無作為ではない。Q40 葉の配列のもっとも重要な原則は，隣り合う葉がなるべく重ならず，それぞれの葉が光を受けるように Q39 配置されているということである。

## 31. 正答：A

The main purpose of the passage is to

(A) describe the function of leaves
(B) offer a definition of a plant
(C) identify different kinds of leaves
(D) demonstrate the importance of plants

このパッセージの主な目的は

(A) 葉の機能を説明すること
(B) 植物の定義を示すこと
(C) さまざまな種類の葉を見分けること
(D) 植物の重要性を明らかにすること

このパッセージは，まず植物学的な意味での「葉」を定義し，続いてその主な機能である「光合成」について説明し，これに適した葉の配列について述べている。よって，(A) が正答。

## 32. 正答：B

The word "them" in line 5 refers to

(A) roots
(B) leaves
(C) other materials
(D) minerals

5 行目の "them" が指し示しているのは

(A) 根
(B) 葉
(C) 他の物質
(D) 無機物

them が to and from という 2 つの前置詞の目的語になっていることに注目。bears water and other materials ... to and from「水と他の物質を葉から出し入れする」対象として文脈上適切なのは，(B) leaves「葉」である。

## 33. 正答：C

The word "conduct" in line 8 is closest in meaning to

(A) absorb
(B) replace
(C) transport
(D) isolate

8 行目の "conduct" にもっとも近い意味を持つのは

(A) ～を吸収する
(B) ～を置き換える
(C) ～を運ぶ
(D) ～を分離する

conduct は「～を伝導する，伝える」という意味。語源的には -duct は「導管，脈管」のこと。water and other materials を目的語としていることからも意味が推定できる。正答の (C) transport は trans「別の離れたところに」＋ port「運ぶ」から成る。

## 34. 正答：A

According to the passage, one function of the roots is to provide

パッセージによれば，根が果たすひとつの機能は

(A) stability to the plant
(B) access to sunlight
(C) synthesis of nutrients
(D) protection from fungi

(A) 植物に安定性を与えること
(B) 日光を受けること
(C) 養分の合成を行うこと
(D) 菌から保護すること

設問の the roots に相当する表現を検索すると，**1** に the roots, which serve to anchor the plant and absorb water とある。よって，下線部を言い換えている (A) が正答。anchor には「錨を下ろす」，転じて「～を固定する」という意味がある。

## 35. 正答：D

According to the first paragraph, all of the following are organs of plants on land EXCEPT

第 1 パラグラフによれば，次のうち陸上の植物の器官として挙げられていないのは

(A) leaves
(B) roots
(C) stems
(D) seeds

(A) 葉
(B) 根
(C) 茎
(D) 種

**1** の冒頭に (A) The leaf is one of the three types of organs that collectively make up a typical plant found on land. The other two are (B) the roots ... and (C) the stem とあるので，言及のない (D) seeds が正答。

## 36. 正答：D

Referring to moss as "having leaves" would most likely be regarded by the author as

コケ類が「葉を持っている」と述べることについて，おそらく筆者が見なしているのは

(A) a misunderstanding of function
(B) an overly strict interpretation
(C) a suitable usage among specialists
(D) technically inappropriate

(A) 機能に関する誤解である
(B) あまりにも厳密な解釈である
(C) 専門家の間では適切な用法である
(D) 専門的に見れば不適切である

設問の moss as "having leaves" に相当する表現を検索すると，**1** に the term is sometimes informally used to refer to the leaf-like structures of mosses ... とあり，直後で they are more properly classified as something other than leaves と述べている。つまり，筆者はコケ類に厳密には「葉」はないと考えている。よって，(D) が正答。technically には「専門的には」という意味がある。

## 37.

正答：B

It can be inferred from the passage that the physical appearance of a leaf primarily depends on

パッセージから推測できるのは，葉の外観が主に決まるのは

(A) the function it is designed to perform
(B) the color of the chlorophyll it contains
(C) the amount of usable sunlight it can receive
(D) the number of leaves attached to one stem

(A) それが果たすべき機能による
(B) それが含む葉緑素の色による
(C) それが受け取る利用可能な日光の量による
(D) 一本の茎に付いている葉の数による

設問の the physical appearance とは「外見」のこと。葉の外見については 2 に They are usually green because the color of the major photosynthetic element, chlorophyll, is green. とある。よって，下線部を言い換えている (B) が正答。

## 38.

正答：A

It can be inferred that a leaf is most similar in operation to which of the following?

葉が機能面でもっとも似ていると推測できるのは，次のどれですか。

(A) A factory
(B) A highway
(C) A warehouse
(D) A conduit

(A) 工場
(B) 高速道路
(C) 倉庫
(D) 水道

1 で The leaf is the plant's photosynthetic organ, the place where light is used to manufacture the food necessary for the plant to live. とあり，葉は光合成を行って，栄養素を manufacture「製造する」部位であると説明されている。よって，製造を主な機能とする (A) が正答。

## 39.

正答：B

The word "oriented" in line 19 is closest in meaning to

19 行目の "oriented" にもっとも近い意味を持つのは

(A) incorporated
(B) aligned
(C) dressed
(D) adhered

(A) 編入された
(B) 整列させられた
(C) 準備の整った
(D) 付着した

oriented の原形 orient は「向きを〜に合わせる」という意味の他動詞。よって，「(一直線に) 整列させる」という意味の他動詞 align の過去分詞形である (B) が正答。

## 40.　　正答：C

According to the passage, how are leaves on a particular stem generally arranged?

(A) In a pattern unique to that particular species of plant
(B) At equal intervals around the circumference of the stem
(C) In a manner that avoids blocking the light to adjacent leaves
(D) With the larger leaves attached highest on the stem

パッセージによれば，特定の茎に生えている葉は一般にどのように配列されていますか。

(A) 植物の種によって特有なパターンで
(B) 茎の周囲に等間隔で
(C) 隣接する葉に当たる光をさえぎらないような方法で
(D) 大きな葉が茎の最上部に生えるように

葉の配列については 2 の最後に言及がある。設問の arranged に相当する表現を検索すると，the most important principle of leaf arrangement is that the leaves are oriented so that each leaf is exposed to the light with a minimum of interference from neighboring leaves とある。よって，下線部を言い換えている (C) が正答。

---

ボキャブラリー
- □ **organ**「器官」
- □ **anchor**「～を固定する」
- □ **stem**「茎」
- □ **photosynthetic**「光合成の」
- □ **vascular plant**「維管束植物」
- □ **liverwort**「コケ」
- □ **facilitate**「～を促進する」
- □ **chlorophyll**「葉緑素」
- □ **orient**「方位を合わせる」
- □ **interference**「干渉」

## Questions 41-50 *Canadian Literature*

| | |
|---|---|
| 1 | カナダでは他国に比肩するような文学が発達していなかった。 |
| 2 | これはひとつには，イギリス，フランス，そしてアメリカ合衆国の影響のもとで成長せざるを得なかったため，もうひとつには国が若く，国民意識の目覚める事件がなかったためである。 |
| 3 | 第二次世界大戦以降には，象徴的で風刺を用いた文学が登場し，今後の発展が期待できる。 |

1 The history of Canadian literature is interesting chiefly as the record of a young nation's attempts to establish its own cultural identity, to find its own language, and to come to terms with its own environment. Q41 There have been no giant literary figures among Canadian writers. To be sure, Q42 a few writers have come to the attention of the world community for their work, but in all cases their reputations have faded with time. The quantity and quality of Canadian writing have made steady progress, even Q44 **spectacular** progress, but Q41 no serious literary critic would claim that the literature of Canada rivals that of England, France, Russia, or the United States.

パラグラフ1 カナダ文学史は何よりもまず，若い国が自国の文化的アイデンティティを確立し，自国の言語を見い出し，自国の状況と折り合いをつける試みの記録として興味深い。Q41 カナダ人作家の中には，文学の巨匠は存在してこなかった。確かに Q42 何人かの作家の作品は国際社会の注目を浴びたが，彼らの評判はどれも時とともに色あせてしまった。カナダの文学作品の量と質は着実に，また Q44 めざましいと言ってよいほどの発展を遂げてきたが，Q41 まっとうな文芸批評家で，カナダ文学がイギリスやフランス，ロシア，あるいはアメリカの文学に比肩すると主張する者は皆無だろう。

2 This fact is partially attributable to Q43 the youth of Canada, which celebrated its first centennial in 1967 and is only around 150 years old today. But there are other reasons. The country and its culture have had to grow up in Q43 the shadow of not one but two founding nations—England and France—and of its great neighbor to the south, the United States. It has been difficult for Canadian authors to avoid imitating the styles of these more established literary traditions and to find a distinctive "Canadianism" which is not a mere compromise among them. This was certainly understandable in the early literature of Canada, since the writers of the 18th and early 19th century were themselves citizens of the colonial powers. In fact, Q45 it was not until the latter half of the 19th century

パラグラフ2 この事実は，部分的には Q43 カナダの若さのためであると言える。カナダは 1967 年に初めて百年祭を祝った国であり，現在でも，たったの建国 150 年ほどである。だが，ほかにも理由はある。この国と文化は，Q43 一つのみならず二つの故国，すなわちイギリスとフランス，さらには南の大きな隣国，アメリカ合衆国の影に隠れて成長しなければならなかった。カナダ人作家にとっては，そうした国のより確立された文学的伝統のスタイルを模倣しないようにすることも，それらのスタイルの単なる折衷ではない固有の「カナダ主義」を見い出すことも難しかったのである。確かにこのことは，初期のカナダ文学においては無理もないことだった。というのも，18 世紀，19 世紀初頭のカナダ人作家たちは，彼ら自身，植民地宗主国の市民だったからだ。事実，Q45 国民文学に多少なりとも近い作品が登場し始めるのは，ようやく 19

that anything even approaching a national literature began to appear. **Furthermore, unlike the United States and France,** Q43 Canada has had no revolution; hence, there has been no great national crisis **to shock** Q46 **it into self-awareness.**

世紀後半になってからであった。さらに，合衆国やフランスと違って，Q43 カナダには革命が起きなかった。それゆえ，Q46 カナダに国民意識を目覚めさせるような重大な国家的危機はなかったのである。

3 Q49 Until very recently, almost all Canadian poetry has been predominantly landscape poetry, strongly influenced by the overpowering presence of the country's magnificent and varied vistas. Q48 Until the 1920's, almost all novels were overly simplified historical romances **designed to give Canadians a sense of their past and some hope for the future. Beginning in the mid-1920's, however,** Q50 Canadian writers at last began to turn towards more realistic themes and the symbolic, even satirical, exploration of contemporary life. **Since the end of World War II, this trend became particularly** Q47 **pronounced and, without question, is a positive sign for the future of Canadian literature.**

パラグラフ3 Q49 ごく最近まで，ほとんどのカナダ詩は主として風景詩であり，自国の壮大で多様な景色の強烈な存在に強く影響されていた。Q48 1920 年代まではほとんどすべての小説が過度に単純化された歴史小説で，過去の意味と未来に対する希望をカナダ人に与えようとするものだった。だが，1920 年代半ばから Q50 ようやくカナダ人作家たちはより現実的なテーマを取り上げ，現代生活について象徴的で，風刺的ですらある探究を開始した。この傾向は第二次世界大戦後に特に Q47 顕著になったが，これはカナダ文学の将来にとって間違いなくよい徴候である。

## 41.

正答：D

What is the main purpose of paragraph 1?

(A) To imply that Canada is incapable of producing high-quality literature
(B) To maintain that Canada has no distinctive national identity
(C) To show that some Canadian writers have gained international attention
(D) To suggest that Canadian literature has yet to achieve a high standing

第 1 パラグラフの主な目的は何ですか。

(A) カナダが質の高い文学を生み出せないと示唆すること
(B) カナダが独自の国家的アイデンティティを持たないと主張すること
(C) 何人かのカナダ人作家が国際的な注目を集めたと明らかにすること
(D) カナダ文学がまだ高い評価を受けていないと主張すること

1 では，There have been no giant literary figures among Canadian writers. また，no serious literary critic would claim that the literature of Canada rivals that of England, France, Russia, or the United States と，カナダ文学が未成熟であると繰り返し強調している。よって，(D) が正答。have yet to *do* は「まだ～していない」という意味。

## 42. 正答：A

What does the author claim has happened to those Canadian writers who have gained international recognition?

筆者は，国際的に認められたカナダ人作家がどうなったと述べていますか。

(A) Their fame did not last long.
(B) Their work was below acceptable standards.
(C) They ignored their own cultural environment.
(D) They rival their counterparts in other countries.

(A) 彼らの名声は短命だった。
(B) 彼らの作品は許容できる基準を満たさなかった。
(C) 彼らは自らの文化的環境を無視した。
(D) 彼らは他の国の作家に比肩する。

設問の Canadian writers who have gained international recognition に相当する表現を検索すると，**1** に a few writers have come to the attention of the world community for their work, but in all cases their reputations have faded with time とある。よって，下線部を言い換えている (A) が正答。

## 43. 正答：D

Which of the following is NOT cited by the author as a reason why it has been difficult for Canada to develop a unique literary tradition?

カナダにとって独自の文学的伝統を育くむのが難しかった理由として，筆者が挙げていないものは次のどれですか。

(A) The influence of other nations
(B) The lack of a defining national crisis
(C) The country's relatively short history
(D) The country's lack of large cities

(A) 他国の影響
(B) 決定的な国家的危機の欠如
(C) 比較的短い歴史
(D) 大都市の欠如

**2** で，the youth of Canada が挙げられ，続いて other reasons として the shadow of not one but two founding nations—England and France—and ... the United States, さらに no revolution, no great national crisis と，3つの理由が列挙されている。よって，言及のない (D) が正答。

## 44. 正答：D

The word "spectacular" in line 7 is closest in meaning to

7行目の "spectacular" にもっとも近い意味を持つのは

(A) visible
(B) compatible
(C) steadfast
(D) striking

(A) 可視的な
(B) 両立できる
(C) 固定した
(D) 著しい

spectacular は「めざましい，著しい」という意味の形容詞。よって，(D) が正答。

## 45. 正答：C

According to the passage, when did Canadian literature first display elements of a national literature?

パッセージによれば，カナダ文学が最初に国民文学の要素を示したのはいつですか。

(A) In the late 18th century
(B) In the early 19th century
(C) In the late 19th century
(D) In the early 20th century

(A) 18世紀末に
(B) 19世紀初頭に
(C) 19世紀末に
(D) 20世紀初頭に

設問の a national literature に相当する表現を検索すると，2 に it was not until the latter half of the 19th century that anything even approaching a national literature began to appear とある。よって，(C) が正答。

## 46. 正答：B

The word "it" in line 20 refers to

20行目の "it" が指し示しているのは

(A) the United States
(B) Canada
(C) revolution
(D) national crisis

(A) アメリカ合衆国
(B) カナダ
(C) 革命
(D) 国家的危機

it は文脈上，shock「ショックを与えられ」，into self-awareness「自己認識を覚醒させられる」ような存在である。よって，革命を経験していない国である (B) が正答。

## 47. 正答：D

The word "pronounced" in line 29 is closest in meaning to

29行目の "pronounced" にもっとも近い意味を持つのは

(A) mentioned
(B) maintained
(C) multiplied
(D) marked

(A) 述べられた
(B) 維持された
(C) 倍増した
(D) 際立った

pronounced は「明白な，際立った」という意味の形容詞。よって (D) が正答。

## 48.

正答：B

The author's attitude toward the early Canadian novels can best be described as

(A) neutral
(B) critical
(C) appreciative
(D) indifferent

初期のカナダの小説に対する筆者の態度をもっともよく表しているのは

(A) 中立的である
(B) 批判的である
(C) 評価している
(D) 無関心である

筆者は全体を通して初期のカナダ文学の未成熟さを指摘し，その理由を説明している。また，3 には Until the 1920's, almost all novels were overly simplified historical romances とある。overly は「過度に」という意味の副詞であり，筆者の批判的な見解が表れている。よって，(B) が正答。

## 49.

正答：D

Where in the passage does the author refer to the major influence on traditional Canadian poetry?

(A) Lines 6-8
(B) Lines 9-10
(C) Lines 17-19
(D) Lines 22-24

このパッセージのどこで筆者は，伝統的なカナダ詩に対する大きな影響について言及していますか。

(A) 6-8 行目
(B) 9-10 行目
(C) 17-19 行目
(D) 22-24 行目

設問の the major influence on traditional Canadian poetry に相当する表現を検索すると，3 に Until very recently, almost all Canadian poetry ... とあり，ここで predominantly landscape poetry, strongly influenced by the overpowering presence of country's magnificent and varied vistas と，自然風景の影響が指摘されている。よって，(D) が正答。

## 50. 正答：A

With which of the following statements would the author most likely agree?

(A) Meaningful literature employs a degree of symbolism.
(B) Contemporary life cannot be realistically portrayed.
(C) Much of Canada's early literature has been unfairly neglected.
(D) The literary trends of the 1920's have unfortunately died out.

筆者は次のどの記述にもっとも同意すると思われますか。

(A) 有意義な文学はある程度，象徴主義を用いる。
(B) 現代の生活は写実主義的には描写できない。
(C) カナダの初期の文学の大半は不当に無視されてきた。
(D) 1920年代の文学的傾向は残念なことに廃れた。

> カナダ文学の最近の傾向を説明して筆者は3で，Canadian writers at last began to turn towards more realistic themes and the symbolic, even satirical, exploration of contemporary life と述べており，さらにこの傾向を a positive sign「よい傾向」と評している。ここから，筆者が象徴主義を成熟した文学の条件としていると推察できる。よって，(A) が正答。

---

ボキャブラリー
- □ **come to terms with ...**「～を甘受する」
- □ **fade**「廃れる，色あせる」
- □ **spectacular**「めざましい」
- □ **rival**「～に匹敵する」
- □ **attributable to ...**「(原因が) ～にある」
- □ **centennial**「百年祭」
- □ **compromise**「妥協，折衷」
- □ **self-awareness**「自己認識」
- □ **predominantly**「大部分は，主に」
- □ **vista**「景観，展望」
- □ **satirical**「皮肉な」
- □ **pronounced**「明白な」

# Practice Test 2
# 第2回実戦問題

## 解説

## 【第２回】実戦問題　正答一覧

### Listening Comprehension

| Part A | | Part B | |
|---|---|---|---|
| 1 | D | 31 | C |
| 2 | A | 32 | B |
| 3 | B | 33 | C |
| 4 | D | 34 | A |
| 5 | B | 35 | D |
| 6 | A | 36 | B |
| 7 | B | 37 | A |
| 8 | C | 38 | D |
| 9 | D | **Part C** | |
| 10 | C | 39 | C |
| 11 | D | 40 | D |
| 12 | C | 41 | A |
| 13 | A | 42 | D |
| 14 | B | 43 | B |
| 15 | C | 44 | A |
| 16 | D | 45 | A |
| 17 | C | 46 | C |
| 18 | A | 47 | B |
| 19 | B | 48 | B |
| 20 | D | 49 | C |
| 21 | D | 50 | D |
| 22 | A | | |
| 23 | B | | |
| 24 | B | | |
| 25 | A | | |
| 26 | C | | |
| 27 | C | | |
| 28 | D | | |
| 29 | C | | |
| 30 | A | | |

### Structure and Written Expression

| Structure | | Written Expression | |
|---|---|---|---|
| 1 | D | | |
| 2 | C | 16 | A |
| 3 | A | 17 | A |
| 4 | B | 18 | B |
| 5 | A | 19 | D |
| 6 | A | 20 | B |
| 7 | B | 21 | D |
| 8 | D | 22 | D |
| 9 | B | 23 | B |
| 10 | B | 24 | D |
| 11 | D | 25 | D |
| 12 | C | 26 | B |
| 13 | A | 27 | D |
| 14 | D | 28 | C |
| 15 | C | 29 | B |
| | | 30 | A |
| | | 31 | C |
| | | 32 | D |
| | | 33 | B |
| | | 34 | C |
| | | 35 | A |
| | | 36 | B |
| | | 37 | A |
| | | 38 | A |
| | | 39 | C |
| | | 40 | C |

### Reading Comprehension

| | | | |
|---|---|---|---|
| 1 | D | 26 | B |
| 2 | A | 27 | C |
| 3 | A | 28 | A |
| 4 | B | 29 | A |
| 5 | D | 30 | B |
| 6 | C | 31 | B |
| 7 | B | 32 | C |
| 8 | C | 33 | C |
| 9 | B | 34 | D |
| 10 | A | 35 | C |
| 11 | A | 36 | C |
| 12 | B | 37 | D |
| 13 | A | 38 | A |
| 14 | B | 39 | D |
| 15 | A | 40 | D |
| 16 | C | 41 | C |
| 17 | D | 42 | B |
| 18 | A | 43 | B |
| 19 | C | 44 | D |
| 20 | B | 45 | B |
| 21 | C | 46 | D |
| 22 | D | 47 | A |
| 23 | C | 48 | B |
| 24 | A | 49 | A |
| 25 | D | 50 | D |

## 1. 演劇についての学生同士の会話　正答：D

045

M This has got to be one of the best plays that the drama department has ever put on.

W It sure is.

M: これは今まで演劇学部が上演した中で最高の芝居のひとつに違いないね。

W: 間違いなくね。

What does the woman mean?

(A) She would like to hear the music play a little longer.
(B) She thinks the design of the department is nice.
(C) She likes the clothes the actors wear in the drama.
(D) She feels the performance is unusually good.

女性は何と言っていますか。

(A) もう少し演奏を聴きたい。
(B) 学科のデザインはよいと思う。
(C) 劇中で役者が着ていた服が気に入っている。
(D) 公演は実にすばらしい。

男性が演劇学部の芝居を高く評価したのを受けて，女性は It sure is. と応じている。これは It sure is (one of the best plays that the drama department has ever put on). の省略で，男性の意見を肯定している。よって，(D) が正答。正答の選択肢では play を performance と言い換えている。play，department，drama といった断片的な単語の繰り返しだけで (A) (B) (C) を選ばないようにしよう。

ボキャブラリー □ **department**「学部」 □ **put on ...**「～を上演する」
□ **performance**「公演」

## 2. 天気についての学生同士の会話　正答：A

046

M The forecast for tomorrow is scattered thunderstorms in the morning and cold and windy in the afternoon.

W Oh no, it sounds just like today.

M: 明日の天気予報は，午前は時折の暴風，午後は寒くて風があるって。

W: いやだわ，今日と同じようね。

What are the speakers discussing?

(A) What the weather will be like tomorrow
(B) What they ate for breakfast this morning
(C) What TV programs will be on this afternoon
(D) What they are planning to do today

話者らは何について話していますか。

(A) 明日はどんな天気になるか
(B) けさ，朝食に何を食べたか
(C) 今日の午後，どんなテレビ番組があるか
(D) 今日何をする予定か

forecast とは weather forecast「天気予報」のこと。scattered thunderstorms in the morning and cold and windy in the afternoon という内容から，この会話が明日の天気についてであることは明らかなので，(A) が正答。

ボキャブラリー □ **forecast**「予測，予報」 □ **scattered**「まばらな」
□ **thunderstorm**「雷雨」

## 3. 今夜の予定についての学生同士の会話　正答：B

047

**W** Everyone's excited about the concert tonight. Did you get your ticket yet?

**M** No. It doesn't look like I'm going to be able to make it. I've only got exams in three classes tomorrow.

**W:** みんな今夜のコンサートを楽しみにしているわ。もうチケットは取った?

**M:** いいや。どうやら行けそうにないんだ。明日は3クラスで試験があるだけなんだけどね。

What does the man imply?

(A) His tests should not be too difficult tomorrow.
(B) He has a lot of studying to do tonight.
(C) He does not think the concert will be very good.
(D) His classes require only a few tests this term.

男性は何を示唆していますか。

(A) 明日のテストはそれほど難しくはないはずだ。
(B) 今夜はたくさん勉強することがある。
(C) コンサートはあまりよくないだろうと思う。
(D) 今学期は授業のテストが少ししかない。

男性がコンサートに行けない理由を，I've only got exams in three classes tomorrow.「たった3つテストがあるだけ」と皮肉まじりに言っていることから，今夜は勉強するつもりだと推測できる。よって，(B) が正答となる。皮肉まじりの調子に気づかずに文字どおり解釈してしまうと，(A) や (D) にひっかかってしまう。

ボキャブラリー □ **make it**「都合をつける」

## 4. 遅刻についての教授と学生の会話　正答：D

048

**W** I'm really sorry for missing class again yesterday, Dr. Greenfield. I just couldn't get out of bed.

**M** I believe I've made it very clear to all the students in my classes how important attendance is. You need to be there, Shirley. Every time. On time. I'm not going to say it again.

**W:** グリーンフィールド博士，昨日もまた授業を欠席してしまってすみません。どうしても起きられなくて。

**M:** 私はクラスの受講生全員に，どれだけ出席が大切かはっきりと言っておいたはずだね。授業には出席しなければならないんだよ，シャーリー。いつも。時間どおりに。もう二度と言いませんよ。

What does the man mean?

(A) He is not going to give the class lecture a second time.
(B) He does not yet know all the students in the class.
(C) He does not understand why so many students are missing class.
(D) He will not give the woman another warning.

男性は何と言っていますか。

(A) 教室での講義は二度としない。
(B) まだクラスの学生全員を知らない。
(C) そんなに多くの学生が欠席する理由がわからない。
(D) 女性に二度と注意しない。

遅刻を重ねる女性に対し，教授は You need to be there, ...「出席しなければいけません」と注意し，最後に I'm not going to say it again.「もう二度と言いませんよ」と念を押している。これを言い換えている (D) が正答となる。

ボキャブラリー □ **get out of bed**「起きる」 □ **attendance**「出席」 □ **warning**「注意，警告」

## 5. 授業についての学生同士の会話　正答：B

049

| | | |
|---|---|---|
| M | Professor Collins's History 327 was definitely one of the hardest classes I've ever taken. I got an A, but I worked my tail off getting it. | M: コリンズ教授の歴史学327は，間違いなく今までで一番たいへんな授業のひとつだったね。Aは取れたけど，そのために懸命にがんばったよ。 |
| W | I know it's hard, but I decided to register for it anyway. Would you mind letting me borrow your notes so I have some idea of what Professor Collins lectures on before the class begins? | W: たいへんなのはわかっているけど，やっぱり私もそのクラスに登録することにしたわ。あなたのノートを貸してもらえないかしら。そうすれば，授業が開講する前にコリンズ教授が何について講義するのかある程度わかるから。 |

What can be inferred from the conversation?　この会話から何が推測できますか。

(A) The man did not work hard last year.　(A) 男性は昨年よく勉強しなかった。
(B) The class requires a lot of effort.　(B) その授業は多くの努力を要する。
(C) The woman missed the last class.　(C) 女性は前回の授業を欠席した。
(D) The professor is an easy grader.　(D) その教授は成績の付け方が甘い。

コリンズ教授の歴史学の授業について男性は ... was definitely one of the hardest classes I've ever taken「今までで一番たいへんな授業だった」, I worked my tail off「懸命にがんばった」と言っている。work *one's* tail off は「猛烈に働く，懸命にがんばる」という意味のイディオム。この授業は宿題など多くの勉強が必要と推測できるので，(B) が正答。

ボキャブラリー □ **definitely**「確かに，間違いなく」
□ **work *one's* tail off**「懸命にがんばる」
□ **register**「登録する」 □ **grader**「採点者」

## 6. 友人についての学生同士の会話　正答：A

050

| | | |
|---|---|---|
| M | Mike says he's getting poor grades in his classes because his professors don't like him. | M: マイクときたら，自分は教授たちに好かれていないからよい成績が取れないなんて言っていたよ。 |
| W | Oh, yeah, right. I saw him at the library once last term. He was reading the newspaper. | W: はいはい，そうね。先学期は一度，図書館で彼を見かけたわ。新聞を読んでいたけどね。 |

What does the woman imply about Mike?
女性はマイクについて何を示唆していますか。

(A) He should study more than he does.
(B) He often goes to the library.
(C) He works for the local newspaper.
(D) He has a lot of classes.

(A) もっと勉強すべきだ。
(B) よく図書館に行く。
(C) 地元の新聞社で働いている。
(D) 授業をたくさん取っている。

成績不振の理由について男性がマイクの言い分を伝えても，女性は Oh, yeah, right. と取り合わない。さらに，図書館で見かけたのは一度きりで，そのときも勉強しないで新聞を読んでいたと言っているので，女性はマイクが不勉強だと思っているとわかる。よって，(A) が正答。Oh, yeah, right. の皮肉の口調に気づかないと，文字どおり「そのとおり」と勘違いしてしまうので注意。

ボキャブラリー □ **grade**「成績，評点」

## 7. 食事当番についての学生同士の会話　正答：B

051

**W** Oh, no. I totally forgot it's my turn to cook dinner tonight. Listen, Ted, is there any chance you could do it instead of me? I've got a chemistry test tomorrow that counts for half the grade in the class.

**M** All right. I'll do it. But the others probably won't be that happy to eat my cooking two days in a row.

**W:** あら，やだ，今夜の料理担当は自分だということをすっかり忘れていたわ。ねえ，テッド，できたら代わってもらえないかしら。明日は化学のテストがあって，それで成績の半分が決まってしまうのよ。

**M:** わかった，やるよ。でも，ぼくの料理を2日続けて食べるなんて，ほかの人たちはあまり喜ばないだろうけどね。

What will the woman probably do tonight?
女性はおそらく今夜何をしますか。

(A) Cook dinner for her roommates
(B) Study for an important examination
(C) Eat dinner at the school cafeteria
(D) Conduct a chemistry experiment

(A) ルームメイトのために夕食を作る
(B) 大切な試験のために勉強する
(C) カフェテリアで夕食をとる
(D) 化学の実験を行う

食事当番であるにもかかわらず，女性は I've got a chemistry test tomorrow「明日化学の試験があるから」と言って，男性に代わりを頼んでいる。もちろん試験勉強をするためなので，(B) が正答。「成績を大きく左右するテスト」を選択肢では an important examination と言い換えていることに留意。dinner, chemistry の繰り返しだけで (A) (C) (D) を選ばないように。

ボキャブラリー □ **turn**「順番」 □ **chemistry**「化学」 □ **count for ...**「～の価値がある」 □ **in a row**「続けて」

## 8. 実験室についての学生同士の会話　正答：C

052

**W** If you're staying late, be sure to lock up the entrance to the lab when you leave.

**M** Don't worry. I'll take care of it. It looks like I'm going to be here a while.

**W:** 遅くまで残るつもりなら，出るときに必ず実験室の入り口の戸締りをしてね。

**M:** 大丈夫，やっておくよ。もうしばらくここにいるつもりだから。

What does the man mean?

(A) The woman should not worry so much.
(B) He will not be in the lab for a while.
(C) He will be sure to lock the facility.
(D) The woman should take care of the laboratory.

男性は何と言っていますか。

(A) 女性はあまり心配すべきではない。
(B) 少しの間，実験室を離れる。
(C) 忘れずに施設の鍵を掛ける。
(D) 女性が実験室の責任を持つべきだ。

実験室を出るときは鍵をかけるように女性が言うと，男性は Don't worry, I'll take care of it. と応じている。よって，(C) が正答。take care of... は「責任をもって～を引き受ける」という意味。この表現の繰り返しだけで (D) を選ばないようにしよう。正答の選択肢では the lab を the facility と言い換えている。(A) の worry，(B) の the lab，a while も繰り返しによるひっかけ。

ボキャブラリー □ **be sure to *do***「必ず～する」 □ **facility**「施設，設備」

## 9. 友人についての学生同士の会話　正答：D

053

**W** I don't think Paul has much of a life outside of studying for class. I think he went to a basketball game one night last winter.

**M** I'm sure his G.P.A. reflects his dedication. He may not have much else going for him, but at least he is a good student.

**W:** ポールって，授業のために勉強すること以外何もしてないんじゃないかしら。去年の冬に一晩，バスケットボールの試合に行ったぐらいだと思うわ。

**M:** 彼の成績がその努力を表しているのは間違いないね。勉強のほかにはほとんど何もしていないようだけど，少なくとも彼はまじめな学生だよ。

What do the speakers imply about Paul?

(A) He is taking too many classes this term.
(B) He enjoys watching basketball.
(C) He has to improve his grades.
(D) He needs some variety in his life.

話者らはポールについて何を示唆していますか。

(A) 今学期授業を取りすぎている。
(B) バスケットボールを見るのが好きだ。
(C) 成績を上げなければならない。
(D) もっといろいろなことをすべきだ。

女性の I don't think Paul has much of a life outside of studying for class.，男性の He may not have much else going for him から，ポールはがり勉気味だとわかる。これは「一晩バスケットボールを見にいったぐらい」「成績が表している」と皮肉っていることからもわかる。よって2人は，ポールは勉強以外のこともすべきだと考えていると推測できる。したがって，正答は (D)。皮肉が理解できないと，誤った推測で (A)(C) を選んでしまう。

ボキャブラリー □ **G.P.A.**「学業平均値」(= **Grade Point Average**)
□ **dedication**「献身，専念」

## 10. 夏休みについての学生同士の会話　正答：C

054

**M** How was your summer vacation, Helen? Did you go down to Florida as you planned?

**W** I wish. I spent the whole summer working in a coffee shop. With the increase in tuition and my moving out of the dorm into an apartment off campus, I realized I needed to make some money rather than spend my savings on a vacation down in Florida.

M: ヘレン，夏休みはどうだった？　計画どおりフロリダに行ったの？

W: そうしたかったんだけどね。夏中ずっとコーヒーショップで働いていたの。学費が上がったし，寮から学外のアパートに引っ越したし，フロリダで遊んで貯金を使うよりも，お金を貯める必要があると思ったの。

What can be inferred about the woman?

(A) She spent her vacation in Florida.
(B) She moved back into the dorm.
(C) She worked over the summer.
(D) She ran out of spending money.

女性について何が推測できますか。

(A) フロリダで休暇を過ごした。
(B) 寮に戻った。
(C) 夏の間ずっと働いた。
(D) 小遣いを使い果たした。

男性からフロリダに行ったのかと尋ねられると，女性はI wish. と応じている。これはI wish (I had done so).「そうだったら［フロリダに行けたら］よかったのだけど」という仮定法過去完了の省略。つまり，フロリダには行っていないということ。代わりに「夏中コーヒーショップで働いた」と述べているので，正答は (C)。vacation，Florida，dorm，money，spend などの断片的な聞き取りで (A) (B) (D) を選ばないように。

ボキャブラリー □ **tuition**「学費」 □ **savings**「貯金」 □ **run out of ...**「～を使い果たす」 □ **spending money**「小遣い」

## 11. 宿題についての学生同士の会話　正答：D

055

**M** Professor Morris sure laid on the homework for tomorrow. I just don't know how I can get all that reading done.

**W** Can anybody?

M: モリス教授ときたら，明日までの宿題をずいぶんとくれたね。あんなにたくさんのリーディング，どうやってこなしたらいいのかわからないよ。

W: こなせる人なんか，だれかいると思う？

What does the woman mean?

(A) Nobody knew what the homework was today.
(B) Somebody must have borrowed her textbook.
(C) Professor Morris stayed home today.
(D) The class assignment is too demanding.

女性は何と言っていますか。

(A) 今日の宿題が何かだれも知らなかった。
(B) だれかが彼女の教科書を借りたに違いない。
(C) モリス教授は今日家にいた。
(D) 授業の課題がきつすぎる。

女性の Can anybody? は男性の発言の一部を受けて，Can anybody get all that reading done? を短縮した修辞疑問文。「こなせる人なんか，だれかいると思う？」（だれもいないでしょうよ）と反語的に応じている。ここから，だれにもこなせないほど大量の宿題が課されたと推測できるので，(D) が正答となる。

ボキャブラリー □ **sure**「確かに，本当に」 □ **lay on** ...「～を課す」
□ **demanding**「過酷な，きつい」

## 12. 休講についての学生同士の会話　正答：C

056

**W** Hi, Patrick. Can you tell me which seminar room the talk will be held in?

**M** You mean you didn't get the message yesterday? The lecture has been postponed until next week.

**W:** こんにちは，パトリック。どのセミナールームで講演があるか教えてくれる?

**M:** 昨日，あなたに残した伝言を聞いていないってこと？　講演は来週まで延期になったんだよ。

What is the problem?

(A) The seminar room is already being used.
(B) The man forgot to contact the woman.
(C) The woman did not receive the man's message.
(D) The lecture was mistakenly canceled.

何が問題ですか。

(A) セミナールームはすでに使われている。
(B) 男性は女性に連絡するのを忘れた。
(C) 女性は男性の伝言を聞かなかった。
(D) 講演は誤って中止された。

男性が You mean you didn't get the message yesterday? と言っていることから，女性は男性の伝言を聞いていなかったとわかる。よって，(C) が正答。seminar room, lecture の繰り返しだけで (A) や (D) を選ばないように。message から誤って連想すると (B) にひっかかってしまう。

ボキャブラリー □ **talk**「講演，講義」 □ **postpone**「～を延期する」

## 13. 用語の定義についての学生同士の会話　正答：A

057

**W** Max, did you write down the definition of an excise tax the other day in the Intro to Economics lecture?

**M** Yeah, let's see. "A tax that is applied to the sale of specific items rather than a general sales tax applied to many products." I think Professor Sutton gave the examples of the extra tax on cigarettes and on luxury cars.

**W:** マックス，この間の経済学入門の講義でやった「物品税」の定義についてノートを取った？

**M:** うん，ええと。「多くの商品にかけられる一般売上税ではなく，特定の物品の売上にかけられる税」。サットン教授は，タバコと高級車にかけられる特別税を例に挙げていたと思うよ。

What does the woman want to know? 女性は何を知りたいのですか。

(A) The meaning of a specialized term (A) 専門用語の定義
(B) The reason for a recent tax increase (B) 最近の増税の理由
(C) The current tax rate on luxury cars (C) 高級車に対する現在の税率
(D) The assignment for an economics class (D) 経済学の授業の宿題

女性は did you write down the definition of an excise tax ...?「物品税の定義を書いた？」と，経済用語の「定義」を尋ねている。よって，definition を the meaning of a specialized term と一般的な表現で言い換えている (A) が正答。tax だけにこだわると (B)(C) にひっかかる。luxury cars，economics の繰り返しにも注意。

ボキャブラリー □ **definition**「定義」 □ **excise tax**「物品税」
□ **specific**「特定の（⇔ **general**：一般の）」□ **assignment**「課題，宿題」

## 14. 就職活動についての学生同士の会話 正答：B

058

**M** Recently I've been leaning toward going to grad school, so I don't think I'll attend the job fair at the student center this weekend.

**M:** 最近は大学院進学のほうに傾いているんだ。だから，今週末に学生センターである就職フェアには行かないつもりさ。

**W** Well, it's the last one of the year. I'd go if I were you, just in case you change your mind about applying to master's programs.

**W:** でも，今年最後のフェアよ。万が一，修士課程に出願する考えが変わった場合に備えて，私だったら行っておくけど。

What does the woman mean? 女性は何と言っていますか。

(A) The man should choose a different graduate program. (A) 男性は別の大学院課程を選ぶべきだ。
(B) The man should consider going to the job fair. (B) 男性は就職フェアに行くことを考えるべきだ。
(C) The man should finish his applications as soon as possible. (C) 男性はできるだけ早く願書を書き終えるべきだ。
(D) There may not be any good jobs available now. (D) 今はよい求人がないかもしれない。

I'd go if I were you. は仮定法過去の表現で「私なら行く」という意味。間接的に男性に就職フェアに行くように勧めている。よって，(B) が正答。

ボキャブラリー □ **grad [graduate] school**「大学院」 □ **job fair**「就職フェア，説明会」
□ **apply to ...**「～に出願する」 □ **master's program**「修士課程」
□ **application**「出願，出願書類」

## 15. 課外活動についての学生同士の会話　正答：C

059

| | |
|---|---|
| **W** Are you going to join our literature discussion group this week, Chris? | **W:** クリス，今週の文学のディスカッション・グループには参加するつもり？ |
| **M** No way. I've got too many papers to write. But I will come next week. | **M:** 絶対無理さ。書かなければいけないレポートがたくさんあるんだ。でも，来週は行くよ。 |

What does the man plan to do?　男性は何をする予定ですか。

(A) Put off writing his papers　(A) レポートを書くのは後にする
(B) Read two newspapers　(B) 新聞２紙を読む
(C) Meet with the group next week　(C) 来週，グループのメンバーと会う
(D) Sign up for a better literature class　(D) もっとよい文学の授業に登録する

男性の I will come next week は，I will come to the discussion group next week という意味なので，(C) が正答となる。ディスカッション・グループとは，学生が授業以外の時間に集まって行う勉強会のこと。(B) の two newspapers は too many papers からのひっかけ。writing，papers，literature などの部分的な繰り返しにも注意が必要。

ボキャブラリー □ **No way.**「（依頼・誘いに対して）とんでもない，それどころじゃない」
□ **put off ...**「～を先延ばしにする」

## 16. 遅刻についての学生と教官の会話　正答：D

060

| | |
|---|---|
| **W** I'm sorry I wasn't on time for class today. | **W:** 今日クラスに遅刻して，すみませんでした。 |
| **M** Shelly, it wouldn't matter so much if it were only once. | **M:** シェリー，1回だけなら問題ないのだがね。 |

What does the man imply?　男性は何を示唆していますか。

(A) It does not matter that the woman missed class.　(A) 女性が授業を休んだことは問題ではない。
(B) He would like to talk to the woman at once.　(B) すぐに女性と話をしたい。
(C) The class did not start on time again today.　(C) 今日も授業は時間どおりに始まらなかった。
(D) The woman is frequently late.　(D) 女性は頻繁に遅刻する。

男性の if it were only once は仮定法過去の表現である。仮定法過去は現在の事実に反することを仮定するので，実際にはマーガレットの遅刻が１回どころではないことがわかる。よって，(D) が正答。not be on time「時間どおりでない」が，be late「遅刻する」と言い換えられていることに注意。

ボキャブラリー □ **matter**「問題となる，重要である」

## 17. 研究計画書についての教授と学生の会話　正答：C

061

**M** Professor Nantz, would you have a second to take a look at my research proposal? I've been working on it day in and day out for the last couple of weeks, but it doesn't seem to be coming together very well.

**W** Normally I'd be happy to, but I'm just on my way out the door. I'm giving a talk later this afternoon as part of the campus lecture series. How about in the morning? Say, around 10:00?

**M:** ナンツ教授，ぼくの研究計画書をちょっと見ていただけますか。ここ何週間か，朝から晩まで取り組んでいたのですが，なかなかうまくまとまらないんです。

**W:** いつもなら喜んで見るところですが，ちょうど出かけるところなんです。午後これから，大学の連続講義で講演をすることになっていて。午前中はどうですか？ そうですね，10時ぐらいは？

What does the woman suggest the man do?

(A) Come back later in the afternoon
(B) Attend her lecture series
(C) Visit her office later
(D) Review the proposal with his research partner

女性は男性に何をするように勧めていますか。

(A) 午後に出直してくる
(B) 連続講義に参加する
(C) 改めてオフィスに来る
(D) 共同研究者と計画を再検討する

学生が教授に研究計画書を見てほしいと頼むと，教授は午後は予定があるのでHow about in the morning?「午前中はどうか」と応じている。ここでthe morningとは当然，明日以降のこと。よって，laterとある(C)が正答。later，afternoon，lecture series，proposal，researchなどの断片的な繰り返しだけで(A)(B)(D)を選ばないように。

ボキャブラリー □ **take a look at ...**「～を見る」 □ **research proposal**「研究計画書」
□ **day in and day out**「一日中，朝から晩まで」 □ **review**「～を再検討する」

## 18. テレビ番組についての学生同士の会話　正答：A

062

**W** Isn't there supposed to be a special documentary on TV this evening?

**M** Yes. I heard it's fantastic. I think it's on Channel 5, at 7 o'clock.

**W:** 今晩TVでドキュメンタリーの特番があるはずじゃなかった？

**M:** うん。すごい番組だって聞いたよ。たしか7時に5チャンネルだと思うよ。

What will the speakers probably do later?

(A) Watch a television program
(B) Take a boat through the channel
(C) Copy some documents
(D) Have dinner around 7 o'clock

話者らはおそらく後で何をしますか。

(A) テレビ番組を見る
(B) 運河を通るボートに乗る
(C) いくつか文書をコピーする
(D) 7時に夕食を食べる

2人がTVのドキュメンタリー番組を見るつもりであることは会話から明らかなので，(A)が正答。(B)のchannelは，テレビの「チャンネル」と同音・同つづりだが，「運河，水路」という意味。(C)のdocumentsはdocumentaryのひっかけ。7 o'clockの繰り返しで(D)にひっかからないように。

ボキャブラリー □ **fantastic**「すばらしい」 □ **document**「文書」

## 19. 学期末レポートについての学生同士の会話　正答：B

063

**W** Francis, you look like you just won the lottery! What happened?

**M** Dr. Bates was so happy with my lab report that he agreed to accept it in lieu of a final paper. So I'm done with everything until next term.

**W:** フランシス，宝くじにでも当たったみたいね。何があったの?

**M:** ベイツ先生がぼくの実験報告書をとても気に入ってくれて，期末レポートの代わりにしてくれるって。だから，ぼくは来学期まで，もうやることは何もないのさ。

Why is the man so happy?

(A) He won a lottery prize.
(B) His vacation has started.
(C) He did well on his finals.
(D) His professor canceled an exam.

男性はなぜそんなに喜んでいるのですか。

(A) 宝くじに当たった。
(B) 休暇が始まった。
(C) 期末試験の成績がよかった。
(D) 教授が試験を取りやめた。

女性の you look like you just won the lottery! は，文字どおり「宝くじに当たった」ではなく，それくらいうれしそうに見えるという比喩。男性がうれしそうな理由は，実験報告書がうまく書けたおかげで期末レポートが免除になったから。つまり，もう長期休暇が始まったということなので，(B) が正答。in lieu of... は「～の代わりに」。be done with... は「～をすませる」という意味。be through ... とも言う。

ボキャブラリー □ **lab [laboratory]**「実験室，実験」 □ **final paper**「期末レポート」

## 20. 履修科目についての教授と学生の会話　正答：D

064

**W** Professor White, I'd really like to enroll in your advanced economics seminar next term, but I'm afraid I haven't taken all of the prerequisites.

**M** I appreciate your enthusiasm, Cathy, but I truly think you need to take all of the required economics courses before you take the seminar. Otherwise, you won't be able to follow the topics we're studying.

**W:** ホワイト教授，来学期の先生の上級経済学セミナーに登録したいのですが，登録に必要な基礎科目のすべてを取ってはいないのですが。

**M:** キャシー，きみの熱心さは感心ですが，やはりセミナーを取る前にまず必修の経済学の授業をすべて取っておくべきだと思いますよ。そうしないと，セミナーで取り上げる内容が理解できないでしょうから。

What does the man suggest the woman do?

(A) Enroll in his course next term
(B) Study harder to follow the course topics
(C) Be more enthusiastic about her studies
(D) Take some more economics classes

男性は女性に何をするように勧めていますか。

(A) 来学期に自分の授業を取る
(B) 授業のトピックが理解できるようもっと勉強する
(C) もっと勉強にやる気を出す
(D) さらにいくつかの経済学の授業を履修する

男性は女性に対して，まず基礎科目を取るように勧めており，そうでないと授業についていけなくなると述べている。よって，(D) が正答。上級レベルのクラス履修の際には，しばしば prerequisites を事前に取っていることが条件となる。なお，大人数に対する講義形式の lecture とは異なり，seminar では少人数での討議が授業の主体となる。(A) の enroll，(B) の follow the course topics，(C) の enthusiastic はいずれも単語の繰り返しによるひっかけ。

ボキャブラリー □ **prerequisite**「基礎科目，必修科目」 □ **enthusiasm**「熱意」
□ **required**「必修の」

## 21. 授業中の学生同士の会話 正答：D

065

| | |
|---|---|
| **M** Do you have an extra sheet of paper I can borrow? | **M:** 借りてもいい余分な紙はあるかな? |
| **W** Here. Just use this notebook. I've got an extra one. | **W:** このノートを使って。別のノートを持ってるから。 |

| | |
|---|---|
| What does the woman mean? | 女性は何と言っていますか。 |
| (A) The man can borrow her notes. | (A) 男性は彼女のメモを借りてもよい。 |
| (B) She does not have any extra paper. | (B) 余分な紙は持っていない。 |
| (C) The man should not use so much paper. | (C) 男性はそんなにたくさん紙を使うべきではない。 |
| (D) She will give the man a notebook. | (D) 男性にノートをあげる。 |

男性が紙を貸してと頼んでいるのに対して，女性は Here. と言ってノートを差し出している。よって，(D) が正答となる。(A) の can borrow, notes は単語の繰り返しよるひっかけ。日本語で言う「ノート」は notebook で，note は「メモ」や「覚書」，「手紙」などを指す。

ボキャブラリー □ **extra**「余分の」

## 22. 専攻についての学生同士の会話 正答：A

066

| | |
|---|---|
| **W** I decided to change majors again. I realize I'm not really cut out for business. And I know that art majors have a tough time finding jobs after graduation. So I decided to give computer science a try. | **W:** 私，また専攻を変えることにしたの。ビジネスにはあまり向いていないとわかったから。それに，美術専攻は卒業後に就職先を見つけるのがたいへんだとわかっているし。だから，コンピュータ科学に挑戦してみることにしたのよ。 |
| **M** Well, good luck. It's the second time you changed majors this year. I hope this isn't just a case of the grass being greener on the other side of the fence. | **M:** まあ，がんばって。だけど，専攻を変えるのは今年これで2回目だよね。これが単に「隣の芝生は青い」ということでなければいいけど。 |

What does the man imply about the woman?
(A) She should not change her major so often.
(B) She would have been successful in business.
(C) She should consider becoming an anthropology major.
(D) She will find her new major too difficult.

男性は女性について何を示唆していますか。
(A) そんなに頻繁に専攻を変えるべきではない。
(B) 彼女はビジネスで成功していただろう。
(C) 人類学を専攻することを考えるべきだ。
(D) 新しい専攻はとても難しいとわかるだろう。

美術，ビジネス，コンピュータ科学と頻繁に専攻分野を変える女性について，男性は Well, good luck. と言っているが，本当に応援しているのではなく，「まあ，せいぜいがんばって」と半ば呆れていることが文脈からわかる。これは続く忠告めいた表現からも確認できる。よって，(A) が正答。The grass is always greener on the other side of the fence.「隣の芝は青い」はことわざ。

ボキャブラリー □ **major**「専攻」 □ **be cut out for ...**「～に適している」
□ **give ... a try**「～に挑戦する」

## 23. レポートについての学生同士の会話 正答：B

067

**M** I've already written more than 25 pages for this modern history report, but I feel like I've just scratched the surface.

**W** Maybe you need to focus your topic a little more.

**M:** この近代史のレポート，もう25ページ以上書いたんだけど，表面をなでただけみたいな気がするんだ。

**W:** もう少しトピックを絞る必要があるんじゃない。

What can be inferred about the man's research paper?
(A) It is already finished.
(B) Its topic may be too broad.
(C) It needs to be more deeply researched.
(D) Its length is inadequate.

男性のリサーチペーパーについて何が推測できますか。
(A) もう仕上がっている。
(B) トピックが漠然としすぎているかもしれない。
(C) もっと徹底的にリサーチする必要がある。
(D) 長さが足りない。

男性が 25 ページ書いてもまだレポートがまとまらないと述べたのに対して，女性は Maybe you need to focus your topic a little more. と助言している。ここから，トピックがまだ漠然としていると推測できるので, (B) が正答。scratch the surface of ... は「～の上っ面をなでる，核心に触れない」ということ。

ボキャブラリー □ **focus**「～の焦点を絞る」 □ **inadequate**「不適切な，不十分な」

## 24. 教授についての学生同士の会話 正答：B

068

**M** Did you hear about Professor Stein? The president just announced that he's making her Vice President for Academic Affairs. So basically she's becoming an administrator.

**M:** スタイン教授のことを聞いた？ 学長が彼女を学務副学長にすると発表したんだ。つまり，彼女は基本的には行政側に回るわけだよ。

**W** Gee, I don't know whether to be happy or sad. She is maybe my favorite professor, and now I won't be able to take any more classes from her.

W: まあ，喜ぶべきか悲しむべきかわからないわ。彼女は結構お気に入りの教授なのに，もうこの先授業を取ることはできないのね。

What does the man tell the woman about Professor Stein?

男性はスタイン教授について女性に何と言っていますか。

(A) She has announced her plans to retire early.
(B) She has been appointed to the university administration.
(C) She is applying to be a full-time researcher.
(D) She will become the vice president of a private company.

(A) 早期退職するという考えを明らかにした。
(B) 大学の行政部の一員として任命された。
(C) 常勤の研究職に志願している。
(D) 民間企業の副社長になる。

男性は，スタイン教授がVice President for Academic Affairs「学務副学長」に任命されたと言っている。これは，続いて説明があるようにan administrator，つまり研究教育ではなく，大学運営に携わる職務のこと。よって，(B) が正答。女性のnow I won't be able to take any more classes from herからの誤った連想で (A)(D) を選ばないように。announced，vice presidentの断片的な繰り返しにも注意。

ボキャブラリー □ **vice president**「副学長，副社長」 □ **administrator**「管理者，理事」
□ **full-time**「常勤の」

## 25. 成績についての学生同士の会話　正答：A

069

**W** Ricardo, you look like you're on cloud nine.

W: リカルド，ご機嫌みたいね。

**M** I just can't believe that Professor Hunt gave me an A in anthropology—she's an incredibly tough grader. I'm ecstatic.

M: 信じられないけど，ハント教授が人類学のクラスでAをくれたんだ。彼女ってすごく成績の付け方が厳しいんだよ。もう有頂天だよ。

How is the man feeling?
(A) Delighted
(B) Disappointed
(C) Nervous
(D) Frustrated

男性はどんな気分ですか。
(A) 喜んでいる
(B) 失望している
(C) 緊張している
(D) 欲求不満である

be on cloud nineは「上機嫌である，有頂天である」という意味の慣用表現。これを知らなくても，tough graderであるハント教授からAをもらったらうれしいであろうことは容易に推測できる。さらに，男性がI'm ecstatic. と述べていることから，(A) が正答。

ボキャブラリー □ **incredibly**「信じられないほど，非常に」
□ **delighted**「大いに喜んで，楽しそうな」 □ **frustrated**「失意の，欲求不満の」

## 26. 授業についての学生同士の会話　正答：C

070

**M** We just had our partners assigned to us for our presentations in Introduction to Communication. I'm really happy that I'm working with Sally.

**W** I'm sorry to say you're in for a surprise. She has to be one of the worst people to work with. She never does anything until the last minute.

M: コミュニケーション概論のプレゼンテーションのパートナーがちょうど決まったところなんだ。ぼくはサリーと一緒にやることになって，すごくうれしいんだ。

W: 冗談でしょ。彼女は一緒にやるには最悪のタイプよ。いつもギリギリまで何もやらないんだから。

---

What does the woman imply about the man's presentation partner?

(A) She is not very good at public speaking.
(B) She is very busy with her part-time work.
(C) She does not prepare well enough in advance.
(D) She is very hard to communicate with.

女性は男性のプレゼンテーションのパートナーについて何を示唆していますか。

(A) 人前で話すのがあまりうまくない。
(B) アルバイトでとても忙しい。
(C) 前もって十分な準備をしない。
(D) コミュニケーションをとるのが難しい。

男性のプレゼンテーションのパートナーであるサリーについて，女性は She never does anything until the last minute.「いつもギリギリまで何もしない」と評している。これを言い換えた (C) が正答。work を「勉強，作業」でなく「仕事」ととると (B) の part-time work にひっかかる。また Communication と communicate の発音の重なりだけで (D) を選ばないように。

ボキャブラリー
☐ **partner**「共同研究者，パートナー」
☐ **I'm sorry to say you're in for a surprise.**「冗談でしょ，驚かせて悪いけど」
☐ **in advance**「前もって」

## 27. 電卓についての学生同士の会話　正答：C

071

**M** By the way, I'm still waiting for you to return my calculator, Mary.

**W** But, Tom, I gave it back to you last week.

M: そういえば，まだ電卓を返してもらってないんだけど，メアリー。

W: でも，トム，先週返したと思うけど。

---

What does the woman mean?

(A) She has finished making the calculations.
(B) She never received the calculations.
(C) She already returned the man's calculator.
(D) She forgot completely about the calculator.

女性は何と言っていますか。

(A) 計算は終えた。
(B) 見積もりを受け取ったことはない。
(C) 男性の電卓はもう返した。
(D) 電卓のことをすっかり忘れていた。

女性は，男性から借りた電卓は gave it back「すでに返した」と言っている。これを returned と言い換えている (C) が正答。

ボキャブラリー ☐ **calculator**「計算機，電卓」

## 28. インターンシップについての学生同士の会話 正答：D

072

**W** I really wanted to get that internship in the mayor's office. I can't believe I missed the deadline to apply.

**W:** 市長のオフィスのインターンシップ，本当にやりたかったんだけどな。自分でも信じられないけど，申し込みの締め切りを忘れてしまったの。

**M** Well, Michele, you're a great student, and the faculty in the political science department all like you. Since you're only a sophomore, you can always try again as a junior.

**M:** ねえ，ミシェル，きみは成績もいいし，政治学部の教授たちもみんなきみをかっているよ。まだ2年生なんだから，3年生になったらいつでも再チャレンジできるよ。

What does the man suggest the woman do? 男性は女性に何をするように勧めていますか。

(A) Talk to the political science faculty (A) 政治学部の教授陣と話す
(B) Contact the mayor's office for an interview (B) 面接のために市長のオフィスに連絡する
(C) Get some advice from the senior students (C) 上級生に助言してもらう
(D) Apply for the position next year (D) その仕事に来年申し込む

締切日を逃してしまった女性に対して，男性は junior でもう一度申し込めばよいと言って慰めている。女性は現在 sophomore「2年生」なので，これは next year「来年」のこと。よって (D) が正答。なお，米国大学の 1，2，3，4 年生はそれぞれ，freshman, sophomore, junior, senior という。

ボキャブラリー □ **deadline**「締め切り」 □ **faculty**「教授陣」 □ **interview**「面接，面談」

## 29. 文房具セールについての学生同士の会話 正答：C

073

**M** The paper says they're having a huge sale on stationery and other school supplies down at Office Station. You want to go down and check it out?

**M:** オフィスステーションで文房具や学用品の大売出しをするって新聞に書いてあったよ。見にいってみる？

**W** I would, but I'm going to be up all night trying to get this paper done. Any chance, though, you could pick up some clear files and a box of staples for me?

**W:** そうしたいけど，このレポートを終わらせるのに徹夜することになりそうなの。できれば，クリアファイル数冊とホチキスの針を1箱買ってきてくれないかしら。

What does the woman plan to do? 女性は何をする予定ですか。
(A) Pick up some office supplies (A) 事務用品を買う
(B) Go shopping with the man (B) 男性と買い物に行く
(C) Stay home and write (C) 家に残って書く
(D) Copy some computer files (D) コンピュータのファイルをコピーする

男性がセールに誘ったところ，女性は I would, but I'm going to be up all night trying to get this paper done. と述べて断っている。I would (go), ... は「レポートがなければ行くのに」という意味の仮定法表現なので，女性がセールに行かずにレポートに取り組むつもりであるとわかる。よって，(C) が正答。Any chance ... は Is there any chance...「～の可能性はありますか」の省略。pick up, supplies, files などの断片的な繰り返しから (A) や (D) にひっかからないように。

ボキャブラリー □ **stationery**「文房具」 □ **school supplies**「学用品」
□ **staple**「ホチキスの針」

## 30. 成績についての学生同士の会話 正答：A

074

| | |
|---|---|
| **M** Mark told me that you are pretty disappointed with your score on the biology final. | **M:** マークが言ってたけど，生物学の期末試験の点数にずいぶんがっかりしてるんだってね。 |
| **W** Disappointed? I'm totally depressed. | **W:** がっかりなんてものじゃないわ。すっかり落ち込んでいるの。 |

What does the woman mean?

(A) She was very disappointed with her test results.
(B) She is glad she finally completed the biology class.
(C) She was sad that Mark was not able to meet her.
(D) She has been under a lot of pressure this term.

女性は何と言っていますか。

(A) テストの結果にとてもがっかりしている。
(B) 生物学の授業をやっと終えてうれしい。
(C) マークに会えなくて悲しかった。
(D) 今学期は多くのプレッシャーを感じていた。

試験結果がよくなかったことについて女性は Disappointed? と返しているが，これは男性のことばを受けて「disappointed（がっかりした）どころではない」という意味。続けて totally depressed「すっかり落ち込んだ」と，もっと重い表現のほうが適切だと述べている。いずれにしてもがっかりしていることは事実なので，(A) が正答。biology, Mark の繰り返しだけで (B) (C) を選んだり，final—finally, depressed—pressure という類似の発音から (B) (D) にひっかかったりしないように。

ボキャブラリー □ **biology**「生物学」 □ **final**「期末試験」 □ **depressed**「意気消沈した」

## Questions 31-34　*Long Conversation 1*

076
キャンパスでの学生同士の会話。これから部の勧誘活動をする男性に，女性は自分も男性の所属するダンス部に興味があると告げる。

| | |
|---|---|
| **Listen to the following conversation between two students.** | **2人の学生による次の会話を聞きなさい。** |
| **W** Hi, Charlie. Where are you headed? | W: こんにちは，チャーリー。どこに行くの？ |
| **M** Hi, Cassandra. Q31 I'm on my way over to the student union. Since it's the beginning of a new term, Q32 our dance club is recruiting new members. We've got a desk set up right outside the student cafe. | M: やあ，カサンドラ。Q31 学生会館に行くところさ。新学期の初めだから，Q32 うちのダンス部が新入部員の勧誘をしているんだ。学生用のカフェのすぐ外に受付デスクを出してね。 |
| **W** I remember. You did the same thing at the beginning of the school year, right? How'd it go? | W: 覚えているわ。年度の初めにも同じことをしていたわよね。あれはどうだったの？ |
| **M** Great. Well, sort of great. We found lots of new members—17 to be exact—but almost all of them were women. That'd be OK if we were a ballet group, but Q33 social dancing is much more fun when there's an equal number of men and women. | M: 成功さ。いや，そこそこかな。たくさんの新メンバー，正確に言えば17人見つかったんだけど，ほぼ全員が女性だったんだ。バレエならそれでもいいけど，Q33 社交ダンスは男女同数のほうがずっと楽しいからね。 |
| **W** So you're not recruiting any more women? That's too bad. I was actually thinking of joining myself. | W: じゃあ，もう女性を募集するつもりはないのね？　残念だわ。実は私も入ろうかと思っていたの。 |
| **M** Oh, we're not restricting the number of women who join. The more, the merrier. It's just that Q33 we hope to find a few more men who might be interested in learning how to dance with a partner. You know anyone? | M: いや，入りたいっていう女性の数は制限していないよ。人数は多いほど楽しいからね。ただパートナーとの踊りを習いたいっていうQ33 男性があと何人かいればなって。だれか心当たりはある？ |
| **W** Well, Q34 my boyfriend's on the football team. Since it's off-season for them now, they should have time. Q34 I bet I can convince some of them that dancing would be a good way for them to stay in shape and meet some nice people at the same time. | W: そうね，Q34 私の彼がフットボール・チームに入ってるの。今はシーズンオフだから，彼らなら時間があるはずね。Q34 体型を保って，しかも同時にすてきな人にもめぐり会うにはダンスがいいって，きっとチームの何人かを説得できると思うわ。 |

## 31.

正答：C

077

Where is the man going?

男性はどこに行くところですか。

(A) To football practice
(B) To a dance performance
(C) To the student center
(D) To a job recruitment fair

(A) フットボールの練習へ
(B) ダンスの公演へ
(C) 学生会館へ
(D) 就職情報フェアへ

行き先を尋ねる女性に対して，男性は I'm on my way over to the student union. と答えている。on *one's* way (over) to ... は「～へ行く途中で」という意味。よって，student union を student center と言い換えている (C) が正答。

## 32.

正答：B

077

What kind of club does the man belong to?

男性はどんな種類の部に所属していますか。

(A) Classical ballet
(B) Social dance
(C) American football
(D) Aerobic exercise

(A) クラシックバレエ
(B) 社交ダンス
(C) アメリカンフットボール
(D) エアロビクス

男性が our dance club と言っていることから，彼自身がダンス部員であるとわかる。また，この後の social dancing，dance with a partner といった表現から，社交ダンス部であるとわかる。よって，(B) が正答。That'd be OK if we were a ballet group が仮定法過去で，現在の事実に反する内容であると理解できないと，(A) を選んでしまう。(C) は女性のボーイフレンドが所属している部。

## 33.

正答：C

077

What kind of problem is the man's club experiencing?

男性の所属する部はどのような問題を抱えていますか。

(A) A shortage of new members
(B) A loss of financial support
(C) An imbalance between sexes
(D) A lack of practice space

(A) 新メンバーの不足
(B) 金銭的な援助の打ち切り
(C) 男女数の不均衡
(D) 練習場所の不足

男性は，女性部員の人数が多いが，社交ダンスは much more fun when there's an equal number of men and women「男女同数だとずっと楽しい」と述べ，we hope to find a few more men「もっと男性がほしい」と答えている。つまり，男性と女性の人数の釣り合いがとれていないのが現状だから，(C) が正答となる。

## 34. 正答：A

077 What does the woman say she will do?

(A) Talk to members of the football team
(B) Take a new exercise course
(C) Telephone the man tomorrow
(D) Reserve a studio for the dance club's practice

女性は何をするつもりだと言っていますか。

(A) フットボール・チームのメンバーに話をする
(B) 新しい運動コースをとる
(C) 明日，男性に電話する
(D) ダンス部の練習のためにスタジオを予約する

会話の最後で女性は，I bet I can convince some of them ...「きっとチームの何人かを説得できると思うわ」と，フットボール・チームのメンバーに話してみると言っている。よって，(A) が正答。

---

ボキャブラリー
- □ **be headed (to ...)**「(〜に) 向かう」
- □ **recruit**「新人を入れる」
- □ **to be exact**「正確には」
- □ **social dancing**「社交ダンス」
- □ **restrict**「〜を制限する」
- □ **merry**「楽しい」
- □ **stay in shape**「体型を保つ」

## Questions 35-38 *Long Conversation 2*

078 学生同士の会話。要する労力に見合わないため，女性は奨学金の申請をあきらめようとしている。男性は，成績優秀者のための別の奨学金があると助言している。

**Listen to the following conversation between two students.**

**2人の学生による次の会話を聞きなさい。**

**M** Hi Tina. Say, how are your scholarship applications coming along? Last time we talked you were in the middle of gathering information on all the different national grants and awards available to students.

M: やあ，ティナ。そういえば，奨学金申請の結果はどうだった？　最後にきみと話したときには，学生が利用できるさまざまな政府助成金や奨学金について情報を集めているところだったよね。

**W** Things have changed. When I realized how much paperwork those scholarship applications required, and I checked out how many people apply for them and how few scholarships are actually awarded, Q36 I decided just to take out an additional loan.

W: 状況が変わったの。そうした奨学金の申請にどれだけ多くの書類が必要かわかったし，それに，応募者はとても多いのに実際に出る奨学金の件数はとても少ないってわかったから，Q36 追加融資を受けることにしたの。

**M** I'm sorry to hear that. It's going to be terrible to graduate with so much debt. Also, I know you've got a high G.P.A. and your professors think very well of you.

M: それは残念だったね。たくさんの借金を抱えて卒業するのはたいへんだろうに。それに，きみは評定平均も高いし，教授たちも評価してくれているのに。

**W** It's nice that you say that, Jimmy. But, in the end, I did a careful cost-benefit analysis, and Q35 when I estimated how much work the applications would require, and how slim my chances were for landing a decent sum of money, it just seemed that my efforts were better put into studying for my courses and graduating on time. That's why I decided to go with a bank loan.

W: そう言ってもらえるとうれしいわ，ジミー。でも結局，慎重に費用対効果分析をしてみると，Q35 申請にかかる労力と，ある程度まとまった金額を手にできる可能性の低さを考えたら，しっかり勉強して予定どおりに卒業するほうがいいと思ったの。だから銀行からお金を借りることにしたわけ。

**M** I see your point. Q37 One recommendation I would make, though, is to talk to your advisor and also maybe some of the professors you are close to in your department. There are some scholarships within the university that departments can award to outstanding students. In these cases, there's no application process at all.

M: なるほどね。Q37 でも，ぼくがひとつアドバイスをするとしたら，きみの指導教官と，あとは学部内の親しい教授何人かに相談してみることだね。優秀な学生に学部が与えることができる学内奨学金がいくつかあるんだ。それなら申請の手続きもまったくいらないしね。

| | | |
|---|---|---|
| W | I hadn't heard about them. | W: そんな奨学金があるなんて初めて聞いたわ。 |
| M | Yeah, I think they're called endowed scholarships. Each department has one or two. I don't know if they involve a lot of money, but I'm sure every little bit would help. | M: うん，たしか奨学基金っていうんだ。各学部がひとつかふたつ用意しているよ。たくさんの額をもらえるかどうかわからないけど，少しでもきっと役には立つと思うよ。 |
| W | You can say that again. Q38 I was on my way to talk to my advisor right now, anyway. You can bet I'm going to ask him about this. | W: そのとおりね。Q38 いずれにせよ，ちょうど指導教官に話しにいくところだったの。もちろんその奨学金のことを聞いてみるわ。 |

## 35.

正答：D

079

Why did the woman decide not to apply for a scholarship?

なぜ女性は奨学金を申請しないことにしたのですか。

(A) She missed the application deadline.
(B) She could not gather enough information.
(C) She found out her grades were too low to qualify.
(D) She did not think it was worth the effort.

(A) 申請期限に間に合わなかった。
(B) 十分な情報を集めることができなかった。
(C) 成績が低すぎて申請資格がないとわかった。
(D) 労力を費やす価値がないと思った。

女性は奨学金申請をやめ，銀行の融資を申し込むことにした理由を，2度繰り返して説明している。要約すれば，how slim my chances were for landing a decent sum of money「まとまった金額を借りられるチャンスが少ない」ということ。したがって，彼女は my efforts were better put into studying「労力を勉強に向けたほうがいい」と結論づけている。これを言い換えている (D) が正答となる。

## 36.

正答：B

079

How did the woman obtain the money she needed?

女性はどのようにして必要なお金を工面しましたか。

(A) She asked her parents.
(B) She borrowed it.
(C) She won a scholarship.
(D) She worked overtime.

(A) 両親に頼んだ。
(B) 借りた。
(C) 奨学金をもらった。
(D) 残業をした。

女性は ... to take out an additional loan と言っている。additional「さらなる，追加の」ということは，以前にもお金を借りていたということ。よって，これを borrowed「借りた」と言い換えている (B) が正答となる。

## 37. 正答：A

079

What does the man recommend that the woman do?

(A) Ask her advisor about scholarships within the university
(B) Discuss her need for funds with the financial aid office
(C) See if her department might grant her a research assistantship
(D) Check with the student services department about part-time jobs

男性は女性に何をするように勧めていますか。

(A) 指導教官に学内奨学金について尋ねる
(B) 学資援助課で資金を必要としていることを相談する
(C) 学科から研究助手の仕事をもらえないか調べてみる
(D) 学生課にアルバイトについて問い合わせる

男性は One recommendation I would make, though, is to talk to your advisor と言って，指導教官に相談に行くよう勧め，There are some scholarships within the university ...「学内奨学金がある」と理由を説明している。よって，(A) が正答。

## 38. 正答：D

079

What does the woman plan to do next?

(A) Apply for a job
(B) Go to the bank
(C) Study at the library
(D) Meet with her advisor

女性は次に何をするつもりですか。

(A) 仕事に申し込む
(B) 銀行に行く
(C) 図書館で勉強する
(D) 指導教官に会う

会話の最後で女性は，I was on my way to talk to my advisor right now ...「ちょうど指導教官に話しにいくところだったの」と述べている。よって，(D) が正答。

---

ボキャブラリー
- □ **scholarship**「奨学金」
- □ **come along**「(仕事などが) 進む」
- □ **grant**「補助金，助成金」
- □ **cost-benefit analysis**「費用対効果分析」
- □ **on time**「予定どおりに」
- □ **I see your point.**「わかりました，ごもっとも」
- □ **advisor**「指導教官」
- □ **outstanding**「優秀な」
- □ **You can say that again.**「そのとおり」

## Questions 39-42 *Principal Research Subjects*

081

1 実験対象となる生物に焦点を当てた生物学の講義。
2 ショウジョウバエは成長が早いため，染色体を基礎とした遺伝学の発展に重要な役割を果たす。
3 マウスも成長，繁殖が早いため重要であり，細胞組織がヒトによく似ており，物質の毒性を調べる研究に特に適している。
4 霊長類，特にチンパンジーは遺伝子構造の99%がヒトと共通しており，ヒトの生体に関わるさまざまな研究に加え，心理学的な実験にも活用される。

**Listen to part of a talk in a biology class. The class has been studying the history of medical research.**

**生物学の授業での講義の一部を聞きなさい。この授業では，医学研究の歴史について学んでいます。**

1 Q39 There are three really important organisms and animals that provide the basis for biological research. In fact, you might call them our principal research subjects in biology: the fruit fly, the mouse and the chimpanzee.

パラグラフ1 Q39 生物学の研究の基礎をなすのは３種のとても重要な生物や動物です。事実，これらが生物学の主たる研究対象であると言えます。ショウジョウバエ，マウス，それからチンパンジーです。

2 First comes the fruit fly. Because fruit flies develop from egg to reproductive adult in just 10 days, they enable researchers to study generational changes in a relatively short period of time. Early in the 20th century, fruit flies were crucial to the establishment of a theory of heredity based upon chromosomes. In 1910, for instance, Thomas Morgan used fruit flies to show how genes control heredity, and Q40 he pointed to changes in the eye color of the flies to confirm Mendel's law that hereditary units occur in pairs. Bet you didn't know that fruit flies have eye colors just like you and me. More recently, fruit flies have also been incredibly important in human genetic research, because 80 percent—that's right, 80 percent—of its genome is also common to humans. I bet you didn't know that either.

パラグラフ2 まず最初にショウジョウバエを取りあげます。ショウジョウバエは，卵から生殖可能な成虫へわずか10日で成長するので，研究者たちは比較的短い期間で発生的変化を調べることができます。20世紀初頭，ショウジョウバエは染色体を基礎とした遺伝学の成立にとって，きわめて重要でした。例えば1910年にトーマス・モーガンは，遺伝子がどのように遺伝を支配しているのかを明らかにするためにショウジョウバエを用いました。Q40 彼はショウジョウバエの目の色の変化に注目し，遺伝単位が２つ一組で生じるというメンデルの法則を確認したのです。みなさんはきっと，ショウジョウバエにも私たちと同じように目に色があることを知らなかったでしょうね。もっと最近でも，ショウジョウバエは人間の遺伝子研究にきわめて重要になっています。というのは，ショウジョウバエのゲノムの80%，そう，なんと80%もがヒトと共通しているからです。このことも，みなさんはきっと知らなかったでしょうね。

3 Another really important creature is the mouse. Q41 Number one, because mice also reproduce quickly and, number two, develop rapidly, they are ideal for research. Yet another advantage that mice have, especially over fruit flies, is that they are warm-blooded mammals and their tissues are quite similar to humans. They are excellent research subjects if one wants to check the toxicity of a substance; that is, for example, whether a chemical is cancer-causing. Like fruit flies, mice have also been terrifically important in genetic research, since they share not 80 percent of their genome with humans, but 95 percent.

パラグラフ3 もうひとつ，とても重要な生物にマウスがあります。Q41 第一に，マウスも早く繁殖し，第二に，急速に成長します。ですから，研究に好都合なのです。しかし，特にショウジョウバエと比べた場合のマウスのもうひとつの利点は，温血の哺乳動物であり，その細胞組織がヒトによく似ていることです。ある物質の毒性を調べたい場合などの研究対象にマウスは適しています。例えば，ある化学物質に発がん性があるかどうかを調べるときなどです。ショウジョウバエと同様に，マウスも遺伝子研究においてきわめて重要でした。なぜならマウスのゲノムは，80% どころかその 95% がヒトと共通しているからです。

4 The third indispensable type of research subject is primates, particularly chimpanzees, since they share nearly 99 percent of their genetic make-up with humans. In fact, primates have been involved in almost every kind of important scientific research that has shed light on how humans work—genetic, anatomical, reproductive, developmental, and so on. Q42 But one of the things that especially distinguishes primates as research subjects is that psychological research can be done on them. Since they share many of the same emotional and psychological states as humans, we can find out a great deal about what motivates men and women, the effect of feeling upon physical condition, and what causes adverse mental health.

パラグラフ4 研究対象として欠かせない第三の生物は霊長類，中でもチンパンジーです。というのも，チンパンジーは，その遺伝子構造のほぼ 99% がヒトと共通しているからです。霊長類は，人間の生態――遺伝，生体構造，生殖，発達などを解明するほぼすべての重要な科学研究に必要とされてきました。Q42 しかし，研究対象として霊長類が特に際立っている理由のひとつは，心理学的研究を行えるということです。チンパンジーはヒトと共通の感情的，心理的状態を数多く有しているので，人間に意欲を起こさせるのは何か，感情が身体に及ぼす影響，精神症状を引き起こすのは何かといったことについて，実に多くを知ることができるのです。

## 39.

正答：C

082

What does the talk mainly discuss?

(A) Designing a research methodology
(B) Choosing a research topic
(C) Types of research subjects
(D) New fields of biological research

この講義は主として何を論じていますか。

(A) 研究方法の設計
(B) 研究主題の選択
(C) 研究対象の種類
(D) 生物学研究の新たな対象分野

講義の冒頭1で，生物学には three really important organisms and animals「3種のとても重要な生物や動物」があり，これらが our principal research subjects in biology「生物学の主たる研究対象」であると説明されている。またこの3種，the fruit fly, the mouse, and the chimpanzee について，順次，具体的に説明されているので，(C) が正答。

## 40.

正答：D

082

According to the professor, what particular characteristic of fruit flies was used to establish principles of heredity?

(A) Size
(B) Sex
(C) Life span
(D) Eye color

教授によれば，遺伝の法則を確立するのに用いられたショウジョウバエの特質は何ですか。

(A) 体長
(B) 性別
(C) 寿命
(D) 目の色

2では，実験対象の生物としてショウジョウバエの特質が解説されている。設問文中の principles of heredity とは，講義で具体的に説明されている Mendel's law のこと。よって，この直前部分で言及された changes in the eye color，すなわち (D) が正答となる。

## 41.

正答：A

082

According to the professor, what advantage do mice offer medical researchers?

(A) They develop quickly.
(B) They require little care.
(C) Their genes mutate more rapidly than humans.
(D) Their nervous systems do not feel pain.

教授によれば，マウスは医学研究者にどのような利点をもたらしますか。

(A) 成長が早い。
(B) ほとんど世話をしなくてよい。
(C) ヒトより早く遺伝子が変異する。
(D) 神経系が痛みを感じない。

マウスの特性は3で，Number one, number two という表現に続いて，reproduce quickly「繁殖が早い」と develop rapidly「成長が早い」の2点が挙げられている。このうち後者を同義表現で言い換えている (A) が正答。

## 42.

正答：D

082

What kind of research does the professor suggest is unique to primates?

(A) Evolutionary
(B) Reproductive
(C) Genetic
(D) Emotional

どのような研究が霊長類に特徴的である，と教授は指摘していますか。

(A) 進化
(B) 生殖
(C) 遺伝
(D) 感情

設問文の unique という表現に留意。霊長類は，genetic, anatomical, reproductive, developmental の側面から研究されているが，問われているのはあくまでも「特徴的」な側面。これについては，especially distinguishes「特に際立っている」という表現を用いて，psychological research「心理学的研究」であると指摘されている。さらに具体的に motivates「動機づける」，feeling「感情」，mental「精神面」ともあるので，これらをまとめている (D) が正答。

---

ボキャブラリー
- ☐ **organism**「生物，有機体」
- ☐ **fruit fly**「ショウジョウバエ」
- ☐ **reproductive**「生殖能力のある」
- ☐ **crucial**「非常に重要な」
- ☐ **heredity**「遺伝」
- ☐ **chromosome**「染色体」
- ☐ **gene**「遺伝子」
- ☐ **Mendel's law**「メンデルの法則」
- ☐ **genome**「ゲノム」
- ☐ **warm-blooded**「温血の」
- ☐ **tissue**「組織」
- ☐ **toxicity**「毒性」
- ☐ **cancer-causing**「発がん性の」
- ☐ **primate**「霊長類」
- ☐ **make-up**「組成，構造」
- ☐ **shed light on ...**「～の解明に役立つ」
- ☐ **anatomical**「解剖学的な，構造上の」
- ☐ **motivate**「～を刺激する」

## Questions 43-46 *Scientific Business Management*

083

1 ビジネスの講義で，近代的企業経営の父とされるフレデリック・テイラーの生涯と業績に焦点を当てる。
2 テイラーは労働者が仕事を効率よく行うための「時間と動作」の研究を行い，一本化された経営哲学を考案した。
3 テイラーは研究を著書『科学的経営の原理』にまとめ，同時に講演によってその哲学を広めようとしたが，その著書は必ずしも客観的な内容とは言えなかった。

**Listen to part of a talk in a business class. The professor is discussing the life and work of Frederick Taylor.**

**ビジネスの授業での講義の一部を聞きなさい。教授はフレデリック・テイラーの生涯と業績について論じています。**

1 Q43 Whenever the topic of factory management comes up, we usually hear the name Frederick Taylor. He was the father of scientific business management. And Taylor and his ideas have, without a doubt, been central to the development of modern managerial techniques.

パラグラフ1 Q43 工場経営の話題が出るたびに，私たちはたいていフレデリック・テイラーという名を耳にします。彼は科学的な企業経営を生み出した人物でした。また，テイラーとその思想は，近代的な経営技法の発達にとって間違いなく中心的なものでした。

2 Beginning in the late 19th century, Taylor initiated what came to be known as "time and motion" studies. Drawing on his background in engineering, he systematically timed and recorded every step of a worker's movement to examine ways in which the worker could perform his or her tasks more efficiently and effectively. He kept track of the time and analyzed the workers' physical actions—their "time and motion" on the factory floor. However, his proposed reforms extended far beyond the assembly line, since his intention was to create a unified philosophy of business that comprised accounting, purchasing, production, and inventory control. Q44 Under Taylor's plan, the traditional factory supervisor would no longer be necessary, because the firm's executives would have access to more detailed and timely information about the factory's operations. Workers would work steadily and energetically, so that ideally the factory would resemble a well-designed, smoothly running machine.

パラグラフ2 19世紀後半からテイラーは，「時間と動作」の研究として知られることになる研究を開始しました。工学の知識を利用して，彼は労働者が仕事をさらに効率よく，かつ効果的に行う方法を調べるために，労働者の動きのすべてを体系的に測定し，記録したのです。彼は時間を計測し，労働者の体の動き，つまり彼らの作業場での「時間と動作」を分析したのです。しかし，彼の改良案は組立ラインにとどまるものではありませんでした。なぜなら，彼の意図は，会計，購買，製造，在庫管理からなる一本化された経営哲学を考案することだったからです。Q44 テイラーの構想では，従来のような工場監督者は不要とされました。というのは，企業の経営陣が工場の操業に関するもっと詳細な情報を逐次手に入れることができることになるからです。労働者が絶え間なく精力的に働くことで，工場は理想的にはうまく設計され，スムーズに作動する機械のようになるのです。

| | |
|---|---|
| 3 Taylor toured the country lecturing to business managers, attempting to publicize his management philosophy. In 1911, he published his standard lecture in the form of a short book entitled *The Principles of Scientific Management*, Q45 which became an immediate best-seller and soon the most popular business book of the first half of the century. Q46 In his book he told many anecdotes taken from his own experience. Partially as a result of including so many personal episodes from his own career, the book was overly subjective and tended to overstate Taylor's own contribution to the emerging field of scientific management. | パラグラフ3 テイラーは，経営者たちに講義しながら国中をまわり，彼の経営哲学を広めようとしました。彼は1911年に，基本的な講義を『科学的経営の原理』という題の小著にまとめて出版しました。Q45 この本はすぐにベストセラーになり，やがて20世紀前半でもっとも人気のあるビジネス書になりました。Q46 本の中で彼は自分の経験から引き出した多くの逸話を語っています。彼自身の経歴からの個人的エピソードが非常に多く書かれていたこともあって，この本は主観的に過ぎ，黎明期にあった科学的経営という分野へのテイラー自身の貢献を誇張する傾向がありました。 |

## 43.

正答：B

084

What was Frederick Taylor's main area of expertise?

(A) Product planning
(B) Factory operations
(C) Finance
(D) Marketing

フレデリック・テイラーの主な専門分野は何でしたか。

(A) 商品企画
(B) 工場操業
(C) 財務
(D) マーケティング

講義の冒頭 1 で，factory management が話題になるときはフレデリック・テイラーの名前が挙がると言われていることから，彼の専門が工場経営，操業であることは明らか。この後に続く彼の生涯についての説明からも確認できる。manufacturing operations, managerial techniques, worker's movement, assembly line, factory といった語が繰り返されていることからも推測可能。よって，(B) が正答。

## 44.

正答：A

084

Under Taylor's plan, which of the following jobs might become unnecessary?

(A) Assembly-line supervisor
(B) Company president
(C) Cost accountant
(D) Production worker

テイラーの構想では，次のうちどの職が不要になりますか。

(A) 組立ライン監督者
(B) 社長
(C) 原価計算係
(D) 製造労働者

設問にある Under Taylor's plan という表現が講義中でも Under Taylor's plan, the traditional factory supervisor would no longer be necessary とそのまま使われていたことを思い出す。ここで factory supervisor「工場監督」とは直前に assembly line の説明があることから，(A) と同義であるとわかる。

## 45. 正答：A

084

What does the professor say about Taylor's book, *The Principles of Scientific Management*?

教授はテイラーの著書『科学的経営の原理』について何と述べていますか。

(A) It was an immediate sensation.
(B) It was widely criticized by business managers.
(C) It was published long after it was written.
(D) It was really authored by someone else.

(A) すぐに大評判になった。
(B) 企業経営者たちに広く批判された。
(C) 執筆後かなり経ってから出版された。
(D) 実は他人によって書かれた。

3 でテイラーの著書 *The Principles of Scientific Management* は an immediate best-seller「すぐにベストセラーに」, the most popular business book of the first half of the century「同世紀前半もっとも人気のあったビジネス本」と描写されているので，非常に広く読まれ，評判になったことがわかる。よって，(A) が正答。

## 46. 正答：C

084

According to the professor, what was one of the shortcomings of Taylor's book, *The Principles of Scientific Management*?

教授によれば，テイラーの著書『科学的経営の原理』の欠点のひとつは何でしたか。

(A) Insufficient data collection
(B) Outdated managerial techniques
(C) Overuse of personal observations
(D) Unsystematic analysis

(A) 不十分なデータ収集
(B) 時代遅れの経営技法
(C) 個人的な逸話の過度の使用
(D) 非体系的な分析

3 のテイラーの著書に関する解説の中で，教授は many anecdotes taken from his own experience「個人的な体験からの逸話の多用」, so many personal episodes from his own career「個人的なエピソードが多い」と繰り返して，この本の問題は個人的体験を過度に引いていることだと指摘している。よって，(C) が正答となる。

---

ボキャブラリー
- ☐ **management**「経営，管理」
- ☐ **managerial technique**「経営手法」
- ☐ **draw on ...**「～を利用する，～を源とする」
- ☐ **systematically**「体系的に」
- ☐ **assembly line**「組立ライン」
- ☐ **philosophy**「哲学」
- ☐ **comprise**「～を含む」
- ☐ **accounting**「会計，経理」
- ☐ **inventory**「在庫」
- ☐ **factory supervisor**「工場監督者」
- ☐ **publicize**「～を宣伝する」
- ☐ **anecdote**「逸話」

## Questions 47-50 *History of Jazz*

085

| | |
|---|---|
| 1 | 音楽鑑賞の講義で，ジャズの歴史から「バップ」を取りあげる。 |
| 2 | 「バップ」は1940年代に始まったエキサイティングなスタイルである。 |
| 3 | 「バップ」では，演奏家のテクニックが脚光を浴びた。特にチャーリー・パーカーが有名である。 |
| 4 | 「バップ」は速いテンポで演奏され，多くの音と急変するハーモニーに満ちたソロを特徴としている。 |
| 5 | また，多彩なスタイルの演奏を残した人物にマイルス・デイビスがいる。 |

**Listen to part of a talk in a music appreciation class. The students have been studying the history of jazz.**

**音楽鑑賞の授業での講義の一部を聞きなさい。学生たちは，ジャズの歴史について学んでいます。**

1 Now that we've covered the origins of jazz in the late 19th-century work chants, spirituals, and folk music of Black Americans, and we've read about, discussed and listened to examples of early blues and ragtime and the great songs played by the big bands of the swing era, Q47 we're ready for my favorite jazz—"bop." I'm happy to say that the next few classes are going to be even more interesting and fun.

パラグラフ1 ジャズの起源が19世紀後半の労働歌，黒人霊歌，アメリカ黒人の民俗音楽にあることを見てきました。それから，初期のブルースやラグタイム，スイング時代のビッグバンドが演奏する名曲について読んだり，議論したり，曲を聞いたりしてきましたね。Q47 次は私のお気に入りのジャズについて話をしましょう。それは「バップ」です。これから数回の授業は，これまでよりもさらにおもしろくて楽しいものになりますよ。

2 "Bop" may be the most spirited and exciting of jazz forms. It arose out of informal performances—jam sessions, as they were called—in New York City's Harlem in 1941 and 1942. Moreover, the bop era was probably the longest-lasting jazz era—stretching from the early 1940's to 1960.

パラグラフ2 「バップ」はおそらくジャズの中でもっとも生き生きして，エキサイティングなスタイルです。それは1941年と1942年にニューヨークのハーレムで行われた，ジャム・セッションと呼ばれる形式ばらない演奏から生まれました。また，バップ時代は，おそらくはもっとも長く続いたジャズの時代で，1940年代から1960年に渡っていました。

3 Although bop began in relaxed settings among small groups of musicians, it required extremely fine, indeed almost virtuoso technique to play. Charlie Parker was the leading bop personality. Q49 It was his exciting alto saxophone flights that won him the popular nickname of "Bird." Parker was perhaps the most skillful of all bop musicians.

パラグラフ3 バップは小グループのミュージシャンらの間で，うち解けた雰囲気の中から生まれたわけですが，それを演奏するにはきわめて繊細で，まさに名人技と言ってよいテクニックが必要でした。チャーリー・パーカーはバップを代表する演奏家でした。Q49 彼がよく知られる「バード」という愛称を得たのは，そのアルトサックスのエキサイティングで羽ばたくような演奏のためでした。パーカーは，おそらくすべてのバップ・ミュージシャンの中でもっとも演奏がうまかったと言えます。

4 As you will notice in a minute, Q48 bop pieces were played at the fastest tempos ever performed in jazz until that time. Bop featured musical solos with many notes and startling, quickly changing harmonies—this is one reason why so many individual bop musicians are famous. Bop gave solo musicians a chance to shine. Even though bop was difficult to sing, a few vocalists such as Sarah Vaughan had the necessary control and voice range. Vaughan did with her voice what other musicians did with their instruments.

パラグラフ4 みなさんもすぐにわかりますが，Q48 バップの曲はそれまでのジャズの中でもっとも速いテンポで演奏されました。バップは，たくさんの音と驚くほど急速に変わるハーモニーに満ちたソロを特徴としており，これが数多くのバップ・ミュージシャンが個人として有名になったひとつの理由です。バップはソロ・ミュージシャンたちに活躍の場を与えたのです。バップを歌うことは難しかったのですが，サラ・ボーンのようないく人かのボーカリストたちは，そのために必要なボイスコントロールの力と声域を持っていました。ボーンは，他のミュージシャンが楽器でやったことを，自分の声で行ったのです。

5 There was one musician who played in almost every possible kind of bop era musical group—Miles Davis. When Davis was 19, he became the trumpeter in Charlie Bird Parker's bop group. Then, in the 1950's, Davis broke away to lead jazz groups that played cool jazz and hard bop. Sometimes Davis's trumpet playing was fast and angry, but at other times it was lonely and haunting. Q50 Next, what I want to do is play diverse selections of bop from Miles Davis's amazing recordings.

パラグラフ5 バップ時代のほとんどありとあらゆる種類のグループで演奏したミュージシャンがひとりいます。マイルス・デイビスです。デイビスは19歳のとき，チャーリー・バード・パーカーのバップ・グループのトランペッターになりました。それから1950年代に，デイビスはそこから離れ，クールジャズとハードバップを演奏するグループを率います。デイビスのトランペット演奏は，あるときは速くて怒りに満ちていましたが，またあるときにはそれはもの悲しくて，心にしみるものでした。Q50 では次に，マイルス・デイビスのすばらしいレコーディングから，さまざまなバップの曲をかけてみたいと思います。

## 47. 正答：B

086

What is the main topic of the talk?

(A) The origin of jazz
(B) Bop music and musicians
(C) Types of bop solos
(D) Miles Davis's musical career

この講義の主題は何ですか。

(A) ジャズの起源
(B) バップとそのミュージシャン
(C) バップ・ソロの種類
(D) マイルス・デイビスの音楽キャリア

教授は冒頭 1 でこれまでの講義の内容を振り返り，今日の授業の内容を紹介して we're ready for my favorite jazz—"bop" と述べている。また，講義の主題が bop であることは，この語が何度も繰り返されていることからも明らか。さらに Charlie Parker，Sarah Vaughan，Miles Davis と具体的なミュージシャンが取りあげられているので，正答は (B) となる。(A) は漠然としすぎており，(C) (D) は解説の一部ではあるが講義全体の主題とは言えない。

## 48. 正答：B

086

According to the professor, what was an unusual characteristic of bop?

(A) It was usually played by large orchestras.
(B) It was often performed at an unusually fast speed.
(C) It emphasized group harmony over individual performance.
(D) It became the most popular music of the 1930's.

教授によれば，バップのまれな特徴は何でしたか。

(A) 通常は大オーケストラで演奏された。
(B) しばしば非常に速いスピードで演奏された。
(C) 個人の演奏よりもグループのハーモニーを強調した。
(D) 1930 年代のもっともポピュラーな音楽となった。

バップの特徴について 4 で ... played at the fastest tempos ever performed in jazz until that time「それまでのジャズの中でもっとも速いテンポで演奏された」，startling, quickly changing harmonies「驚くほど急激に変わるハーモニー」と説明されている。よって，(B) が正答。

## 49. 正答：C

086

What instrument did Charlie Bird Parker play?

(A) The piano
(B) The trombone
(C) The saxophone
(D) The trumpet

チャーリー・バード・パーカーはどんな楽器を演奏しましたか。

(A) ピアノ
(B) トロンボーン
(C) サクソフォーン
(D) トランペット

3 に，It was his exciting alto saxophone flights that won him the popular nickname of "Bird"「彼がよく知られる「バード」という愛称を得たのは，そのアルトサックスのエキサイティングで羽ばたくような演奏のためだった」とあるので，(C) が正答。

## 50.

正答：D

086

What will the professor do next?

(A) Personally perform a Miles Davis song
(B) Talk about Charlie Parker's career
(C) Discuss the post-bop era
(D) Play various examples of bop

教授は次に何をしますか。

(A) マイルス・デイビスの曲を自分で演奏する
(B) チャーリー・パーカーの生涯について話す
(C) バップ後の時代について論じる
(D) さまざまなバップの曲をかける

最後の部分で教授は Next, what I want to do is play diverse selections of bop from Miles Davis's amazing recordings.「マイルス・デイビスの曲をかけたいと思います」と言っているので，(D) が正答。various examples と diverse selections が同義である。この play は「演奏する」ではなく，CD やレコードを「かける」の意味。Miles Davis という固有名詞だけで (A) を選ばないように注意。

---

ボキャブラリー
- □ **chant**「歌，聖歌」
- □ **spiritual**「(黒人) 霊歌」
- □ **folk music**「民俗音楽」
- □ **swing era**「スイング時代」
- □ **arise**「生まれる」
- □ **virtuoso**「名人 (の)」
- □ **piece**「曲」
- □ **note**「音」

## Structure

### 1.
正答：D

**Although** Jackson Pollock was widely regarded as an accomplished painter, he abandoned the use of brushes and began pouring the paint straight onto the canvas.

ジャクソン・ポロックは卓越した画家として広く知られていたが，彼は絵筆の使用をやめ，キャンバスに絵の具を直接注ぐ手法を始めた。

Jackson Pollock was ... と he abandoned ... の2つの節があるので，空所にはこれらをつなぐ従位接続詞が入る。よって，(D) が正答。despite は「～にもかかわらず」という意味の前置詞。that は接続詞で名詞節を導くが，従位接続詞ではないので，2つの節を接続できない。nonetheless は「それにもかかわらず」という意味の副詞。

ボキャブラリー □ **accomplished**「熟達した」

### 2.
正答：C

A musical suite is a set of instrumental pieces **often assembled** from a stage work such as a ballet or an opera.

組曲とは，器楽曲を組み合わせたものであり，バレエやオペラのような舞台作品からまとめられることが多い。

空所前の名詞 instrumental pieces を後ろから形容詞的に修飾し，かつ後ろの from に正しくつながるのは (C)。assembled は過去分詞の形容詞用法の後置修飾。(A) は節なので，接続詞なしに文中に挿入できない。(B) の関係詞節は文中に挿入できるが，assemble が「～を集める」という能動態なので文意に即さない。(D) は which are often assembled であれば可。

ボキャブラリー □ **suite**「組曲，ひとそろい」 □ **instrumental**「楽器の」

### 3.
正答：A

**Even before the invention of antibiotics** many indigenous cultures used germ-killing medicines made from plants.

抗生物質が発明される以前ですら，多くの土着文化は植物から作った殺菌剤を使用していた。

文意が通るように，正しい語順の選択肢を選ぶ。副詞 Even「～でさえも」は，副詞句 before the invention of antibiotics を強調している。(A) が正答。

ボキャブラリー □ **antibiotic**「抗生物質」 □ **indigenous**「土着の，土地固有の」
□ **germ-killing**「殺菌作用のある」

### 4.
正答：B

Destruction of habitat is **one of the greatest threats** to many endangered species.

生息環境の破壊は，多くの絶滅危惧種にとって最大の脅威のひとつである。

選択肢中，正しく意味が通るのは (B) のみ。《one of the+ 可算名詞の複数形》で「～の中のひとつ」。

ボキャブラリー □ **habitat**「（居住・生息の）環境」 □ **threat**「脅威」
□ **endangered species**「絶滅危惧種」

## 5.

正答：A

In economics, the decline in the domestic purchasing power of a nation's currency **is referred to** as inflation.

経済学では，国の通貨が持つ国内購買力の低下はインフレーションと呼ばれる。

主語 the decline に続く述語動詞が欠落しているので，適切な動詞を補う。refer to *A* as *B*「A を B と呼ぶ」の受動態 *A* be referred to as *B*「A は B と呼ばれる」を完成させるには (A) が適切。

ボキャブラリー □ **domestic**「国内の」 □ **currency**「通貨」 □ **inflation**「インフレーション」

## 6.

正答：A

As most of its **soil is too infertile or thin** for farming, northern Minnesota's economy is largely dependent upon tourism and timber.

土壌のほとんどが農業を行うにはやせすぎており不毛なので，ミネソタ州北部の経済は観光と木材に大きく依存している。

接続詞 As ... 以下の従属節内を完成させるのに適切な語順の選択肢を選ぶ。主語 most（soil は不可算扱いなので，most も不可算扱い）に対応する述語動詞が is であること，所有格の代名詞 its には名詞が続くことに着目する。(A) が正答。

ボキャブラリー □ **infertile**「不毛の」 □ **timber**「材木」

## 7.

正答：B

According to botanists, a plant species **flourishes** depending upon air temperature, sunlight exposure, and soil fertility.

植物学者によれば，草木の成長は気温，日当り，土地の肥え具合にかかっている。

主語 a plant species に対応する述語動詞を選ぶ。species は単複同形だが，ここでは不定冠詞 a があるので単数扱いとわかる。よって，三単元の -s を伴う (B) が正答。

ボキャブラリー □ **botanist**「植物学者」 □ **temperature**「温度」

## 8.

正答：D

The value of a company's stock is determined by both its current financial strength **and** its expected future performance.

企業の株式価値は，現在の財務体質と，将来期待される業績によって決まる。

both と相関的に用いる等位接続詞は and である。(D) が正答。both *A* and *B* で「A も B も両方とも」。その他の選択肢を相関接続詞として使うときは，either *A* or *B*，not *A* but *B*，neither *A* nor *B* である。

ボキャブラリー □ **determine**「～を決める」 □ **current**「現在の」

## 9.

正答：B

The chemical composition of a substance can vary from being made up of a single pure element to a combination of many different elements in a compound.

物質の化学的な構造は，ひとつの純元素から成るものから，多くの異なる元素が化合しているものまで，さまざまである。

名詞 composition「構造, 組成」を修飾するのは形容詞である。よって, (B) が正答。(A) は副詞，(C) は名詞である。composition は「構造」という意味では不可算扱いなので，不定冠詞 A を含む (D) も誤り。

ボキャブラリー □ **composition**「構造」 □ **substance**「物質」 □ **element**「元素」

## 10.

正答：B

The question of whether alien species can play a positive role in an ecological system is still the subject of much controversy among biologists.

生態系において外来種が望ましい役割を果たしうるかという問題は，生物学者の間でいまだ多くの議論を呼んでいる。

controversy「論争，議論」は，一般的な意味では不可算扱い。よって，不可算名詞を修飾する (B) が正答。(A) (D) は可算名詞の複数形しか修飾できない。(C) は文脈に合致しない。

ボキャブラリー □ **controversy**「論争」

## 11.

正答：D

During a recession, both the increase in unemployment rate and the decrease in tax collection rate exert stress on an economy.

景気後退期には，失業の増加と税収の低下はともに経済を圧迫する。

等位接続詞 and で並列される語や句は文法的に等しくなければならない。the increase in unemployment rate ともっともバランスよく並列するのは (D) である。

ボキャブラリー □ **recession**「不景気」 □ **unemployment**「失業」

## 12.

正答：C

Of all of the Indo-European languages still spoken in Europe, Welsh is the oldest.

ヨーロッパで今日でも話されているすべての印欧基語のなかで，ウェールズ語がもっとも古い。

文脈上，最上級を用いるのが正しい。よって，(C) が正答。最上級の形容詞には通例，定冠詞 the が必要。

ボキャブラリー □ **Indo-European language**「印欧基語」

## 13.

**正答：A**

The Federal Reserve Board **is composed** of seven members who are appointed by the president of the United States and who serve fourteen-year terms.

連邦準備制度理事会は 7 人の委員によって構成され，彼らは合衆国大統領によって任命されて 14 年の任期を務める。

主語 The Federal Reserve Board に対応する述語動詞がないので，適切な動詞を含む選択肢を選ぶ。(A) か (C) に絞られるが，compose は「～を構成する」という意味の他動詞なので，ここでは受動態が適切。よって，(A) が正答となる。

ボキャブラリー □ **be composed of ...**「～から構成されている」□ **appoint**「～を任命する」
□ **term**「任期」

## 14.

**正答：D**

**In 1961**, the New Democratic Party was formed in Canada in a merger between two other political parties.

1961 年，カナダで 2 つの政党が合併し，新民主党が結成された。

空所に続く部分が文として成立しているため，独立してその文を修飾する副詞句 (D) が正答。(A) は従属接続詞 When に続く節がないので誤り。また，(B) (C) のように it was が含まれる場合は It is ... that の強調構文の可能性があるが，It was in 1961 that ... の形にならなくてはならない。

ボキャブラリー □ **merger**「合併」

## 15.

**正答：C**

**Since** the discovery of the electron, hundreds of kinds of particles have been found.

電子の発見以降，何百種もの粒子が発見された。

空所の後には節ではなく句が続いていることを確認し，正しい前置詞を選ぶ。まず接続詞の (B)，副詞の (D) を除き，(A) (C) に絞る。... have been found「(これまでに) 発見された」という述語動詞の意味と時制に合うのは，「～以来」を意味する (C)。since には前置詞のほか接続詞，副詞もあるが，いずれも主動詞は完了時制でなければならない。

ボキャブラリー □ **particle**「粒子，微分子」

## 16. is を入れて Manganese is used にする　正答：A

**Manganese is used** chiefly in the making of steel alloys, but it also has several important agricultural uses.

マンガンは主に合金鋼の製造に用いられるが，いくつかの重要な農業用の用途もある。

(A) Manganese used ... では能動態で「マンガンが～を用いた」の意味になってしまう。文意に合うように Manganese is used ...「マンガンは～に用いられる」と受動態にするのが正しい。

ボキャブラリー □ **manganese**「マンガン」　□ **alloy**「合金」

## 17. small または miniature を削除する　正答：A

The **small**［または **miniature**］size of solid-state circuits makes them ideally suited for use in the cockpits of space vehicles and aircraft.

ソリッドステート回路は小型なので，宇宙船や航空機のコックピットでの使用に適している。

(A) は small「小さい」，miniature「小型の」と意味の同じ形容詞が重複しているので，どちらか一方を削除する。このように意味の重複した不要な語を除く問題は TOEFL ITP 頻出項目のひとつ。この文の主語は circuits ではなく size なので，(B) の makes は三人称単数形で正しい。

ボキャブラリー □ **circuit**「回路」　□ **space vehicle**「宇宙船」　□ **aircraft**「航空機」《単複同形》

## 18. their を his または her もしくは his or her にする　正答：B

It is difficult for an author to detect minor errors in **his**［または**her**もしくは**his or her**］own work, so a copy editor is usually asked to perform that task.

著者が自作の細かな誤りを見つけることは難しいので，たいてい編集者がこの役目を任される。

an author を指す代名詞として数が対応するように，(B) の their を his または her，もしくは his or her とするのが正しい。文頭の It は形式主語で，対応する真主語は to detect である。

ボキャブラリー □ **copy editor**「編集者，原稿整理係」

## 19. he was also an を削除する　正答：D

Though he attended school only through the ninth grade, Richard Wright became a novelist, short-story writer, and **essayist**.

リチャード・ライトは９年生までしか学校に通わなかったものの，長編小説家，短編作家，エッセイストになった。

*A* and *B* や *A*, *B*, and *C* で並列される語や句は文法的に等しくなければならない。よって，a novelist, short-story writer と並列するように (D) he was also an essayist《節》を単に essayist とするのが正しい。

ボキャブラリー □ **attend**「～に通学する」

## 20. furnitures を furniture にする　正答：B

Early American Colonial is a style of making **furniture** which primarily utilizes maple wood.

アーリー・アメリカン・コロニアルとは家具作りの様式のひとつであり，主としてカエデ材を用いる。

furnitureは不可算名詞として扱われる集合名詞なので，常に単数形で用いる。よって，(B) furnitures は furniture とする。物質名詞と同様，量の多少は much/little で示し，数えるときには a piece of ... を用いる。baggage，luggage，machinery なども同様。

ボキャブラリー □ **primarily**「主として」 □ **utilize**「～を用いる」

## 21. the を入れて of the Southwest にする　正答：D

Perhaps the most skilled Native American horseback riders were the Apache tribe **of the Southwest**.

アメリカ先住民でもっとも馬術に長けていたのは，おそらく南西部のアパッチ族であった。

(D) の southwest は形容詞，副詞なら「南西の［へ］」だが，ここでは Southwest「南西部地方」という固有名詞で，定冠詞 the を伴う。the West「西部地方」, the South「南部地方」も同様。

ボキャブラリー □ **skilled**「熟練の」 □ **tribe**「部族」

## 22. them を it にする　正答：D

From 1978 to 1981 the Einstein telescope made important discoveries by using a complex set of reflecting surfaces to form an image of the sky and transmit **it** back to Earth.

1978 年から 1981 年にかけてアインシュタイン望遠鏡は，複雑に組み合わせた反射鏡を使って天体の像をとらえて地球に送り返す方法で重要な発見を行った。

(D) them は文脈上，an image を指すので，数を対応させて it とするのが正しい。代名詞に下線が引かれている場合，必ずそれに対応する名詞を文中に探し，数・性・格を確認する。

ボキャブラリー □ **telescope**「望遠鏡」 □ **transmit**「～を伝達する」

## 23. that abandoned または who abandoned にする　正答：B

It was the painters of the Ashcan School **that**［または **who**］**abandoned** romanticism for realism and rural beauty for urban reality.

ロマン主義を捨て写実主義をとり，田園の美しさではなく都会の現実を描いたのは，アシュカン派の画家たちだった。

設問文は It is ... that の強調構文だが，it is に対応する that が欠落しているので，(B) abandoned の前にこれを補うのが正しい。強調の対象がこの文のように「人」の場合には that の代わりに who,「もの」の場合には which が用いられることもある。

ボキャブラリー □ **romanticism**「ロマン主義」 □ **realism**「写実主義，現実主義」

## 24. usual を usually にする　正答：D

Solubility is a measure of the amount of solid or gas that will dissolve in a given amount of solvent, **usually** a liquid.

溶解度とは一定量の溶媒，たいていは液体に解ける固体もしくは気体の量を示す単位である。

文脈から判断して，liquid は a given amount of solvent の代表例であり，付加的に挙げられている。よって，(D) の形容詞 usual「通例の」を副詞形 usually「通例は」とするのが正しい。

ボキャブラリー □ **solubility**「溶解度」 □ **solid**「固体」 □ **gas**「気体」
□ **dissolve**「溶ける，～を溶かす」
□ **solvent**「溶剤；溶解力のある，支払い能力のある」□ **liquid**「液体」

## 25. on which を by which にする　正答：D

Nomination by a political party is typically the first step in a process **by which** a candidate gains political office.

政党による指名は通例，候補者が行政職に就くための過程の第一歩である。

(D) の which の先行詞は a process であり，この文のように「～の過程を経て」という意味で用いる場合，伴う前置詞は on ではなく，by または through である。

ボキャブラリー □ **nomination**「指名，任命」 □ **candidate**「候補者」

## 26. it を削除する　正答：B

Sugarcane, classified as a grass, **annually** yields over nine tons of sugar per acre.

サトウキビは草本に分類されるが，毎年１エーカーあたり９トン以上の砂糖を産出する。

主語は Sugarcane，これに対応する述語動詞は yields なので，主語として重複している (B) it を削除する。カンマにはさまれている classified as a grass は分詞構文の挿入なので，省いて考えると文構造がわかりやすくなる。

ボキャブラリー □ **sugarcane**「サトウキビ」 □ **yield**「～を産する，生ずる」 □ **acre**「エーカー」

## 27. qualities を quality にする　正答：D

Albert Ryder developed one of the most original painting styles of his time, using yellowish colors that gave his works an eerie, haunting **quality**.

アルバート・ライダーは当時もっとも独創的な画風のひとつを生み出し，黄色がかった色を作品に用いて，不気味で忘れがたい特徴を加えた。

(D) の前に不定冠詞 an があるので，quality と単数形に直すのが正しい。

ボキャブラリー □ **eerie**「不気味な，不可解な」

## 28. or を and にする　正答：C

Great care must be taken when producing silicon chips, both to prevent contamination by dust **and** to avoid manufacturing defects.

シリコンチップを製造する際は，ほこりによる汚染を防ぎ，また製造欠陥を避けるために慎重を期さなければならない。

both と相関的に用いる等位接続詞は and であるから，(C) or を and にする。both *A* and *B* で「A と B の両方とも」。or は either *A* or *B* のように用いて「A または B のいずれか」。and，or はともに等位接続詞なので，A と B は文法的に等しくなければならない。ここでは to prevent と to avoid がともに to 不定詞。

ボキャブラリー □ **contamination**「汚染」 □ **manufacturing**「製造の」 □ **defect**「欠陥」

## 29. himself を his にする　正答：B

Richard Feynman won the Nobel prize in physics for **his** work in developing principles to reliably predict the outcomes of sub-atomic events.

リチャード・ファインマンは，素粒子の作用を的確に予測する原理を打ち立てた業績で，ノーベル物理学賞を受賞した。

文脈から判断して，work「研究」は Richard Feynman のものである。よって，(B) は再帰代名詞ではなく，所有格の his とするのが正しい。誤って for himself「彼自身のために」と解釈すると，work 以下の文構造がとれなくなる。

ボキャブラリー □ **physics**「物理」 □ **principle**「原理」

## 30. property を properties にする　正答：A

In biology, there are some unusual **properties** associated with micro-organisms, such as rapid mutation and asexual reproduction.

生物学では，微生物には急速な突然変異や無性生殖などの珍しい特性があるとされている。

述語動詞が are であること，形容詞 some「いくつかの～」によって修飾されていることから，主語の (A) property は複数形にすべきである。associated 以下は過去分詞の形容詞用法で，properties を後ろから修飾している。

ボキャブラリー □ **property**「特質」 □ **reproduction**「生殖」

## 31. great を greater にする　正答：C

Typically, the weaker the immune system of an organism is, the **greater** its susceptibility to infection.

通例，生物の免疫システムが弱ければ弱いほど，伝染病に感染しやすくなる。

《the ＋比較級 , the ＋比較級》の構文「～すればするほど, ますます…する」を完成させる。(C) great は比較級にする。この構文では語順が倒置されるが，元々は the immune system of an organism is the weaker と its susceptibility to infection (is) the greater という 2 つの節がカンマをはさんで並んでいる。後節内の述語動詞は前節と重複するので省略されている。

ボキャブラリー □ **immune**「免疫の」 □ **susceptibility**「感染しやすさ」

## 32. methodically を methodical にする　正答：D

Some composers are spontaneous and imaginative in the way they create their music, while others are more orderly and **methodical**.

作曲家には，作曲の仕方が気まぐれで想像性に富む者もいれば，もっと整然として方法論的な者もいる。

等位接続詞 and, but, or によって並列される語や句は文法的に等しくなければならない。(D) は前の orderly「秩序だった，規律正しい」が形容詞なので，methodical と形容詞にする。orderly の語形 -ly から副詞と勘違いすると，誤りを見落としてしまう。

ボキャブラリー □ **spontaneous**「自発的な」 □ **imaginative**「想像力に富む」

## 33. **them** を **themselves** にする 正答：B

Throughout American history, immigrants have typically been able to support **themselves** only by taking the lowest paying jobs.

アメリカではいつの時代も，移民はたいてい，最低賃金の仕事をするだけで生計を立てることができた。

文脈上，support の目的語が指すのは主語 immigrants であるので，再帰代名詞でなければならない。よって，(B) は themselves とするのが正しい。

ボキャブラリー □ **immigrant**「移民」

## 34. **a** を **the** にする 正答：C

Jazz, which began to emerge at the end of the 19th century, is considered **the** first major musical form to originate in the United States.

ジャズは 19 世紀末に登場したが，アメリカで誕生した初めての主要な音楽形式であると考えられている。

first は「第一番目の，最初の」という意味では，通例，定冠詞 the が必要である。(C) a を the とする。

ボキャブラリー □ **originate**「生まれる」

## 35. **its** を **their** にする 正答：A

Because of **their** poor topsoil and sparse rainfall, the plains of eastern Montana are utilized more for grazing than farming.

やせた表土と少ない降雨のため，モンタナ州東部の平原は農業よりも放牧に用いられている。

文脈から判断して，poor topsoil and sparse rainfall は the plains のものなので，(A) は単数を受ける its ではなく，複数を受ける their とするのが正しい。

ボキャブラリー □ **sparse**「まばらな」 □ **grazing**「放牧」

## 36. **possible** を **possibly** にする 正答：B

According to zoologists, the horseshoe crab is **possibly** the oldest living animal species on Earth.

動物学者によれば，おそらく，カブトガニが地球上で最古の生物種である。

文脈から判断して，the horseshoe crab is ... に続く補語は species であるべき。(B) possible は形容詞だと補語になってしまうので，possibly「たぶん」と副詞形にして，文全体を修飾させるのが正しい。

ボキャブラリー □ **zoologist**「動物学者」

## 37. during を when にする　正答：A

It was not until 1920 **when** the Nineteenth Amendment was ratified that American women were finally granted the right to vote.

憲法修正 19 条が批准されて，ようやくアメリカで女性に選挙権が認められたのは 1920 年のことだった。

1920 という時を表す名詞と the Nineteenth Amendment 以下の節を接続できるのは，関係副詞 when である。(A) during は前置詞なので，後にとれるのは語・句のみ。

ボキャブラリー □ **ratify**「〜を批准する」 □ **grant**「〜を授ける」

## 38. supporter を supporters にする　正答：A

One of the most vocal **supporters** of the principle of civil disobedience, the philosopher Henry David Thoreau spent a night in jail in 1846 for refusing to pay taxes.

市民的不服従の原則をもっとも積極的に支援した人物のひとりである哲学者のヘンリー・デイビッド・ソローは，1846 年，納税を拒否したかどで一晩，留置された。

「〜の中のひとつ」は《one of the ＋可算名詞の複数形》で表す。よって，(A) は supporters と複数形にするのが正しい。

ボキャブラリー □ **civil disobedience**「市民的不服従」 □ **jail**「留置場」

## 39. awarded を was awarded にする　正答：C

For his study of the regulation of cholesterol and fatty acid in the body, Conrad Bloch **was awarded** a Nobel Prize in medicine in 1964.

コンラッド・ブロックは，体内のコレスレロールと脂肪酸の抑制に関する研究で，1964 年にノーベル医学賞を受賞した。

文意から award「(賞・メダルなどを) 授与する」は能動態ではなく受動態にすべきである。よって, (C) は was awarded とするのが正しい。なお, award は《award ＋人＋賞》または《awarad ＋賞＋ to 人》の形で用いる。

ボキャブラリー □ **acid**「酸」 □ **medicine**「医学」

## 40. lose を losing にする　正答：C

William Jennings Bryan, an American populist politician, is best known for **losing** presidential elections in 1896, 1900, and 1908.

アメリカの人民主義の政治家, ウィリアム・ジェニングズ・ブライアンは，1896 年，1900 年, 1908 年の大統領選挙に落選したことでよく知られている。

前置詞 for に続く語は名詞形でなければならない。よって (C) lose を losing と動名詞にするのが正しい。

ボキャブラリー □ **populist**「人民主義者の」 □ **election**「選挙」

## Questions 1-10 *Minerals*

1 ミネラルは人体と食物に含まれる栄養素である。
2 体内では生理的な触媒として，栄養の摂取や抗体の供給などに重要な役割を果たす。
3 ミネラルは食事で摂取しなくてはならない。特に不足しがちなのはカルシウム，鉄分などである。ミネラル不足は健康に深刻な影響を及ぼすが，ミネラルは互いに影響し合うので，個別に考えることはできない。

1 Q2 Minerals are nutrients that exist in the body and in food in organic and inorganic combinations. Q2 All tissues and internal fluids of living things contain varying quantities of them. Q2 Q3 **They** are constituents of bones, teeth, soft tissue, muscle, blood, and nerve cells. They are important factors in maintaining physiological processes, strengthening skeletal structures, and preserving the vigor of the heart and brain as well as all muscle and nerve systems.

パラグラフ 1 Q2 ミネラルは人体，また有機性，無機性の化合物に含まれる栄養素である。Q2 生命体の全組織と体液には，さまざまな分量のミネラルが含まれている。Q2 Q3 ミネラルは骨，歯，柔組織，筋肉，血液，神経細胞の構成要素である。ミネラルは生理的プロセスを維持し，骨格を強化し，心臓と脳および筋肉と神経系統の活力を保つうえで重要な成分である。

2 Within the body, minerals play a variety of significant roles. They act as a Q4 **catalyst** for many biological reactions, Q5 including muscle response, the transmission of messages through the nervous system, digestion, and the utilization of nutrients in foods. Q5 Furthermore, they are important in the production of hormones and thus influence physical growth. On a daily basis, they are necessary for the absorption of vitamins. Zinc, iron, copper, magnesium, and potassium are five minerals that are particularly involved in digestion and metabolism. Minerals also keep blood and tissue fluids from becoming either too acidic or too alkaline, and they permit other nutrients to pass into the bloodstream. In addition, they help draw chemical substances in and out of the cells, and Q6 they aid in the distribution of antibodies when a foreign or toxic element enters the body.

パラグラフ 2 ミネラルは，体内でさまざまな重要な役割を果たしている。Q5 筋反応，神経組織を通しての命令の伝達，消化，食物中の栄養素の利用といった，多くの生物学的反応の Q4 触媒として働く。Q5 さらにミネラルは，ホルモンの生成において重要であり，そのため体の成長に影響する。毎日の生活で，ミネラルはビタミンを摂取するうえで欠かせない。亜鉛，鉄分，銅，マグネシウム，カリウムは，特に消化と代謝にかかわる５大ミネラルである。ミネラルはまた，血液と体液が酸性になりすぎたり，アルカリ性になりすぎたりしないように働き，他の栄養分が血液中に摂取されるようにする。さらにミネラルは，細胞内に化学物質を出し入れしたり，Q6 体内に異物や毒物が入ったときに抗体を供給したりするのに役立つ。

| | |
|---|---|
| 3 Q7 All the minerals known to be needed by the human body must be supplied in the diet: the body does not produce them. This is one of the underlying suppositions of sound diet and healthy nutrition. Among the most important minerals sometimes missing from diets are calcium, iron, and iodine. Shortages of these essential minerals over a long period of time can have serious health consequences. Q8 For example, calcium deficiency can cause bones to be brittle and to heal slowly when broken. Q9 **Adequate** calcium especially needs to be absorbed by middle-aged women and by both men and women as they progress into old age. Although the various minerals can be recognized individually, Q10 minerals cannot be considered separate with respect to their utilization since they influence each other. Simply stated, every mineral affects the function of other minerals. | パラグラフ3 Q7 人体に必要だと知られているミネラルはすべて，食物で供給されなければならない。体がミネラルを作り出すわけではないのである。このことは，しっかりした食事と健全な栄養摂取の大前提のひとつである。食事で不足しがちなもっとも重要なミネラルには，カルシウム，鉄分，ヨウ素がある。これらの不可欠なミネラルが長年にわたって不足すると，健康に深刻な影響が出る恐れがある。Q8 たとえば，カルシウム不足によって骨はもろくなり，骨折したときに治るのが遅くなることがある。Q9 十分な量のカルシウム摂取は特に，中年女性，また男女問わず高齢になってからは欠かせない。さまざまなミネラルを個別に見ることはできるが，Q10 ミネラルは互いに影響し合うので，その利用に関しては分けて考えることはできない。簡単に言えば，どのミネラルも，他のミネラルの機能に影響を及ぼすのである。 |

## 1.

正答：D

What does the passage mainly discuss?

このパッセージは主に何を論じていますか。

(A) The chemical make-up of minerals　(A) ミネラルの化学構造
(B) The diseases caused by lack of minerals　(B) ミネラルの不足によって生じる病気
(C) The minerals lacking in the common diet　(C) 普通の食事に不足しているミネラル
(D) The use of minerals in the body　(D) 体内におけるミネラルの役割

全体を通して体内でのミネラルの働きが説明されている。よって，(D) が正答。(A) (B) (C) に関連する言及はあるが，いずれもこのパッセージの主目的とは言えない。

## 2.

正答：A

In the first paragraph, the author implies that minerals are found

第1パラグラフで，ミネラルがあると筆者が示唆しているのは

(A) throughout the body　(A) 体全体
(B) mainly in the bone and skeletal system　(B) 主に骨と骨格系の中
(C) largely in fluid form　(C) 主に体液の中
(D) in a limited number of combinations　(D) 限られた数の化合物の中

1 には Minerals are nutrients that exist in the body, さらに All tissues and internal fluids of living things contain varying quantities of them. とあり，より具体的に They are constituents of bones, teeth, soft tissue, muscle, blood, and nerve cells. と，ミネラルが体内のいたるところに含まれると説明されている。よって，(A) が正答。(B) (C) はそれぞれ mainly「主として」, largely「主に」という表現があるために誤り。

## 3.

正答：A

The word “They” in line 3 refers to

(A) minerals
(B) organic and inorganic combinations
(C) all tissues
(D) living things

3 行目の “They” が指し示しているのは

(A) ミネラル
(B) 有機的・無機的な化合物
(C) 全組織
(D) 生物

They の対象となりうる複数形の名詞を文脈に留意して検討すれば，Minerals are ... = varying quantities of them = They are constituents ... であるとわかる。よって，(A) が正答。

## 4.

正答：B

The word “catalyst” in line 8 is closest in meaning to

(A) barrier
(B) stimulant
(C) reversal
(D) foundation

8 行目の “catalyst” にもっとも近い意味を持つのは

(A) 障壁
(B) 刺激物
(C) 反転
(D) 基礎

catalyst は「触媒」という意味の名詞。触媒とは，化学反応に際し，反応物質以外のもので，それ自身は化学変化を受けず，反応速度を変化させる物質。つまり，一定の化学的「刺激」により化学反応を促進させる物質のこと。よって，(B) が正答。

## 5.

正答：D

In paragraph 2, the author mentions that minerals influence all of the following functions EXCEPT

(A) the sending of nerve impulses
(B) the digesting of food
(C) the producing of hormones
(D) the creation of new cells

第 2 パラグラフで，ミネラルが影響を及ぼさないと筆者が述べているのは

(A) 神経的刺激の送信
(B) 食物の消化
(C) ホルモンの生成
(D) 新しい細胞の生成

2 に including muscle response, the transmission of messages through the nervous system, digestion, and the utilization of nutrients in foods. Furthermore, they are important in the production of hormones とあり，(A) (B) (C) に対応している。よって，言及されていない (D) が正答。

## 6.

正答：C

What does paragraph 2 imply about the relation between minerals and diseases?

(A) An excessive amount of a specific mineral can cause diseases.
(B) Diseases can enter the body with minerals.
(C) Minerals play a role in fighting diseases.
(D) Physicians prescribe particular minerals to treat diseases.

第2パラグラフはミネラルと病気の関係について，何を示唆していますか。

(A) 特定のミネラルが多すぎると病気の原因となる。
(B) 病気はミネラルとともに体内に入ってくる。
(C) ミネラルは病気からの回復に役立つ。
(D) 医師は病気治療のために特定のミネラルを処方する。

> 設問にある diseases に相当する表現を 2 で検索すると，when a foreign or toxic element enters the body が見つかる。ここで a foreign or toxic element とは具体的には病原菌のこと。これに関してミネラルは，they aid in the distribution of antibodies ... とあるので，これを言い換えている (C) が正答。

## 7.

正答：B

According to the passage, what is the main reason that minerals are so closely related to diet?

(A) They are essential to digesting food.
(B) They are only obtained through food.
(C) They can be lost during food digestion.
(D) They may not be present in most foods.

パッセージによれば，ミネラルが食物に非常に密接に関係している主な理由は何ですか。

(A) 食物を消化するのに欠かせない。
(B) 食物からのみ摂取できる。
(C) 消化の段階で失われることがある。
(D) ほとんどの食物に含まれていないかもしれない。

> 食物とミネラルの関係は 3 で述べられている。設問の diet に相当する表現を検索すると，All the minerals known to be needed by the human body must be supplied in the diet: the body does not produce them. とある。よって，下線部を言い換えている (B) が正答。

## 8.

正答：C

Which mineral appears to play the most important role in maintaining healthy bones?

(A) Iron
(B) Zinc
(C) Calcium
(D) Potassium

健康な骨を維持するうえでもっとも重要な役割を果たすと思われるミネラルはどれですか。

(A) 鉄分
(B) 亜鉛
(C) カルシウム
(D) カリウム

> 設問の bones に相当する表現を検索すると，3 に For example, calcium deficiency can cause bones to be brittle and to heal slowly when broken. とある。よって，(C) が正答。

## 9. 正答：B

The word "Adequate" in line 25 is closest in meaning to

(A) abundant
(B) sufficient
(C) diminished
(D) vigorous

25 行目の "Adequate" にもっとも近い意味を持つのは

(A) 豊富な
(B) 十分な
(C) 減少した
(D) 精力的な

adequate は「十分な，適切な」という意味の形容詞。よって，(B) が正答。

## 10. 正答：A

What does the author conclude about minerals?

(A) They have a complex relation to one another.
(B) They are the single most important factor in health.
(C) They are produced naturally by the body.
(D) They have the greatest importance during illness.

筆者はミネラルについてどのように結論づけていますか。

(A) 相互に複雑に関係している。
(B) 健康にとって唯一のもっとも重要な成分である。
(C) 人体によって自然に作り出される。
(D) 病気の際，もっとも重要である。

結論を問う問題なので，最後の部分に注目する。3 の最後に minerals cannot be considered separate with respect to their utilization since they influence each other とあり，さらに，これを要約して Simply stated, every mineral affects the function of other minerals. とある。よって，下線部をまとめて言い換えている (A) が正答。

---

ボキャブラリー

- ☐ **nutrient**「栄養素」
- ☐ **inorganic**「無機物の」
- ☐ **tissue**「(細胞) 組織」
- ☐ **nerve cell**「神経組織」
- ☐ **skeletal**「骨格の」
- ☐ **catalyst**「触媒」
- ☐ **hormone**「ホルモン」
- ☐ **acidic**「酸性の」
- ☐ **cell**「細胞」
- ☐ **toxic**「有毒の，毒性の」
- ☐ **iodine**「ヨウ素」
- ☐ **organic**「有機物の」
- ☐ **combination**「化合物」
- ☐ **constituent**「構成要素」
- ☐ **physiological**「生理（学）上の」
- ☐ **vigor**「力」
- ☐ **digestion**「消化」
- ☐ **metabolism**「代謝」
- ☐ **alkaline**「アルカリ性の」
- ☐ **antibody**「抗体」
- ☐ **supposition**「仮説」
- ☐ **brittle**「もろい」

## Questions 11-20 *Corporations*

1 世界の企業の70%以上は個人経営だが，事業形態としてもっとも重要なのは株式会社である。
2 株式会社は独立した存在で，所有者や社員が交代しても会社は存続する。
3 株式会社が重要になった理由のひとつは，巨額の資金調達が可能となることである。
4 さらに，経営者と事業主が分かれていることが挙げられる。

1 More than 70 percent of the world's businesses are owned and operated by a single person, mainly due to the ease of formation this type of business affords. Nevertheless, while the "sole proprietorship" remains by far the most common type of business organization today, there is no doubt that Q11 the dominant form of business in the world is the corporation. Although not all corporations are huge multi-national organizations, it can generally be said that Q11 the ability of corporations to influence the economy, politics, and culture of a nation greatly surpasses that of any other form of business.

パラグラフ1 世界の企業の70%以上は，ひとりの人間によって所有され，経営されている。これは何よりもまず，このタイプの企業は設立しやすいためである。とは言え，現在でも「個人事業」が依然としてもっとも一般的な事業体形式である一方で，Q11 世界における主要な事業形態は間違いなく株式会社である。すべての株式会社が巨大な多国籍企業というわけではないが，一般的には，Q11 一国の経済，政治，文化に対する株式会社の影響力は，その他の事業形態をはるかに上回っていると言ってよい。

2 The association of human beings in pursuit of a common Q13 **objective** is as old as history. However, the concept of Q12 a corporation as an entity separate and distinct from the individuals who constitute it occurred at the beginning of the colonial era, roughly the early 17th century. Q14 Legally, the corporation is an **artificial "person,"** capable of conducting business transactions in the same way as the owner of a sole proprietorship would. Unlike the business owned by a single individual, though, Q15 the life of a corporation is potentially perpetual. It does not end when the owner dies or when its members change.

パラグラフ2 共通の Q13 目的の追求のために人間が共同することは，古来からある。しかし Q12 株式会社を，それを構成する各個人から分離した独立の存在として考えるようになったのは，初期植民地時代のことであり，おおよそ17世紀初頭である。Q14 法的には株式会社とは，人工的な「人」（法人）のことであり，個人事業主と同じように商取引を行うことができる。しかし，一個人によって所有される事業とは違って，Q15 株式会社の命は潜在的には永久に続く。所有者が死んだり構成員が交代したりしても，会社は存続するのである。

3 The principal reason why the corporation has become the most important form of business in the world is that it is the most practical type of organization for Q16 raising

パラグラフ3 株式会社が世界でもっとも重要な事業形態になった主な理由は，株式会社は Q16 資本を調達するのにもっとも実用的な組織形態であることだ。Q19 他の大企業と

capital. Q19 Obtaining the manufacturing plants, the equipment, and the marketing outlets necessary to compete with other large concerns Q16 requires capital that may Q17 **run into** hundreds of millions of dollars, far more than any individual or even groups of individuals could supply. The system of shareholding, which allows for multiple owners, in conjunction with the development of a capital market for the impersonal purchase and sale of stock, has significantly assisted corporations to obtain the funds they need to operate on a wide scale.

競合するのに必要な工場，設備，販路を獲得するには，Q16 何億ドルにも Q17 のぼる資本が必要になることがあるが，これは個人や小集団が供給できるものではない。株式所有という仕組みによって複数名による所有が可能になり，同時に株式の個人購入以外の売買のための資本市場が発達し，株式会社が大規模に活動するために必要な資金を獲得するうえでこの仕組みが大きな助けとなってきた。

4 Another advantage the corporation has over other forms of business enterprise is that it provides independent management; that is, Q18 business executives who, separate from the owners or shareholders, are paid to oversee and operate the company. This typically results in more professional and expert management and Q18 has evolved to be an increasingly important feature in corporate profitability.

パラグラフ4 株式会社がその他の事業形態に対して有しているもうひとつの利点は，それが独立した経営を可能にすることである。すなわち，Q18 経営者は，事業保有者や株主とは分かれており，企業の監督・運営のため雇われている。それゆえ経営は一般的に，より専門的かつ高度なものとなり，Q18 事業収益においてますます重要な特徴をなすようになってきた。

## 11.

正答：A

What is the main idea of the passage?

(A) The corporation is the most influential type of business organization.

(B) The corporation is the most common type of business organization.

(C) Corporations must be very carefully managed.

(D) Corporations have accumulated too much power.

このパッセージの論旨は何ですか。

(A) 株式会社はもっとも影響力のある企業組織の種類である。

(B) 株式会社はもっとも一般的な企業組織の種類である。

(C) 株式会社は非常に慎重に経営されなければならない。

(D) 株式会社はあまりにも力を蓄えすぎた。

1 には個人事業と比較する形で the dominant form of business in the world is the corporation, また the ability of corporations to influence the economy, politics, and culture of a nation greatly surpasses that of any other form of business とあり，株式会社の影響力の大きさが強調されている。よって，(A) が正答。

## 12. 正答：B

Which of the following is true of corporations?

(A) They are as old as history.
(B) They are distinct from their owners.
(C) They can easily be separated into smaller entities.
(D) They exist primarily in the Western world.

株式会社について正しいのは次のどれですか。

(A) 有史以来存在する。
(B) 所有者から独立している。
(C) より小さい事業体に簡単に分割できる。
(D) 主に西洋世界において存在する。

> 2 に a corporation as an entity separate and distinct from the individuals who constitute it とある。よって，(B) が正答。as old as history であるのは corporation ではなく The association なので (A) は誤り。

## 13. 正答：A

The word "objective" in line 9 is closest in meaning to

(A) aim
(B) value
(C) norm
(D) belief

9 行目の "objective" にもっとも近い意味を持つのは

(A) 目的
(B) 価値
(C) 規範
(D) 信念

> objective は「目的」という意味の名詞。よって, (A) が正答。ほかに形容詞で「客観的な」という意味もある。

## 14. 正答：B

In line 13, the author's use of the phrase "artificial 'person'" implies that

(A) more than one person owns a corporation
(B) a corporation is not a human entity
(C) corporations are unfeeling and inhumane
(D) many individuals combine to make up a corporation

13 行目の "artifical 'person'" という句を用いて筆者が示唆しているのは

(A) 複数の人が株式会社を所有すること
(B) 株式会社が人間ではないこと
(C) 株式会社は無感情で非人道的であること
(D) 多くの個人が集まって株式会社を構成すること

> 2 には Legally, the corporation is an artificial "person," とあり，株式会社はあくまでも法律上の「人」であると説明されている。よって，(B) が正答。「法人」とはいわゆる人間,「自然人」とは異なるということ。

## 15.　正答：A

Which of the following can be inferred about a sole proprietorship?

(A) It could cease to exist upon the death of its owner.
(B) It is less inventive than a corporation.
(C) It has a hard time attracting qualified managers.
(D) It is difficult to establish and administer.

個人事業について推測できることは次のどれですか。

(A) 所有者が死んだ時点で存在しなくなる。
(B) 株式会社よりも独創性が低い。
(C) 有能な経営陣を集めづらい。
(D) 設立して管理するのが難しい。

2 に個人事業と対比する形で，the life of a corporation is potentially perpetual. It does not end when the owner dies or when its members change. と株式会社の永続性が指摘されている。ここから逆に，個人事業は永続性がなく，所有者の死によって消滅するかもしれないと推測できる。よって，(A) が正答。

## 16.　正答：C

Which of the following aspects of a corporation is most extensively discussed in paragraph 3?

(A) Determining how much stock to issue
(B) Appointing managers to run the business
(C) Acquiring the capital necessary to operate
(D) Deciding which types of assets to purchase

第 3 パラグラフでもっとも詳しく論じられている企業の側面は次のどれですか。

(A) 株式の発行数を決めること
(B) 会社を経営するための経営陣を任命すること
(C) 活動するのに必要な資本を獲得すること
(D) どのような種類の資産を購入するかを決めること

raising capital，requires capital that may run into hundreds of millions of dollars, a capital market などの語句からも明らかなように，3 は事業展開のために必要な資本の調達について論じている。よって，(C) が正答。

## 17.　正答：D

The phrase “run into” in line 21 is closest in meaning to

(A) collide with
(B) compete with
(C) attain
(D) approach

21 行目の “run into” にもっとも近い意味を持つのは

(A) ～と衝突する
(B) ～と競う
(C) ～を達成する
(D) ～に近付く

run into は続く hundreds of millions of dollars からも推測できるように「(数量などが) ～に達する」の意味。よって，(D) が正答。

## 18. 正答：A

With which of the following statements would the author most likely agree?

筆者は次のどの記述にもっとも同意すると思われますか。

(A) There is an increasing separation of stockholders and management in modern corporations.
(B) Managers are more highly motivated if they also own stock in the corporation.
(C) Stockholders are not usually very interested in how the corporation is managed.
(D) A smaller number of shareholders allows the firm to be managed more efficiently.

(A) 現代の株式会社では，株主と経営者がより分離されるようになってきている。
(B) 経営者も自社株を持てば，よりいっそうやる気を起こす。
(C) 株主は普通は，その株式会社の経営状態にあまり関心がない。
(D) 株主の数が少ないほうが，企業を効率よく経営できる。

> 4 で，株式会社においては business executives「経営者」と the owners or shareholders「事業主や株主」が分離しており，この事業形態が has evolved to be an increasingly important feature ... と説明されている。よって，(A) が正答。

## 19. 正答：C

Which of the following is NOT mentioned as an important use of the capital raised by the corporation?

株式会社によって集められる資本の重要な用途として言及されていないのは次のどれですか。

(A) The building of production facilities
(B) The acquisition of machinery
(C) The training of corporate managers
(D) The establishment of distribution outlets

(A) 製造設備の建造
(B) 機械類の獲得
(C) 企業経営陣の養成
(D) 販路の確立

> 3 に Obtaining the manufacturing plants, the equipment, and the marketing outlets necessary to compete with other large concerns と資本の用途が列挙されており，(A) (B) (D) に対応している。よって，言及のない (C) が正答。

## 20.　正答：B

What is probably discussed in the paragraph that precedes the passage?

(A) Further advantages provided by the corporate form of business
(B) Characteristics of the single-owner form of business
(C) Reasons why the corporation has recently become popular
(D) Different types of multi-national business organizations

このパッセージの前のパラグラフでは，おそらく何が論じられていますか。

(A) 株式会社という企業形態によってもたらされるさらなる利点
(B) 個人所有という企業形態の特徴
(C) 株式会社が最近になって人気が出た理由
(D) さまざまな種類の多国籍企業

1 の冒頭の2文ではthe sole proprietorship「個人事業」と比較する形でcorporations「株式会社」が紹介されている。しかし，それ以降は後者の特徴だけを説明しており，前者についての解説はない。これは直前のパラグラフですでに説明されているためと推測できる。よって，(B) が正答。

---

ボキャブラリー
- □ **proprietorship**「所有していること，所有権」
- □ **dominant**「支配的な」
- □ **corporation**「（株式）会社」
- □ **surpass**「～に勝る，～をしのぐ」
- □ **in pursuit of ...**「～を求めて」
- □ **transaction**「業務，取引」
- □ **perpetual**「永続的な」
- □ **raise capital**「資本を集める」
- □ **plant**「工場」
- □ **in conjunction with ...**「～に関連して」
- □ **management**「経営」
- □ **shareholder**「株主」

## Questions 21-30 *Phillis Wheatley*

**1 奴隷出身の詩人であったフィリス・ウィートリーは，本を出版した最初のアフリカ系アメリカ人であった。**
**2 アフリカから売られてきた彼女は主人たちに教育を受けさせてもらい，すぐに才能を開かせた。**
**3 彼女はイギリスに理解者を得て，処女作をロンドンで出版し，さらに奴隷の身分から自由になった。**

1 Phillis Wheatley, Q24 ignored as a poet for almost two hundred years, was Q23 Q24 not only a talented writer, recognized in Europe more than in the United States, but she was also the first African American to publish a book, the first woman writer whose publication was promoted and nurtured by a community of women, and the first American woman author who for a while earned a living by means of her writing. She was also a slave and survived the Q22 **horrific** "middle passage" from Africa to North America.

パラグラフ1 フィリス・ウィートリーは，Q24 およそ200年にわたって詩人としては無視されてきたが，Q23 Q24 アメリカ合衆国よりもヨーロッパで認められた才能ある作家であったというだけではなく，本を出版した最初のアフリカ系アメリカ人であり，その著作が女性のコミュニティによって広められ，育まれた最初の女性作家であり，一定期間，文筆活動で生計を立てた最初のアメリカ人女性作家でもあった。彼女はまた奴隷でもあり，アフリカと北アメリカを結ぶあの Q22 恐るべき「中間航路」を生き延びたのである。

2 Phillis Wheatley was born in West Africa, along the fertile lowlands of the Gambia River. But when she was seven or eight, she was captured by slave traders, transported to Boston, and on July 11, 1761, sold to John and Susanna Wheatley. Q25 Unlike most slave owners of the time, the Wheatleys permitted the young girl to learn to read her new language, and soon after, her poetic talent began to emerge. Her earliest published poem appeared when she was fourteen and relates how two men narrowly escaped being drowned off Cape Cod in Massachusetts. Q27 Much of her Q26 **subsequent** poetry also deals with mortality. Of her surviving fifty-five poems, for instance, nineteen are Q27 Q30 elegies, poems written in the memory of people who have passed away. Q30 Her last poem is an elegy written about herself and her career.

パラグラフ2 フィリス・ウィートリーは西アフリカ，ガンビア川沿いの肥沃な低地で生まれた。だが，7歳か8歳のときに奴隷商人に捕らえられてボストンに連れてこられ，1761年7月11日にジョン・ウィートリー，スザンナ・ウィートリー夫妻に売られた。Q25 当時の大半の奴隷所有者とは違って，ウィートリー夫妻はその少女に，彼女にとって新しい言葉の読み方を学ぶことを許した。すると，じきに彼女の詩の才能が開花し始めたのである。最初に発表された彼女の詩は14歳のときに書かれたもので，2人の男がマサチューセッツ州ケープコッド沖でかろうじて溺死から逃れた様子を詠っている。Q27 彼女は Q26 その後の詩の多くでも，人間の死すべき運命を題材にしている。たとえば，残っている55編の詩のうち19編が Q27 Q30 エレジー，すなわち亡くなった人々を追憶して書かれた詩である。Q30 彼女の最後のエレジーは，彼女自身と彼女の生涯について書かれている。

3 Q28 Wheatley's first book, simply entitled *Poems*, having been turned down

パラグラフ3 単に『詩』と題された Q28 ウィートリーの最初の本は，彼女の人種と性別を理

for publication in Boston because of her race and sex, Q28 appeared in London in 1773. The following year Q29 she was granted her freedom, probably because a group of British women, her literary patrons, paid for her release from slavery. In 1778 Wheatley married John Peters, a free African American who managed a store and sometimes represented African Americans in the courts of law. But neither her writing nor her husband's work could protect their family from tragedy, and in 1784, she died after a difficult child-birth with her newborn infant in a shack on the edge of Boston.

由にボストンでの出版を断られ，Q28 1773年にロンドンで出版された。その翌年 Q29 彼女は自由の身となったが，これはおそらく彼女の文学を評価したパトロンであった英国の女性らのグループが，彼女を奴隷身分から自由にするためにお金を支払ったためである。1778年にウィートリーは，ジョン・ピータースと結婚した。彼は商店を経営する自由身分のアフリカ系アメリカ人で，しばしば法廷でアフリカ系アメリカ人たちの弁護を行っていた。しかし，彼女の作品も，彼女の夫の仕事も彼女の家族を悲劇から守ることはできず，1784年，彼女はボストンの外れにある小さな小屋で，生まれたばかりの子どもとともに亡くなった。

## 21. 正答：C

What is the main purpose of the passage?

(A) To analyze the main themes of Phillis Wheatley's poems
(B) To illustrate the cruelty of slavery in colonial America
(C) To describe Phillis Wheatley's life and work as a writer
(D) To show that Phillis Wheatley was one of America's most talented poets

このパッセージの主な目的は何ですか。

(A) フィリス・ウィートリーの詩の主要なテーマを分析すること
(B) 植民地時代のアメリカの奴隷制の残酷さを説明すること
(C) フィリス・ウィートリーの作家としての生涯と作品を描写すること
(D) フィリス・ウィートリーがアメリカのもっとも才能ある詩人のひとりだったと示すこと

このパッセージがフィリス・ウィートリーの誕生，成長，執筆活動，死去と，彼女の生涯についての概説であることは全体から明らか。よって，(C) が正答。(A) (B) (D) に関連する言及はあるが，いずれもパッセージ全体の主旨とは言えない。

## 22. 正答：D

The word "horrific" in line 6 is closest in meaning to

(A) long
(B) deserted
(C) liberal
(D) dreadful

6行目 "horrific" にもっとも近い意味を持つのは

(A) 長い
(B) さびれた
(C) 自由な
(D) 恐ろしい

"horrific" は動詞 horrify「怖がらせる」の形容詞形である。同様に動詞 dread「～を恐れる」の形容詞形である (D) dreadful が正答。

## 23.　正答：C

Which of the following is NOT mentioned as one of Phillis Wheatley's accomplishments?

(A) She was the first African American to publish a book.
(B) She was the first female writer supported mainly by other women.
(C) She was the first slave who earned her freedom through her writing.
(D) She was the first professional woman writer in America.

フィリス・ウィートリーの業績のひとつとして述べられていないのは，次のうちのどれですか。

(A) 本を出版した最初のアフリカ系アメリカ人だった。
(B) 主に他の女性たちに支持された最初の女性作家だった。
(C) 執筆活動を通して自由を手にした最初の奴隷だった。
(D) アメリカで最初の本職の女性作家だった。

1 でフィリス・ウィートリーは，not only a talented writer, recognized in Europe more than in the United States, but she was also the first African American to publish a book, the first woman writer whose publication was promoted and nurtured by a community of women, and the first American woman author who for a while earned a living by means of her writing. と紹介されており，下線部はそれぞれ (A) (B) (D) に対応している。よって，言及のない (C) が正答。

## 24.　正答：A

The author implies in the first paragraph that Phillis Wheatley's

(A) writing has not received as much attention as it deserves
(B) interest in writing began when she was a child in Africa
(C) poetry was rejected by many contemporary women writers
(D) poems were better known in America than in Europe

第1パラグラフで筆者が示唆しているのは，フィリス・ウィートリーの

(A) 著述活動が相応の注目を集めていないこと
(B) 著述活動に対する興味は，アフリカでの少女時代に始まっていたこと
(C) 詩は多くの同時代の女性作家に認められなかったこと
(D) 詩はヨーロッパよりもアメリカでより知られていたこと

1 で筆者はフィリスが ignored as a poet for almost two hundred years と指摘し，設問 23 で見たように注目に値する理由を列挙している。ここから，筆者はウィートリーをもっと評価すべきと考えていると推測できる。よって，(A) が正答。

## 25.

**正答：D**

It can be inferred from the second paragraph that

第 2 パラグラフから推測できるのは

(A) Phillis Wheatley tried to escape from her captors
(B) many people in Boston opposed slavery
(C) Phillis Wheatley had a difficult time learning English
(D) few slaves at that time learned how to read

(A) フィリス・ウィートリーは奴隷商人から逃げようと試みた
(B) ボストンの多くの人が奴隷制に反対していた
(C) フィリス・ウィートリーは英語を学ぶのに苦労した
(D) 読み方を学んだ奴隷は当時ほとんどいなかった

2 で Unlike most slave owners of the time「他の奴隷所有者とは異なって」ウィートリー夫妻がフィリスが英語を学ぶことを許したとの指摘がある。ここから，他の奴隷所有者は奴隷に英語を学ばせなかったと推測できるので，(D) が正答。

## 26.

**正答：B**

The word "subsequent" in line 15 is closest in meaning to

15 行目の "subsequent" にもっとも近い意味を持つのは

(A) substantial
(B) later
(C) best
(D) misplaced

(A) 実質的な
(B) もっと後の
(C) 最善の
(D) 見当違いの

subsequent は「続いて起こる，その後の」という意味の形容詞。よって，(B) が正答。

## 27.

**正答：C**

What appears to be one of the main themes of Phillis Wheatley's poetry?

フィリス・ウィートリーの詩の主要テーマのひとつと考えられるのはどれですか。

(A) Love
(B) Race
(C) Death
(D) Religion

(A) 愛
(B) 人種
(C) 死
(D) 宗教

設問の the main themes of Phillis Wheatley's poetry に相当する表現を検索すると，2 に Much of her subsequent poetry also deals with mortality. とあり，elegies, poems written in the memory of people who have passed away. とある。下線部，すなわち「死すべき運命」「エレジー（悲歌）」「亡くなった人を追憶して」はいずれも人の死に関するものである。よって，(C) が正答。

## 28.　　　正答：A

When was Phillis Wheatley's first volume of poetry published?

(A) 1773
(B) 1774
(C) 1778
(D) 1784

フィリス・ウィートリーの最初の詩集が出版されたのはいつですか。

(A) 1773年
(B) 1774年
(C) 1778年
(D) 1784年

設問の Phillis Wheatley's first volume of poetry published に相当する表現を検索すると，3 に Wheatley's first book ... appeared in London in 1773. とある。よって，(A) が正答。

## 29.　　　正答：A

According to the author, how did Phillis Wheatley gain her freedom?

(A) Her friends purchased her liberty.
(B) Her masters recognized her talent.
(C) She married a white landowner.
(D) She refused to serve anymore as a slave.

筆者によれば，フィリス・ウィートリーはどのようにして自由を得ましたか。

(A) 彼女の友人たちが彼女の自由を買った。
(B) 彼女の主人たちが彼女の才能を認めた。
(C) 彼女は白人の土地所有者に嫁いだ。
(D) 彼女は奴隷として仕え続けるのを拒んだ。

設問の gain her freedom に相当する表現を検索すると，3 に she was granted her freedom, probably because a group of British women, her literary patrons, paid for her release from slavery. とある。よって，下線部を言い換えている (A) が正答。

## 30.　　　正答：B

What is true of Phillis Wheatley's final poem?

(A) It was simply called *Poems*.
(B) It concerned her own death.
(C) It was discovered after she had died.
(D) It was about her husband and newborn child.

フィリス・ウィートリーの最後の詩作に当てはまるのはどれですか。

(A) 単に「詩」と題された。
(B) 彼女自身の死に関連していた。
(C) 彼女の死後，発見された。
(D) 彼女の夫と新しく誕生した子についてであった。

2 の最後の文に Her last poem is an elegy written about herself and her career. とある。そして彼女の書いた elegy は poems written in the memory of people who have passed away と説明されているので，最後の詩作は自分自身の死についてのものとわかる。よって，(B) が正答。

---

ボキャブラリー
□ **mortality**「死すべき運命」
□ **pass away**「死ぬ」
□ **court of law**「裁判所」
□ **shack**「小屋」
□ **elegy**「悲歌」
□ **entitle**「～を題する」
□ **tragedy**「悲劇」

## Questions 31-40 *Volcanoes*

1 火山の分類には噴出した物質の種類，噴出の速度，噴出の時間の長さが用いられる。
2 楯上火山は，溶岩流出の繰り返しによりできる。
3 複合火山は，複数の溶岩ドームがひとつになってできる。
4 複成火山は成層火山とも呼ばれ，ひとつの火山の最上部の火口から流出される岩片から形成される。

1 Q40 The world's volcanoes are classified into types based mainly upon how they have formed. This itself is a result of Q32 the types of materials that have erupted from them, the velocity at which the materials have been ejected, and the length of time over which the eruptions have occurred.

パラグラフ1 Q40 世界の火山は，主として，それがどのようにできたかに基づいて，いくつかの種類に分類される。この分類は，Q32 火山が噴出した物質の種類，この物質が放出された速度，また噴火が続いた時間の長さに基づく。

2 The most common type of volcano, the shield volcano, is a gently sloping dome gradually built up over time by thin layers of volcanic ash and a series of lava flows. These flows are relatively thin, Q34 **rarely** exceeding seven meters in thickness, and made from lava that flowed out slowly. Q35 Any fragmental materials such as volcanic rock and volcanic boulders thrown out by explosions are insignificant and have virtually no effect on the shape of the mountain. As a shield volcano grows, eruptions of lava gradually cease to originate from the volcano's central vent and instead lava flows out of secondary fissures on the slopes of the mountain. Eventually, the main column of lava is no longer capable of reaching the summit of the volcano, and all the eruptions come from the secondary vents. Q33 From then on the volcano increases in diameter but not in height.

パラグラフ2 もっとも一般的な火山のタイプである楯状火山は，火山灰の薄い層と溶岩流出の繰り返しにより長い時間をかけて徐々にできた，傾斜のなだらかなドームである。この溶岩流は比較的薄く，厚さ７メートルを超えることは Q34 まずなく，ゆっくりと流れ出てくる溶岩でできている。Q35 噴火によって放出される火山岩や火山礫岩のような火山砕屑物は少なく，火山の形状にほとんど影響しない。楯状火山が大きくなるにつれて溶岩は徐々に火山の中心火口から噴出しなくなり，代わって溶岩が火山の山腹の亀裂から流出する。やがて溶岩の中央の柱が火山の頂上に届かなくなり，溶岩はすべて二次的にできた口から噴出するようになる。Q33 それ以降は，火山の高さではなく，その直径が拡大していく。

3 The second type of volcano is created when several smaller lava domes unite as they grow in size, forming a compound volcano. Q36 The island of Hawaii, for example, has been formed by the union of five such lava domes. In a compound

パラグラフ3 第二のタイプの火山は，複数の小さな溶岩ドームが規模が大きくなるにつれてひとつになり，複合火山を形成することでできあがる。Q36 例えば，ハワイ島はそうした溶岩ドーム５つからできたものである。複合火山の場合，溶岩ドームはそれ

volcano, lava domes are built up by thick lava that flows down from the vent at the top of each dome; over time a compound volcano can grow to a tremendous size as its various vents build up its base. Some compound volcanoes have risen from thousands of meters below the sea's surface to form islands or island chains.

それのドームの頂点にある火口から流れ出てくる厚みのある溶岩によってできる。複数の火口がそれぞれベースを作るので，複合火山は，時間とともに，巨大な大きさになることがある。複合火山のなかには，海底数千メートルから隆起し，海面上に島や列島を作り出すものもある。

4 In contrast, the third type, Q37 a composite volcano, which is also sometimes called a "stratovolcano," develops a form dominated by rock fragments exploded from the topmost crater of a single volcano that are interspersed with the lava that flows from its central vent. Compared to the size of the entire mountain, which may rise more than 3,000 meters above its base, the crater that forms the central vent is quite small, hardly ever more than a few hundred meters in diameter. A volcano of this kind normally exhibits a Q38 **steep** slope and appears symmetrical when viewed from a distance. Mt. St. Helens in the United States, Mt. Vesuvius in Italy, and Mt. Fuji in Japan are perhaps Q39 the most famous examples of composite volcanoes.

パラグラフ4 これに対して第三のタイプである Q37 複成火山は，しばしば「成層火山」とも呼ばれるが，ひとつの火山の最上部の火口から放出される岩片を主として形成されるもので，これらの岩片は中心火口から流れ出る溶岩流の中に散在している。ふもとから 3, 000 メートル以上にも達することがある山全体の大きさに比べると，この噴火口はかなり小さく，直径 200-300 メートルを超えることはほとんどない。この種の火山は通常傾斜が Q38 急で，遠くから眺めると左右対称に見える。アメリカのセントヘレナ山，イタリアのベスビオ山，日本の富士山がおそらく，Q39 もっとも有名な複成火山の例である。

## 31.

正答：B

What does the passage mainly discuss?

このパッセージは主に何を論じていますか。

(A) The worldwide distribution of volcanoes
(B) The physical forms of volcanoes
(C) The dangers posed by volcanoes
(D) The creation of new volcanoes

(A) 火山の世界分布
(B) 火山の形状
(C) 火山によって生じる危険
(D) 新しい火山の形成

1 では火山の分類方法が示され，以降の3パラグラフでそれぞれの火山の発生メカニズムと形状について説明されている。よって，(B) が正答。(D) は漠然としすぎている。

## 32.

正答：C

What factor is NOT mentioned in paragraph 1 as playing a role in the formation of a volcano?

(A) How long a volcano has been active
(B) What kinds of materials a volcano has discharged
(C) The place a volcano has occurred
(D) How fast lava and rock have erupted

火山の生成に関して，第1パラグラフで言及されていないのはどれですか。

(A) 火山がどれくらいの期間にわたって活発か
(B) 火山がどんな種類の物質を吹き出すか
(C) 火山が生じる場所
(D) どれくらいの早さで溶岩や岩石が噴出するか

1 は，火山の分類基準として，the types of materials that have erupted from them, the velocity at which the materials have been ejected, the length of time over which the eruptions have occurred の3点を挙げている。よって，ここで言及がない (C) が正答。

## 33.

正答：C

According to the passage, at some point a shield volcano will

(A) merge with adjacent lava domes
(B) be destroyed by explosions
(C) cease growing in height
(D) be subject to fragmentation

パッセージによれば，楯状火山はある時点で

(A) 隣接する溶岩ドームと合体する
(B) 爆発によって破壊される
(C) 高くならなくなる
(D) 分裂しやすくなる

設問に a shield volcano とあるので 2 の The most common type of volcano, the shield volcano, is ... 以下の記述を検討すると，From then on the volcano increases in diameter but not in height. とある。よって，(C) が正答。

## 34.

正答：D

The word “rarely” in line 7 is closest in meaning to

(A) hardly
(B) periodically
(C) ordinarily
(D) seldom

7行目の “rarely” にもっとも近い意味を持つのは

(A) ほとんど～ない
(B) 定期的に
(C) 通常は
(D) めったに～しない

rarely は頻度を表し「めったに～（し）ない」という意味の準否定語。正答は同じく準否定語の (D)。(A) も準否定語だが程度を表し「ほとんど～（し）ない」という意味。

## 35.

正答：C

What materials are unlikely to be present in a shield volcano?

(A) Lava flows
(B) Volcanic ash
(C) Large rocks
(D) Lava layers

楯状火山に含まれている可能性が低い物質は何ですか。

(A) 溶岩流
(B) 火山灰
(C) 大きな岩
(D) 溶岩層

2 の中盤に，楯状火山を形成する物質についての説明があるが，ここで ...volcanic rock and volcanic boulders ... are insignificant と，火山性の岩石や巨礫が insignificant「取るに足らない」と指摘されている。よって，(C) が正答。

## 36.

正答：C

It can be inferred from the passage that which type of volcano may be most commonly seen in the Pacific Ocean?

(A) Shield volcanoes
(B) Stratovolcanoes
(C) Compound volcanoes
(D) Composite volcanoes

このパッセージから，太平洋でもっとも一般的な火山の種類はどれだと推測できますか。

(A) 楯状火山
(B) 成層火山
(C) 複合火山
(D) 複成火山

設問の Pacific Ocean についての直接的な言及はないが，3 の compound volcano「複合火山」に関する記述の中に，太平洋上にある島，ハワイの事例がある。よって，(C) が正答。

## 37.

正答：D

Rock fragments play a major role in the formation of

(A) shield volcanoes
(B) lava domes
(C) compound volcanoes
(D) composite volcanoes

その生成過程で，岩石の破片が大きな役割を果たすのは

(A) 楯状火山
(B) 溶岩ドーム
(C) 複合火山
(D) 複成火山

設問の Rock fragments に相当する表現を検索すると，4 に，a composite volcano, ... develops a form dominated by rock fragments とある。よって，(D) が正答。

## 38. 正答：A

The word "steep" in line 29 is closest in meaning to

(A) sharp
(B) slow
(C) beautiful
(D) gentle

29行目の "steep" にもっとも近い意味を持つのは

(A) 急勾配の
(B) 遅い
(C) 美しい
(D) やさしい

文中にあるように, steep は slope「斜面, 坂」の勾配が「急である」という意味。(A) が正答。

## 39. 正答：D

Why does the author mention Mt. Vesuvius?

(A) To explain a famous volcano
(B) To imply the danger that volcanoes pose
(C) To suggest how beautiful volcanoes can be
(D) To illustrate a composite volcano

筆者はなぜベスビオ山に言及しているのですか。

(A) 有名な火山を説明するため
(B) 火山活動停止の危険性を示唆するため
(C) 火山がいかに美しくありうるかを示唆するため
(D) 複成火山について説明するため

Mt. Vesuvius は，アメリカの Mt. St. Helens，日本の Mt. Fuji と並んで，the most famous examples of composite volcanoes とある。よって，複成火山の例なので (D) が正答。

## 40. 正答：D

Which of the following best characterizes the organization of the passage?

(A) Cause and effect
(B) Chronological development
(C) An extended narrative
(D) A classification of types

このパッセージの構成をもっともよく特徴づけているのは次のどれですか。

(A) 原因と結果
(B) 年代順の発展
(C) 長い物語
(D) 種類の分類

1 の冒頭で The world's volcanoes are classified into types と述べ，続く部分で The most common type ..., The second type ..., the third type ... と火山の種類を列挙している。よって，(D) であることは明らかに。

---

ボキャブラリー
- □ **eruption**「噴火」
- □ **lava**「溶岩」
- □ **vent**「火口」
- □ **diameter**「直径」
- □ **intersperse**「～を散在させる」
- □ **symmetrical**「左右対称の」

1 グレートプレーンズは約100万平方マイルの広大な空間である。
2 アメリカ先住民「プレーンズインディアン」はそこで生活する術を身につけていた。
3 彼らは「バンド」を活動単位としていた。
4 彼らは道徳的な部族社会を営んでいた。部族の子どもや若い男女には，それぞれ異なるしつけが行われた。

1 The Great Plains of North America cover about a million square miles. The Plains' immense size and few natural barriers create almost inconceivable space that seems to reach in all directions. Q42 Persistent winds sweeping through this vastness meet little resistance.

パラグラフ1 北アメリカのグレートプレーンズ（大平原）は，約100万平方マイルの広さを持つ。グレートプレーンズは広大で，自然の障害物がほとんど存在せず，想像を絶するほどの空間であり，全方位に広がっているように見える。Q42 この広大な空間を絶えず吹き抜ける風をさえぎるものはほとんど何もない。

2 Q43 Coping with the extremes of this environment was a skill that the Native Americans commonly called "Plains Indians" perfected, **and** Q45 it was only during unusually bitter winters, or when an accident of fate created a dangerous situation, that there was any real threat to the survival of their nomadic communities. Q44 In a sheltered wooded valley with the teepees tucked well back into a grove of cottonwoods and banked high with brush, a Plains Indian camp was secure against all but the most severe winter storms.

パラグラフ2 Q43 一般に「プレーンズインディアン」と呼ばれるアメリカ先住民たちは，こうした環境の極端な状態にうまく対応する技術に熟達していた。Q45 彼らの遊牧生活共同体の存続が本当に脅かされるのは，並はずれて厳しい冬の間か，もしくは運命の偶然によって危険な状況が生じたときだけだった。Q44 プレーンズインディアンの集落は樹木の茂る安全な谷間にあり，ティピはハコヤナギの木立の奥に隠れ，低木でしっかりと囲まれていたので，非常に厳しい冬の嵐を除けば，あらゆるものからしっかりと守られていた。

3 Since families were usually too small to offer adequate protection and tribes too large to be supported by the conditions of Plains' environment, Q46 the band was the basic unit to which a person belonged. It was a social entity consisting of a series of families united both politically and economically under the leadership of a chief and a council; it averaged about three hundred members. The security offered by the band was of essential economic importance in winter when Q47 **unpredictable** and often extremely harsh weather could make it impossible to hunt or travel.

パラグラフ3 家族では，十分な庇護を与えるのに普通は小さすぎるし，部族ではグレートプレーンズの環境下でやっていくのには大きすぎるので，Q46 個人が所属する基本的単位はバンドだった。バンドは首長と会議の統率の下に，政治的かつ経済的に統合された複数の家族から成る集団だった。そこには平均300人ほどの構成員がいた。バンドが与えてくれる安全は，冬の間，Q47 突発的に，また時として非常に厳しくなる天候のために狩りや移動ができなくなったとき，欠くことのできない経済的重要性を持っていた。

4 The children of the Plains tribes were encouraged to follow the moral values that emphasized respect for tribal rules and elders and to avoid greed, Q48 **egotism**, and irresponsibility. Q50 The young men were taught that it was their duty to provide food and to protect the community, while young women were instructed to uphold a virtuous life of service to Q49 **their** parents, **their** future husbands, **their** children, and **their** tribe.

パラグラフ4 プレーンズインディアン諸部族の子どもたちは，部族の決め事と年長者を尊重し，貪欲，Q48 利己主義，無責任を避けることを重んじる道徳的価値に従うようしつけられた。Q50 若い男は，食料を供給し，共同体を守ることが彼らの義務であると教えられ，若い女は，Q49 自分の両親，未来の夫，子どもたち，そして部族全体に仕える高潔な生活を支えるよう教えられた。

## 41.

正答：C

What does the passage mainly discuss?

(A) The geography of the Great Plains
(B) The climate of the Great Plains
(C) The society of the Plains Indians
(D) The leadership of Plains Indian tribes

このパッセージは主に何を論じていますか。

(A) グレートプレーンズの地理
(B) グレートプレーンズの気候
(C) プレーンズインディアンの社会
(D) プレーンズインディアン諸部族の指導力

2 以降のプレーンズインディアンの社会や構成に関する記述から，このパッセージの主題が (C) であるのは明らか。1 にはグレートプレーンズの地勢描写があるが，主題ではない。(D) に関する記述も 4 にあるが，中心的な内容ではない。

## 42.

正答：B

It can be concluded from paragraph 1 that the Great Plains are unusually

(A) moist
(B) windy
(C) fertile
(D) dry

第1パラグラフから推測すると，グレートプレーンズは非常に

(A) 湿気が多い
(B) 風が強い
(C) 肥沃である
(D) 乾燥している

1 に Persistent winds sweeping through this vastness meet little resistance. とあるので，(B) が正答。

## 43. 正答：B

What is most likely the main reason why the author describes in detail the physical characteristics of the Great Plains?

筆者がグレートプレーンズの自然の特徴を詳細に述べている主な理由は何であると考えられますか。

(A) Because they are unique to the North American continent.
(B) Because they affected the social structure of Plains Indian culture.
(C) Because they are subject to some of the world's harshest weather.
(D) Because they influenced the worldview of the Plains Indians.

(A) 北アメリカ大陸特有のものだから。
(B) プレーンズインディアン文化の社会構造に影響を与えたから。
(C) 世界でもっとも厳しい気候にさらされているから。
(D) プレーンズインディアンの世界観に影響を及ぼしたから。

> 2 の Coping with the extremes of this environment was a skill that the Native Americans commonly called "Plains Indians" perfected からわかるように，筆者はプレーンズインディアンはグレートプレーンズの環境に適応するように社会を築いたと考えている。3 ではより具体的に，この環境に適合した社会的単位はバンドであったと説明されている。よって，(B) が正答。

## 44. 正答：D

According to the passage, where did the Plains Indians typically make their camps?

このパッセージによれば，プレーンズインディアンはたいがいどこに居住地を設けましたか。

(A) On mountain slopes
(B) Next to rivers
(C) In open spaces
(D) Among trees

(A) 山の斜面に
(B) 川沿いに
(C) 何もない場所に
(D) 木々の間に

> 設問の their camps に相当する表現を検索すると，2 の最後に，In a sheltered wooded valley ..., a Plains Indian camp ... とある。よって，wooded「樹木の茂る」を言い換えている (D) が正答。

## 45. 正答：B

According to the passage, what presented the greatest danger to Plains Indians?

パッセージによれば，プレーンズインディアンにとって最大の危険は何でしたか。

(A) Drought
(B) Winter
(C) Disease
(D) War

(A) 日照り
(B) 冬
(C) 病気
(D) 戦争

設問の the greatest danger to Plains Indians に相当する表現を検索すると，**2** に it was only during unusually bitter winters ... that there was any real threat to the survival of their nomadic communities. とある。また the most severe winter storms, in winter when unpredictable and often extremely harsh weather ... と冬の厳しさが繰り返し強調されている。よって，(B) が正答。

## 46.

正答：D

According to the passage, what was the principal group in which Plains Indians were organized?

(A) The family
(B) The tribe
(C) The clan
(D) The band

パッセージによれば，プレーンズインディアンを組織する主な集団は何ですか。

(A) 家族
(B) 部族
(C) 氏族
(D) バンド

設問の the principal group に相当する表現を検索すると，**3** に the band was the basic unit to which a person belonged とある。よって，(D) が正答。

## 47.

正答：A

The word “unpredictable” in line 17 is closest in meaning to

(A) unforeseeable
(B) unfamiliar
(C) furious
(D) frantic

17 行目の “unpredictable” にもっとも近い意味を持つのは

(A) 予見できない
(B) 見慣れない
(C) 怒り狂った
(D) 半狂乱の

unpredictable は，un-「～できない」＋ predict「予測する」＋ able「～できる」から成る。つまり「予測不可能な」という意味の形容詞。語源的に同じ構造の (A) が正答。unforeseeable は un ＋ foresee ＋ able。foresee は fore「予め」＋ see「見る」で「予見する」という意味。

## 48.

正答：B

The word “egotism” in line 20 is closest in meaning to

(A) sin
(B) selfishness
(C) disrespect
(D) violence

20 行目の “egotism” にもっとも近い意味を持つのは

(A) 罪
(B) 自己中心
(C) 無礼
(D) 暴力

“egotism” は，ego「自我，エゴ」から推測されるように，「利己主義，うぬぼれ」のこと。同様に self「自己」を含む (B) が正答。

## 49.　正答：A

The word "their" in line 23 refers to

(A) young women
(B) parents
(C) future husbands
(D) children

23 行目の "their" が指し示しているのは

(A) 若い女
(B) 両親
(C) 未来の夫
(D) 子どもたち

等位接続詞 and を介して their ... の形が並列にあるので，この their はすべて同一であるとわかる。よって，(A) が正答。

## 50.　正答：D

It can be inferred from the author's discussion of Plains Indian children that

(A) males and females fought side-by-side during war
(B) women were also expected to hunt for food
(C) girls matured more quickly than boys
(D) male and female roles were quite different

プレーンズインディアンの子どもたちに関する筆者の解説から推測すると

(A) 戦闘時に男性と女性が並んで戦った
(B) 女性も食料のため狩りをするよう期待されていた
(C) 女の子は男の子よりも早く大人になった
(D) 男性と女性の役割が大きく異なっていた

4 で対比対照を表す接続詞 while をはさんで, The young men ... と young women ... に期待される異なる役割が具体的に説明されている。よって，(D) が正答。

---

ボキャブラリー
- □ **extreme**「極端さ」
- □ **nomadic**「遊牧の」
- □ **tribe**「部族」
- □ **social entity**「社会共同体」
- □ **harsh**「厳しい」
- □ **greed**「貪欲さ」
- □ **uphold**「～を支える」
- □ **virtuous**「道徳的な」

Practice Test 3

# 第3回実戦問題

## 解説

## 【第 3 回】実戦問題　正答一覧

### Listening Comprehension

| Part A | | Part B | |
|---|---|---|---|
| 1 | C | 31 | C |
| 2 | B | 32 | A |
| 3 | D | 33 | B |
| 4 | A | 34 | D |
| 5 | C | 35 | C |
| 6 | C | 36 | A |
| 7 | C | 37 | B |
| 8 | D | 38 | D |
| 9 | A | **Part C** | |
| 10 | D | 39 | B |
| 11 | D | 40 | A |
| 12 | A | 41 | C |
| 13 | D | 42 | D |
| 14 | A | 43 | A |
| 15 | B | 44 | D |
| 16 | B | 45 | B |
| 17 | A | 46 | D |
| 18 | B | 47 | B |
| 19 | A | 48 | C |
| 20 | B | 49 | A |
| 21 | B | 50 | C |
| 22 | C | | |
| 23 | B | | |
| 24 | A | | |
| 25 | B | | |
| 26 | D | | |
| 27 | D | | |
| 28 | C | | |
| 29 | C | | |
| 30 | C | | |

### Structure and Written Expression

| Structure | | Written Expression | |
|---|---|---|---|
| 1 | A | | |
| 2 | C | 16 | B |
| 3 | D | 17 | D |
| 4 | B | 18 | A |
| 5 | A | 19 | C |
| 6 | D | 20 | C |
| 7 | D | 21 | C |
| 8 | A | 22 | B |
| 9 | B | 23 | D |
| 10 | C | 24 | B |
| 11 | B | 25 | C |
| 12 | A | 26 | A |
| 13 | B | 27 | D |
| 14 | C | 28 | B |
| 15 | D | 29 | D |
| | | 30 | A |
| | | 31 | D |
| | | 32 | C |
| | | 33 | B |
| | | 34 | C |
| | | 35 | C |
| | | 36 | A |
| | | 37 | D |
| | | 38 | C |
| | | 39 | D |
| | | 40 | C |

### Reading Comprehension

| | | | |
|---|---|---|---|
| 1 | B | 26 | D |
| 2 | C | 27 | A |
| 3 | D | 28 | B |
| 4 | A | 29 | C |
| 5 | D | 30 | D |
| 6 | A | 31 | D |
| 7 | B | 32 | A |
| 8 | D | 33 | C |
| 9 | D | 34 | B |
| 10 | D | 35 | A |
| 11 | C | 36 | B |
| 12 | C | 37 | C |
| 13 | A | 38 | B |
| 14 | B | 39 | D |
| 15 | C | 40 | C |
| 16 | A | 41 | C |
| 17 | C | 42 | B |
| 18 | D | 43 | B |
| 19 | A | 44 | A |
| 20 | D | 45 | B |
| 21 | D | 46 | A |
| 22 | A | 47 | B |
| 23 | C | 48 | A |
| 24 | B | 49 | C |
| 25 | C | 50 | B |

## 1. 大学院進学についての学生同士の会話 正答：C

088

| | | |
|---|---|---|
| M | Say, Helen, did you hear back on your graduate school application yet? | M: そういえば，ヘレン，大学院への願書の結果は来た？ |
| W | Just this morning I got the acceptance letter I'd been waiting for. | W: けさ，ずっと待っていた合格通知が届いたわ。 |

What does the woman mean?
女性は何と言っていますか。

(A) She filed the application earlier in the morning.
(B) Her acceptance letter has not arrived yet.
(C) Her application to graduate school was successful.
(D) She decided not to apply to graduate school.

(A) けさ早くに願書を提出した。
(B) 合格通知はまだ届いていない。
(C) 大学院への出願がうまくいった。
(D) 大学院に出願しないことに決めた。

男性に願書出願の結果を聞かれ，女性は the acceptance letter「合格通知」が届いたと応じている。よって，出願が successful であったと言い換えている (C) が正答。hear back は「返事をもらう」という意味。(A) の file an application は「願書を提出する，申請を出す」という意味。acceptance letter の繰り返しで (B) にひっかからないように。

ボキャブラリー □ **application**「出願，出願書類」 □ **acceptance letter**「合格通知」

## 2. 待ち合わせについての学生同士の会話 正答：B

089

| | | |
|---|---|---|
| W | Mark, I'm really sorry for keeping you waiting. My history class didn't finish on time. | W: マーク，待たせてしまってごめんなさい。歴史学のクラスが時間どおりに終わらなかったの。 |
| M | No sweat, Margaret. I've got an essay exam later today, and it gave me time to review my notes. | M: 気にしなくていいよ，マーガレット。今日は後から論述式のテストがあるので，ノートを見直す時間ができたから。 |

What did the man do while he was waiting for the woman?
男性は女性を待っている間，何をしましたか。

(A) He wrote a note.
(B) He studied for a test.
(C) He prepared for a presentation.
(D) He outlined an essay.

(A) メモを書いた。
(B) 試験勉強をした。
(C) 発表の準備をした。
(D) レポートのアウトラインを作成した。

女性が待ち合わせに遅れたことを謝ったのに対して，男性は essay exam「論述式テスト」のために review my notes「ノートを見直す」ことができたと応じている。これをまとめて言い換えている (B) が正答となる。essay exam を test と言い換えている。No sweat. は「平気だ」という意味の口語表現。

ボキャブラリー □ **essay exam**「論述式試験」 □ **review**「～を復習する」

## 3. 舞台についての学生同士の会話 正答：D

090

M What are you still doing here in the dorm? I thought the play you're doing for your acting class starts at seven—it's almost 5:45 now. Don't you need to get ready?

M: まだ寮に残って何しているの？ 演劇のクラスのためにきみがやる予定の舞台は7時に始まると思っていたけど。もうすぐ5時45分だよ。準備しなくていいの？

W No hurry. They pushed the starting time back one hour because a special lecture by a visiting scholar is being given in the auditorium. As long as I leave by six, I'll be there in plenty of time.

W: 急がなくていいのよ。講堂では客員教授が特別講義をやっていて，開演時間が1時間遅れることになったの。6時までに出れば，十分間に合うわ。

What does the woman imply?

女性は何を示唆していますか。

(A) Her performance has been canceled.
(B) She plans on going to a lecture later.
(C) The man is welcome to attend the play.
(D) She will leave the dorm soon.

(A) 公演は中止になった。
(B) 後で講義に行こうと思っている。
(C) 男性が演劇に参加するのは歓迎である。
(D) もうすぐ寮を出る。

男性の it's almost 5:45 now から，この会話が交わされているのは6時少し前だとわかる。演劇に出る予定の女性は As long as I leave by six ...「6時までに出れば」と言っているので，まもなく出かけるはずである。よって，(D) が正答。公演が中止されたわけではないので (A) は誤り。lecture，play の繰り返しだけで (B) (C) を選ばないように。

ボキャブラリー □ **dorm**「寮」 □ **push ... back**「～を遅らせる，後退させる」
□ **visiting scholar**「客員教授」 □ **auditorium**「講堂」

## 4. 実験についての学生同士の会話 正答：A

091

W I'm having a really hard time scheduling lab time for my biology experiment. In the laboratories, faculty have first priority, then graduate students. Undergraduate students like us don't have much opportunity to get into the lab. Except late at night, of course.

W: 生物学の実験のために実験室を使う時間がうまく取れないでいるのよ。実験室では教授が最優先で，その次が大学院生なの。私たち学部生は実験室を使える機会があんまりないの。もちろん，夜遅くを除いてね。

M I had the same problem. And when I complained, everybody just said that that's the way it's always been in the biology department.

M: ぼくも同じ問題を抱えていたよ。それでぼくが苦情を言ったら，みんな，生物学部では昔からずっとそうだったって言うだけなんだよ。

What problem is the woman having?

(A) The research facilities she needs are seldom available.
(B) The biology department does not hire undergraduates.
(C) The biology laboratory is closed at night.
(D) The biology faculty are too busy to help the students.

女性はどんな問題を抱えていますか。

(A) 必要な研究施設がめったに使えない。
(B) 生物学部は学部生を雇わない。
(C) 生物実験室は夜は閉まっている。
(D) 教授たちが忙しくて学生を手伝えない。

女性は生物学の実験について，I'm having a really hard time scheduling lab time.「実験室を使う時間がうまく取れずにいる」と説明し，その理由は実験室使用の優先順位が決まっているためだと述べている。よって，(A) が正答。lab を The research facilities she needs，having a really hard time scheduling を seldom available「めったに空いていない」に言い換えている。

ボキャブラリー □ **faculty**「（集合的に）教員」 □ **priority**「優先」 □ **undergraduate**「学部の」

## 5. 友人についての学生同士の会話 正答：C

092

M Robert has been spending a lot of time in the library lately.
W You would too if you were failing in three classes.

M: ロバートは最近，ずいぶんと図書館にいるね。
W: 3つも授業を落としそうだったら，あなたもそうするでしょ。

What does the woman imply about Robert?

(A) He likes studying in the library.
(B) He took too many courses this term.
(C) He is not a very good student.
(D) He is taking a class in library research.

女性はロバートについて何を示唆していますか。

(A) 彼は図書館で勉強するのが好きだ。
(B) 彼は今学期，授業を取りすぎた。
(C) 彼はあまり模範的な学生ではない。
(D) 彼は図書館リサーチのクラスを取っている。

「ロバートが図書館にずっといる」理由について，女性は彼が were failing in three classes「3つも授業を落としそうだ」と，仮定法で示唆している。ここから，ロバートがあまり勉強熱心な学生ではないとわかるので，(C) が正答。

ボキャブラリー □ **fail**「落第する」

## 6. レポートについての学生同士の会話 正答：C

093

M Mary, I really need a favor. Would you have any time to proofread my research report?
W How does tomorrow sound?

M: メアリー，ぜひお願いしたいことがあるんだけど。ぼくのリサーチレポートを校正してもらう時間あるかな？
W: 明日ではどう？

What does the woman mean?

(A) She is rather busy tomorrow.
(B) She is planning to go downtown.
(C) She can check his report the next day.
(D) She hopes the man will finish his research soon.

女性は何と言っていますか。

(A) 明日はとても忙しい。
(B) 町に行く予定である。
(C) 翌日に彼のレポートをチェックできる。
(D) 男性にすぐにリサーチを終えてほしい。

レポートを校正してくれる時間があるか尋ねた男性に対して，女性は How does tomorrow sound?「明日ではどう？」と応じている。よって，(C) が正答。proofread を check に，tomorrow を the next day に言い換えている。tomorrow，research などの断片的な聞き取りで (A) (D) を選ばないように。tomorrow から明日の予定の話だと誤った連想をすると，(B) にひっかかってしまう。

ボキャブラリー □ **favor**「親切な行為，世話」 □ **proofread**「〜を校正する」

## 7. お金の貸し借りについての学生同士の会話　正答：C

094

**W** Peter, I know I haven't paid you back the $50 I borrowed from you last month, but I was wondering if maybe you could lend me another $20 to go to a movie tonight?

**M** Come on, Mary. You've got to be kidding!

**W:** ピーター，先月借りた50ドルをまだ返してないことはわかっているのだけど，今夜映画に行くのにまた20ドル貸してもらえたらって，思っているの。

**M:** いいかげんにしてよ，メアリー。冗談だろ！

What can be inferred from the conversation?

(A) The man enjoys the woman's sense of humor.
(B) The woman will go to see a film later in the evening.
(C) The man does not intend to loan money to the woman.
(D) The woman has not seen the man for several months.

この会話から何が推測できますか。

(A) 男性は女性のユーモアを楽しんでいる。
(B) 女性は今夜映画を観に行くだろう。
(C) 男性は女性にお金を貸すつもりはない。
(D) 女性は何か月も男性に会っていなかった。

女性が男性に再三の借金を頼むと，男性は Come on, Mary. You've got to be kidding! と言って呆れている。Come on. は，ここでは反語的に「いいかげんにしろ，よしてくれ」という意味。つまり男性は，女性にまたお金を貸すつもりはないと断っているので，(C) が正答。kidding を文字どおりにとると，(A) の sense of humor にひっかかってしまう。お金を借りられなかったこの女性が実際に映画に行くかどうかは不明なので，(B) は誤り。

ボキャブラリー □ **come on**「よせよ，いいかげんにしろ」 □ **sense of humor**「ユーモア」

## 8. 教授についての学生同士の会話　正答：D

095

**M** I'm having a hard time following Dr. Dacy's lectures. The organization of the lectures is clear, but her handwriting is illegible. I can't read anything she writes on the board.

**W** Me, neither. I tried sitting closer to the front, but I still can't make out anything she writes down.

M: デイシー博士の講義についていくのはたいへんだよ。講義の構成は明確なんだけど，彼女の字は読みにくいね。彼女の板書はまったく読めないよ。

W: 私もよ。前に近い席に座ったけど，それでも彼女の書くことは何もわからなかったわ。

What problem are the speakers discussing?

(A) The professor speaks too softly.
(B) The professor's pronunciation is unclear.
(C) The professor's lectures are disorganized.
(D) The professor has poor handwriting.

話者らはどんな問題について話していますか。

(A) 教授は声が小さすぎる。
(B) 教授の発音は不明瞭である。
(C) 教授の講義はまとまりがない。
(D) 教授は字がへただ。

教授の板書は illegible「読みにくい」ため，I can't read anything she writes「まったく読めない」と男性が言ったのに対して，女性も Me, neither.「私もよ」と同意している。よって，2人とも教授の字が汚いと感じているとわかるので，これを poor handwriting「字がへただ」と言い換えている (D) が正答。(B) の unclear，(C) の disorganized は部分的な音の重なりによるひっかけ。

ボキャブラリー □ **handwriting**「筆跡，書体」 □ **make out**「(文字などを) 判読する，理解する」

## 9. レポートについての学生同士の会話　正答：A

096

**W** My research paper is due tomorrow, and I haven't even started it yet. I guess it will be another all-nighter for me.

**M** Not again!

W: リサーチペーパーは明日が締め切りなのに，まだ始めてもいないのよ。また徹夜になりそうな気がするわ。

M: まさか，また？

What can be inferred about the woman?

(A) She completes assignments at the last minute.
(B) She is an excellent researcher.
(C) She enjoys writing term papers.
(D) She plans to go to an all-night party.

女性について何が推測できますか。

(A) ギリギリで課題を仕上げる。
(B) 優秀な研究者である。
(C) 期末レポートを書くことを楽しんでいる。
(D) オールナイトのパーティーに行く予定だ。

女性が another all-nighter「また徹夜」と言い，男性は Not again!「まさか，また？」と応じている。ここから，女性がギリギリまで課題を終えないのは今回が初めてでないとわかるので，(A) が正答。research paper が assignment と言い換えられている。

ボキャブラリー □ **due**「期限の」 □ **all-nighter**「徹夜，一晩中続くもの」

## 10. 外国語学習についての学生同士の会話　正答：D

097

**M** The self-study lab for our French course is fantastic. It has all kinds of materials that help with everything from pronunciation to vocabulary building. I've been there every day this week, and I can already see the improvement in my listening skill.

**M:** フランス語のコースの自習用ラボってすごいよ！　発音から語彙の増強まで，役に立つ教材が何でもあるんだ。ぼくは今週毎日通ってるけど，もうリスニングの力が伸びているのが実感できるよ。

**W** I guess I'd better go check it out then. Thanks for the tip.

**W:** じゃあ私も行ってみるべきね。アドバイスをありがとう。

What does the woman mean?

女性は何と言っていますか。

(A) She will try to check out the book later.
(B) Use of the self-study lab should not be required.
(C) Her pronunciation in French is already good enough.
(D) She will visit the self-study lab herself.

(A) 後で本を借りてみるだろう。
(B) 自習室の使用は義務付けられるべきでない。
(C) 自分のフランス語の発音はもう十分うまい。
(D) 自分も自習用ラボに行ってみる。

男性が語学独習用ラボのメリットを説明すると，女性は I guess I'd better go check it out then.「私も行ってみるべきね」と応じている。check out とは「～の様子を見る，試す」という意味で，ここでの it は語学ラボのこと。よって，彼女も語学ラボに行くつもりだとわかるので (D) が正答。なお check out には図書館などで本を「借り出す」という意味もあり，この意味でとると (A) にひっかかる。

ボキャブラリー □ **self-study lab**「自習用ラボ」 □ **material**「教材，資料」
□ **pronunciation**「発音」 □ **tip**「アドバイス」

## 11. 週末の予定についての学生同士の会話　正答：D

098

**M** If you don't have any plans for this weekend, I was wondering if you'd like to drive up the coast with me to meet my family.

**M:** 今週末，特に予定がないなら，海岸沿いにドライブしながら，ぼくの家族に会いに来ないかなって思ったんだけど。

**W** I'd love to. You've been bragging about your mother's cooking all semester.

**W:** ぜひそうしたいわ。今学期中ずっとお母さんの手料理を自慢してたわよね。

What will the speakers do this weekend?

話者らは今週末，何をしますか。

(A) Invite the man's family for dinner
(B) Help the man's mother cook a meal
(C) Take a hike on the coast
(D) Visit the man's family

(A) 男性の家族を夕食に招く
(B) 男性の母親が料理するのを手伝う
(C) 海岸沿いをハイキングする
(D) 男性の家族を訪問する

男性が実家に来ないかと誘ったのに対して，女性が I'd love to.「ぜひそうしたいわ」と応じているので，2人は男性の実家に行くつもりであるとわかる。よって，(D) が正答。mother，cook，coast など断片的な聞き取りでは (B) (C) にひっかかってしまう。

ボキャブラリー □ **brag about ...**「～を自慢する」 □ **take a hike**「ハイキングする」

## 12. 教授についての学生同士の会話 正答：A

099

**W:** Is my watch slow, or did Professor Salazar let us out early again?

**M:** There's nothing wrong with your watch. And to tell the truth, Salazar's lectures are ones I don't mind at all getting out of early.

**W:** 私の時計が遅れているのかしら。それとも，サラザール教授がまた早めにクラスを終わらせてくれたのかしら。

**M:** きみの時計には問題ないよ。それにはっきり言って，サラザール先生の講義は早く終わってくれて，いっこうにかまわないし。

What does the man imply about Professor Salazar?

(A) His lectures are not very interesting.
(B) His lectures often run overtime.
(C) He often comes early to his lectures.
(D) He does not mind if students miss his lectures.

男性はサラザール教授について何を示唆していますか。

(A) 講義があまりおもしろくない。
(B) 講義がよく長引く。
(C) よく講義に早めにくる。
(D) 学生が講義を欠席しても気にしない。

男性がこの教授のクラスが早く終わるのはいっこうにかまわないと言っていることから，このクラスが退屈であると推測できる。よって，(A) が正答。watch からの誤った連想で (B) や (C) を選ばないように。not mind や lectures などの断片的な聞き取りでは (D) にひっかかってしまう。

ボキャブラリー □ **overtime**「規定時間を超えて」

## 13. 午後の天気についての学生同士の会話 正答：D

100

**M:** I sure hope it doesn't rain. We've got a tennis meet scheduled for this afternoon.

**W:** Well, you'll be lucky if it doesn't. The forecast is for showers.

**M:** 絶対に雨が降ってほしくないんだ。今日の午後，テニスの予定があるから。

**W:** 降らなければ運がいいわよ。天気予報ではにわか雨ですって。

What does the woman mean?

(A) The man should take a shower after playing tennis.
(B) The tennis team changed its practice schedule.
(C) The man will be lucky to win his tennis match.
(D) The weather may not be very good for tennis.

女性は何と言っていますか。

(A) 男性はテニス後にシャワーを浴びるべきだ。
(B) テニスのチームは練習の予定を変更した。
(C) 男性はテニスの試合に勝てれば運がよい。
(D) 天気はおそらくテニスにはあまりよくない。

テニスをするので雨が降らないでほしいと言う男性に対して，女性は The forecast is for showers.「天気予報ではにわか雨」と応じている。この天気がテニスに適さないのは明らかなので，(D) が正答。(A) の shower，(B) の schedule，(C) の will be lucky など，部分的な繰り返しにひっかからないよう注意。

ボキャブラリー □ **meet**「競技会，集まり」

## 14. 宿題についての学生同士の会話 正答：A

101

**M** This term I'm really going to get organized. No more all-nighters! I'm going to do the readings on time, and, above all, I'm going to get my reports and essays done even before they are due.

**M:** 今学期はちゃんと計画的になるんだ。もう徹夜はしないよ！ リーディングの予習は予定どおりにやるし，それに何より，レポートやエッセイは締切前に終わらせるつもりさ。

**W** Give me a break, David. When was the last time you actually finished a paper before the deadline?

**W:** ちょっと待ってよ，デイビッド。あなたが締切前にちゃんとレポートを終わらせたのはいつのことだったかしら？

What does the woman imply about the man? 女性は男性について何を示唆していますか。

(A) His plans are unrealistic.
(B) He ought to take a short break from his reading.
(C) He should begin reading the class textbook.
(D) He studies more than he actually needs to.

(A) 計画が非現実的だ。
(B) 宿題をやめて短い休憩を取るべきだ。
(C) 授業の教科書を読み始めるべきだ。。
(D) 必要以上に勉強する。

男性が新学期の決意表明をすると，女性は Give me a break と言って驚いている。これは「冗談はやめて」程度の軽い口語表現。続いて When was the last time ... ? と言っているが，これは反語的な疑問文で「～はいつ？（そんなことはなかったでしょう）」という意味。ここから，男性はいつも締切を過ぎてレポートを提出していたと推測できる。よって，(A) が正答。

ボキャブラリー □ **Give me a break.**「ちょっと待ってよ，勘弁して」 □ **deadline**「締切」

## 15. コンサートについての学生同士の会話 正答：B

102

**M** Did you pick up the tickets to tonight's concert at the student center?

**M:** 今夜のコンサートのチケット，学生センターで買ってくれたかい？

**W** Sure did. You owe me $50.

**W:** ええ，もちろんよ。50ドル，私に返してね。

What can be inferred from the conversation? 会話から何が推測できますか。

(A) The tickets for the concert were sold out.
(B) The woman paid for the man's concert ticket.
(C) The concert will start just before 8 o'clock.
(D) The man decided not to attend the concert.

(A) コンサートのチケットは売り切れていた。
(B) 男性のコンサートチケット代は女性が払った。
(C) コンサートは８時少し前に始まる。
(D) 男性はコンサートに行かないことにした。

女性は男性に対して，You owe me $50「50ドル貸しがある」と言っていることから，女性が男性のチケット代を立て替えたと推測できる。よって，(B) が正答。女性の Sure did. は Sure, I did pick up the tickets ... という意味。

ボキャブラリー □ **pick up**「～を手に入れる」 □ **be sold out**「売り切れている」

## 16. カフェテリアでの学生同士の会話 正答：B

103

M Do you mind if I sit here? The cafeteria's packed today.

W I'm saving this seat for my friend. But you can sit here until she comes.

M: ここに座ってもいいですか？ 今日はカフェテリアがいっぱいなので。

W: この席は友人のために取ってあるのですが，彼女が来るまでなら，どうぞ。

What does the woman mean?

(A) The man needs to move to another seat right away.
(B) The man can sit there for the time being.
(C) She would like the man to meet her friend.
(D) She is unsure whether her friend is coming.

女性は何と言っていますか。

(A) 男性はすぐに別の席に移る必要がある。
(B) 男性はしばらくの間そこに座っていてよい。
(C) 男性に自分の友人に会ってほしい。
(D) 友人が来るかどうかわからない。

カフェテリアで空席を探している男性に対して，女性は until she comes「彼女が来るまでなら」座ってもかまわないと応じている。よって，これを for the time being「しばらくの間」と言い換えている (B) が正答。

ボキャブラリー □ **packed**「満員で」

## 17. 実験についての学生同士の会話 正答：A

104

W I'm quite excited about the next chemistry lab. We're pairing up to do some original research, and the professor assigned me to work with Bill. I think we'll make a good team.

M Bill? You've got to be kidding. He never follows through on anything.

W: 次の化学の実験がすごく楽しみなの。ペアを組んでそれぞれ独自のリサーチをするんだけど，教授は私とビルを組ませたの。いいコンビになるわ。

M: ビル？ 冗談だろ。彼は何も最後までやり通さないよ。

What does the man imply about the woman's research partner?

(A) He is not very reliable.
(B) He has a very good sense of humor.
(C) He can do just about anything.
(D) He is more of a leader than a follower.

男性は女性のリサーチパートナーについて何を示唆していますか。

(A) あまり頼りにならない。
(B) ユーモアのセンスがある。
(C) ほとんど何でもできる。
(D) 人についていくよりも引っ張っていくタイプだ。

自分の研究パートナーはビルだと言った女性に対して，男性は He never follows through on anything. と応じている。follow through は「最後までやり通す」という意味。ここから，ビルがあまり頼りにならない人物だと推測できるので，(A) が正答。kidding からの誤った連想で (B) を選ばないように。

ボキャブラリー □ **assign**「～を割り当てる」 □ **follower**「追随者」

## 18. 予習課題についての学生同士の会話　正答：B

105

**M** Do you know by what day we have to have read those supplementary readings?

**W** Beats me. Professor Cox hands those articles out sometimes, but then he isn't really clear on when they're actually going to be covered in class. I wish he would put this kind of information on the syllabus.

M: この追加の予習課題，何曜日までに読み終えなきゃいけないか知ってる？

W: 知らないわ。コックス教授はこういう論文をときどき配っておいて，実際いつ授業で扱うのかはあんまりはっきりしないのよね。こういう情報は講義予定表に載せてくれるといいんだけど。

What are the speakers complaining about?

(A) Their professor's lectures are not very clear.
(B) They do not know when their reading assignments are due.
(C) They did not receive a copy of the course syllabus.
(D) The articles they are reading are difficult to understand.

話者らは何について不満を述べていますか。

(A) 教授の講義はあまり明解でない。
(B) 予習課題の期限がいつなのかわからない。
(C) 講義予定表をもらっていない。
(D) 今読んでいる論文は理解するのが難しい。

男性が追加の予習課題の期限を尋ねると，女性は Beats me. と応じている。これは「さあね，わからない」という意味の口語表現。ここから，2 人ともこの宿題の期限を知らないとわかる。よって期限を due という語で言い換えている (B) が正答。

ボキャブラリー □ **supplementary reading**「追加教材」 □ **Beats me.**「わからない」
□ **hand ... out**「～を配る」 □ **article**「記事，論文」
□ **syllabus**「講義要項，シラバス」

## 19. 成績についての学生同士の会話　正答：A

106

**M** Do you think you'll be able to persuade your parents to let you have a car during your last year in school?

**W** It'll be really tough, especially considering how demanding my classes are this semester. But if I work hard and maintain a high grade point average this term, I think I'll be able to convince them.

M: きみが最終学年に在籍している間に車を持たせてくれるように両親を説得できると思う？

W: かなりきついと思うわ。特に今学期どれだけ授業がたいへんかを考えるとね。でも，がんばって勉強して今学期よい成績を維持できたら，説得できると思うわ。

What does the woman imply?

(A) She will have to study especially hard this semester.
(B) She probably will not be able to persuade her parents.
(C) She does not really need to have a car on campus.
(D) She is worried that her grades may drop this term.

女性は何を示唆していますか。

(A) 今学期は特にがんばって勉強しなくてはならない。
(B) おそらく両親を説得できないだろう。
(C) 学内ではあまり車を持つ必要がない。
(D) 今学期成績が下がるかもしれないと不安だ。

女性は，車を持てるように親を説得するには maintain a high grade point average this term「今学期よい成績を維持すること」が条件だと言っている。また，今学期の授業について considering how demanding my classes are this semester「授業がどれだけたいへんかを考えると」と述べている。難しい授業をとりながら好成績を維持するということは，一生懸命に勉強しなければならないということ。よって，(A) が正答。

ボキャブラリー □ **persuade**「～を説得する」 □ **demanding**「要求の厳しい」 □ **semester**「学期」 □ **convince**「～を説得する」

## 20. 大学進学についての学生同士の会話 正答：B

107

**M** Have you sent off all of your applications for graduate school yet?

**W** Almost. I'm still waiting for my advisor to finish writing a letter of recommendation to one of the schools. He said he'd finish it later this week.

**M:** 大学院の願書はもう全部送ったの？

**W:** ほとんどね。指導教官が志望校のひとつへの推薦状を書いてくれるのを待っているの。今週後半には書き終えるって言ってたわ。

What does the woman mean?

(A) All of her applications have been submitted.
(B) She will be able to submit the last application soon.
(C) She has decided against going to graduate school.
(D) All of her professors wrote recommendations.

女性は何と言っていますか。

(A) 願書はすべて提出した。
(B) もうすぐ最後の願書を提出できるだろう。
(C) 大学院には行かないことにした。
(D) 教授は全員推薦状を書いてくれた。

大学院への願書送付はすべて終わったか男性が尋ねると，女性は Almost.「ほとんど」，つまり，まだ終わってはいないと答えている。続いて女性は，今週中にあと 1 通推薦状を書いてもらうのを待っていると説明しているので，彼女はまもなく最後の出願書類を送ることができるとわかる。よって，(B) が正答。

ボキャブラリー □ **application**「願書」 □ **graduate school**「大学院」 □ **advisor**「指導教官」 □ **letter of recommendation**「推薦状」

## 21. 勉強会についての学生同士の会話 正答：B

108

**W** Do you know where we're supposed to get together for our study group tonight?

**M** I don't have a clue. I wish we would just pick one spot and stay with it.

W: 今夜の勉強会はどこで集まることになっているか知ってる？

M: 見当もつかないよ。いつも同じ場所に決めておけばいいのにね。

What does the man imply about the study group?

男性は勉強会について何を示唆していますか。

(A) It is much too difficult for him.
(B) It has no regular meeting place.
(C) It has too many members.
(D) It always meets at the same time.

(A) 自分にとっては難しすぎる。
(B) 決まった集合場所がない。
(C) メンバーが多すぎる。
(D) いつも同じ時間に集合している。

女性が勉強会の場所を尋ねると，男性は I don't have a clue. と答えている。これは口語で「さっぱりわからない，見当もつかない」という意味。また，I wish we would just pick one spot and stay with it. と述べていることから，勉強会には決まった場所がないとわかるので，(B) が正答。

ボキャブラリー □ **get together**「集まる」

## 22. キャンプ用品についての学生同士の会話 正答：C

109

**W** Did you know that it only costs $5 a night to rent tents from the student recreation center?

**M** That sounds like a real bargain. No wonder so many students go camping on weekends.

W: レクリエーションセンターからテントを借りるのに一泊5ドルしかかからないって知ってた？

M: それは格安だね。道理で多くの学生が週末にキャンプに行くわけだ。

What are the speakers discussing?

話者らは何について話していますか。

(A) The high fees to use the student recreation center
(B) The new campground that has been built
(C) The low cost of renting camping gear
(D) The sale of tents at a camping supply shop

(A) レクリエーションセンターの高い利用料
(B) できたばかりの新しいキャンプ場
(C) キャンプ用品のレンタル料の安さ
(D) キャンプ用品店でのテントのセール

女性が学生レクリエーションセンターのテント貸し出しが it only costs $5 a night「一泊５ドルしかかからない」と言ったのに対して，男性は That sounds like a real bargain. と応じている。real bargain は「掘り出し物，お買い得品」という意味なので，2人がキャンプ用品レンタル料の安さについて話していることは明らか。よって，正答は (C)。student recreation center，camp，tents などの断片的な聞き取りで (A) (B) (D) にひっかからないように注意。

ボキャブラリー □ **recreation center**「娯楽・研修施設」 □ **campground**「キャンプ場」
□ **gear**「用具，道具」

## 23. 通学手段についての学生同士の会話　正答：B

110

M The carpool sure worked great while it lasted. No one ever missed a day, and it certainly helped us to cut commuting costs.

W Yes, but with the weather getting warmer, we'll all be switching over to bicycles anyway. We can start the carpool up in the fall again when the weather gets cold.

M: 車の相乗りをやっている間，すごくうまくいっていたね。だれもサボらなかったし，確実に通学費用も抑えられたし。

W: そうね。でも，気候も暖かくなってきているから，いずれにしてもみんな自転車に代えることになるわね。秋になって寒くなってきたら，また相乗りを始めればいいわよ。

What can be inferred from the conversation?

(A) The carpool was unsuccessful.
(B) The carpool will resume later in the year.
(C) The woman would like to join the carpool.
(D) The carpool was expensive to maintain.

この会話から何が推測できますか。

(A) 相乗りはうまくいかなかった。
(B) 相乗りは今年の後半に再開する。
(C) 女性は相乗りに参加したい。
(D) 相乗りを続けるには費用がかかった。

女性は，We can start the carpool up in the fall again「秋になればまた乗り合いを再開できる」と述べている。よって，(B) が正答。start up again が resume，the fall が later in the year と言い換えられている。carpool とは，ガソリン代の節約のために，車を持つ何人かが組んで，通学や買い物のときに輪番で自分の車に他人を相乗りさせること。cut ... costs からの誤った連想で (D) を選ばないように。

ボキャブラリー □ **last**「続く」　□ **commute**「通学・通勤する」

## 24. 私物の貸し借りについての学生同士の会話　正答：A

111

W Dan, you're welcome to borrow my backpack when you go hiking this weekend, but if you don't mind my asking, what happened to your own backpack?

M The straps broke on it. And I'm short on money this month, so I won't be able to buy a new one until at least next month.

W: ダン，今週末ハイキングに行くのに私のバックパックを借りていくのはかまわないけど，自分のバックパックはどうしたのか聞いてもいい？

M: ぼくのはストラップが壊れたんだ。それに，今月はちょっとお金が足りなくて，少なくとも来月にならないと新しいのは買えないんだよ。

What does the man tell the woman?

(A) His backpack is unusable.
(B) He will buy a new backpack this weekend.
(C) His backpack is not big enough.
(D) He will pay back the money next month.

男性は女性に何と言っていますか。

(A) 自分のバックパックは使えない。
(B) 今週末に新しいバックパックを買う。
(C) 自分のバックパックでは大きさが足りない。
(D) 来月お金を返す。

「自分のバックパックはどうしたの？」と尋ねる女性に対して，男性は The straps broke on it.「ストラップが壊れた」と答えている。よって，これを unusable「使えない」と言い換えている (A) が正答。buy a new や money，next month の断片的な聞き取りで (B) や (D) を選ばないように注意。

ボキャブラリー □ **backpack**「バックパック，リュックサック」
□ **be short on money**「お金が足りない」

## 25. カフェテリアについての学生同士の会話　正答：B

112

W No way I want to eat at the student cafeteria again tonight. I've eaten there three nights in a row.

M Gee. I can understand the way you feel. Overcooked beef and rubber carrots are not my idea of a good meal, either.

W: 今夜もまたカフェテリアで食べるなんて絶対いやよ。このところ3晩続けてそこで食べているんだから。

M: それはたいへんだ。その気持ち，ぼくにもわかるよ。ガチガチのビーフや，ゴムみたいなニンジン，ぼくにもごちそうには思えないさ。

What do the speakers imply about the cafeteria?

(A) Its prices are unreasonably high.
(B) Its food is not very delicious.
(C) It closes too early in the evening.
(D) It serves rather healthy meals.

話者らはカフェテリアについて何を示唆していますか。

(A) 値段が法外に高い。
(B) 食事があまりおいしくない。
(C) 夜の閉店が早すぎる。
(D) とても健康的な食事を提供している。

女性がカフェテリアで続けて食事をしたくないと言ったのに対して，男性も同感だと応じ，Overcooked beef and rubber carrots とまずい食事を具体的に挙げている。よって，(B) が正答。No way. は「絶対にありえない，いやだ」という強い拒否の気持ちを表す口語表現。相手からの誘いに対して「絶対いやだ」と断るときにも使う。Gee はもともと Jesus を遠回しに略した語で，「おや，まあ！」と驚きや称賛の気持ちを示す。

ボキャブラリー □ **student cafeteria**「学生食堂」 □ **in a row**「続けて」
□ **unreasonably**「法外に」

## 26. 寮生活についての学生同士の会話　正答：D

113

W I am really upset. The darned washer in our dorm is on the blink again, and I have nothing to wear to the dance tonight.

M This is your lucky day. I was just on my way to the laundromat on 5th Avenue. Go get your wash, and I'll give you a ride there.

W: まったく頭に来るわ。寮のポンコツ洗濯機の調子がまたおかしくて，今夜のダンスに着ていく服が何もないのよ。

M: きみ，今日はついているよ。ちょうど5番通りのコインランドリーに行くところだったんだ。洗濯物を持っておいでよ。そこまで車で送ってあげるから。

Why is the woman upset?

(A) She will not be able to attend the dance.
(B) She does not have time to go to the laundromat.
(C) She does not know where the dance will be held.
(D) She cannot use the washing machine in her dorm.

女性はなぜ怒っているのですか。

(A) ダンスに参加できそうにない。
(B) コインランドリーに行く時間がない。
(C) どこでダンスが行われるかわからない。
(D) 寮の洗濯機が使えない。

女性は，The darned washer in our dorm is on the blink again「寮のポンコツ洗濯機の調子がまたおかしくて」と述べており，寮の洗濯機が使える状態ではないとわかる。よって，(D) が正答。washer を washing machine と言い換えている。dance，laundromat といった断片的な単語の繰り返しだけで (A) (B) (C) を選ばないように。

ボキャブラリー □ **darned**「しゃくにさわる，いまいましい」 □ **on the blink**「(機械などが) 調子が悪い」 □ **laundromat**「コインランドリー」

## 27. 成績についての教授と学生の会話 正答：D

114

**M** Dr. Quincy, you sent me an e-mail to come and see you during your office hour tomorrow. What's up?

**W** To be honest, Karl, I'd rather wait until tomorrow to talk about it with you in detail. But I should let you know that I'm extremely concerned about how you performed on the mid-term exam. It was totally out of character for you.

**M:** クィンシー博士，明日オフィスアワーにオフィスに来るようメールをくださいましたが，何でしょうか？

**W:** 正直なところ，カール，詳しく話すのは明日にしたいわ。でも，あなたの中間試験の結果についてとても心配しているということは伝えておきましょう。まったくあなたらしくない成績でしたよ。

What does the woman imply about the man?

(A) He is often late for appointments.
(B) He did rather well on the mid-term test.
(C) He needs to include more details in his writing.
(D) He is usually a very good student.

女性は男性について何を示唆していますか。

(A) よく約束の時間に遅れる。
(B) 中間試験のできがかなりよかった。
(C) レポートにもっと詳細を含める必要がある。
(D) 普段はとてもよくできる学生である。

男性を呼び出す理由について教授は明言を避けているが，I'm extremely concerned about how you performed on the mid-term exam.「あなたの中間試験の結果について，とても心配している」と試験結果が悪かったことを示唆している。また，そのことについて It was totally out of character for you.「あなたらしくない」と言っていることから，この学生は普段は成績がよいと推測できる。よって，(D) が正答。

ボキャブラリー □ **office hour**「オフィスアワー，内勤時間」 □ **to be honest**「正直なところ」 □ **in detail**「詳しく」 □ **be out of character for ...**「～らしくない」

## 28. イベントについての学生同士の会話　正答：C

115

W I'm afraid I've got bad news about using the dorm lounge for John's birthday party. Somebody's already got it booked for both Saturday and Sunday night.

M Oh, no. I've been telling everyone—except John, of course—that we're going to have the birthday bash there. Well, I'm not sure what to do. Maybe we could try to reserve a room in the student union.

W: ジョンの誕生日パーティーのために寮のラウンジを使う件だけど，残念なことに，だれかがもう土曜日も日曜日も夜を押さえてしまっているのよ。

M: 困ったな。誕生パーティーをそこでやるとみんなに，もちろんジョン以外にだけど，伝えちゃったよ。どうすればいいかわからないな。学生会館で部屋を予約できるかあたってみようか。

What problem do the speakers have?

(A) The woman forgot to reserve the dorm lounge.
(B) The man told John about the surprise party.
(C) The room they wanted to use is already taken.
(D) They made a mistake on the time of the party.

話者らの問題は何ですか。

(A) 女性が寮のラウンジの予約を忘れた。
(B) 男性がサプライズパーティーのことをジョンに話してしまった。
(C) 使いたかった部屋がすでに予約されていた。
(D) パーティーの時間を間違えた。

女性は誕生パーティーのための場所について Somebody's already got it booked ...「だれかがもう予約してしまった」と答えている。これを言い換えている (C) が正答。reserve, the dorm lounge, John, party という単語の繰り返しだけで (A) (B) (D) を選ばないように。surprise party とは，当人を驚かせるために本人に内緒で企画するパーティーのこと。

ボキャブラリー □ **bash**「パーティー」　□ **student union**「学生会館」

## 29. 住まいについての学生同士の会話　正答：C

116

W It doesn't matter that you really want to live off campus. You know, the Housing Office isn't going to let you out of your contract. There would be no one left in the dorms after fall semester if they did that.

M Well, next year I won't make the same mistake of applying for campus housing.

W: どれだけあなたがキャンパス外に引っ越したいかなんて関係ないわよ。ハウジングオフィスが契約を解約させてくれないのは知ってるでしょ。そんなことしたら，秋学期の終わりには寮にはだれも残っていないわよ。

M: そうだね，来年はキャンパス内の寮に申し込むようなミスは繰り返さないよ。

What does the man mean?

(A) He would like to have a different roommate.
(B) He thinks more students should live in the dormitory.
(C) He plans to live outside the university next year.
(D) He believes the housing office made a mistake.

男性は何と言っていますか。

(A) 別のルームメイトがほしい。
(B) もっと多くの学生が寮に住むべきだと思う。
(C) 来年は大学の外に住むつもりだ。
(D) ハウジングオフィスがミスをしたと信じている。

契約により寮を解約してキャンパス外に引っ越すことはできないと言う女性に対して，男性は next year I won't make the same mistake「来年は同じ過ちを繰り返さない」と応じている。ここで「過ち」とは寮に申し込んだこと。ここから，男性が来年は学外に住むつもりとわかるので，(C) が正答。Housing Office は，学内の寮に関する事務手続きや管理などを行う部署。

ボキャブラリー □ **off campus**「キャンパス外で」 □ **contract**「契約」
□ **dorm [dormitory]**「学生寮」

## 30. 期末セールについての学生同士の会話　正答：C

117

| | |
|---|---|
| **W** Hey, did you see the announcement that the bookstore is having a 50 percent off, end-of-term sale on all of its pens, paper, notebooks, and sketchbooks? Man, I'd like to pick some up. | **W:** ねえ，書店の期末セールでペン，紙，ノート，スケッチブックが全品半額になるって告知見た? すごいじゃない，いくつか買いたいんだけど。 |
| **M** Me, too. I could really use some envelopes. Let's head over there right now while there's still a decent selection. | **M:** ぼくもだよ。いくつか封筒が必要なんだ。まだいろいろ選べるうちに，今すぐ行こうよ。 |

What are the speakers planning to do?
話者らは何をしようとしていますか。

(A) Visit an art exhibit　(A) 美術展に行く
(B) Send some packages at the post office　(B) 郵便局で荷物を送る
(C) Buy some stationery supplies on sale　(C) セール中の文房具を買う
(D) Purchase some books at a bookstore　(D) 書店で本を購入する

男性の発話の最後にある Let's head over there right now ... から，2人がこれから there = the bookstore に向かうとわかる。ただし目的は pens, paper, notebooks, and sketchbooks や envelopes など stationery supplies「文房具」の購入である。よって，(C) が正答。断片的な聞き取りで sketchbooks から (A) an art exhibit，envelopes から (B) the post office，bookstore から (D) books を連想しないよう注意。

ボキャブラリー □ **man**「〔間投詞〕うわあ」 □ **on sale**「セール中の」

## Questions 31-34　*Long Conversation 1*

119 学生同士の会話。男性の参加したインターンシップについて話が進んでいる。

| | |
|---|---|
| **Listen to the following conversation between two students.** | ２人の学生による次の会話を聞きなさい。 |
| **W** George, Q31 long time no see! | **W:** ジョージ，Q31 久しぶり！ |
| **M** Hi, Theresa. Q31 It's been almost half a year, hasn't it? | **M:** やあ，テレザ。Q31 半年ぶりくらいかな？ |
| **W** Probably. So what's the reason Q31 you dropped out of sight for an entire term? | **W:** たぶんね。で，Q31 学期中まったく見かけなかったのはどうして？ |
| **M** Well, Q32 Q34 I had this really great internship at the city planning office all fall. I actually worked with the city planners and architects—looking at different proposed developments, like where new parks should be, how they should be designed, the size and scope of the buildings, all that stuff. | **M:** 実は，Q32 Q34 この秋はずっと，都市計画局でとてもいいインターンシップをしていたんだ。都市計画者や建築家たちと実際に一緒に仕事をしたのさ。どこに公園を造るか，それをどう設計するか，建物の大きさや規模をどうするか，とか何とか，いろいろな開発案に目を通したよ。 |
| **W** It sounds great. | **W:** それはすごいわね。 |
| **M** Yeah, and Q33 the best thing was I not only got course credit for it, but I also got paid. | **M:** ああ，Q33 何が一番よかったかと言えば，それで授業単位を取ったばかりか給料までもらえたんだ。 |
| **W** Let me get this right. You got paid to go to school? | **W:** ちょっと待って。勉強に行って給料がもらえたっていうわけ？ |
| **M** Sure did. Of course, Q33 almost all internships are unpaid, but there are some rare ones that you can get a salary or stipend for. The urban planning program that I'm in apparently has some pretty good connections in government and private industry, so they are able to place students in some great situations. Q33 Q34 You get course credit plus a salary. The cash was helpful. But, frankly, I learned about ten times more working in the planning department than I would have learned in a classroom. | **M:** そうさ。もちろん Q33 たいていのインターンシップは無給だけど，給料や奨学金がもらえるものもまれにあるんだ。ぼくのいる都市計画プログラムは，どうやら役所や民間企業といいコネクションがあるらしくてね，学生にいい仕事を回せるみたいだよ。Q33 Q34 単位に加えて給料までもらえるんだ。お金は助かったな。でも，はっきり言って，都市計画課で働くほうが，教室で学ぶより10倍は勉強になったね。 |

**W** Boy, that sounds like a great program. So how does it feel to be back in the ivory tower?

**W:** へえ，すごくよさそうなプログラムね。で，象牙の搭（大学）に戻ってみてどう？

**M** Not too bad, actually. Anyway, I'm going to graduate at the end of this term.

**M:** 悪くないね，実際。いずれにしても，学期末には卒業する予定だし。

## 31. 正答：C

120

What can be inferred about the speakers?

(A) They are both enrolled in the same program.
(B) They started the university at the same time.
(C) They have not seen each other for quite a while.
(D) They both hope to graduate at the end of the term.

話者らについて何が推測できますか。

(A) 同じプログラムに登録している。
(B) 同じ時期に大学に入学した。
(C) 長いことお互い会っていなかった。
(D) 2 人とも今学期末に卒業したいと願っている。

女性は冒頭で Long time no see!「久しぶり」と声をかけ，男性も It's been almost half a year, hasn't it?「半年ぶりくらいだね」と応じている。また，女性は，you dropped out of sight for an entire term「学期中まったく見かけなかった」と述べている。よって，2 人が久しぶりに会っているとわかるので，(C) が正答。

## 32. 正答：A

120

Where has the man been working?

(A) A government office
(B) A private company
(C) A university planning department
(D) An urban studies program

男性はどこで働いていましたか。

(A) 役所
(B) 民間企業
(C) 大学の企画課
(D) 都市研究プログラム

男性は the city planning office「都市計画局」でインターンシップをしていたと説明している。これを government office「役所」と言い換えている (A) が正答。

## 33. 正答：B

120

What was unusual about the man's internship?

(A) It lasted an entire year.
(B) He received money for doing it.
(C) It was unrelated to his major.
(D) He obtained it after he graduated.

男性のインターンシップに関して，特別なことは何でしたか。

(A) まる一年に及んだ。
(B) それを行うことでお金を得た。
(C) 自分の専攻に無関係だった。
(D) 卒業した後に獲得した。

会話の後半で，インターンシップについて get paid「給料がもらえた」と繰り返され，さらに get a salary or stipend for「給料や奨学金がもらえる」，plus a salary「加えて給料まで」，the cash「お金」と，有給であることが強調されている。よって，(B) が正答。

## 34. 正答：D

120

How does the man feel about his internship experience?

(A) Nervous
(B) Regretful
(C) Frustrated
(D) Enthusiastic

男性はインターンシップの経験についてどう感じていますか。

(A) 緊張している
(B) 後悔している
(C) 不満を抱いている
(D) とても喜んでいる

男性は自分のインターンシップを really great internship と述べており，またその理由を You get course credit plus a salary. The cash was helpful.「単位に加えて給料までもらえるんだ。お金は助かったな。」と説明している。さらに I learned about ten times more working in the planning department「10倍もためになった」と述べている。よって，(D) が正答。

---

ボキャブラリー
- □ **Long time no see.**「久しぶりですね」
- □ **city planning office**「都市計画局」
- □ **scope**「規模」
- □ **credit**「単位，評定」
- □ **stipend**「奨学金，手当」

## Questions 35-38

*Long Conversation 2*

🔊 121 学生と指導教官の会話。経済学を学ぶ女性は進路に迷い，指導教官に助言を求めている。

| | |
|---|---|
| **Listen to the following conversation between a student and her academic advisor.** | **学生と指導教官による次の会話を聞きなさい。** |
| **W** Professor Wittenburg, I'd really like your advice about something that's been on my mind. Could I talk to you? | **W:** ウィッテンバーグ教授，ずっと考えていることについて，ぜひ先生の助言をいただきたいのですが。お話ししてもよろしいですか。 |
| **M** Sure, Susan, have a seat. Right now it's my office hour anyway, and you know I'm always happy to talk to an advisee. | **M:** もちろんです，スーザン。どうぞ座って。いずれにせよ，ちょうどオフィスアワーですし，あなたも知ってのとおり，指導学生とはいつでも喜んで話しますよ。 |
| **W** I'm graduating in May and, well, Q35 I'm trying to decide what to do afterward. | **W:** わたしは5月に卒業するのですが，それで，Q35 その後何をするか決めようとしているところです。 |
| **M** Yes, and given Q36 your performance here as an economics major—Q37 you had straight A's I think in your economics courses—you'll have a lot of opportunities. | **M:** なるほど。Q36 経済学専攻生としてのあなたの成績を考えれば，Q37 たしか経済学のコースはオールAでしたよね，いくつもの可能性がありますね。 |
| **W** That's the problem. Q35 I'm having a difficult time making up my mind about what I want to do. I'd like to go right on to graduate school, Q36 either in economics or business. But maybe it would be good for me to work for a while and get some experience before continuing my studies. | **W:** それが問題なんです。Q35 自分が何をしたいのか決めかねていて。Q36 経済学かビジネスを専攻にして，このまま大学院に進学しようかとも思います。でも，しばらく働いて，少し経験を積んでから研究を続けるのもよいかもしれません。 |
| **M** Q37 This is the same struggle many of our best students go through. I'm afraid there's no single answer. It depends on you. | **M:** Q37 優秀な学生の多くは，同じような悩みを抱えるものですよ。残念ながら，答えはひとつではありません。あなた次第ですよ。 |
| **W** That's what I thought you'd say. | **W:** そうおっしゃると思っていました。 |
| **M** I do have one suggestion. Q38 Maybe you are thinking about this too much as an either/or choice. Maybe you could both work and continue your studies? | **M:** ひとつアドバイスがあります。Q38 この件に関して，AかBかの選択で考えすぎているかもしれませんよ。仕事と研究の継続は両立できるのでは？ |
| **W** What do you mean? | **W:** どういうことですか。 |

| | |
|---|---|
| **M** Q38 Why not take an interesting job with a company and at the same time enroll part-time in an evening program, such as an MBA program? Take some night classes. | M: Q38 企業でおもしろい仕事をしながら，同時にパートタイムの学生として，MBAプログラムなど，夜間プログラムに入学してみたらどうですか。夜間のクラスをいくつか取るのです。 |
| **W** I never thought about that. That sounds really promising. Maybe I'll go over to the Career Planning Office right now and check out the part-time graduate programs in this area. | W: 考えたこともありませんでした。大いに可能性が広がりそうですね。すぐにキャリア・プランニング・オフィスに行って，この地域のパートタイム大学院プログラムについて調べてみます。 |

## 35.

正答：C

122

Why did the woman go to talk to the man?

女性はなぜ男性に話をしに行きましたか。

(A) She cannot get into the graduate program she wants to enter.
(B) She is having a difficult time finding a job.
(C) She does not know what she wants to do when she graduates.
(D) She has been unable to complete all of the requirements for her major.

(A) 入学したい大学院プログラムに入れない。
(B) なかなか仕事が見つからない。
(C) 卒業してから何をしたいのかわからない。
(D) 専攻の全必修科目を終えられずにいる。

女性は卒業後の進路に関して，I'm trying to decide what to do afterward「その後何をするか決めようとしているのです」と相談の内容を説明している。また，I'm having a difficult time making up my mind about what I want to do.「自分で何をしたいのか，決めかねています」とも繰り返している。よって，(C) が正答。

## 36.

正答：A

122

What field is the woman studying?

女性はどの分野を学んでいますか。

(A) Economics
(B) Mathematics
(C) Engineering
(D) Linguistics

(A) 経済学
(B) 数学
(C) 工学
(D) 言語学

教授は女性について an economics major「経済学専攻生」と述べており，また your economics courses「経済学のコース」の成績がよかったと指摘している。学生もまた大学院に進学する場合には，either in economics or business「経済学かビジネス」の勉強を継続したいと述べている。よって，(A) が正答。

## 37.

正答：B

122

What can be inferred about the woman?

(A) She seldom meets with her advisor.
(B) She is probably a very good student.
(C) She may decide to change her major again.
(D) She will not be able to graduate this spring.

女性について何が推測できますか。

(A) 指導教官にはめったに会わない。
(B) おそらくたいへん優秀な学生である。
(C) 専攻を再度変更するかもしれない。
(D) この春には卒業できない。

教授は女性の学業成績について，you had straight A's I think in your economics courses「たしか経済学のコースはオールAでしたよね」と述べている。また，彼女の悩みについても This is the same struggle many of our best students go through.「優秀な学生の多くは同じような悩みを抱えるものですよ」と述べている。よって，(B) が正答。

## 38.

正答：D

122

What does the man suggest the woman do?

(A) Consult with an academic counseling office
(B) Contact as many potential employers as possible
(C) Concentrate more on her current courses
(D) Consider working and studying at the same time

男性は女性に何をするように勧めていますか。

(A) アカデミック・カウンセリング・オフィスに相談する
(B) できるだけ多くの求人企業に接触する
(C) 現在のコースにもっと集中する
(D) 仕事と学業の両立を検討する

教授は，仕事か進学かと either/or choice「Aか，Bか」で悩むのではなく，Maybe you could both work and continue your studies?「仕事と研究の継続を両立できるのでは？」と指摘し，Why not take an interesting job with a company and at the same time enroll part-time in an evening program, such as an MBA program?「企業でおもしろい仕事をしながら，同時にパートタイムの学生として，MBAプログラムなど，夜間プログラムに入学してみたらどうですか」と具体的に助言している。よって，(D) が正答。

---

ボキャブラリー
- □ **make up *one's* mind**「決心する」
- □ **go through ...**「～を体験する」
- □ **either/or choice**「二者択一」
- □ **MBA**「経営学修士（= **Master of Business Administration**）」
- □ **check out ...**「～を調べる」

## Questions 39-42 *Gold Rush*

124

1 歴史学の講義で，ゴールドラッシュを扱う。金はその希少価値から需要が多く，古くから採掘されていた。1848年，カリフォルニアで金が発見されたのをきっかけにゴールドラッシュが始まった。
2 ゴールドラッシュの結果，さまざまな民族が肩を並べ，それぞれの個人の利益のために働いた。その結果，ゴールドラッシュは鉱業そのものの発展に結び付いた。

**Listen to part of a talk in a history class.**

**歴史学の授業での講義の一部を聞きなさい。**

1 Although humans have valued gold since the dawn of early civilizations, the world's first true gold rush didn't happen until gold was discovered in California in 1848. That first gold rush lasted from 1848 to 1853. Five years. And during that five years, at least a quarter of a million people moved to California to try to strike it rich. No such mass movement of people in search of economic gain had ever been witnessed in the world up until that time. So what was Q39 the most important reason behind the gold rush besides a desire for wealth, which was hardly new? Basically, Q39 improved means of communication, especially widely circulated newspapers. Those newspapers were what you might call the first mass media. Only because people found out relatively quickly about the discovery of gold were they able to decide to try to take advantage of it.

パラグラフ1 古代文明の夜明け以来，人類はずっと金を高く評価してきましたが，世界初の本格的なゴールドラッシュが起きたのは，1848年にカリフォルニアで金が発見されてからのことでした。最初のゴールドラッシュは1848年から1853年まで続きました。5年間です。そしてこの5年の間，少なくとも25万人が一攫千金をねらってカリフォルニアに移ってきました。これほどまでに多くの人々が経済的利得を求めて移動したことは，未曾有でした。それでは，Q39 富への欲求は当然として，これ以外で，このゴールドラッシュの背景にあるもっとも重要な要因は何だったのでしょうか。基本的には，Q39 コミュニケーション手段の発達，特に広く流通するようになった新聞です。こうした新聞は，最初のマスメディアと言えるでしょう。金の発見について比較的早く知りえたからこそ，人々はこれを利用しようと決断できたのです。

2 To understand the California gold rush—and the other gold rushes in America that came after it—you have to realize that this was an unplanned, uncoordinated migration of large numbers of people. They were free and independent individuals of varied ethnic backgrounds who were subject to no other force than the desire to better themselves. They simply wanted a better life, and that meant more money. Q40 Whites, Blacks, Chinese, Mexicans, Native Americans—they all worked next to each other trying to strike it rich. Q41 And the innovation and creativity that this freedom and diversity resulted in directly

パラグラフ2 カリフォルニアのゴールドラッシュや，それに続くアメリカのその他のゴールドラッシュを理解するには，これが計画的でも組織的でもない大移住であったということを認識しなければなりません。彼ら移住者は民族的背景の異なる，自由で独立した個人であり，裕福になりたいという欲求だけに従っていたのです。彼らはただ，もっと豊かな生活を望んでいたのであり，それにはもっと多くのお金が必要だったのです。Q40 白人，黒人，中国人，メキシコ人，アメリカ先住民——彼らはみな一山当てようとして，肩を並べて働いたのです。Q41 また，こうした自由と多様性が生み出した革

led to the development of a major industry, mining, that had been virtually unknown to Americans before the middle of the 19th century. By the end of the 19th century, though, Q42 American mining engineers and manufacturers of mining equipment were in high demand throughout the entire world. And American companies were opening mines on almost every continent around the globe.

新性と創造性は直接的に，19 世紀半ばまでアメリカ人にはほとんど知られていなかった鉱業という産業の発達に結び付きました。もっとも，19 世紀の終わりには，Q42 アメリカの鉱山技師と採掘機材製造業者に対する需要が世界中で高まっていました。そして，アメリカ企業は地球上のほとんどすべての大陸で鉱山を開発していました。

## 39.

正答：B

125

Why did so many people suddenly move to California in 1848?

(A) Gold had become a more valuable commodity.
(B) People had more access to current information.
(C) Mining equipment was cheaper in price.
(D) More rapid forms of transportation were available.

多くの人々が 1848 年に突然カリフォルニアに移住したのはなぜですか。

(A) 金がさらに価値のあるものになった。
(B) 人々が最新の情報をより多く入手できるようになった。
(C) 採掘機材がもっと安価だった。
(D) より速い交通形態が利用できた。

1 で，the most important reason behind the gold rush「ゴールドラッシュの背景にあるもっとも重要な要因」として，a desire for wealth「富への欲求」以外に指摘されているのは，improved means of communication「コミュニケーション手段の発達」，特に widely circulated newspapers「広く流通するようになった新聞」という mass media「マスメディア」の出現であったと説明されている。よって，これを言い換えている (B) が正答。

## 40.

正答：A

125

How can the people who mined gold in North America best be described?

(A) They were an ethnically diverse group of people.
(B) They had little idea of how to mine gold effectively.
(C) They coordinated their activities carefully.
(D) They mainly worked for large mining corporations.

北アメリカで金を採掘した人々についてどのように説明するのがもっとも適切ですか。

(A) 人種的に多様な人々の集団だった。
(B) 効率のよい金の採掘法についてほとんど知らなかった。
(C) 自分たちの活動を注意深く調整した。
(D) 主に大きな採鉱会社で働いていた。

2 で教授は採掘者について Whites, Blacks, Chinese, Mexicans, Native Americans と複数の人種名を列挙し，これをすぐ後で diversity「多様性」という語で表現しているので，(A) が正答となる。

## 41.

正答：C

125

With which of the following statements would the professor most likely agree?

(A) Gold has been the source of many conflicts between nations.
(B) It is extremely difficult to measure the concept of wealth.
(C) There is a close relationship between freedom and creativity.
(D) Europe is more socially progressive than North America.

教授は次のどの記述にもっとも同意するでしょうか。

(A) 金は国家間の多くの対立の原因であり続けてきた。
(B) 富の概念を判定することはきわめて難しい。
(C) 自由と創造性の間には密接な関連がある。
(D) ヨーロッパは北アメリカよりも社会的に進んでいる。

教授は 2 で ... the innovation and creativity that this freedom and diversity resulted in ... と述べ,「革新性と創造性」が「自由と多様性」によって可能になったと説明している。つまり，両者は相互に関連していたということ。よって，(C) が正答。

## 42.

正答：D

125

According to the professor, what was one result of the gold rush?

(A) The value of the dollar became based upon gold.
(B) California became the most populated state.
(C) The cross-continental railroad became profitable.
(D) American mining companies became international.

教授によれば，ゴールドラッシュのもたらした結果のひとつは何でしたか。

(A) ドルの価値が金に基づくようになった。
(B) カリフォルニアがもっとも人口の多い州になった。
(C) 大陸横断鉄道が大きな収益を上げるようになった。
(D) アメリカの採掘企業が国際的になった。

講義の最後に，19 世紀末には，American mining engineers and manufacturers of mining equipment were in high demand throughout the entire world「アメリカの鉱山技師と採掘機材製造業者に対する需要が世界中で高まっていました」とある。さらに And American companies were opening mines on almost every continent around the globe.「アメリカ企業は地球上のほとんどすべての大陸で鉱山を開発していました」とも説明されている。よって，(D) が正答。throughout the entire world と every continent around the globe が international と言い換えられていることに留意。

ボキャブラリー

- ☐ **strike it rich**「一攫千金をねらう」
- ☐ **mass movement**「大移動」
- ☐ **witness**「～を目撃する」
- ☐ **circulate**「～を流通させる」
- ☐ **take advantage of ...**「～を利用する」
- ☐ **migration**「移住」
- ☐ **ethnic background**「民族的背景」
- ☐ **mining**「鉱業」

## Questions 43-46 *Don Coles*

126

1 文学の講義で，カナダ出身の詩人ドン・コールズを取り上げる。
2 コールズは詩のテーマに「時間」を取りあげ，人はある程度時間を制することができると主張した。
3 その一方でコールズは時間が前進することも認めており，それを表現するために，詩の中で句読点を避けるなどの巧妙な技法を用いた。

| | |
|---|---|
| **Listen to part of a talk in an American literature class.** | **アメリカ文学の授業での講義の一部を聞きなさい。** |
| 1 Q43 I'd like to talk to you today about one of my favorite writers: Don Coles. Coles comes from Canada and has lived for a long time in Toronto. Like other poets, Coles addresses many different themes in his poems, such as love, ambition, passion, and betrayal. But the theme Don Coles seems most concerned with, in poem after poem, is time. | パラグラフ1 Q43 今日は，私のいちばん好きな作家のひとり，ドン・コールズについてお話ししたいと思います。コールズはカナダ出身で，長くトロントに住んでいました。他の詩人のように，コールズもその詩の中で，愛，野心，情熱，裏切りなど，さまざまな主題について詠っています。しかし，ドン・コールズが実に多くの詩で採り上げており，もっとも関心を持っていたように思われるテーマは時間です。 |
| 2 Certainly, many poets going back to the ancient Greeks have written about time. And maybe the most common view of time is that it is always moving forward and can't be stopped. Don Coles's treatment of this theme is utterly new. Q44 He believes that we can, and must, try to find some way to manage time, to control time, even if only briefly. Perhaps my favorite line from Coles's poetry is the following: "an hour is immortal even if a life isn't." Isn't that beautiful? It means that an hour can seem to last forever even if our individual lives must come to an end. | パラグラフ2 もちろん，古代ギリシャ人にまでさかのぼる多くの詩人が，時間について書いてきました。そして，おそらくもっともありふれた時間観とは，時間とは常に進んでおり，止めることはできない，というものでしょう。このテーマに対するドン・コールズの取り組みは，まったく新しいものです。Q44 私たちは，たとえほんの一瞬でも，時間を制する方法を見つけようとできるし，また，そうしなければならない，と彼は考えているのです。たぶんコールズの詩の中で私が一番好きな詩句はこうです。「人生は滅すれど，時は不滅だ」美しいと思いませんか？ これは，私たちの人生はたとえ必ず終わるとしても，時が永遠に続くように思われることもあるということを意味しています。 |
| 3 Coles uses a very clever technique to convey this view of time. In many of his poems Q45 he avoids punctuating his sentences in the normal way—we find almost no commas or even periods until the last sentence of the poem. In one example, he | パラグラフ3 こうした時間観念を表現するために，コールズは実に巧妙な手法を用いています。多くの作品の中で Q45 彼は，通常の方法で文に句読点を付けることを避けています。詩の最後の一行までカンマも，ピリオドすらもほとんどないのです。一例を挙げ |

presents an imaginary dialog between his own imaginative language and his father's polite, middle-class silence. Three sentences span 19 lines, with not even a comma to separate the thoughts. In the process he manages to convey the effect of being swept along as he demonstrates the reasons for his father's love and, at the same time, Q46 tries desperately to justify to his father his own decision to pursue a life devoted to writing poetry, rather than work at a more conventional job. I'm sure that if his father reads this poem, he will be convinced that his son made the right career decision.

ると，彼は，彼自身の想像性に富んだ言語と，彼の父親の上品な中産階級風の沈黙との間の，架空の対話を繰り広げています。3つの文が19行に及んでおり，思考を区切るカンマすら使われていません。こうした方法で彼は，父親の愛情の理由を示しながら時に押し流されている雰囲気を表現し，また同時に Q46 父親に対して，もっと普通の仕事をするのではなく，詩作にふける生き方を追求する道を自分で選んだことを，なんとか正当化しようと試みているのです。彼の父親がこの詩を読めば，息子は正しい職業を選択したと納得するに違いありません。

## 43.

正答：A

127

What is the topic of the talk?

(A) An important Canadian poet
(B) The origin of Canadian poetry
(C) Themes of North American poetry
(D) One of Don Coles's best-known poems

この講義の主題は何ですか。

(A) カナダのある重要な詩人
(B) カナダ詩の起源
(C) 北アメリカの詩の主題
(D) ドン・コールズのもっともよく知られている詩のひとつ

1 の冒頭で教授は Don Coles について話すと述べ，Coles comes from Canada と彼がカナダ出身であると説明している。よって，(A) が正答。Don Coles という名前にこだわると (D) を選んでしまうが，その作品のひとつが講義の中心的な考察対象ではない。

## 44.

正答：D

127

According to the professor, how does Coles view the power of time?

(A) As an illusion
(B) As overwhelming
(C) As thoroughly reversible
(D) As temporarily controllable

教授によれば，コールズは時間の力をどのように見ていますか。

(A) 幻想として
(B) 圧倒的なものとして
(C) 完全に可逆的なものとして
(D) 一時的に制御できるものとして

コールズの時間意識について，2 で He believes that we can, and must, try to find some way to manage time, to control time, even if only briefly.「私たちは，たとえほんの一瞬でも，時間を制する方法を見つけようとできるし，また，そうしなければならない，と彼は考えているのです」と説明されている。よって，(D) が正答。

## 45.

正答：B

127

What technique does Coles use to convey his view of time?

(A) Short sentences
(B) Lack of punctuation
(C) Repeated phrases
(D) Unconnected words

コールズは，彼の時間観を伝えるのにどのような技法を用いていますか。

(A) 短文
(B) 句読点の不使用
(C) フレーズの反復
(D) 単語の羅列

コールズの詩作の特徴について 3 で教授は，he avoids punctuating his sentences in the normal way「通常の方法で句読点を付けることを避けた」と，句読点の使い方に特徴があったと指摘し，すぐに we find almost no commas or even periods「カンマも，ピリオドすらもほとんどないのです」と具体的に説明している。よって，これを言い換えている (B) が正答。

## 46.

正答：D

127

What does the professor imply about Coles's father?

(A) He worked hard to educate his son.
(B) He was also a successful writer.
(C) He was rarely involved in family affairs.
(D) He initially disapproved of his son's career.

教授はコールズの父について何を示唆していますか。

(A) 息子の教育に熱心だった。
(B) 自分も成功した物書きだった。
(C) 家庭内のことにはめったに関わらなかった。
(D) 最初は息子の職業を認めていなかった。

3 でコールズが作品の中で tries desperately to justify to his father his own decision to pursue a life devoted to writing poetry「詩を書く仕事を選んだことを父親に対して正当化しようとしている」と説明されているところから，父親は詩人になるという彼の選択に反対していたと推測できる。よって，(D) が正答。

---

ボキャブラリー
- □ **address**「～に対処する」
- □ **poem**「(一編の) 詩」
- □ **ambition**「野心」
- □ **betrayal**「裏切り」
- □ **treatment**「扱い」
- □ **immortal**「不滅の，不死の」
- □ **punctuate**「～に句読点を付ける」
- □ **devote**「(時間，努力を) 捧げる」
- □ **conventional**「伝統的な，型にはまった」

## Questions 47-50 *Geology*

128

1 地質学の講義で，外的な力である風と水に焦点を当てる。
2 湖は消失する。その原因は第一に水の喪失であり，第二に堆積物による湖盆の破壊である。
3 水の喪失の原因は，侵食による流出河川の地形変化である。
4 一方，堆積物が湖盆にたまると，湖は泥沼や湿地になり，最終的には草地となって塞がってしまう。

**Listen to part of a talk in a geology class.**

**地質学の授業での講義の一部を聞きなさい。**

1 As you know from our course syllabus, Q48 in our last class we concluded our study of earthquakes and other features of the Earth that are shaped by forces from inside the planet. Today, we'll begin our study of wind and water, which are largely external forces that shape the land from outside.

パラグラフ1 コース・シラバス（予定表）でもわかるように，Q48 先回のクラスで，地震と，惑星内部からの力によって形成されたその他の地球の諸特徴についての学習は終了しています。今日からは，風と水について学びますが，これらは主として外的な力であり，外部から地形を形作ります。

2 Because our human life span is relatively short, we often don't realize that Q47 most lakes are temporary features of a landscape. Even the largest lake is likely to exist for a much shorter time than many other physical features, such as mountains. There are basically Q47 two reasons for the disappearance of lakes. First, the lake may lose its water, leaving its basin empty. Second, the lake basin itself may gradually be destroyed—usually by being filled up with sediment.

パラグラフ2 人間の寿命は比較的短いので，私たちはしばしば，Q47 多くの湖は一時的な地形にしかすぎないということに気づきません。もっとも大きな湖ですらも，それ以外の多くの地形，例えば山などに比べればずっと短い期間しか存在しないことが多いのです。基本的に Q47 湖の消失には，2つの原因があります。第一に，水がなくなって湖盆が空になってしまうことです。第二に，湖盆そのものが，多くの場合，堆積物が溜まって次第に破壊されてしまうことです。

3 To begin with, Q49 let me address the loss of water—this is the most common reason why lakes disappear. What often happens with lakes is that Q49 their outlet stream simply empties all the water from the lake. This happens when the stream cuts its bed below the level of the lake floor. Basically, a healthy outlet stream helps control the water level of a lake and keeps the water fresh, like water running from a faucet. However, over time, as a result of erosion, the outlet stream will cut deeper and deeper into the surrounding soil as it runs downward. When the bottom of the outlet stream gets lower than the bottom of the lake, it effectively functions like a drain at

パラグラフ3 まず Q49 水の喪失から説明しましょう。これは湖が消失する一番の原因です。どうなるかというと，Q49 流出側の河川からその湖の水がすべて流れ出てしまうのです。これは，河川の河床が水流に削られ，湖底よりも低くなるときに起こります。本来，きちんとした流出河川は湖の水位を維持するのに役立ち，水をきれいに保ちます。蛇口から流れ出る水のようにです。ところが，時間が経つと侵食が起こり，その結果流出河川は下流へ流れるにつれて周囲の土壌をどんどん深く削り取っていくのです。流出河川の河床が湖底よりも低くなったとき，流出河川は，ちょうどキッチンシンクの底の排水溝のような役割を果たしま

| | | |
|---|---|---|
| | the bottom of a kitchen sink. All of the water drains out just like when you finish washing dishes and let the water out. | す。食器洗いを終えて排水するときとちょうど同じように，水がすべて排出されてしまうわけです。 |
| 4 | This brings us to a secondary reason for the disappearance of lakes: excessive sediment. Sediment is basically sand and dirt that are carried in by the in-bound streams that keep the lake alive by bringing it water. Q50 These bits of earth and dirt settle at the bottom of the lake and gradually fill in its basin. Slowly, more and more sediment is deposited around the edges of the lake, and the lake becomes a bog or a marsh. In the end, the basin fills in completely and turns into a grassy meadow. | パラグラフ4 ここで，湖が消失してしまう二番目の原因，すなわち過度の堆積の話になります。堆積物とは要は砂や泥であり，これらは湖に水を運び入れ，枯れないようにしている川の流れによって運ばれてきます。Q50 こうした土や泥が湖底に堆積し，徐々に湖盆を埋めていきます。湖の周縁に集まる堆積物は徐々に増え，湖は泥沼もしくは湿地になってしまいます。最後には湖盆は完全に塞がり，草地と化してしまうのです。 |

## 47.

正答：B

129

What is the main topic of the talk?

この講義の主題は何ですか。

(A) When lakes are formed
(B) Why lakes vanish
(C) Where lakes occur
(D) What function lakes have

(A) 湖はいつできるか
(B) 湖はなぜ消失するか
(C) 湖はどこにできるか
(D) 湖はどんな機能を果たすか

冒頭 1 で湖について取り上げると述べた後，教授は 2 で湖は temporary features「一時的な地形」，exist for a much shorter time「短い時間しか存在しない」としたうえで，two reasons for the disappearance of lakes「湖が消失する 2 つの理由」の説明を始めている。よって，(B) が正答となる。

## 48.

正答：C

129

What have the students in this class previously been studying?

学生らはこのクラスでこれまで何について学んでいましたか。

(A) Storms
(B) Climate
(C) Earthquakes
(D) Oceans

(A) 嵐
(B) 気候
(C) 地震
(D) 大洋

1 で教授は，前回までの授業内容を振り返り，in our last class we concluded our study of earthquakes ...「先回のクラスで，地震…についての学習は終了しています」と述べている。よって，(C) が正答となる。

## 49.　正答：A

129 According to the professor, what is the most common reason for the disappearance of a lake?

教授によれば，湖が消失するもっとも一般的な理由は何ですか。

(A) Its outlet stream empties its water.
(B) Its water evaporates into air.
(C) Its basin gradually fills in.
(D) Its bottom is taken over by plants.

(A) 流出河川が水を排出する。
(B) 水が大気中に蒸発する。
(C) 湖盆が徐々に埋まってしまう。
(D) 湖底が植物に覆われてしまう。

> 3 で the most common reason とされているのは the loss of water「水の喪失」である。直後で their outlet stream simply empties all the water from the lake「流出側の河川からその湖の水がすべて流れ出てしまうのです」と，さらに具体的に説明されているので，(A) が正答となる。

## 50.　正答：C

129 According to the professor, why do the basins of some lakes gradually fill in?

教授によれば，一部の湖盆はなぜ徐々に埋まってしまうのですか。

(A) An outlet stream becomes blocked.
(B) An earthquake changes the basin level.
(C) Sediment is deposited at the lake bottom.
(D) The amount of rainfall in an area decreases.

(A) 湖から流れ出る流水が堰き止められる。
(B) 地震が湖盆の深さを変える。
(C) 堆積物が湖底に溜まる。
(D) その地域の降雨量が減る。

> 設問文中の gradually fill in が，4 で These bits of earth and dirt settle at the bottom of the lake and gradually fill in its basin.「こうした土や泥が湖底に堆積し，徐々に湖盆を埋めていきます」と講義中で述べられている。よって，(C) が正答となる。

---

ボキャブラリー
- □ **disappearance**「消失」
- □ **basin**「盆，湖底，流域」
- □ **sediment**「堆積物」
- □ **outlet stream**「流出河川」
- □ **bed**「土台，床」
- □ **erosion**「侵食」
- □ **soil**「土壌」
- □ **drain**「排水管；～を排出する」
- □ **let ... out**「～を排出する」
- □ **excessive**「過度の」
- □ **in-bound**「流入してくる」
- □ **deposit**「～を積む」
- □ **bog**「沼，湿地」
- □ **marsh**「湿地」
- □ **meadow**「牧草地」

## Structure

### 1. 正答：A

**Iron, the main component of the Earth's core, is also present in the crust.**

鉄は地核の主たる成分であり，地殻にも含まれる。

同格の挿入句として意味が通るのは (A) のみ。Iron = the main component (of the Earth's core) である。(B) (C) (D) はいずれも語順が誤りで，意味をなさない。

ボキャブラリー □ **component**「構成要素」 □ **core**「核」 □ **crust**「地殻，外皮」

### 2. 正答：C

The doctrine of the expanding universe is based on the observation that the light from all of the galaxies is red-shifted, **indicating** that they are moving away from us.

宇宙膨張論は，あらゆる銀河が発する光は赤方偏移しており，地球から遠ざかっていることを示しているという観測を論拠としている。

この文にはすでに主語（The doctrine）と述語動詞（is based）がそろっているため，動詞形である (A) や (B) は入らない。(C) (D) はともに分詞形で，分詞構文を作るが，後に that 節をとるのは (C) のみ。

ボキャブラリー □ **doctrine**「論，主張」 □ **galaxy**「銀河」

### 3. 正答：D

Female oysters may discharge **as many as** a million eggs during a single spawning season.

雌のカキは一回の産卵期に 100 万もの卵を産むことがある。

as ... as には「～と同じくらい」という比較のほか，「～もの，～しか」という数量などを強調する用法がある。ここでは a million eggs が可算名詞の複数形なので，many を含む (D) が正答。(A) は as much as 40 percent「40 パーセントもの」のように不可算名詞に用いる。

ボキャブラリー □ **discharge**「～を排出する，荷降ろしをする」 □ **spawn**「産卵する」

### 4. 正答：B

**The analyzing of carbon compounds** is the principal focus of organic chemistry.

炭素化合物の分析は有機化学の主要なテーマである。

述語動詞の is に対応する主語が欠けているので，これを補う。主語になるのは名詞相当の語句なので，動名詞で始まる (B) が正答となる。is から主語は単数とわかるので，Compounds で始まる (D) は初めから除外できる。

ボキャブラリー □ **carbon compound**「有機物，炭素化合物」 □ **organic chemistry**「有機化学」

## 5.
正答：A

In Arctic latitudes the fur of the ermine is usually white, **while** in warmer regions the fur on the back of the animal tends to be brown.

北極地方ではオコジョの毛は通常白いが，暖かい地域では背中の毛は茶色い傾向にある。

カンマをはさんで2つの節があり，かつ内容がIn Arctic latitudesとin warmer regionsの対比であることに着目する。対照を表す接続詞(A)が正答。(B)は「～にもかかわらず」，(C)は「～と対照的に」という類似の意味を持つが，ともに群前置詞なので，後には節ではなく，名詞をとる。

ボキャブラリー □ **latitude**「緯度」＊「経度」はlongitude。 □ **ermine**「オコジョ」

## 6.
正答：D

**Ergonomics is the** study of the relationship between people and the furniture, tools, and machinery they use at work.

人間工学とは，人間と，人間が仕事で用いる家具，道具，機械との関係を扱う学問である。

この文には《主語＋述語動詞》が欠落しているので，これを補う。よって，(D)が正答となる。(B)には動詞がないので除く。(A) (C) (D)はいずれも《主語＋動詞》を含むが，(C)はThat ergonomics「エルゴノミクス」が文意に即さない。(A)はIt is ... which強調構文の可能性を考えても，which以下の関係詞節が成り立たない。which studies the relationship ... なら可。ergonomicsはeconomicsやmathematicsなどと同様に学問の名前なので，複数形の-sが付いても単数扱いである。

ボキャブラリー □ **ergonomics**「人間工学」

## 7.
正答：D

After being eaten, food passes through the alimentary canal where it is digested **and absorbed**.

食物は，食べられると消化管を通り，そこで消化されて吸収される。

(B) (C) (D)にandが含まれるが，空所前のdigested《過去分詞》とバランスよく並列するのは(D)のみ。

ボキャブラリー □ **alimentary canal**「消化管」 □ **digest**「～を消化する」
□ **absorb**「～を吸収する」

## 8.
正答：A

**Few** bird species have survived from the Miocene Age, but one that has is the Sandhill Crane.

現在まで生き残った中新世期の鳥類はほとんどいないが，そうした種のひとつにカナダヅルがいる。

but以下の文脈から前節が否定的な内容であるべきとわかる。よって，準否定語の(A)が正答。a fewは「少しはある」と肯定的だが，fewは「少ししかない，ほとんどない」と否定的（不可算名詞の修飾に用いるa littleとlittleも同様）。なお，one that hasはone that has survivedの省略である。

ボキャブラリー □ **species**「（動植物分類上の）種」 □ **survive**「生き延びる」

## 9.

正答：B

**Orion is** the most easily identified constellation in the winter sky of the Northern Hemisphere.

オリオン座は，北半球の冬空でいちばん見つけやすい星座だ。

この文には《主語＋述語動詞》が欠落しているので，正答は《名詞＋動詞》を含む (B) または (C) のいずれか。(C) は that が含まれていないので，It is ... that 強調構文にはできない。よって，(B) が正答。

ボキャブラリー □ **constellation**「星座」

## 10.

正答：C

Evolutionary psychology **assumes that** all human emotions arise because they increase the chance of survival in some way.

発達心理学は，人間のあらゆる感情は，何らかの点で生存の可能性を高めるからこそ生じる，と仮定している。

主語 Evolutionary psychology に続く述語動詞が欠落しているので，これを補う。述語動詞にならない -ing 形の (A)，関係詞節の (D) を除く。(B) (C) はいずれも動詞を含むが，ここでは文脈から判断して能動でなければならない。よって，(C) が正答。(B) だと assume の目的語が Evolutionary psychology となってしまい，that 以下が成り立たない。

ボキャブラリー □ **evolutionary**「進化（論）的な」

## 11.

正答：B

Some scholars argue that the first Thanksgiving celebration was not that of the British colonists at the Plymouth Colony in Massachusetts in 1621, **but** that of the Spanish settlers in St. Augustine, Florida in 1565.

最初の感謝祭は，1621 年のマサチューセッツ州プリマス植民地におけるイギリス人入植者によるものではなく，1565 年フロリダ州セントオーガスティンでのスペイン人入植者によるものだ，と一部の学者は主張している。

not *A* but *B*「A ではなく B」という相関接続詞を用いた表現を完成させる。よって，(B) が正答。なお，but は等位接続詞なので，A と B とは文法的に等しくなければならない。ここでは that of ... と that of ... が並列しており，that はいずれも Thanksgiving celebration を受ける。

ボキャブラリー □ **celebration**「祝賀（会）」 □ **colonist**「入植者」

## 12.

正答：A

Not unless one uses special instruments during a solar eclipse **is it possible** to view the chromosphere of the Sun.

特別な道具を使用しない限り，日食時に太陽の彩層を観察することはできない。

本来この文は It is not possible to ... unless ...「～じない限り…は不可能だ」の語順だが，not，never，seldom など否定の副詞が文頭にくると倒置が起こる。よって，正しく倒置されている (A) が正答。

ボキャブラリー □ **solar eclipse**「日食」＊「月食」は lunar eclipse。 □ **chromosphere**「彩層」

## 13.

**正答：B**

The larger the area of a heated surface, **the greater** is the rate of evaporation.

加熱される面が広ければ広いほど，蒸発の速度も速くなる。

《the＋比較級, the＋比較級》「～すればするほどますます…する」という TOEFL ITP 頻出の重要構文を完成させる。よって，(B) が正答。

ボキャブラリー □ **evaporation**「蒸発」

## 14.

**正答：C**

The Sioux Indians were one of the first Native American tribes to win **compensation** from the United States government for the loss of the natural resources on their tribal homelands.

スー族インディアンは，部族領地内の天然資源を失った代償として合衆国政府から賠償金を勝ち取った，最初の先住アメリカ部族のひとつである。

win が「～を勝ち取る」という意味の他動詞なので，空所には目的語となる名詞が入る。よって，(C) が正答。(A) は形容詞，(B) は現在分詞・動名詞，(D) は動詞で，いずれも目的語にならない。

ボキャブラリー □ **tribe**「部族」 □ **compensation**「賠償，代償」
□ **natural resources**「天然資源」

## 15.

**正答：D**

New York's Carnegie Hall, originally known as Music Hall, was renamed in 1891 because of Andrew Carnegie's large contribution to **its** construction.

ニューヨークのカーネギーホールは，もともとは「音楽堂」の名称で知られていたが，アンドリュー・カーネギーが多額の建設費を寄付したことにより，1891 年に改称された。

文脈から判断して，空所には construction「建設」の意味上の目的語を表す代名詞が入る。ここでは建設されたのは Carnegie Hall なので，これを受ける代名詞として適切な (D) が正答となる。

ボキャブラリー □ **contribution**「寄付（金）」

## 16. 語順を main source にする 正答：B

Carbohydrates serve as the **main source** of nutrition for herbivorous, or plant-eating, animals.

炭水化物は草食性，すなわち植物を食べる動物にとって主たる栄養源である。

語順が転倒している (B) source main を main source とするのが正しい。形容詞が単独で名詞を修飾するとき，名詞の前にくる場合（前置）と後にくる場合（後置）があるが，ほとんどの形容詞は前に置かれる。後置するのは，後置が慣用的に決まっている一部の形容詞や強意などの場合のみ。

ボキャブラリー □ **carbohydrate**「炭水化物」 □ **nutrition**「栄養」 □ **herbivorous**「草食性の」

## 17. animal を animals にする 正答：D

Despite being excellent swimmers, penguins are one of the most awkward **animals** on land.

ペンギンは泳ぎはうまいにもかかわらず，陸上ではもっともぎこちない動物の一種である。

「～の中のひとつ」は《one of the ＋可算名詞の複数形》で表す。よって，(D) animal を animals と複数形に直すのが正しい。

ボキャブラリー □ **awkward**「ぶざまな，ぎこちない」

## 18. who を whose にする 正答：A

William Seward, **whose** purchase of Alaska in 1867 was ridiculed as Seward's Folly, is now credited with one of the most important land acquisitions in American history.

1867 年のアラスカ購入は「スーアードの愚行」と嘲笑されたが，ウィリアム・スーアードは現在では，アメリカ史上もっとも重要な領土取得のひとつを行ったと評価されている。

主格の関係詞 (A) who に続くのは動詞でなければならない。purchase「購入」のような名詞をとるのは所有格の whose である。先行詞の William Seward を whose に代入すると，Seward's purchase of Alaska となるが，所有格は続く動作名詞の意味上の主語になるので，Seward purchased Alaska を意味する。

ボキャブラリー □ **ridicule**「～をあざける」 □ **folly**「愚行」 □ **acquisition**「取得」

## 19. compose を composed にする 正答：C

It has now been widely confirmed that neutrons and protons are **composed** of smaller particles called quarks.

中性子や陽子がクォークと呼ばれるさらに小さな粒子で構成されていることは，現在では広く認知されるようになった。

(C) compose は「～を構成する」という他動詞なので，are compose と原形のまま be 動詞と並ぶのは誤り。composed と過去分詞にして，be composed of ...「～で構成されている」とするのが正しい。

ボキャブラリー □ **neutron**「中性子」 □ **proton**「陽子」 □ **particle**「粒子，微分子」

## 20. complete を completely にする 正答：C

When certain substances are kept at very low temperatures, electrical resistance **completely** disappears, resulting in superconductivity.

ある種の物質は極低温に保たれると電気抵抗が完全になくなり，超伝導性となる。

(C) complete は形容詞であり，直後の動詞 disappears を修飾するには completely と副詞形にしなくてはならない。result in ... は「(結果的に) ～になる，～で終わる」という意味。ここでは resulting in ... と分詞構文を作っている。

ボキャブラリー □ **electrical resistance**「電気抵抗」 □ **superconductivity**「超伝導性」

## 21. it produces を producing にする 正答：C

Mammal embryos tend to develop in two stages, dividing into highly versatile cells such as brain stem cells in the first, and **producing** highly specific cells such as organ cells in the second.

哺乳類の胚は２段階の発達をする傾向があり，第１段階では脳幹細胞などの多くの働きをする細胞に分裂し，第２段階では器官細胞などのように機能の特化した細胞を作り出す。

two stages の具体的な内容として，等位接続詞 and によって並列される divide と produce は同じ形でなければならない。よって，現在分詞形の dividing に合わせて，(C) it produces を producing とするのが正しい。

ボキャブラリー □ **embryo**「胚」 □ **versatile**「融通のきく，多用な」
□ **brain stem cell**「脳幹細胞」

## 22. it を削除する 正答：B

Herring, an important commercial fish, **has been fished** virtually to the point of extinction.

ニシンは商業的に重要な魚だが，絶滅しそうになるほど濫獲されてきた。

この文には Herring has been fished ... と《主語＋述語動詞》がそろっている。よって，主語として重複する (B) it を削除するのが正しい。Herring と挿入部分の an important commercial fish は同格である。

ボキャブラリー □ **herring**「ニシン」 □ **to the point of ...**「～と言ってよいほどまでに」
□ **extinction**「絶滅」

## 23. raising を rising にする 正答：D

By the early 1980's, the consumer price index had climbed from a value of 100 in 1967 to more than 300, **rising** more than 200 percent.

1980 年代初頭までに，消費者物価指数は 1967 年を 100 とすると 300 以上にまで上がり，200 パーセント以上も上昇した。

(D) raising は他動詞 raise「～を上昇させる」の現在分詞である。ここでは文脈から「上昇する」と自動詞であるべきなので，rising とするのが正しい。なお，rise の変化は rise–rose–risen，raise の変化は raise–raised–raised である。

ボキャブラリー □ **consumer price index**「消費者物価指数」

## 24. the を a にする　正答：B

Beginning in the 1950's, a number of American composers began experimenting with non-musical sounds in their compositions.

1950年代以降，多くのアメリカ人作曲家は，作品の中に非音楽的な音を使う試みを始めた。

the number of ... は「～の数」という意味。しかし，ここでは文脈から「たくさんの～」という意味であるべきなので，(B) a (number of) と直すのが正しい。a number of ... は，many あるいは several と同義で，後に複数形の可算名詞を伴う。不可算名詞の場合は a good [great] deal of ... を用いる。

ボキャブラリー □ **composition**「作曲，作品」

## 25. in を among にする　正答：C

Economics can be defined as the study of how people choose **among** the various possible uses of their scarce resources.

経済学とは，限られた資源のさまざまな活用法の中で人々がどのような選択をするかを研究する学問であると定義できる。

複数の選択肢や種類について「～の中で，～の間で」という意味を表す前置詞は (C) in ではなく，among である。among の後には通例三者以上のものがくる。二者の場合には between を用いる。

ボキャブラリー □ **economics**「経済学」

## 26. their を its にする　正答：A

As its name indicates, Gulfport, Mississippi is a major shipping point for the entire Gulf of Mexico region.

ミシシッピー州ガルフポートはその名のごとく，メキシコ湾岸全域への主要な運送拠点である。

文脈上 name は Gulfport のもの，つまり Gulfport's name なので，所有代名詞の数を合わせて (A) their は its とするのが正しい。

ボキャブラリー □ **gulf**「湾」

## 27. and を or にする　正答：D

The best known of the saber-toothed cats, the Smilodon of California, was much larger than either the Asian tiger or African lion.

もっとも知られている剣歯虎であるカリフォルニアのスミロドンは，アジアのトラやアフリカのライオンよりもずっと大型である。

相関接続詞の正しい組み合わせは either *A* or *B*「A または B のいずれか」である。よって，(D) and を or とするのが正しい。and は both *A* and *B* の形で用いる。

ボキャブラリー □ **saber-toothed**「剣歯を持った」

## 28.　it を削除する　正答：B

Graphite, widely used in pencils, **is** a form of carbon that is soft enough to form a line on paper.

鉛筆で広く使われている黒鉛は炭素の一種であり，紙上に線を引けるだけの柔らかさがある。

分詞構文の挿入句 widely used in pencils を除いて文構造を検討すると，Graphite, it is ... となり，述語動詞 is に対応する主語が重複していることがわかる。よって，(B) it を削除する。

ボキャブラリー □ **carbon**「炭素」

## 29.　humor that is colorful を colorful humor にする　正答：D

The novels of Mark Twain are known for their memorable characters, accurate dialect, and **colorful humor**.

マーク・トウェインの小説は，その印象的な登場人物，緻密な方言描写，また豊かなユーモアで知られている。

等位接続詞 and を含む *A*, *B*, and *C* で並列される語や句は文法的に等しくなければならない。A，B に相当する memorable characters，accurate dialect がともに《形容詞＋名詞》なので，(D) の下線部もこの形にそろえる。

ボキャブラリー □ **memorable**「忘れられない」　□ **accurate**「正確な」

## 30.　fast を fastest にする　正答：A

The **fastest** land animal is the cheetah, which can achieve speeds of more than 110 kilometers an hour.

もっとも足が速い陸生動物はチーターであり，時速 110 キロ以上の速度を出せる。

形容詞 fast は文脈上，最上級とすべきである。よって，(A) fast は fastest とするのが正しい。The fast land animal のままだと「その足が速い陸生動物は」と特定の一匹の描写，または「足の速い陸生動物はみな」と総称的な意味になってしまう。

ボキャブラリー □ **achieve**「～を達成する」

## 31.　there を削除する　正答：D

When South Dakota became a state in 1889, the city of Pierre was established as its **capital**.

1889 年にサウスダコタが州になったとき，ピア市が州都に定められた。

文末の副詞 (D) there「そこで」は，文脈から判断して不要なので削除する。

ボキャブラリー □ **capital**「首都・州都」

## 32.　are を is にする　正答：C

The turnip, though not as widely consumed as the potato or the radish, **is** still one of the most important root vegetables.

カブはジャガイモやダイコンほど消費されないが，それでも貴重な根菜のひとつである。

though が導く挿入節を省いて考えれば The turnip are ... となり，主語と述語動詞 (C) are の数が一致していないとわかる。The turnip は単数なので is とするのが正しい。

ボキャブラリー □ **consume**「～を消費する」

## 33. 語順を **air pollution** にする　正答：B

Environmental destruction caused by **air pollution** and water contamination costs major urban areas millions of dollars in annual clean-up costs.

大気汚染や水質汚染によって生じる環境破壊のため，大都市部は毎年，多額の浄化費用を要している。

(B) の「大気汚染」は air pollution の語順が正しい。この語順は，等位接続詞 and で並列されている water contamination「水質汚染」からも推測できる。

ボキャブラリー □ **destruction**「破壊」 □ **pollution**「汚染」

## 34. **entirely** を **entire** にする　正答：C

Emily Dickinson, one of the most famous 19th-century American poets, lived almost her **entire** life in seclusion in Amherst, Massachusetts.

エミリー・ディキンソンはもっとも有名な 19 世紀アメリカの詩人のひとりであるが，生涯のほとんどをマサチューセッツ州アマーストでの隠遁生活で過ごした。

名詞 life を修飾できるのは形容詞。(C) entirely は副詞なので，entire とするのが正しい。

ボキャブラリー □ **seclusion**「隠遁，隔離」

## 35. **in** を **on** にする　正答：C

During the 1960's, a large shift occurred in media as more people watched the news **on** TV rather than reading it in the newspaper.

1960 年代，ますます多くの人々がニュースを，新聞で読むのではなく，テレビで見るようになったのにつれ，メディアでは大きな変化が生じた。

「新聞で」は前置詞 in を使って in the newspaper だが，(C) の「TV で」は 前置詞 on を用いて on TV と表現する。なお「ラジオで」も on を用いて on the radio である。

ボキャブラリー □ **shift**「変化」

## 36. **influence** を **influential** にする　正答：A

Frank Lloyd Wright was **influential** in not only the designing of individual homes but also the planning of public facilities.

フランク・ロイド・ライトは，個人住宅の設計のみならず，公共施設の立案にも影響を与えた。

主語の Frank Lloyd Wright という人物を形容する補語に相当するので，(A) は名詞 influence「影響」ではなく，形容詞 influential「影響力がある」とするのが正しい。

ボキャブラリー □ **facility**「施設」

## 37. expends を expend にする　正答：D

The principle of successful weight loss for both men and women is for them to consume fewer calories than they **expend**.

男女を問わず，減量に成功するための基本は，カロリーの摂取量を消費量以下に抑えることである。

than に続く節で《主語＋述語動詞》の数が対応していないので，(D) expends は expend と直すのが正しい。

ボキャブラリー □ **expend**「～を消費する」

## 38. itself を it にする　正答：C

Although some of Iowa's corn crop is consumed by humans, much of **it** is used as animal feed.

アイオワ州産のトウモロコシの一部は人間によって消費されるが，その多くは家畜の餌として使われる。

文脈から判断して，much of ... に続くのは，Iowa's corn crop を指す代名詞であるが，再帰形である必要はない。よって，(C) は目的格の it とするのが正しい。

ボキャブラリー □ **crop**「作物」

## 39. the computer を computer にする　正答：D

The development of the electrical circuit led to the invention of the radio, television, and **computer**.

電気回路の開発は，ラジオ，テレビ，コンピュータの発明につながった。

等位接続詞 and によって並列される語や句は，文法的に等しくなければならない。よって，radio, television に合わせて (D) computer とするのが正しい。定冠詞 the は，radio，television，computer のすべてにかかっている。

ボキャブラリー □ **electrical**「電気を用いた」

## 40. among を between にする　正答：C

Through her experiments with radiation, Madame Curie was the first to identify the difference **between** a non-radioactive element and a radioactive isotope.

放射線を用いる実験によって，キュリー夫人は初めて，非放射性物質と放射性アイソトープの違いを特定した。

「～の間の，～の中で」という意味の前置詞には，between と among があるが，通例，between は「2つのもの」，among は「3つ以上のもの」について用いる。ここでは $A$ and $B$ の形で2つなので，(C) among ではなく，between を用いる。

ボキャブラリー □ **experiment**「実験」　□ **radiation**「放射線」

## Questions 1-10 *Underground Railroad*

1 奴隷制反対運動組織「地下鉄道」はアフリカ系アメリカ人により運営され，多くの黒人奴隷の逃亡に協力した。
2 「地下鉄道」という名称には，奴隷解放の交通システムを準備するという比喩的な意味合いがある。
3 「地下鉄道」は北部，南部北方で広範な活動を行い，逃亡した黒人奴隷に安全を提供した。
4 大胆にも，活動拠点の「駅」は連邦議会議事堂のすぐそばにまで存在した。

1 In the years before the Civil War, the Underground Railroad smuggled thousands of Black slaves from the South to freedom in the North. Q3 Although White abolitionists who opposed slavery contributed to this effort, Q10 the Underground Railroad was primarily run, maintained, and Q2 **funded by** African Americans. Q3 Black working-class men and women collected the bulk of the food and clothing and provided the shelter and transportation for the run-away slaves, and wealthier, better educated Blacks arranged for legal assistance and offered leadership and financial support.

パラグラフ1 南北戦争以前の時期，地下鉄道は何千人もの黒人奴隷を南部から北部に密かに脱出させ，自由にした。Q3 奴隷制度に反対していた白人の奴隷制廃止論者らもこの運動に貢献したが，Q10 地下鉄道は主にアフリカ系アメリカ人らによって運営され，維持され，Q2 資金が提供されていた。Q3 黒人の労働者階級の人々が大量の食料や衣服を集め，逃亡した奴隷に隠れ場と交通手段を与え，また裕福で教育のある黒人たちは，法的な支援を手配したり，リーダーシップや財政的援助を提供したりした。

2 Although the origins of the term are uncertain, by 1850 both those who participated in the Underground Railroad and those who sought to destroy it freely employed metaphors from the railroad business to describe its activities and operations. More important, Northerners and Southerners understood both its symbolic and real meaning. The number of African Americans who fled or were smuggled out of the South was never large enough to threaten the institutional stability of slavery. Q4 Yet the number actually freed was, in a way, less significant than the heroic and symbolic value of the fact that a metaphorical transportation system was in place to free slaves. In other words, the Underground Railroad was an indictment of the institution of slavery and the true character of the institutions that supported it.

パラグラフ2 地下鉄道という言葉の起源は定かではないが，1850年までには，地下鉄道に参加していた人々と，それを壊滅させようとしていた人々の双方が，その活動と運動を言い表すのに鉄道業から取った比喩をおのずと使うようになっていた。さらに重要なのは，北部の人も南部の人も，その象徴的な意味と本当の意味の両方を理解していたことである。南部から逃亡または密かに連れ出されたアフリカ系アメリカ人の数は，奴隷制度の安定性を脅かすほど多くはなかった。Q4 しかし，ある意味では，実際に逃亡した人の数は，奴隷を解放する比喩的な意味での「交通システム」が用意されていたという事実が持つ，英雄的で象徴的な意味合いほど重要ではない。言い換えれば，地下鉄道は，奴隷制とそれを支えていた社会制度の本質に対する告発だったのだ。

3 Q5 Most of the slaves who reached freedom in the North actually initiated their own escapes. After their initial flight, however, fugitives needed guidance and assistance to keep their hard-won liberty. Although the effectiveness of the Black underground varied depending upon the time and place, there was an Q6 **astonishingly** large number of semi-autonomous networks that operated across the North and the upper South. They were especially active and efficient in Ohio, Pennsylvania, and New York, and Q7 surprisingly effective networks, often centered in local Black churches, existed in most northern and border states.

パラグラフ3 Q5 北部で自由になった奴隷の大半は，実際には，最初は自分の力で逃げ出した。だが，逃げ出した後で，やっと手にした自由を守るために，逃亡者たちは指導と援助を必要とした。黒人の地下活動の効果は，時と場所によってまちまちだったが，Q6 驚異的な数の半自治的なネットワークが，北部と南部北方の全域で活動していた。それらは，特にオハイオ州，ペンシルバニア州，ニューヨーク州で活発かつ効果的に機能しており，Q7 しばしば地域の黒人教会を拠点として，驚くほど効果的なネットワークが北部諸州の大半と境界諸州に存在していた。

4 Q8 The most daring and best organized "station" was operated in the very shadow of the U.S. Capitol. Run by free Blacks from Washington, D.C., this underground network was remarkably successful in rescuing a huge number of slaves from plantations in Maryland and Virginia at considerable risk to its operators. Q9 It was one of the bravest and most noble ventures in American history.

パラグラフ4 Q8 もっとも大胆で，もっともよく組織されていた「駅」は，連邦議会議事堂のすぐ近くにあった。この地下ネットワークは，ワシントン DC の自由身分の黒人たちによって運営されており，関係者らは大きな危険を冒しながらも，メリーランド州とヴァージニア州の農園から膨大な数の奴隷を助け出した。Q9 それはアメリカ史上，もっとも勇気にあふれた崇高な企てのひとつであった。

## 1.

正答：B

What is the passage mainly about?

(A) How the Underground Railroad helped slaves to escape
(B) The operation and support of the Underground Railroad
(C) The place where the Underground Railroad functioned most effectively
(D) Famous people who contributed to the Underground Railroad

このパッセージは主に何について述べていますか。

(A) 地下鉄道はどのように奴隷の脱走を助けたか
(B) 地下鉄道の運営と支援
(C) 地下鉄道がもっとも効果的に機能した場所
(D) 地下鉄道に貢献した有名な人々

このパッセージは「地下鉄道」を概説的に説明しているので，もっとも総論的な (B) が正答。(A) (C) (D) に関する言及もあるが，いずれもパッセージ全体の主題とは言えない。

## 2. 正答：C

The phrase "funded by" in line 4 is closest in meaning to

4行目の "funded by" にもっとも近い意味を持つのは

(A) led by
(B) founded by
(C) paid for by
(D) overseen by

(A) ～により率いられた
(B) ～により設立された
(C) ～のために資金が支払われた
(D) ～により監督された

動詞 fund は事業や企画に「資金を提供する」。選択肢中，金銭に関する表現は (C) のみ。発音・綴りが似ている found「設立する」と混同しないように。

## 3. 正答：D

All of the following are referred to in the passage as supporters of the Underground Railroad EXCEPT

次のうち，地下鉄道の支持者としてパッセージ中で挙げられていないのは

(A) White abolitionists
(B) Black workers
(C) educated African Americans
(D) northern Catholics

(A) 白人の奴隷制廃止論者
(B) 黒人労働者
(C) 教育を受けたアフリカ系アメリカ人
(D) 北部のカトリック教徒

1 に地下鉄道の運営者として，white abolitionists ..., Black working-class men and women ..., wealthier, better educated Blacks ... の三者が挙げられている。よって，言及のない (D) が正答。

## 4. 正答：A

According to the author, what was the main significance of the term "Underground Railroad"?

筆者によれば，「地下鉄道」という語の第一の重要性は何でしたか。

(A) Its symbolism
(B) Its accuracy
(C) Its secrecy
(D) Its deception

(A) その象徴性
(B) その正確さ
(C) その秘密主義
(D) その欺瞞

「地下鉄道」という名称の由来については 2 に言及があり，逃亡に成功した奴隷の実数よりも the heroic and symbolic value のほうが重要だったと指摘されている。よって，(A) が正答。ほかにも metaphors，metaphorical と類似の表現が繰り返されている。

## 5.

正答：D

In paragraph 3, the author implies that

(A) many slaves had little desire to escape from their masters
(B) most northern governments officially supported slavery
(C) the Underground Railroad eventually caused the slave system to collapse
(D) most slaves had to undertake their own initial escapes

第３パラグラフで筆者が示唆しているのは

(A) 多くの奴隷は主人から逃げたいとはあまり思っていなかった
(B) 大半の北部の政府が公式に奴隷制を支持していた
(C) 地下鉄道が最終的に奴隷制を崩壊させた
(D) ほとんどの奴隷は最初は自分で脱走しなければならなかった

3 に Most of the slaves ... actually initiated their own escapes. とあるので，これを言い換えている (D) が正答。(A) (B) を示唆する言及はない。また，(C) は 2 の「実際に逃亡を助けられた黒人の数は，制度を脅かすほど多くはなかった」との記述と矛盾するので誤り。

## 6.

正答：A

The word “astonishingly” in line 22 is closest in meaning to

(A) amazingly
(B) increasingly
(C) slightly
(D) deceptively

22 行目の “astonishingly” にもっとも近い意味を持つのは

(A) 驚くばかりに
(B) ますます
(C) わずかに
(D) 人を欺くように

astonishingly は動詞 astonish「驚かす，びっくりさせる」の副詞形。同様に動詞 amaze「びっくりさせる」の副詞形である (A) が正答。

## 7.

正答：B

According to the passage, what particular organizations played a significant role in the Underground Railroad?

(A) White law firms
(B) Black churches
(C) Local governments
(D) Northern newspapers

このパッセージによれば，どの特定の組織が，地下鉄道において重要な役割を果たしましたか。

(A) 白人の法律事務所
(B) 黒人教会
(C) 地方政府
(D) 北部の新聞社

3 の最後に，surprisingly effective networks, often centered in local Black churches, とある。よって，(B) が正答。

## 8. 正答：D

According to the passage, where was the Underground Railroad boldest and most efficient?

(A) New York
(B) Pennsylvania
(C) Maryland
(D) Washington, D.C.

パッセージによれば，地下鉄道はどこでもっとも大胆かつ効率的でしたか。

(A) ニューヨーク州
(B) ペンシルバニア州
(C) メリーランド州
(D) ワシントン DC

設問の boldest and most efficient に相当する表現を検索すると，4 に The most daring and best organized "station" was operated in the very shadow of the U.S. Capitol. とある。the U.S. Capitol「連邦議会議事堂」が Washington, D.C. にあるのは常識であり，直後の文からも明らか。よって，(D) が正答。

## 9. 正答：D

In which paragraph does the author most clearly express an opinion?

(A) Paragraph 1
(B) Paragraph 2
(C) Paragraph 3
(D) Paragraph 4

筆者がもっともはっきりと意見を表明しているのはどの段落ですか。

(A) 第 1 パラグラフ
(B) 第 2 パラグラフ
(C) 第 3 パラグラフ
(D) 第 4 パラグラフ

1 2 3 は地下鉄道の実態についての客観的な説明だが，4 には It was one of the bravest and most noble ventures in American history. とあり，筆者自身の見解が明示されている。よって，(D) が正答。

## 10.

**正答：D**

With which of the following statements would the author most likely agree?

(A) The support of wealthy whites was crucial to the operation of the Underground Railroad.
(B) The Underground Railroad played a major role in starting the Civil War.
(C) The Underground Railroad seriously threatened the slavery system in the South.
(D) African Americans were mainly responsible for running the Underground Railroad.

筆者は次のどの記述にもっとも同意すると思われますか。

(A) 裕福な白人の支援が地下鉄道の運動にとって重要だった。
(B) 地下鉄道は南北戦争を開始させるうえで重要な役割を果たした。
(C) 地下鉄道は南部の奴隷制を非常に脅かした。
(D) アフリカ系アメリカ人が地下鉄道を運営する責任を主に担っていた。

> 1 に the Underground Railroad was primarily run, maintained, and funded by African Americans. とあるので，下線部を言い換えている (D) が正答。(A)(B) を示唆する言及はない。(C) は 2 の記述と矛盾するので誤り。

---

**ボキャブラリー**

- □ **abolitionist**「奴隷制廃止論者」
- □ **the bulk of ...**「大量の～」
- □ **metaphor**「隠喩」
- □ **flee**「～を逃れる」
- □ **smuggle**「～を密かに持ち運ぶ」
- □ **indictment**「告発」
- □ **daring**「大胆な」
- □ **the U.S. Capitol**「連邦議会議事堂」

## Questions 11-20 *Dolls in North America*

1 ヨーロッパからの移民が北アメリカに人形を持ち込み，19 世紀以降それらに話す，食べるといった人間の動作を付加していった。
2 20 世紀には新素材の開発とともに，そっくり人形，バービー人形などの新しい人形が誕生した。

1 When the early European immigrants arrived in North America in the late 16th century, they brought their dolls with them. It was not until 1858, however, that the first original North American doll was patented by Ludwig Greiner, a German-born toy-maker in Philadelphia. By 1862, several designers had developed Q13 dolls that could walk and Q12 say simple words or phrases, such as "mama" or "papa." Q15 The next two decades saw a flurry of activity by doll-makers to try to get them to Q13 perform actions typical of human children, like Q12 nursing, swimming, or consuming food. Q15 Even the famous inventor Thomas Edison became involved. In the early 1880's, he succeeded in reducing the size of the record player he had invented so one could fit inside the body of a doll, making it able to "speak." Other patents were issued for dolls that could wave their hands or wink.

パラグラフ 1 初期のヨーロッパ移民は，16 世紀末に北アメリカにやってきたときに人形を一緒に持ってきた。しかし，ドイツ生まれのフィラデルフィアの玩具職人ルートヴィヒ・グライナーが最初の北アメリカ製人形で特許を取ったのは，1858 年になってのことだった。1862 年までには何人かのデザイナーが，Q13 歩いたり，「ママ」「パパ」といった Q12 簡単な言葉をしゃべったりできる人形を完成させた。Q15 続く 20 年間には，人形師たちは，Q13 人間の子どもに特徴的な Q12 あやす，泳ぐ，食べるといった動作を人形にさせようと，次々に試みた。Q15 有名な発明家トーマス・エジソンまでがそのひとりだった。1880 年代初頭に，彼は自分が発明したレコードプレーヤーの小型化に成功しており，人形の胴体に入れて人形が「しゃべる」ことができるようにした。ほかにも手を振ったり，まばたきしたりできる人形にも特許が与えられた。

2 Q14 During the first half of the 20th century, the emphasis among doll-makers was on developing new types of materials for the construction of dolls. Q14 Consumers demanded durability and realism, both in form and feel. Dolls modeled after newborn babies were popular in the 1920's, and Q16 in the 1930's the rising popularity of motion pictures led to the creation of portrait dolls, dolls made to resemble well-known people, especially movie stars. Q17 The late 1940's represented a watershed in the history of dolls. With the development of modern plastics, notably vinyl, the degree of realism doll manufacturers could

パラグラフ 2 Q14 20 世紀前半には，人形師の間では，人形を作るための新種の素材の開発に重点が置かれた。Q14 消費者は，形と手触りの両方の点で耐久性とリアルさとを求めた。1920 年代には，生まれたばかりの赤ん坊をモデルにした人形が流行し，Q16 1930 年代には映画の人気の高まりによって，特に映画スターなどの有名人に似せた「そっくり人形」が作られた。Q17 1940 年代末は人形の歴史の転換期となった。新素材プラスチック，特にビニールが開発されたことで，人形製作者が表現できるリアルさの度合いは Q18 劇的に高まった。1950 年代終りになると，バービー人形が登場した。前世紀の着せ替え人形と同じく，バー

attain increased Q18 **dramatically**. The close of the 1950's saw the introduction of the Barbie doll. Like the fashion dolls of the previous century, these dolls had huge wardrobes. Unlike their predecessors, however, Q20 these newer dolls were Q19 **first and foremost** meant to be played with, rather than being intended mainly as way of displaying clothing fashions.

ビー人形にはたくさんの衣装が付いていた。しかし，前世紀のはやりの人形とは違って，Q20 これらの新しい人形は主に洋服を見せるためではなく，Q19 何よりも使って遊ぶためのものとして作られた。

## 11.

正答：C

What does the passage mainly discuss?

(A) The origin of dolls in American life
(B) The uses of dolls in the United States
(C) The development of dolls in American society
(D) Materials used in making dolls in the United States

このパッセージは主に何を論じていますか。

(A) アメリカ人の生活における人形の起源
(B) アメリカにおける人形の用途
(C) アメリカ社会における人形の発達
(D) アメリカにおいて人形製作に使われた材料

このパッセージは時間軸に沿って展開されており，1 では16世紀末から19世紀まで，2 では20世紀前半から中期にかけての，アメリカにおける人形製作とその展開が説明されている。よって，(C) が正答。(A) (B) (D) は，全文にわたる主な考察対象ではないので誤り。

## 12.

正答：C

Which of the following is NOT mentioned in the passage as an example of human behaviors performed by dolls during the 1800's?

(A) Eating
(B) Swimming
(C) Crying
(D) Speaking

1800年代の人形が行った人間行動の例として，パッセージ中で言及されていないのは次のどれですか。

(A) 食べること
(B) 泳ぐこと
(C) 泣くこと
(D) しゃべること

19世紀の人形については 1 に説明があり，この時期の人形の技術的進歩が，say simple words or phrases, nursing, swimming, or consuming food と列挙されている。よって，言及のない (C) が正答。

## 13.

正答：A

Which aspect of dolls does paragraph 1 mainly discuss?

(A) Function
(B) Composition
(C) Usage
(D) Realism

第 1 パラグラフが主に論じているのは人形のどのような側面ですか。

(A) 機能
(B) 構成
(C) 用途
(D) リアリズム

前問で見たように，**1** では人形の技術的発達について説明されており，食べる，泳ぐなど，人形の仕掛けが多様になったとある。よって，(A) が正答。

## 14.

正答：B

People who purchased dolls in the early 1900's were greatly concerned that a doll should

(A) be relatively inexpensive
(B) appear as human as possible
(C) have an educational use
(D) exhibit a wide range of abilities

1900 年代初期に人形を買った人々が人形について関心を示したのは

(A) 比較的安価であること
(B) できるだけ人間に似ていること
(C) 教育的用途を持っていること
(D) さまざまな能力を示すこと

設問の the early 1900's に相当する表現を検索すると，**2** に During the first half of the 20th century 以下に Consumers demanded durability and realism, both in form and feel. とあり，具体的に赤ん坊や有名人の人形が流行したと指摘されている。よって，(B) が正答。

## 15.

正答：C

Why does the author mention the famous inventor Thomas Edison?

(A) To explain the reason why dolls were becoming increasingly smaller
(B) To show that there had previously been little interest in producing dolls
(C) To illustrate how important the manufacture of dolls had become
(D) To reveal a well-known inventor's unexpected fondness for dolls

なぜ筆者は有名な発明家トーマス・エジソンに言及しているのですか。

(A) 人形の小型化が進んだ理由を説明するため
(B) それ以前は人形作りにほとんど関心が持たれていなかったことを示すため
(C) 人形の製作がいかに重要になっていたかを例証するため
(D) 有名な発明家が意外にも人形好きだったことを明らかにするため

エジソンは The next two decades saw a flurry of activity by doll-makers の象徴的な例として紹介されている。flurry とは「疾風，突風」のこと。ここでは「活況，盛況」という意味で使われている。よって，エジソンへの言及は，人形製作が活発になったことを表していると考えられる。(C) が正答。

## 16.　正答：A

What can be inferred about many dolls in the 1930's?

1930 年代の人形の多くについて何が推測できますか。

(A) They resembled film actors and actresses.
(B) They looked like newborn babies.
(C) They were extremely small in size.
(D) They were made of new lightweight materials.

(A) 映画俳優や女優に似ていた。
(B) 新生児のような見かけだった。
(C) きわめて小さかった。
(D) 新しい軽量素材でできていた。

設問の dolls in the 1930's に相当する表現を検索すると，**2** に in the 1930's the rising popularity of motion pictures led to the creation of portrait dolls, dolls made to resemble well-known people, especially movie stars とある。よって，movie stars を film actors and actresses と言い換えている (A) が正答。

## 17.　正答：C

According to the passage, the biggest breakthrough in doll construction occurred during

パッセージによれば，人形製作にもっとも飛躍的な発展が生じたのは

(A) the 1920's
(B) the 1930's
(C) the 1940's
(D) the 1950's

(A) 1920 年代
(B) 1930 年代
(C) 1940 年代
(D) 1950 年代

設問の the biggest breakthrough に相当する表現を検索すると，**2** に The late 1940's represented a watershed in the history of dolls. とある。よって，(C) が正答。watershed とは「分水嶺，転機」のこと。

## 18.　正答：D

The word "dramatically" in line 20 is closest in meaning to

20 行目の "dramatically" にもっとも近い意味を持つのは

(A) progressively
(B) instantaneously
(C) marginally
(D) radically

(A) 段々と
(B) 即座に
(C) わずかに
(D) 徹底的に

dramatically は「劇的に」という意味の副詞。よって，(D) が正答。

## 19.

**正答：A**

The phrase "first and foremost" in line 22 is closest in meaning to

(A) above all
(B) at the beginning
(C) practically speaking
(D) in many respects

22 行目の "first and foremost" にもっとも近い意味を持つのは

(A) とりわけ
(B) 当初は
(C) 実際的に言えば
(D) 多くの点で

first and foremost は字義どおりには「第一であり，かつ主要な」で，通例「まっさきに，いの一番に」と訳す。これと類義の (A) above all は字義どおりには「すべてを越えて，すべてに勝って」

## 20.

**正答：D**

Compared to the fashion dolls of the late 19th century, Barbie dolls were

(A) furnished with more expensive wardrobes
(B) primarily meant to display the newest fashions
(C) popular with both children and adults
(D) mainly intended to be used as toys

19 世紀末の着せ替え人形に比べて，バービー人形は

(A) より高価な衣装が付いていた
(B) 主に最新のファッションを見せるためのものだった
(C) 子どもと大人の両方に人気があった
(D) 主におもちゃとして使うためのものだった

Barbie dolls については 2 で，these newer dolls were first and foremost meant to be played with と説明されている。よって，(D) が正答。(A) は 19 世紀の人形とバービー人形の類似点。尋ねられているのは相違点なので不適。(B) は rather than being intended mainly as way of displaying clothing fashions と否定されている。(C) に関する言及はない。

---

ボキャブラリー
- ☐ **flurry**「活況，混乱」
- ☐ **nurse**「～を授乳する，～を看病する」
- ☐ **newborn baby**「新生児」
- ☐ **watershed**「分水点，重大な時機」
- ☐ **vinyl**「ビニール」
- ☐ **first and foremost**「まっさきに」

## Questions 21-30 *Uranus and Neptune*

1 天王星と海王星は太陽系外郭にあるガス性の惑星である。
2 天王星は主に水素，ヘリウム，水で構成されており，少量のメタンのため青緑色をしている。
3 天皇星は他の惑星に比べ自転軸が傾いており，時計回りに自転する。さらに土星同様，環を持っている。
4 海王星は謎が多いが，質量，構成ともに天王星に類似している。

1 Uranus and Neptune, rather similar in size and make-up, lie Q30 beyond Jupiter and Saturn towards the outer edge of the Solar System. They are much smaller than these two giant planets, but Q22 **they** are still huge bodies in comparison with the inner planets nearer the Sun: Mercury, Venus, Earth, and Mars. Like Jupiter and Saturn, both Uranus and Neptune are gaseous and dense.

パラグラフ1 天王星と海王星は規模と組成がたいへん似ており，Q30 木星と土星の外側，太陽系の外郭にある。天王星と海王星はこの２つの巨大惑星よりはるかに小さいが，Q22 両星はそれでもより太陽に近い内惑星の水星，金星，地球，火星に比べれば巨大である。木星や土星と同様に，天王星と海王星はともにガスでできていて密度が高い。

2 Q25 Uranus is composed of hydrogen, helium, substantial amounts of water, and probably some methane and ammonia. Q24 Quite likely it is the trace amounts of methane in its upper atmosphere that give it a blue-green color. Underneath the thick clouds over the planet's surface, Q23 there may well be an immense ocean of water that, though it is heated to several thousand degrees Kelvin, does not boil away because of the Q26 **intense** pressure from the atmosphere above it. Q25 The core of the planet is most likely rock and metal.

パラグラフ2 Q25 天王星は，水素，ヘリウム，大量の水，そしておそらく少量のメタンとアンモニアで構成されている。Q24 天王星が青緑色をしているのは，ほぼ間違いなく，大気の上層に微量のメタンがあるためである。惑星の表面を覆っている厚い雲の下には Q23 広大な海があると思われるが，この海は絶対温度数千度に達しているにもかかわらず，その上にある大気の Q26 強い圧力のために，沸騰して蒸発してしまうことはない。Q25 天王星の中心核は，おそらくは岩石と金属とでできていると思われる。

3 One unusual feature of Uranus is that in contrast to most other planets Q27 its rotational axis is tilted, and the planet lies on its side with its north pole pointing slightly below the plane. During the course of its 84-year orbit around the Sun, Uranus points first one pole toward the Sun, then its equator, and then the other pole. Many astronomers believe that a catastrophic collision between Uranus and another body, perhaps a large comet, may have knocked the planet on its side. Another unusual feature is that it rotates in retrograde, or clockwise, motion about once every 17 hours. The planet has 15 known satellites, which are composed mostly

パラグラフ3 天王星のひとつの特徴は，他の大半の惑星に比べて Q27 自転軸が傾いていることであり，北極が黄道面のわずかに下を向く形で斜めになっている。84 年の公転周期の間に，天王星のまず一方の極が，次に赤道が，そして最後にもう一方の極が太陽に向く。多くの天文学者は，天王星と他の天体，おそらくは巨大な彗星との大衝突が，天王星を傾かせたと考えている。もうひとつの特徴は，天王星は約 17 時間周期で逆向きに，つまり時計回りに自転することである。天王星には 15 個の既知の衛星があり，それらはほとんど氷でできており，非常にクレーターが多い。土星と同じく，天王星にも幅が狭い円形の細い環があるが，

| | |
|---|---|
| of ice and are heavily cratered. Like Saturn, Uranus has a system of narrow, circular, sharp-edged rings, but instead of being bright and icy they are made of some unusually dark material; moreover, in some places the rings are so thin that they disappear. | それらは明るい氷状ではなく，非常に暗いなんらかの物質でできている。さらに，それらの環はところどころで非常に薄く，消えてしまっている。 |
| **4** Neptune is even more of a mystery than Uranus. Q28 Little was known about it at all until the spacecraft Voyager 2 flew by in 1989. The planet's mass is comparable to that of Uranus, and it has a similar composition. Its thick atmosphere of hydrogen, helium, and some methane gives it a bluish color. Like Uranus, Neptune rotates rapidly, once every 16.1 hours; however, the planet's high temperature suggests that Q29 Neptune by contrast has an internal, heat source. | パラグラフ4 海王星は天王星よりもはるかに謎が多い。Q28 1989年に探査機ボイジャー2号が接近するまでは，海王星についてはほとんど何も知られていなかった。海王星の質量は天王星と同等で，その構成も似ている。水素，ヘリウム，少量のメタンから成る厚い大気があるため，海王星は青みがかった色をしている。天王星と同様に海王星も高速で自転し，16.1時間で一周する。しかし，海王星の温度が高いということは，Q29 天王星とは違って内部に熱源を持っていることを示唆している。 |

## 21. 正答：D

What is the main topic of the passage?

(A) The contrast between Uranus and Neptune
(B) Outer planets of the Solar System
(C) The physical make-up of Uranus
(D) Features of Uranus and Neptune

このパッセージの主題は何ですか。

(A) 天王星と海王星の対比
(B) 太陽系の外惑星
(C) 天王星の物理的構成
(D) 天王星と海王星の特徴

1 は天王星と海王星についての概説，2 3 は天王星の特徴についての説明，4 は海王星の特徴の説明であり，パッセージ全体が (D) を主題としているのは明らか。4 では確かに海王星と天王星の比較が見られるが，パッセージ全体の主題とは言えない。

## 22. 正答：A

The word "they" in line 3 refers to

(A) Uranus and Neptune
(B) Jupiter and Saturn
(C) two giant planets
(D) inner planets

3行目の "they" が指し示しているのは

(A) 天王星と海王星
(B) 木星と土星
(C) 2つの巨大惑星
(D) 内惑星

they をさかのぼって追跡すると前文に，They are much smaller than these two giant planets とある。この They はさらに前の文の Uranus and Neptune を受けている。よって，(A) が正答。these two giant planets の指す Jupiter and Saturn との混同に注意。

## 23. 正答：C

In what way is Uranus similar to the Earth?

(A) They are roughly the same size.
(B) They have comparable atmospheres.
(C) They are both probably covered by seas.
(D) They each rotate once every 24 hours.

天王星はどのような点で地球に似ていますか。

(A) だいたい同じ大きさである。
(B) 同等の大気がある。
(C) どちらもおそらく海で覆われている。
(D) どちらも 24 時間で一周する。

2 の天王星の特徴についての記述の中に there may well be an immense ocean of water とあるので，(C) が正答。

## 24. 正答：B

According to the passage, why does Uranus appear to be blue-green in color?

(A) Because of its high temperature
(B) Because of the methane in its atmosphere
(C) Because of its thick cloud cover
(D) Because of the metal found in its soil

パッセージによれば，なぜ天王星は青緑色に見えるのですか。

(A) 高温のため
(B) 大気中のメタンのため
(C) 惑星を覆う厚い雲のため
(D) 土壌中にある金属のため

設問の blue-green in color に相当する表現を検索すると，2 に Quite likely it is the trace amounts of methane in its upper atmosphere that give it a blue-green color. とある。よって，下線部に相当する (B) が正答。

## 25. 正答：C

According to the passage, Uranus is composed of all of the following EXCEPT

(A) hydrogen
(B) ammonia
(C) lava
(D) metal

このパッセージによれば，次のうち天王星を構成する物質ではないのは

(A) 水素
(B) アンモニア
(C) 溶岩
(D) 金属

設問の Uranus is composed of に相当する表現を検索すると，2 に Uranus is composed of hydrogen, helium, substantial amounts of water, and probably some methane and ammonia. とある。さらに 2 の最後に The core of the planet is most likely rock and metal. とある。よって，言及のない (C) が正答。

## 26. 正答：D

The word "intense" in line 11 is closest in meaning to

(A) faint
(B) direct
(C) variable
(D) high

11 行目の "intense" にもっとも近い意味を持つのは

(A) かすかな
(B) 直接的な
(C) 変わりやすい
(D) 高い

intense は光や温度が「激しい，強烈な」という意味。よって，この文脈でこれにもっとも近いのは (D) である。(A) faint「かすか」は対義語。

## 27. 正答：A

What does paragraph 3 mainly discuss?

(A) The manner in which Uranus spins
(B) The collision between Uranus and an asteroid
(C) The moons of Uranus
(D) The composition of Uranus's ring

第 3 パラグラフは主に何を論じていますか。

(A) 天王星の回転の様子
(B) 天王星と小惑星の衝突
(C) 天王星の衛星
(D) 天王星の環の構成

3 の its rotational axis，orbit，rotates などの表現から，天王星の自転と公転，つまり spin（回転）について述べているのは明らか。よって，(A) が正答。

## 28. 正答：B

What can be inferred about the spacecraft Voyager 2?

(A) It passed close by the planet Uranus.
(B) It provided important information about Neptune.
(C) It made the first accurate measurement of Neptune's rotation.
(D) It used Uranus's gravity to swing around to Neptune.

探査機ボイジャー 2 号について何が推測できますか。

(A) 天王星の近くを通り過ぎた。
(B) 海王星について重要な情報をもたらした。
(C) 海王星の自転を初めて正確に測定した。
(D) 天王星の重力を利用して海王星に接近した。

設問にある the spacecraft Voyager 2 を検索すると，4 に Little was known about it at all until the spacecraft Voyager 2 flew by in 1989. とある。ここから探査機ボイジャー 2 号によって海王星の謎の解明が進んだとわかる。よって，(B) が正答。Uranus と Neptune を混同して (A) を選ばないように。

## 29.

**正答：C**

According to paragraph 4, how does Neptune differ from Uranus?

(A) It has a denser mass.
(B) It has a thicker atmosphere.
(C) It generates its own heat.
(D) It rotates more slowly.

第４パラグラフによれば，海王星は天王星とどのように異なっていますか。

(A) 質量の密度がより大きい。
(B) 大気がより厚い。
(C) 自ら熱を発生する。
(D) もっとゆっくり自転する。

海王星と天王星の相違点についての設問なので，対比を表す表現に留意。4 に Neptune by contrast has an internal, heat source. とある。ここで by contrast は「(天王星とは) 異なって」という意味で使われている。よって，下線部を言い換えている (C) が正答。

## 30.

**正答：D**

What does the paragraph preceding the passage probably discuss?

(A) The make-up of Uranus and Neptune
(B) Mercury, Venus, Earth, and Mars
(C) The size of the Solar System
(D) Jupiter and Saturn

このパッセージの直前のパラグラフでは，おそらく何を論じていますか。

(A) 天王星と海王星の組成
(B) 水星，金星，地球，火星
(C) 太陽系の大きさ
(D) 木星と土星

1 では，beyond Jupiter and Saturn，these two giant planets，Like Jupiter and Saturn と，天王星と海王星が「土星と木星」と比較される形で紹介されている。ここから，直前のパッセージでは「土星と木星」についての記述があったと推測できる。よって，(D) が正答。

---

ボキャブラリー

□ **Uranus**「天王星」
□ **Neptune**「海王星」
□ **make-up**「組成，構造」
□ **hydrogen**「水素」
□ **trace**「僅少」
□ **Kelvin**「ケルビン〔絶対温度の単位〕」
□ **rotational axis**「自転軸」
□ **tilted**「傾いた」
□ **equator**「赤道」
□ **astronomer**「天文学者」
□ **collision**「衝突」
□ **in retrograde**「逆行して」
□ **mass**「質量」

## Questions 31-40 *Jacob Lawrence*

**1** ジェイコブ・ローレンスはアフリカ系アメリカ人の生活を描いた画家で，連作を特徴としていた。
**2** ローレンスはニューヨークのハーレムで活動を始め，「トゥーサン・ルーヴェルチュール」や「黒人の移住」などの有名な作品を生み出した。また，さまざまな題材による単一作品も描いた。

**1** Most of the artwork produced by the American painter Jacob Lawrence depicted the lives of African Americans in the United States during the middle of the 20th century. His paintings portray contemporary Black history, culture, and significant events or people. Q32 His style can be thought of as expressive and direct, made more so by the bold colors he chose to employ. Q33 The most interesting feature of Lawrence's painting is the narrative format he used. Rather than confining himself to a single painting, his signature mark was creating a series of paintings related to a central theme. These multiple images were often accompanied by Q34 **relevant** text researched by the artist.

パラグラフ1 アメリカ人画家ジェイコブ・ローレンスによって描かれた作品の大半は，20世紀半ばのアメリカ合衆国におけるアフリカ系アメリカ人の生活を描写している。彼の絵は，同時代の黒人の歴史，文化，そして重要な出来事を描いている。Q32 彼の手法は，表現豊かで直接的と見なすことができるが，これは彼の大胆な色使いによっていっそう際立っている。Q33 ローレンスの絵のもっとも興味深い特徴は，彼が用いる連続物語的な形式である。彼の特徴は，一枚の絵にとらわれずに，ある中心的なテーマに関連して複数の作品を描くことだった。こうした連続ものの絵にはたいてい，彼が調査した，絵に Q34 関連のある文章が付されていた。

**2** Q36 When Lawrence was nine, his family moved to Harlem in New York City, whose museums and art centers provided him with his first real exposure to art and a chance to develop his emerging artistic talents. By the time he was fifteen, Q35 he was studying under the leading African American artist of the day, Charles Alston, at the Harlem Art Workshop. Lawrence then attended the prestigious American Artists School on a two-year scholarship, where he first exhibited his *Toussaint L'Ouverture* series. Soon after he painted his Frederick Douglass and Harriet Tubman series, he started Q37 what would Q38 **eventually** become his most celebrated work, "The Migration of the Negro," a monumental series comprising 60 paintings that chronicle the exodus of southern Blacks to the urban North after World War I. Q40 The themes

パラグラフ2 Q36 ローレンスが9歳のとき，一家はニューヨーク市のハーレムへ移ったが，ハーレムの美術館やアートセンターは，芸術との初めての本格的な出会いと，芽生えつつあった芸術的才能を開花させる機会とを彼に与えた。15歳までに，ハーレム・アート・ワークショップで，Q35 彼は当時の代表的なアフリカ系アメリカ人芸術家，チャールズ・アルストンの下で学んでいた。ローレンスはその後，2年間の奨学金を得て有名なアメリカン・アーティスト・スクールへ通い，そこで彼はトゥーサン・ルーヴェルチュール・シリーズを初めて出品した。ほどなくして，彼はフレデリック・ダグラスとハリエット・タブマンを描いた連作を発表し，さらに Q37 Q38 後に彼のもっとも有名な作品となる「黒人の移住」を描き始めた。この不朽の作品は，第一次世界大戦後に南部の黒人が北の都市部へと大挙して移動する様子を描いた，60枚の絵で構

of subsequent series included hospitals, theater, Nigeria, and Hiroshima. Q39 In addition to those narrative series for which he is best known, throughout his career Q40 he also painted single works, whose subjects ranged from pool parlors to jazz musicians to self portraits. An image of Jesse Jackson painted by Lawrence became the cover of *Time* magazine in 1970.

成されている。Q40 その後の連作のテーマには，病院，映画館，ナイジェリア，ヒロシマなどがあった。Q39 もっともよく知られている物語シリーズに加え，その生涯を通じて Q40 彼は単一作品も描いたが，その題材は玉突き場からジャズ・ミュージシャンや自画像と，多岐に渡っている。ローレンスの描いたジェシ・ジャクソンの絵は，1970年にタイム誌の表紙を飾った。

## 31.

正答：D

What topic does the passage mainly discuss?

(A) The development of American modernism
(B) Twentieth-Century African American artists
(C) The struggles of Jacob Lawrence
(D) The life and work of a notable American artist

このパッセージは主にどんなトピックについて論じていますか。

(A) アメリカン・モダニズムの発展
(B) 20世紀のアフリカ系アメリカ人画家たち
(C) ジェイコブ・ローレンスの奮闘
(D) ある著名なアメリカ人画家の生涯と作品

このパッセージの主題が，ジェイコブ・ローレンスという一人の芸術家の the life and work「生涯と作品」であることは明らか。よって，(D) が正答。ローレンスが a notable American artist と言い換えられていることに留意。(A)(B) は漠然としすぎている。(B) の artists が複数であることにも留意。

## 32.

正答：A

How can the style of Jacob Lawrence's paintings best be described?

(A) Assertive
(B) Ambiguous
(C) Subdued
(D) Sparse

ジェイコブ・ローレンスの絵の様式をもっともよく言い表しているのはどれですか。

(A) 強い色彩を持つ
(B) 不明瞭な
(C) やわらかな
(D) 希薄な

設問の the style of Jacob Lawrence's paintings に相当する表現を検索すると，1 に His style can be thought of as expressive and direct, made more so by the bold colors he chose to employ. とある。よって，下線部を言い換えている (A) が正答。assertive は「断定的な」のほかに「強い色彩［香り］を持つ」という意味がある。

## 33. 正答：C

According to paragraph 1, what was the distinctive feature of Jacob Lawrence as a painter?

(A) He always based his paintings upon a written text.
(B) He preferred to paint using shades of black and white.
(C) He composed multiple paintings around a single theme.
(D) He mainly used events in his own life to illustrate his paintings.

第 1 パラグラフによれば，ジェイコブ・ローレンスの画家としての際立った特徴は何でしたか。

(A) 常に書かれたテキストに基づいて絵を描いた。
(B) 白黒の色調を用いて絵を描くことを好んだ。
(C) 単一のテーマについて多数の絵を描いた。
(D) 自分の絵を説明するため，自分の人生における出来事を主に用いた。

設問の the distinctive feature of Jacob Lawrence に相当する表現を検索すると，1 に The most interesting feature of Lawrence's painting is the narrative format he used. とある。よって，下線部を言い換えている (C) が正答。2 ではこの連作の具体的な例が紹介されている。

## 34. 正答：B

The word "relevant" in line 9 is closest in meaning to

(A) written
(B) related
(C) personal
(D) visual

9 行目の "relevant" にもっとも近い意味を持つのは

(A) 書かれた
(B) 関係している
(C) 個人的な
(D) 視覚的な

形容詞 relevant は問題や主題に「関連して，関係があって」。名詞 relation「関係」から推測できるように，分詞形容詞である (B) related も同じく「関係がある」という意味がある。

## 35. 正答：A

It can be inferred that the author mentions Charles Alston because

(A) he was an important influence on Jacob Lawrence's art
(B) he was the subject of a Jacob Lawrence painting
(C) he helped Jacob Lawrence win a scholarship
(D) he gave Jacob Lawrence significant financial support

筆者がチャールズ・アルストンに言及している理由として推測できるのは

(A) 彼はジェイコブ・ローレンスの芸術に重要な影響を与えた
(B) 彼はジェイコブ・ローレンスの作品の主題だった
(C) 彼はジェイコブ・ローレンスの奨学金獲得を助けた
(D) 彼はジェイコブ・ローレンスにかなりの額の財政的支援を与えた

Charles Alstonについては 2 に he was studying under the leading African American artist of the day, Charles Alston とある。study under は「～の下で学ぶ」という意味である。よって，これを言い換えている (A) が正答。

## 36.

正答：B

Moving to Harlem was important for the young Jacob Lawrence because it was the first time that he

(A) lived among African Americans
(B) encountered serious artwork
(C) was able to attend school
(D) attempted to draw and paint

ハーレムへ移ったことは幼いジェイコブ・ローレンスにとって重要なことだった。なぜなら，そこで初めて

(A) アフリカ系アメリカ人の間で生活したからである
(B) 本格的な美術作品に出会ったからである
(C) 学校に通うことができたからである
(D) 絵を描こうとしたからである

設問の Moving to Harlem に相当する表現を検索すると，2 に When Lawrence was nine, his family moved to Harlem in New York City, whose museums and art centers provided him with his first real exposure to art とある。よって，下線部を言い換えている (B) が正答。

## 37.

正答：C

Which of Lawrence's works apparently received the greatest critical acclaim?

(A) His Toussaint L'Ouverture
(B) The Harriet Tubman series
(C) The Migration of the Negro
(D) His portrait of Jesse Jackson

もっとも高い評価を受けたと思われるローレンスの作品はどれですか。

(A) トゥーサン・ルーヴェルテュール
(B) ハリエット・タブマン・シリーズ
(C) 黒人の移住
(D) ジェシ・ジャクソンの肖像画

設問の the greatest critical acclaim に相当する表現を検索すると，2 に what would eventually become his most celebrated work, "The Migration of the Negro" とある。よって，(C) が正答。

## 38.

正答：B

The word "eventually" in line 17 is closest in meaning to

(A) in reality
(B) in time
(C) unexpectedly
(D) potentially

17 行目の "eventually" にもっとも近い意味を持つのは

(A) 現実には
(B) やがて
(C) 思いがけなく
(D) 潜在的に

eventually は一連の経緯を表して「結局は，ついに，やがて」という意味。(B) in time にも同じく，時の経過を経て「やがて，早晩」という意味がある。なお in time にはほかに，時間に「間に合って」という意味もある。

## 39. 正答：D

Which of the following can be inferred from the passage about the single works of Jacob Lawrence?

ジェイコブ・ローレンスの単一作品について，パッセージから推測できるのは次のうちどれですか。

(A) They were primarily concerned with foreign themes.
(B) They were mostly commissioned by famous people.
(C) They were mainly painted near the end of his life.
(D) They were secondary to his multiple image paintings.

(A) 主に外国に関するテーマを取り扱っていた。
(B) 多くは著名な人々によって依頼されたものだった。
(C) 主に彼の晩年に描かれた。
(D) 連作作品に比して二次的なものだった。

設問の the single works に相当する表現を検索すると，2 に In addition to those narrative series for which he is best known, throughout his career he also painted single works, とあり，彼が連作によってもっとも知られていたとわかる。ここから，単一作品は彼の主要な仕事ではないと推測できる。よって，(D) が正答。

## 40. 正答：C

All of the following are mentioned as subjects of Lawrence's paintings EXCEPT

次のうち，ローレンスの絵画の主題として言及されていないのは

(A) hospitals
(B) jazz musicians
(C) landscapes
(D) himself

(A) 病院
(B) ジャズミュージシャン
(C) 景色
(D) 自分自身

設問の subjects に相当する語を検索すると，2 の最後近くに，he also painted single works, whose subjects ranged from pool parlors to jazz musicians to self portraits とある。さらに subjects と類義の themes という語を含む直前の文では，The themes of subsequent series included hospitals, theater, Nigeria, and Hiroshima. とある。よって，言及がない (C) が正答。

---

ボキャブラリー
- □ **depict**「～を描く」
- □ **portray**「～を描く」
- □ **narrative**「物語（的な）」
- □ **confine**「～を制限する，閉じ込める」
- □ **prestigious**「名声高い」

1 甲殻類にはカニや小エビなどが含まれ，多くは海洋に生息している。
2 甲殻類は概して5対の付属肢を持ち，それぞれが異なる機能を持つ。
3 多くの種には聴覚器官がないが，体の表面にある刺毛で震動を感知する。

1 There are more than 26,000 species of crustaceans, Q50 ranging from crabs to sea lice and barnacles to krill. Q42 They can be found in almost every type of habitat except the most arid of deserts. The vast majority, however, are found in the sea, where they live from the surface layers all the way down to the greatest depths of the ocean. Crustaceans Q43 **exhibit** an almost infinite variety of colors and patterns. Q44 Some of the smaller varieties of plankton have completely transparent bodies with little or no pigment. Q50 On the other hand, deep-sea shrimps are often a uniformly brilliant red. Q45 Some marine crustaceans, like particular kinds of krill, are self-luminescent, emitting their own light; land and freshwater crustaceans may become luminous if infected with bright-colored bacteria but are unable to produce the light by themselves.

パラグラフ1 甲殻類は2万6千種以上が存在し，Q50 カニ，フナムシ，フジツボ，オキアミなどさまざまな種が含まれる。Q42 甲殻類は，非常に乾燥した砂漠を除いて，ほとんどあらゆる環境に生息している。しかし，大部分は海に棲んでおり，そこでは甲殻類は海面層から最深部まで，あらゆるところに生息している。甲殻類は，数限りないほどに多様な色と形状をQ43 示している。Q44 プランクトンの中には，色素がほとんど，もしくはまったくなく，完全に透明な体をしている種類がある。Q50 その一方で，深海に棲む小エビは，一様に鮮やかな赤色をしているものが多い。Q45 海洋甲殻類の中には，ある種のオキアミなど，自ら光を発する自己発光性のものがある。陸生甲殻類と淡水甲殻類は，明るい色をしたバクテリアが寄生していると発光することがあるが，自分で光を作り出すことはできない。

2 Crustaceans typically have five pairs of appendages protruding from their heads, the function of which varies depending on the species. In general, Q46 the first two are primarily sensory antennae, though they may also assist in locomotion or feeding. The third set is the mandibles used to chew food. The latter two pairs are mainly used to set up feeding currents designed to propel food toward the mandibles.

パラグラフ2 甲殻類には概して頭胸部から突き出ている5対の付属肢があるが，その機能は種によって異なる。一般には，Q46 最初の2対は主に触角であるが，これらが移動や摂食を助けることもある。3対目は大顎で，餌をかむのに使われる。残りの2対は，主に餌を大顎に送り込むための水流を起こすのに使われる。

3 Q49 No special hearing organ, or ear, has been found among the various species of crustaceans, but numerous hollow, hair-like bristles, supplied with nerves, are present on the surface of the body and the appendages.

パラグラフ3 Q49 甲殻類の多くの種には特定の聴覚器官，つまり耳がないことがわかっているが，神経が通っている中空の毛のような刺毛が体と付属肢の表面にたくさん生えている。Q47 これらは触れると動くので，

Q47 **These** move when touched, making it possible for the organism to respond to and Q48 **discern** vibrations, including sound.

それによって甲殻類は音などの振動に反応し，それを Q48 識別することができるのである。

## 41. 正答：C

What does the passage mainly discuss?

このパッセージは主に何を論じていますか。

(A) The types of crustaceans
(B) The evolution of crustaceans
(C) Characteristics of crustaceans
(D) Origins of crustaceans

(A) 甲殻類の種別
(B) 甲殻類の進化
(C) 甲殻類の諸特徴
(D) 甲殻類の起源

甲殻類に関して，1 はその生息域，2 は体構造，3 は感覚器官について説明している。よって，これらを characteristics「諸特徴」とまとめている (C) が正答。(A) は 1 にしか該当しない。(B) (D) についての言及はない。

## 42. 正答：B

It can be inferred from the passage that crustaceans would NOT likely be found

甲殻類が生息していないであろうことがパッセージから推測できるのは

(A) at the lower levels of the ocean
(B) in places with very limited rainfall
(C) in conditions of high humidity
(D) at high mountain elevations

(A) 海底付近
(B) 降雨量がごく限られている場所
(C) 湿度の高い状態
(D) 海抜の高いところ

甲殻類の生息地は 1 で説明されている。They can be found in almost every type of habitat except the most arid of deserts. とあるので，下線部に相当する (B) が正答。

## 43. 正答：B

The word “exhibit” in line 5 is closest in meaning to

5 行目の “exhibit” にもっとも近い意味を持つのは

(A) perform
(B) display
(C) proclaim
(D) distinguish

(A) ～を遂行する
(B) ～を表示する
(C) ～を宣言する
(D) ～を識別する

exhibit は「～を示す」という意味の他動詞。よって，(B) が正答。

## 44.

正答：A

According to paragraph 1, some varieties of plankton are

(A) devoid of color
(B) found only near the surface
(C) consumed by sea shrimps
(D) extremely numerous

第1パラグラフによれば，ある種のプランクトンは

(A) 無色である
(B) 海面近くにしか生息していない
(C) 海エビに食べられる
(D) きわめて数が多い

プランクトンの色に関して 1 で Some of the smaller varieties of plankton have completely transparent bodies with little or no pigment. とある。よって，下線部を言い換えている (A) が正答。

## 45.

正答：B

Which of the following is true of self-luminescent crustaceans?

(A) They are present in nearly every environment.
(B) They usually live only in salt water.
(C) They emit a bright red glow.
(D) They are often infected by bacteria.

自己発光性の甲殻類について正しいのは次のどれですか。

(A) ほとんどあらゆる環境に生息している。
(B) たいていは海水中にのみ生息している。
(C) 明るい赤色光を発する。
(D) しばしばバクテリアに寄生されている。

設問の self-luminescent crustaceans に相当する表現を検索すると，1 に Some marine crustaceans ... are self-luminescent とあり，自己発光性の甲殻類は「海洋甲殻類」であるとされている。よって，(B) が正答。

## 46.

正答：A

The main function of the first two pairs of crustacean appendages is to allow the organism to

(A) perceive its surroundings
(B) move from one place to another
(C) digest its food
(D) gather essential nutrients

最初の2対の付属肢の主な機能によって甲殻類ができるのは

(A) 周囲の環境を知覚すること
(B) ある場所から別の場所へ移動すること
(C) 食物を消化すること
(D) 不可欠の栄養物を集めること

設問の the first two pairs of crustacean appendages に相当する表現を検索すると，2 に the first two are primarily sensory antennae, とある。よって，下線部を言い換えている (A) が正答。

## 47.

正答：B

The word "These" in line 20 refers to

(A) species of crustaceans
(B) hair-like bristles
(C) nerves
(D) appendages

20 行目の "These" が指し示しているのは

(A) 甲殻類の種
(B) 毛のような刺毛
(C) 神経
(D) 付属肢

These の直前には複数形の名詞がいくつかあるが，これが文の主語であることから，まず前文の主語，numerous hollow, hair-like bristles を指示対象として検討する。これを These に代入した場合，続く move when touched ... と問題なくつながるので，(B) が正答。

## 48.

正答：A

The word "discern" in line 21 is closest in meaning to

(A) detect
(B) resemble
(C) avoid
(D) calculate

21 行目の "discern" にもっとも近い意味を持つのは

(A) ～を検出する
(B) ～に似ている
(C) ～を避ける
(D) ～を計算する

動詞 discern は，はっきりと「～を見分ける，識別する」。(A) detect にも同様に「見つける，発見する」という意味がある。

## 49.

正答：C

Which of the following is true about a crustacean's sense of hearing?

(A) It can only hear loud noises.
(B) It responds primarily to chemical stimuli.
(C) It utilizes no specific hearing organ.
(D) It functions better under water than on land.

甲殻類の聴覚について正しいのは次のどれですか。

(A) 大きな音だけを感知する。
(B) 主に化学的刺激に対して反応する。
(C) 特定の聴覚器官を使用しない。
(D) 陸上よりも水中でうまく機能する。

3 に No special hearing organ, or ear, has been found among the various species of crustaceans とある。よって，(C) が正答。

## 50. 正答：B

What type of crustacean is NOT mentioned in the passage?

このパッセージで言及されていない甲殻類はどれですか。

(A) Crabs　(A) カニ
(B) Lobsters　(B) ロブスター
(C) Krill　(C) オキアミ
(D) Shrimp　(D) エビ

> 1 に ranging from crabs to sea lice and barnacles to krill .... On the other hand, deep-sea shrimps ...,　とあり，これらは (A) (C) (D) に相当する。しかし，(B) Lobsters への言及はない。

---

ボキャブラリー
- □ **crustacean**「甲殻類」
- □ **barnacle**「蔓脚類」
- □ **arid**「乾燥した」
- □ **infinite**「無数の，無限の」
- □ **pigment**「色素」
- □ **uniformly**「一様に」
- □ **luminescent**「発光性の」
- □ **appendage**「外肢，付属物」
- □ **protrude**「突き出る」
- □ **antennae**「触覚〔単数形：**antenna**〕」
- □ **locomotion**「運動，移動」
- □ **mandible**「下あご」
- □ **hollow**「空洞の」
- □ **bristle**「とげ，剛毛」
- □ **discern**「～を識別する」

**Paul Wadden, Ph.D.**（ポール・ワーデン）

順天堂大学国際教養学部教授。ヴァーモント大学大学院修了（修辞学）。イリノイ州立大学大学院修了（英米文学博士）。

著述家・文学者。ニューヨーク・タイムズ，ウォールストリート・ジャーナル，ワシントン・ポストなど，多数の新聞および雑誌に執筆。著作に *A Handbook for Teaching English at Japanese Colleges and Universities* (Oxford University Press), *Teaching English at Japanese Universities: A New Handbook* (Routledge), TESOL Quarterly, College Composition, College Literature に掲載の言語教育に関する論文，70 冊を超える TOEFL® TEST, TOEIC® TEST, GRE 対策教材など多数。

**Robert A. Hilke**（ロバート・A・ヒルキ）

(株)リンクアンドモチベーション　プリンシパル。(株)ヒルキコミュニケーションズ代表取締役社長。旭化成，ホンダ，富士通，NGK などで異文化間コミュニケーションのコンサルタントとして活躍。カリフォルニア大学サンディエゴ校大学院（言語学）修士課程修了。元国際基督教大学専任講師。

異文化コミュニケーションおよび言語能力テストのスペシャリストで，TOEIC，TOEFL，GRE 対策教材などの著書多数。いずれのテストも繰り返し受験し，その傾向，特徴を詳細に把握したうえでの模擬問題の執筆と受験指導で定評がある。ほかに，『国際ビジネス感覚養成講座』など，語学教育に関する著書や論文多数。

**松谷偉弘［博士］Takehiro Matsutani, Ph.D.**

（まつたに・たけひろ）

国際基督教大学 (ICU)，ペンシルヴェニア大学，アマースト大学で英米思想史を専攻。日米の有名予備校を経て，現在はリベラルアーツ＋英学専門の私塾「武蔵野自由英学塾」MILE: Musashino Institute for Liberal arts and English を主宰。

**【翻訳協力】**

**城座沙蘭［博士］　Saran Shiroza, Ph.D.**

（しろざ・さらん）

国際基督教大学 (ICU)，ペンシルヴェニア大学，東京大学大学院で社会言語学を専攻。専門は国際英語論 (World Englishes)。博士（東京大学）。東京大学教養学部，上智大学英文学科を経て，現在は国際基督教大学教養学部アーツ・サイエンス学科で応用英語学・社会言語学関連の科目を担当。



**TOEFL ITP® TEST 実戦問題集【改訂版】**

2011 年 12 月 15 日　初版第 1 刷発行
2024 年 5 月 10 日　改訂初版第 1 刷発行

著　者　Paul Wadden ／ Robert A. Hilke ／松谷 偉弘
制　作　ツディブックス株式会社
発行者　田中 稔
発行所　株式会社 語研
〒 101 – 0064
東京都千代田区神田猿楽町 2 – 7 – 17
電　話　03 – 3291 – 3986
ファクス　03 – 3291 – 6749
組　版　ツディブックス株式会社
印刷・製本　シナノ書籍印刷株式会社

ISBN978-4-87615-431-9 C0082
書名　トーフルアイティーピーテスト　ジッセンモンダイシュウ　カイテイバン
著者　ポール・ワーデン／ロバート・ヒルキ／マツタニ　タケヒロ


定価：本体 3,000 円＋税（10%）（税込定価：3,300 円）
乱丁本，落丁本はお取り替えいたします。

語研ホームページ https://www.goken-net.co.jp/

本書の感想は
スマホから↓

## SECTION 1

| | | | | | |
|---|---|---|---|---|---|
| 1 | Ⓐ Ⓑ Ⓒ Ⓓ | 21 | Ⓐ Ⓑ Ⓒ Ⓓ | 41 | Ⓐ Ⓑ Ⓒ Ⓓ |
| 2 | Ⓐ Ⓑ Ⓒ Ⓓ | 22 | Ⓐ Ⓑ Ⓒ Ⓓ | 42 | Ⓐ Ⓑ Ⓒ Ⓓ |
| 3 | Ⓐ Ⓑ Ⓒ Ⓓ | 23 | Ⓐ Ⓑ Ⓒ Ⓓ | 43 | Ⓐ Ⓑ Ⓒ Ⓓ |
| 4 | Ⓐ Ⓑ Ⓒ Ⓓ | 24 | Ⓐ Ⓑ Ⓒ Ⓓ | 44 | Ⓐ Ⓑ Ⓒ Ⓓ |
| 5 | Ⓐ Ⓑ Ⓒ Ⓓ | 25 | Ⓐ Ⓑ Ⓒ Ⓓ | 45 | Ⓐ Ⓑ Ⓒ Ⓓ |
| 6 | Ⓐ Ⓑ Ⓒ Ⓓ | 26 | Ⓐ Ⓑ Ⓒ Ⓓ | 46 | Ⓐ Ⓑ Ⓒ Ⓓ |
| 7 | Ⓐ Ⓑ Ⓒ Ⓓ | 27 | Ⓐ Ⓑ Ⓒ Ⓓ | 47 | Ⓐ Ⓑ Ⓒ Ⓓ |
| 8 | Ⓐ Ⓑ Ⓒ Ⓓ | 28 | Ⓐ Ⓑ Ⓒ Ⓓ | 48 | Ⓐ Ⓑ Ⓒ Ⓓ |
| 9 | Ⓐ Ⓑ Ⓒ Ⓓ | 29 | Ⓐ Ⓑ Ⓒ Ⓓ | 49 | Ⓐ Ⓑ Ⓒ Ⓓ |
| 10 | Ⓐ Ⓑ Ⓒ Ⓓ | 30 | Ⓐ Ⓑ Ⓒ Ⓓ | 50 | Ⓐ Ⓑ Ⓒ Ⓓ |
| 11 | Ⓐ Ⓑ Ⓒ Ⓓ | 31 | Ⓐ Ⓑ Ⓒ Ⓓ | | |
| 12 | Ⓐ Ⓑ Ⓒ Ⓓ | 32 | Ⓐ Ⓑ Ⓒ Ⓓ | | |
| 13 | Ⓐ Ⓑ Ⓒ Ⓓ | 33 | Ⓐ Ⓑ Ⓒ Ⓓ | | |
| 14 | Ⓐ Ⓑ Ⓒ Ⓓ | 34 | Ⓐ Ⓑ Ⓒ Ⓓ | | |
| 15 | Ⓐ Ⓑ Ⓒ Ⓓ | 35 | Ⓐ Ⓑ Ⓒ Ⓓ | | |
| 16 | Ⓐ Ⓑ Ⓒ Ⓓ | 36 | Ⓐ Ⓑ Ⓒ Ⓓ | | |
| 17 | Ⓐ Ⓑ Ⓒ Ⓓ | 37 | Ⓐ Ⓑ Ⓒ Ⓓ | | |
| 18 | Ⓐ Ⓑ Ⓒ Ⓓ | 38 | Ⓐ Ⓑ Ⓒ Ⓓ | | |
| 19 | Ⓐ Ⓑ Ⓒ Ⓓ | 39 | Ⓐ Ⓑ Ⓒ Ⓓ | | |
| 20 | Ⓐ Ⓑ Ⓒ Ⓓ | 40 | Ⓐ Ⓑ Ⓒ Ⓓ | | |

## SECTION 2

| | | | |
|---|---|---|---|
| 1 | Ⓐ Ⓑ Ⓒ Ⓓ | 21 | Ⓐ Ⓑ Ⓒ Ⓓ |
| 2 | Ⓐ Ⓑ Ⓒ Ⓓ | 22 | Ⓐ Ⓑ Ⓒ Ⓓ |
| 3 | Ⓐ Ⓑ Ⓒ Ⓓ | 23 | Ⓐ Ⓑ Ⓒ Ⓓ |
| 4 | Ⓐ Ⓑ Ⓒ Ⓓ | 24 | Ⓐ Ⓑ Ⓒ Ⓓ |
| 5 | Ⓐ Ⓑ Ⓒ Ⓓ | 25 | Ⓐ Ⓑ Ⓒ Ⓓ |
| 6 | Ⓐ Ⓑ Ⓒ Ⓓ | 26 | Ⓐ Ⓑ Ⓒ Ⓓ |
| 7 | Ⓐ Ⓑ Ⓒ Ⓓ | 27 | Ⓐ Ⓑ Ⓒ Ⓓ |
| 8 | Ⓐ Ⓑ Ⓒ Ⓓ | 28 | Ⓐ Ⓑ Ⓒ Ⓓ |
| 9 | Ⓐ Ⓑ Ⓒ Ⓓ | 29 | Ⓐ Ⓑ Ⓒ Ⓓ |
| 10 | Ⓐ Ⓑ Ⓒ Ⓓ | 30 | Ⓐ Ⓑ Ⓒ Ⓓ |
| 11 | Ⓐ Ⓑ Ⓒ Ⓓ | 31 | Ⓐ Ⓑ Ⓒ Ⓓ |
| 12 | Ⓐ Ⓑ Ⓒ Ⓓ | 32 | Ⓐ Ⓑ Ⓒ Ⓓ |
| 13 | Ⓐ Ⓑ Ⓒ Ⓓ | 33 | Ⓐ Ⓑ Ⓒ Ⓓ |
| 14 | Ⓐ Ⓑ Ⓒ Ⓓ | 34 | Ⓐ Ⓑ Ⓒ Ⓓ |
| 15 | Ⓐ Ⓑ Ⓒ Ⓓ | 35 | Ⓐ Ⓑ Ⓒ Ⓓ |
| 16 | Ⓐ Ⓑ Ⓒ Ⓓ | 36 | Ⓐ Ⓑ Ⓒ Ⓓ |
| 17 | Ⓐ Ⓑ Ⓒ Ⓓ | 37 | Ⓐ Ⓑ Ⓒ Ⓓ |
| 18 | Ⓐ Ⓑ Ⓒ Ⓓ | 38 | Ⓐ Ⓑ Ⓒ Ⓓ |
| 19 | Ⓐ Ⓑ Ⓒ Ⓓ | 39 | Ⓐ Ⓑ Ⓒ Ⓓ |
| 20 | Ⓐ Ⓑ Ⓒ Ⓓ | 40 | Ⓐ Ⓑ Ⓒ Ⓓ |

## SECTION 3

| | | | | | |
|---|---|---|---|---|---|
| 1 | Ⓐ Ⓑ Ⓒ Ⓓ | 21 | Ⓐ Ⓑ Ⓒ Ⓓ | 41 | Ⓐ Ⓑ Ⓒ Ⓓ |
| 2 | Ⓐ Ⓑ Ⓒ Ⓓ | 22 | Ⓐ Ⓑ Ⓒ Ⓓ | 42 | Ⓐ Ⓑ Ⓒ Ⓓ |
| 3 | Ⓐ Ⓑ Ⓒ Ⓓ | 23 | Ⓐ Ⓑ Ⓒ Ⓓ | 43 | Ⓐ Ⓑ Ⓒ Ⓓ |
| 4 | Ⓐ Ⓑ Ⓒ Ⓓ | 24 | Ⓐ Ⓑ Ⓒ Ⓓ | 44 | Ⓐ Ⓑ Ⓒ Ⓓ |
| 5 | Ⓐ Ⓑ Ⓒ Ⓓ | 25 | Ⓐ Ⓑ Ⓒ Ⓓ | 45 | Ⓐ Ⓑ Ⓒ Ⓓ |
| 6 | Ⓐ Ⓑ Ⓒ Ⓓ | 26 | Ⓐ Ⓑ Ⓒ Ⓓ | 46 | Ⓐ Ⓑ Ⓒ Ⓓ |
| 7 | Ⓐ Ⓑ Ⓒ Ⓓ | 27 | Ⓐ Ⓑ Ⓒ Ⓓ | 47 | Ⓐ Ⓑ Ⓒ Ⓓ |
| 8 | Ⓐ Ⓑ Ⓒ Ⓓ | 28 | Ⓐ Ⓑ Ⓒ Ⓓ | 48 | Ⓐ Ⓑ Ⓒ Ⓓ |
| 9 | Ⓐ Ⓑ Ⓒ Ⓓ | 29 | Ⓐ Ⓑ Ⓒ Ⓓ | 49 | Ⓐ Ⓑ Ⓒ Ⓓ |
| 10 | Ⓐ Ⓑ Ⓒ Ⓓ | 30 | Ⓐ Ⓑ Ⓒ Ⓓ | 50 | Ⓐ Ⓑ Ⓒ Ⓓ |
| 11 | Ⓐ Ⓑ Ⓒ Ⓓ | 31 | Ⓐ Ⓑ Ⓒ Ⓓ | | |
| 12 | Ⓐ Ⓑ Ⓒ Ⓓ | 32 | Ⓐ Ⓑ Ⓒ Ⓓ | | |
| 13 | Ⓐ Ⓑ Ⓒ Ⓓ | 33 | Ⓐ Ⓑ Ⓒ Ⓓ | | |
| 14 | Ⓐ Ⓑ Ⓒ Ⓓ | 34 | Ⓐ Ⓑ Ⓒ Ⓓ | | |
| 15 | Ⓐ Ⓑ Ⓒ Ⓓ | 35 | Ⓐ Ⓑ Ⓒ Ⓓ | | |
| 16 | Ⓐ Ⓑ Ⓒ Ⓓ | 36 | Ⓐ Ⓑ Ⓒ Ⓓ | | |
| 17 | Ⓐ Ⓑ Ⓒ Ⓓ | 37 | Ⓐ Ⓑ Ⓒ Ⓓ | | |
| 18 | Ⓐ Ⓑ Ⓒ Ⓓ | 38 | Ⓐ Ⓑ Ⓒ Ⓓ | | |
| 19 | Ⓐ Ⓑ Ⓒ Ⓓ | 39 | Ⓐ Ⓑ Ⓒ Ⓓ | | |
| 20 | Ⓐ Ⓑ Ⓒ Ⓓ | 40 | Ⓐ Ⓑ Ⓒ Ⓓ | | |

## SECTION 1

| | | |
|---|---|---|
| 1 Ⓐ Ⓑ Ⓒ Ⓓ | 21 Ⓐ Ⓑ Ⓒ Ⓓ | 41 Ⓐ Ⓑ Ⓒ Ⓓ |
| 2 Ⓐ Ⓑ Ⓒ Ⓓ | 22 Ⓐ Ⓑ Ⓒ Ⓓ | 42 Ⓐ Ⓑ Ⓒ Ⓓ |
| 3 Ⓐ Ⓑ Ⓒ Ⓓ | 23 Ⓐ Ⓑ Ⓒ Ⓓ | 43 Ⓐ Ⓑ Ⓒ Ⓓ |
| 4 Ⓐ Ⓑ Ⓒ Ⓓ | 24 Ⓐ Ⓑ Ⓒ Ⓓ | 44 Ⓐ Ⓑ Ⓒ Ⓓ |
| 5 Ⓐ Ⓑ Ⓒ Ⓓ | 25 Ⓐ Ⓑ Ⓒ Ⓓ | 45 Ⓐ Ⓑ Ⓒ Ⓓ |
| 6 Ⓐ Ⓑ Ⓒ Ⓓ | 26 Ⓐ Ⓑ Ⓒ Ⓓ | 46 Ⓐ Ⓑ Ⓒ Ⓓ |
| 7 Ⓐ Ⓑ Ⓒ Ⓓ | 27 Ⓐ Ⓑ Ⓒ Ⓓ | 47 Ⓐ Ⓑ Ⓒ Ⓓ |
| 8 Ⓐ Ⓑ Ⓒ Ⓓ | 28 Ⓐ Ⓑ Ⓒ Ⓓ | 48 Ⓐ Ⓑ Ⓒ Ⓓ |
| 9 Ⓐ Ⓑ Ⓒ Ⓓ | 29 Ⓐ Ⓑ Ⓒ Ⓓ | 49 Ⓐ Ⓑ Ⓒ Ⓓ |
| 10 Ⓐ Ⓑ Ⓒ Ⓓ | 30 Ⓐ Ⓑ Ⓒ Ⓓ | 50 Ⓐ Ⓑ Ⓒ Ⓓ |
| 11 Ⓐ Ⓑ Ⓒ Ⓓ | 31 Ⓐ Ⓑ Ⓒ Ⓓ | |
| 12 Ⓐ Ⓑ Ⓒ Ⓓ | 32 Ⓐ Ⓑ Ⓒ Ⓓ | |
| 13 Ⓐ Ⓑ Ⓒ Ⓓ | 33 Ⓐ Ⓑ Ⓒ Ⓓ | |
| 14 Ⓐ Ⓑ Ⓒ Ⓓ | 34 Ⓐ Ⓑ Ⓒ Ⓓ | |
| 15 Ⓐ Ⓑ Ⓒ Ⓓ | 35 Ⓐ Ⓑ Ⓒ Ⓓ | |
| 16 Ⓐ Ⓑ Ⓒ Ⓓ | 36 Ⓐ Ⓑ Ⓒ Ⓓ | |
| 17 Ⓐ Ⓑ Ⓒ Ⓓ | 37 Ⓐ Ⓑ Ⓒ Ⓓ | |
| 18 Ⓐ Ⓑ Ⓒ Ⓓ | 38 Ⓐ Ⓑ Ⓒ Ⓓ | |
| 19 Ⓐ Ⓑ Ⓒ Ⓓ | 39 Ⓐ Ⓑ Ⓒ Ⓓ | |
| 20 Ⓐ Ⓑ Ⓒ Ⓓ | 40 Ⓐ Ⓑ Ⓒ Ⓓ | |

## SECTION 2

| | |
|---|---|
| 1 Ⓐ Ⓑ Ⓒ Ⓓ | 21 Ⓐ Ⓑ Ⓒ Ⓓ |
| 2 Ⓐ Ⓑ Ⓒ Ⓓ | 22 Ⓐ Ⓑ Ⓒ Ⓓ |
| 3 Ⓐ Ⓑ Ⓒ Ⓓ | 23 Ⓐ Ⓑ Ⓒ Ⓓ |
| 4 Ⓐ Ⓑ Ⓒ Ⓓ | 24 Ⓐ Ⓑ Ⓒ Ⓓ |
| 5 Ⓐ Ⓑ Ⓒ Ⓓ | 25 Ⓐ Ⓑ Ⓒ Ⓓ |
| 6 Ⓐ Ⓑ Ⓒ Ⓓ | 26 Ⓐ Ⓑ Ⓒ Ⓓ |
| 7 Ⓐ Ⓑ Ⓒ Ⓓ | 27 Ⓐ Ⓑ Ⓒ Ⓓ |
| 8 Ⓐ Ⓑ Ⓒ Ⓓ | 28 Ⓐ Ⓑ Ⓒ Ⓓ |
| 9 Ⓐ Ⓑ Ⓒ Ⓓ | 29 Ⓐ Ⓑ Ⓒ Ⓓ |
| 10 Ⓐ Ⓑ Ⓒ Ⓓ | 30 Ⓐ Ⓑ Ⓒ Ⓓ |
| 11 Ⓐ Ⓑ Ⓒ Ⓓ | 31 Ⓐ Ⓑ Ⓒ Ⓓ |
| 12 Ⓐ Ⓑ Ⓒ Ⓓ | 32 Ⓐ Ⓑ Ⓒ Ⓓ |
| 13 Ⓐ Ⓑ Ⓒ Ⓓ | 33 Ⓐ Ⓑ Ⓒ Ⓓ |
| 14 Ⓐ Ⓑ Ⓒ Ⓓ | 34 Ⓐ Ⓑ Ⓒ Ⓓ |
| 15 Ⓐ Ⓑ Ⓒ Ⓓ | 35 Ⓐ Ⓑ Ⓒ Ⓓ |
| 16 Ⓐ Ⓑ Ⓒ Ⓓ | 36 Ⓐ Ⓑ Ⓒ Ⓓ |
| 17 Ⓐ Ⓑ Ⓒ Ⓓ | 37 Ⓐ Ⓑ Ⓒ Ⓓ |
| 18 Ⓐ Ⓑ Ⓒ Ⓓ | 38 Ⓐ Ⓑ Ⓒ Ⓓ |
| 19 Ⓐ Ⓑ Ⓒ Ⓓ | 39 Ⓐ Ⓑ Ⓒ Ⓓ |
| 20 Ⓐ Ⓑ Ⓒ Ⓓ | 40 Ⓐ Ⓑ Ⓒ Ⓓ |

## SECTION 3

| | | |
|---|---|---|
| 1 Ⓐ Ⓑ Ⓒ Ⓓ | 21 Ⓐ Ⓑ Ⓒ Ⓓ | 41 Ⓐ Ⓑ Ⓒ Ⓓ |
| 2 Ⓐ Ⓑ Ⓒ Ⓓ | 22 Ⓐ Ⓑ Ⓒ Ⓓ | 42 Ⓐ Ⓑ Ⓒ Ⓓ |
| 3 Ⓐ Ⓑ Ⓒ Ⓓ | 23 Ⓐ Ⓑ Ⓒ Ⓓ | 43 Ⓐ Ⓑ Ⓒ Ⓓ |
| 4 Ⓐ Ⓑ Ⓒ Ⓓ | 24 Ⓐ Ⓑ Ⓒ Ⓓ | 44 Ⓐ Ⓑ Ⓒ Ⓓ |
| 5 Ⓐ Ⓑ Ⓒ Ⓓ | 25 Ⓐ Ⓑ Ⓒ Ⓓ | 45 Ⓐ Ⓑ Ⓒ Ⓓ |
| 6 Ⓐ Ⓑ Ⓒ Ⓓ | 26 Ⓐ Ⓑ Ⓒ Ⓓ | 46 Ⓐ Ⓑ Ⓒ Ⓓ |
| 7 Ⓐ Ⓑ Ⓒ Ⓓ | 27 Ⓐ Ⓑ Ⓒ Ⓓ | 47 Ⓐ Ⓑ Ⓒ Ⓓ |
| 8 Ⓐ Ⓑ Ⓒ Ⓓ | 28 Ⓐ Ⓑ Ⓒ Ⓓ | 48 Ⓐ Ⓑ Ⓒ Ⓓ |
| 9 Ⓐ Ⓑ Ⓒ Ⓓ | 29 Ⓐ Ⓑ Ⓒ Ⓓ | 49 Ⓐ Ⓑ Ⓒ Ⓓ |
| 10 Ⓐ Ⓑ Ⓒ Ⓓ | 30 Ⓐ Ⓑ Ⓒ Ⓓ | 50 Ⓐ Ⓑ Ⓒ Ⓓ |
| 11 Ⓐ Ⓑ Ⓒ Ⓓ | 31 Ⓐ Ⓑ Ⓒ Ⓓ | |
| 12 Ⓐ Ⓑ Ⓒ Ⓓ | 32 Ⓐ Ⓑ Ⓒ Ⓓ | |
| 13 Ⓐ Ⓑ Ⓒ Ⓓ | 33 Ⓐ Ⓑ Ⓒ Ⓓ | |
| 14 Ⓐ Ⓑ Ⓒ Ⓓ | 34 Ⓐ Ⓑ Ⓒ Ⓓ | |
| 15 Ⓐ Ⓑ Ⓒ Ⓓ | 35 Ⓐ Ⓑ Ⓒ Ⓓ | |
| 16 Ⓐ Ⓑ Ⓒ Ⓓ | 36 Ⓐ Ⓑ Ⓒ Ⓓ | |
| 17 Ⓐ Ⓑ Ⓒ Ⓓ | 37 Ⓐ Ⓑ Ⓒ Ⓓ | |
| 18 Ⓐ Ⓑ Ⓒ Ⓓ | 38 Ⓐ Ⓑ Ⓒ Ⓓ | |
| 19 Ⓐ Ⓑ Ⓒ Ⓓ | 39 Ⓐ Ⓑ Ⓒ Ⓓ | |
| 20 Ⓐ Ⓑ Ⓒ Ⓓ | 40 Ⓐ Ⓑ Ⓒ Ⓓ | |

## SECTION 1

| | | | | | |
|---|---|---|---|---|---|
| 1 | Ⓐ Ⓑ Ⓒ Ⓓ | 21 | Ⓐ Ⓑ Ⓒ Ⓓ | 41 | Ⓐ Ⓑ Ⓒ Ⓓ |
| 2 | Ⓐ Ⓑ Ⓒ Ⓓ | 22 | Ⓐ Ⓑ Ⓒ Ⓓ | 42 | Ⓐ Ⓑ Ⓒ Ⓓ |
| 3 | Ⓐ Ⓑ Ⓒ Ⓓ | 23 | Ⓐ Ⓑ Ⓒ Ⓓ | 43 | Ⓐ Ⓑ Ⓒ Ⓓ |
| 4 | Ⓐ Ⓑ Ⓒ Ⓓ | 24 | Ⓐ Ⓑ Ⓒ Ⓓ | 44 | Ⓐ Ⓑ Ⓒ Ⓓ |
| 5 | Ⓐ Ⓑ Ⓒ Ⓓ | 25 | Ⓐ Ⓑ Ⓒ Ⓓ | 45 | Ⓐ Ⓑ Ⓒ Ⓓ |
| 6 | Ⓐ Ⓑ Ⓒ Ⓓ | 26 | Ⓐ Ⓑ Ⓒ Ⓓ | 46 | Ⓐ Ⓑ Ⓒ Ⓓ |
| 7 | Ⓐ Ⓑ Ⓒ Ⓓ | 27 | Ⓐ Ⓑ Ⓒ Ⓓ | 47 | Ⓐ Ⓑ Ⓒ Ⓓ |
| 8 | Ⓐ Ⓑ Ⓒ Ⓓ | 28 | Ⓐ Ⓑ Ⓒ Ⓓ | 48 | Ⓐ Ⓑ Ⓒ Ⓓ |
| 9 | Ⓐ Ⓑ Ⓒ Ⓓ | 29 | Ⓐ Ⓑ Ⓒ Ⓓ | 49 | Ⓐ Ⓑ Ⓒ Ⓓ |
| 10 | Ⓐ Ⓑ Ⓒ Ⓓ | 30 | Ⓐ Ⓑ Ⓒ Ⓓ | 50 | Ⓐ Ⓑ Ⓒ Ⓓ |
| 11 | Ⓐ Ⓑ Ⓒ Ⓓ | 31 | Ⓐ Ⓑ Ⓒ Ⓓ | | |
| 12 | Ⓐ Ⓑ Ⓒ Ⓓ | 32 | Ⓐ Ⓑ Ⓒ Ⓓ | | |
| 13 | Ⓐ Ⓑ Ⓒ Ⓓ | 33 | Ⓐ Ⓑ Ⓒ Ⓓ | | |
| 14 | Ⓐ Ⓑ Ⓒ Ⓓ | 34 | Ⓐ Ⓑ Ⓒ Ⓓ | | |
| 15 | Ⓐ Ⓑ Ⓒ Ⓓ | 35 | Ⓐ Ⓑ Ⓒ Ⓓ | | |
| 16 | Ⓐ Ⓑ Ⓒ Ⓓ | 36 | Ⓐ Ⓑ Ⓒ Ⓓ | | |
| 17 | Ⓐ Ⓑ Ⓒ Ⓓ | 37 | Ⓐ Ⓑ Ⓒ Ⓓ | | |
| 18 | Ⓐ Ⓑ Ⓒ Ⓓ | 38 | Ⓐ Ⓑ Ⓒ Ⓓ | | |
| 19 | Ⓐ Ⓑ Ⓒ Ⓓ | 39 | Ⓐ Ⓑ Ⓒ Ⓓ | | |
| 20 | Ⓐ Ⓑ Ⓒ Ⓓ | 40 | Ⓐ Ⓑ Ⓒ Ⓓ | | |

## SECTION 2

| | | | |
|---|---|---|---|
| 1 | Ⓐ Ⓑ Ⓒ Ⓓ | 21 | Ⓐ Ⓑ Ⓒ Ⓓ |
| 2 | Ⓐ Ⓑ Ⓒ Ⓓ | 22 | Ⓐ Ⓑ Ⓒ Ⓓ |
| 3 | Ⓐ Ⓑ Ⓒ Ⓓ | 23 | Ⓐ Ⓑ Ⓒ Ⓓ |
| 4 | Ⓐ Ⓑ Ⓒ Ⓓ | 24 | Ⓐ Ⓑ Ⓒ Ⓓ |
| 5 | Ⓐ Ⓑ Ⓒ Ⓓ | 25 | Ⓐ Ⓑ Ⓒ Ⓓ |
| 6 | Ⓐ Ⓑ Ⓒ Ⓓ | 26 | Ⓐ Ⓑ Ⓒ Ⓓ |
| 7 | Ⓐ Ⓑ Ⓒ Ⓓ | 27 | Ⓐ Ⓑ Ⓒ Ⓓ |
| 8 | Ⓐ Ⓑ Ⓒ Ⓓ | 28 | Ⓐ Ⓑ Ⓒ Ⓓ |
| 9 | Ⓐ Ⓑ Ⓒ Ⓓ | 29 | Ⓐ Ⓑ Ⓒ Ⓓ |
| 10 | Ⓐ Ⓑ Ⓒ Ⓓ | 30 | Ⓐ Ⓑ Ⓒ Ⓓ |
| 11 | Ⓐ Ⓑ Ⓒ Ⓓ | 31 | Ⓐ Ⓑ Ⓒ Ⓓ |
| 12 | Ⓐ Ⓑ Ⓒ Ⓓ | 32 | Ⓐ Ⓑ Ⓒ Ⓓ |
| 13 | Ⓐ Ⓑ Ⓒ Ⓓ | 33 | Ⓐ Ⓑ Ⓒ Ⓓ |
| 14 | Ⓐ Ⓑ Ⓒ Ⓓ | 34 | Ⓐ Ⓑ Ⓒ Ⓓ |
| 15 | Ⓐ Ⓑ Ⓒ Ⓓ | 35 | Ⓐ Ⓑ Ⓒ Ⓓ |
| 16 | Ⓐ Ⓑ Ⓒ Ⓓ | 36 | Ⓐ Ⓑ Ⓒ Ⓓ |
| 17 | Ⓐ Ⓑ Ⓒ Ⓓ | 37 | Ⓐ Ⓑ Ⓒ Ⓓ |
| 18 | Ⓐ Ⓑ Ⓒ Ⓓ | 38 | Ⓐ Ⓑ Ⓒ Ⓓ |
| 19 | Ⓐ Ⓑ Ⓒ Ⓓ | 39 | Ⓐ Ⓑ Ⓒ Ⓓ |
| 20 | Ⓐ Ⓑ Ⓒ Ⓓ | 40 | Ⓐ Ⓑ Ⓒ Ⓓ |

## SECTION 3

| | | | | | |
|---|---|---|---|---|---|
| 1 | Ⓐ Ⓑ Ⓒ Ⓓ | 21 | Ⓐ Ⓑ Ⓒ Ⓓ | 41 | Ⓐ Ⓑ Ⓒ Ⓓ |
| 2 | Ⓐ Ⓑ Ⓒ Ⓓ | 22 | Ⓐ Ⓑ Ⓒ Ⓓ | 42 | Ⓐ Ⓑ Ⓒ Ⓓ |
| 3 | Ⓐ Ⓑ Ⓒ Ⓓ | 23 | Ⓐ Ⓑ Ⓒ Ⓓ | 43 | Ⓐ Ⓑ Ⓒ Ⓓ |
| 4 | Ⓐ Ⓑ Ⓒ Ⓓ | 24 | Ⓐ Ⓑ Ⓒ Ⓓ | 44 | Ⓐ Ⓑ Ⓒ Ⓓ |
| 5 | Ⓐ Ⓑ Ⓒ Ⓓ | 25 | Ⓐ Ⓑ Ⓒ Ⓓ | 45 | Ⓐ Ⓑ Ⓒ Ⓓ |
| 6 | Ⓐ Ⓑ Ⓒ Ⓓ | 26 | Ⓐ Ⓑ Ⓒ Ⓓ | 46 | Ⓐ Ⓑ Ⓒ Ⓓ |
| 7 | Ⓐ Ⓑ Ⓒ Ⓓ | 27 | Ⓐ Ⓑ Ⓒ Ⓓ | 47 | Ⓐ Ⓑ Ⓒ Ⓓ |
| 8 | Ⓐ Ⓑ Ⓒ Ⓓ | 28 | Ⓐ Ⓑ Ⓒ Ⓓ | 48 | Ⓐ Ⓑ Ⓒ Ⓓ |
| 9 | Ⓐ Ⓑ Ⓒ Ⓓ | 29 | Ⓐ Ⓑ Ⓒ Ⓓ | 49 | Ⓐ Ⓑ Ⓒ Ⓓ |
| 10 | Ⓐ Ⓑ Ⓒ Ⓓ | 30 | Ⓐ Ⓑ Ⓒ Ⓓ | 50 | Ⓐ Ⓑ Ⓒ Ⓓ |
| 11 | Ⓐ Ⓑ Ⓒ Ⓓ | 31 | Ⓐ Ⓑ Ⓒ Ⓓ | | |
| 12 | Ⓐ Ⓑ Ⓒ Ⓓ | 32 | Ⓐ Ⓑ Ⓒ Ⓓ | | |
| 13 | Ⓐ Ⓑ Ⓒ Ⓓ | 33 | Ⓐ Ⓑ Ⓒ Ⓓ | | |
| 14 | Ⓐ Ⓑ Ⓒ Ⓓ | 34 | Ⓐ Ⓑ Ⓒ Ⓓ | | |
| 15 | Ⓐ Ⓑ Ⓒ Ⓓ | 35 | Ⓐ Ⓑ Ⓒ Ⓓ | | |
| 16 | Ⓐ Ⓑ Ⓒ Ⓓ | 36 | Ⓐ Ⓑ Ⓒ Ⓓ | | |
| 17 | Ⓐ Ⓑ Ⓒ Ⓓ | 37 | Ⓐ Ⓑ Ⓒ Ⓓ | | |
| 18 | Ⓐ Ⓑ Ⓒ Ⓓ | 38 | Ⓐ Ⓑ Ⓒ Ⓓ | | |
| 19 | Ⓐ Ⓑ Ⓒ Ⓓ | 39 | Ⓐ Ⓑ Ⓒ Ⓓ | | |
| 20 | Ⓐ Ⓑ Ⓒ Ⓓ | 40 | Ⓐ Ⓑ Ⓒ Ⓓ | | |